NEGATIVE CERTAINTIES

RELIGION AND POSTMODERNISM

A series edited by Thomas A. Carlson

RECENT BOOKS IN THE SERIES

Heidegger's Confessions: The Remains of Saint Augustine in "Being and Time" and Beyond
by Ryan Coyne (2015)

Arts of Wonder: Enchanting Secularity—Walter De Maria, Diller + Scofidio, James Turrell, Andy Goldsworthy
by Jeffrey L. Kosky (2012)

God Without Being : Hors-Texte, Second Edition
by Jean-Luc Marion (2012)

Secularism in Antebellum America
by John Lardas Modern (2011)

The Figural Jew : Politics and Identity in Postwar French Thought
by Sarah Hammerschlag (2010)

The Indiscrete Image : Infinitude and Creation of the Human
by Thomas A. Carlson (2008)

NEGATIVE CERTAINTIES

Jean-Luc Marion

Translated by Stephen E. Lewis

The University of Chicago Press
Chicago and London

JEAN-LUC MARION, member of the Académie française, is professor emeritus of philosophy at the Université Paris-Sorbonne (Paris IV), the Andrew Thomas Greeley and Grace McNichols Greeley Professor of Catholic Studies and Professor of the Philosophy of Religions and Theology and professor in the Committee on Social Thought and the Department of Philosophy at the University of Chicago, and holds the Dominique Dubarle chair at the Institut Catholique of Paris. He is the author of many books, including *The Erotic Phenomenon* and *God without Being*, both also published by the University of Chicago Press. STEPHEN E. LEWIS is professor and chair of the English department at the Franciscan University of Steubenville. He has translated several works by Jean-Luc Marion.

The University of Chicago Press, Chicago 60637
The University of Chicago Press, Ltd., London

Printed in the United States of America.

24 23 22 21 20 19 18 17 16 15 1 2 3 4 5

ISBN-13: 978-0-226-50561-9 (cloth)

Library of Congress Cataloging-in-Publication Data

Marion, Jean-Luc, 1946– author.
[Certitudes négatives. English]
Negative certainties / Jean-Luc Marion ; translated by Stephen E. Lewis.
pages cm
"Originally published as Certitudes négatives. © Editions Grasset & Fasquelle"—Title page verso.
Includes bibliographical references and index.
ISBN 978-0-226-50561-9 (cloth : alkaline paper) 1. Certainty. 2. Knowledge, Theory of. 3. Phenomenology. 4. Negative theology. I. Lewis, Stephen E. (Stephen Evarts), translator. II. Title.
B2430.M283C4713 2015
121′.63—dc23

2015003618

∞ This paper meets the requirements of ANSI/NISO Z39.48-1992 (Permanence of Paper).

The Philosopher lives on problems as man does on food. An insoluble problem is an indigestible food.

—NOVALIS[1]

CONTENTS

Foreword *ix*
Translator's Acknowledgments *xi*

INTRODUCTION
§ 1. Attempt to Introduce the Concept of Negative Certainties into Philosophy 1

CHAPTER I: THE UNDEFINABLE, OR THE FACE OF MAN
§ 2. "What Is Man?" 8
§ 3. "*Ipse mihi magna quaestio*" 15
§ 4. What It Costs to Know (Oneself) 22
§ 5. Proscription 26
§ 6. The Fund of Incomprehensibility 37
§ 7. The Indefinite and the Unstable 41

CHAPTER II: THE IMPOSSIBLE, OR WHAT IS PROPER TO GOD
§ 8. The Impossible Phenomenon 51
§ 9. The Irreducible 57
§ 10. Possibility without Conditions 64
§ 11. The (Im)possible: From Contradiction to Event 71
§ 12. The (Im)possible from My Point of View 74
§ 13. The (Im)possible from God's Point of View 76

CHAPTER III: THE UNCONDITIONED, OR THE STRENGTH OF THE GIFT
§ 14. The Contradictions of the Gift 83
§ 15. The Terms of Exchange 87
§ 16. Reducing the Gift to Givenness 93

§ 17. Without the Principle of Identity 103
§ 18. Without the Principle of Sufficient Reason 106

CHAPTER IV: THE UNCONDITIONED AND THE VARIATIONS OF THE GIFT

§ 19. Sacrifice According to the Terms of Exchange 115
§ 20. Regiving, Beginning from the Recipient 120
§ 21. The Confirmation of Abraham 128
§ 22. Forgiveness According to the Terms of Exchange 132
§ 23. Regiving, Beginning from the Giver 140
§ 24. The Return of the Prodigal Son 147

CHAPTER V: THE UNFORESEEABLE, OR THE EVENT

§ 25. What the Object Excludes 155
§ 26. The Condition of the Object 162
§ 27. Concerning the Distinction of Phenomena into Objects and Events 173
§ 28. Without Cause 181
§ 29. The Original Unknown 188
§ 30. The Double Interpretation 194

CONCLUSION

§ 31. In Praise of Paradox 201

Bibliographical Note 209
Notes 211
General Index 265
Index to Biblical Passages 277

FOREWORD

This book concludes, at least for now, the unfolding of the theoretical possibilities opened in 1997 by *Being Given: Toward a Phenomenology of Givenness* and brought to light by *In Excess: Studies of Saturated Phenomena* (2001); by *The Erotic Phenomenon* (2003); and, in another direction, by *In the Self's Place: The Approach of Saint Augustine* (2008). In each case, the goal has simply been to work at broadening the theater of phenomenality: here, after givenness and saturation, I attempt to introduce into philosophy the concept of negative certainties. Usage alone will determine the legitimacy of these attempts.

The arguments and the descriptions that follow of course owe a great deal to my friends, my students, and my colleagues, whether at the Sorbonne or in Chicago, in Rome or in Lecce. May they receive the assurance of my gratitude.

Paris
July 3, 2009

TRANSLATOR'S ACKNOWLEDGMENTS

My work on this translation was helped by the fact that several parts of this book had already been capably translated into English by other accomplished translators. In the course of translating this book, I referred often to this material, and I have therefore acknowledged the valuable work of these individuals in a note at the beginning of each pertinent chapter.

I would also like to thank Christina M. Gschwandtner, Michelle Rebidoux, and Donald Wallenfang for helpful advice and suggestions, and express my gratitude to Jean-Luc Marion for his trust, patience, and friendly encouragement.

Steubenville, Ohio
July 2014

INTRODUCTION

§ 1. Attempt to Introduce the Concept of Negative Certainties into Philosophy

To know means to know with certainty. To know without certainty would in fact mean knowing while doubting, and thus not knowing at all. To know always means to know for certain, with "certain science," for there is no uncertain science. This equivalence between knowledge and science and between science and certainty has the status of evidence. This evidence alone allows us to distinguish the exact or "hard" sciences from the approximate or human and social sciences: strictly speaking, the former alone deserve the title of science because they produce (or claim to produce) certainties, while the latter only reach certainty at a distance, approximately. Such is the case, to the point that we still lay claim to certainty even if nihilism often makes us almost give up on the ambition of attaining to a genuine science: we no longer truly know, but we mean to keep hold of certainty. We remain essentially Cartesian, whether we want to be or not, and whether we know it or not.

However, there is an obstacle. If knowing is equivalent to knowing certainly, then we do not know as much as we are able to think, because the criterion of certainty rules out most of our thoughts from inclusion in the field of science. Indeed, how do we reach certainty? By two paths. Either by an a priori, formal knowledge, as in logic and mathematics: but here certainty has a price, tautology and absolute ideality, which do not allow us access to any individualized entity or any entity having a real status (of a thing). Thus, we have a first abstraction. Or, in order to avoid paying this price, we take another path, this time a posteriori, and thus experimental. But this path requires an experience reduced precisely to that which, regarding a thing or a state of affairs, can satisfy certainty (see below, § 26). Indeed, in its spontaneous course, experience imposes an uncontrolled manifold of intuitions, which never stop developing and varying, so that the contingency of the thing or the state of affairs affects the knowledge, which itself becomes variable, changing, and thus uncertain. It is therefore necessary—and here again we find ourselves to be Cartesians—to reduce the material of the experience: to reduce the material to that in it which can be known with certainty, and to abandon the remainder to the darkness of the unknowable. Where does the line of demarcation lie? Between, on the one side, the exigencies of certain science and, on the other, the pure variability of matter. For if certain science succeeds in producing certainty, it is only in the field of that which certain science can reduce to its criteria: the field of that which can be put in order (the order that orders according to knowledge, indifferent to the natural disposition of the presumed essence of the entities), that is to say, all that which can be modeled; and therefore the field of what can be measured (what is naturally measurable, like the three dimensions of space, but above all what is not in itself measurable, but must be transcribed into measurable space, like time, speed, acceleration, weight, etc.), which is to say, all the parameters. What remains, because it cannot be reduced to the criteria of certainty, must be abandoned to the domain of undetermined matter, lacking in exactitude and without a homeland in certain science. In the end, an exact science is only established by *giving up* on knowing that which decidedly cannot satisfy the criteria of certainty, the order of the models, and the measure of the parameters. Consequently, a science secures its certainty only by *reducing* the thing in itself to an object—to that which the gaze can throw before itself in plain sight [*s'objecter face à face en pleine évidence*]. Nothing becomes certain that does not also become an object. By definition, the object appears knowable without remainder because it retains nothing more than that which can be known of the thing.

In this way there seems to be an identity among knowledge in general, certain knowledge by exact science, and knowledge of the object. And yet, it is precisely this triple equivalence among knowledge, certainty, and object that must be questioned. For we have access to *knowledge without an object*, because the knowable does not reduce completely to an object but extends by right to that which remains a thing *in itself*, that which has not satisfied the conditions of objectification and its reduction. Constantly, and without always being fully aware of it, we come across something that happens to us without recurring or belonging to us. For instance, it could be the thing, not as something present-at-hand or subsistent, identical to its persistent presence (*vorhanden*), but handled straightaway as something that we have to-hand, without having it before our eyes (*zuhanden*), according to Heidegger's distinction. It could be the difference between the object synthesized by apperception according to the a priori conditions of experience (and thus of its objects), on the one hand, and, on the other, the irreducible in-itself of the thing that is free not to appear according to our finite criteria, as distinguished by Kant. Or, finally, it could be the gap between the thing understood and the infinite, the incomprehensibility of which is implied by formal reason, according to Descartes's distinction. In each case, we undergo on a daily basis the unavailability of that which is an exception to objectification, not as a distant domain, reserved for strange experiences, but in the daily and banal proximity of what happens to us without identifiable cause, without foreseeable reason, in a virginal contingency, banal and familiar. In each event, we undergo this mode of happening, which requires nothing of anyone and above all no authorization from a transcendental I (chapter V). And this is especially so in the event that admits no precondition—neither the principle of contradiction, nor the principle of sufficient reason: the gift (chapters II and IV). We cannot deny this banal proximity, particularly as it puts into operation phenomena as close to us—closer to us than ourselves—as our birth and the paternity that engenders it. This inevitable phenomenon is always already there. A mode of knowledge—that of the object—that cannot do justice to it retains its legitimacy, but thus reveals its limit. But it also loses all legitimacy if it does not recognize this limit—an epistemological limit, which attests more essentially to ontic finitude. The object has value only as finite and in finitude, which, moreover, it presupposes without being able to conceive of it. To conceive of our finitude thus demands that we no longer claim to know only objects, and that we allow for a knowledge without an object.

But there is more. The equivalence between certainty and knowledge can also be contested. And must be, because it can be. Indeed, there is also *knowledge without certainty*, because without object. Certainty admittedly works, above all and most often, with objects and in view of objects.

It does so by exercising the predicative and thus affirmative (categorical) use of language: speaking consists of speaking in order to say something (we were often told: don't speak without saying anything!); speaking in order to say something amounts to saying something about something, attributing a property to a subject: the sky is blue, the earth is round, two and two are four, he who doubts exists, God is not visible, the future is unknown, and so forth. Even if all of these propositions are not proved, even if they do not all lead to the constituting of an object, their potential certainty will result from their categorical ambition. The potential certainty will always affirm it. Such seems to be the case for the assertions of the exact sciences, according to their proper and constant claim: to say something certain about something, by an affirmative assertion. And yet, the positive and affirmative certainties of the sciences also claim a second privilege: their progress. The sciences say and realize a progress, they even claim to be the only means to reach progress, in opposition to the repetition of errors or approximations in the other figures of knowing (doesn't philosophy amount to the sum of all thinkable and even unthinkable errors, ceaselessly repeated?). However, these two claims—positive certainty and indefinite progress—do not proceed without a contradiction, at least one that is apparent enough to take seriously. If every affirmation can and must submit itself at the least to revision by a new, more comprehensive affirmation (putting aside the challenge or the refutation of one theory by another); if the falsification of a scientific assertion about some objects remains by definition always possible (and no one contests the rigor, the fruitfulness, and the honesty of this scientific self-discipline); in short, if every categorical affirmation about one or more objects exposes itself in principle to a possible revision, and can, in the best of cases, only be valid provisionally as a final truth, or more precisely as a final state of the known truth, then affirmative knowledge cannot claim to be absolutely certain. The positive certainty of a scientific assertion about an object thus remains provisional, because this object remains finite, and above all because the thought that constitutes it remains finite. The point here is not to contest (after all, by what right?) the certainty of positive statements, but to emphasize, or at least to admit, that this certainty remains inevitably provisional, revisable, in a sense radically contingent. From this it follows that positive certainty does not exhaust all certainty—that certainty requires more than its categorical and affirmative formulation; that is to say, it requires more than knowledge of the object.

But could another certainty than positive certainty by predication and affirmation be conceived? In this desperate ambition isn't there a kind of triumphant return of the preeminent metaphysical attempt at absolute knowledge, with all the illusions and dangers to which history so clearly attests? Or wouldn't there be an irrational exaltation here (dubbed *Schwärmerei* by the language of the Enlightenment), reviving the fantasies of an intellectual, or worse, "mystical" intuition? Such would probably be the case if we claimed to surpass and complete provisional, affirmative certainty by another affirmative, definitive, and dogmatic certainty. But in philosophy, there is a completely different path: that of *negative certainty*. Here, Descartes and Kant, little known for precritical dogmatism and unbridled irrationalism, are proposed as fairly sure guides. — Descartes first of all, who concludes his doctrine of the constitution of the object (the first of its kind: a constitution through positive affirmations of something over something, and through subtraction of the uncertain in the thing experienced, so as to retain from it only the certifiable objective) with a decisive remark on the limits of positive science. He who has

> mastered this whole method [. . .] may see [. . .] that his lack of further knowledge is not due to any want of intelligence or art. As often as he applies his mind to acquire knowledge of something, either he will be entirely successful, or at least he will realize that success depends upon some observation which it is not within his power to make—so he will not blame his intelligence, even though he is forced to come to a halt; or, finally, he will be able to demonstrate that the thing he wants to know wholly exceeds the grasp of the human mind—in which case he will not regard himself as more ignorant on that account, for this discovery amounts to no less a knowledge (*quia non minor scientia est*) than any other.[1]

Put otherwise: when I know that I cannot know the answer to a question "because of the obstacle which the nature of the problem itself or the human condition presents" ("*ipsius difficultatis natura, vel humana conditio*"), then "this point is no less a knowledge [science] than that which reveals the nature of the thing itself" ("*quae cognitio non minor scientia est, quam illa quae rei ipsius naturam exhibet*").[2] In this way, we can attain certain knowledge [*une science*] not only through positive certainty, by objectifying the nature of a thing as yet unknown, but also, if this affirmation proves to be unattainable, through *negative* certainty that either the thing itself, or our finite condition, renders the experience impossible and the answer unknowable. And this latter result—the knowledge of unknowability—amounts to "no less a knowledge [*science*]" than the affirmative answer to the question; for, precisely because this affirmation cannot be made with certainty, it is necessary to hold it in a purely negative certainty. Recognizing negatively the "limits of the mental powers" ("*ingenii limites*")[3] constitutes, negatively, a certainty comparable to the positive knowledge of any object. And the rather difficult-to-conceive *cogito* could in the end offer the most complete example of such a negative certainty, as it is articulated on the border of the finite and the infinite.

Kant, even more than Descartes, devotes his entire *Critique* to the recognition of the boundaries of reason. Or rather, he devotes it especially to the consideration of ignorance or nonknowing in a more radical mode than that of banal skepticism (in this instance, that of Hume): "The consciousness of my nonknowing (*Unwissenheit*) (if this nonknowing is not at the same time known to be necessary) should not end my inquiries, but is rather the proper cause to arouse them."[4] And it is true that such a "nonknowing" is in no way univocal, or simple: it can bear "either on things or on the determination and boundaries of my knowledge (*Grenzen meiner Erkenntnis*)."[5] In other words, it can effect a positive certainty through a categorical assertion on an object, or a negative certainty on the boundaries of the power of knowing. The knowledge of these boundaries must not, indeed, be confused with the a posteriori perception of my powerlessness to resolve such or such question, which is mere consciousness of the de facto "limits" ("*Schranken*") of my mind (as I would discover the limits of my country by pushing out toward its empirical borders); at issue instead are the boundaries (*Grenze*) that I know a priori, by "investigating in a *critical manner*" what my power of knowing can and cannot do (just as I would calculate the dimensions, and thus the boundaries, of the sphere of the earth on the basis of the principle of its rotundity and the measure of the longitudinal and latitudinal degrees of its surface). At issue here is an "absolutely necessary" nonknowing, as certain as a categorical knowledge: "This [. . .] cognition of nonknowing, which is possible only by means of the critique of reason itself, is thus *science*."[6] At the end of the *Critique*, the philosopher attains a priori a *negative certainty* of the impossibility of certain areas of knowledge, a certainty without an object, yet absolute and scientific.[7]

Against Duns Scotus ("*Negationes . . . non summe amamus*"[8]), we will therefore say, following Descartes and Kant, that we prefer negations provided that they *also* give certainties. And I have another reason for invoking the name of Kant here. In his attempt "to introduce into philosophy the concept of negative magnitudes," he distinguishes between logical opposition and real opposition. The former obtains where a thing contradicts itself with respect to the principle of contradiction: a body can be in motion (which is thinkable), or at rest (which is also thinkable), but no body can be, at the same time and in the same respect, in motion and at rest: this is not thinkable or representable, and so the object is annulled (*nihil negativum irrepraesentabile*). But there is also a real opposition, "that where two predicates of a thing are opposed to each other, but not through the law of contradiction. Here, too, one thing cancels that which is posited by the other; but the consequence is *something* (*cogitabile*)."[9] Two real forces that annul each other (for example, attraction and repulsion) produce a null result (immobility of the body), yet one that is nevertheless still real. Thus, even if nothing is seen or known as an object, two forces in a sense perfectly invisible confront each other at a heightened degree of reality. Negative magnitudes can be known without making a new object visible. Their certainty, as negative as can be, remains established. Thus, the negative itself can give rise to certainty.

We will therefore examine a hypothesis. If a question endowed with sense, formulated correctly and without logical contradiction, remains without a possible answer for a finite mind, and even for a priori reasons *must not* receive an answer according to the criteria of finite (metaphysical) rationality (the two principles of contradiction and of sufficient reason)—then, insofar as such a question is always being asked and left without an answer, and it survives this absence, does it not give a reality to be thought (*cogitabile*)? And does it not merit the rank of a negative certainty? For even denegation can be a matter of givenness.[10]

I. THE UNDEFINABLE, OR THE FACE OF MAN

Prince I know all things
I know the rosy-cheeked and the pale
I know Death who devours all
I know everything but myself.

—FRANÇOIS VILLON[1]

§ 2. "What Is Man?"

I am and I think. Admittedly, I am not always exactly insofar as I think, since I do not think exclusively that I am, nor clearly what I am, nor, for that matter, on the basis of where I am. But despite everything, from this mere fact that I think, it follows without any doubt that I am. Even if it is not always, or even often, I who decide what I think, even if I do not often think what I will, and even if I must on the contrary recognize that what is thought (for *it* thinks) in and through me imposes itself on me without *me* deciding or willing it in any way, nevertheless, by the mere fact that thought happens to me, it follows inevitably that I am. For, when it thinks in me, the issue is not the mere acknowledgment that every man thinks ("*Homo cogitat*," as Spinoza remarks without further commentary),[2] but instead the principle that the thought thinks itself in any case in the first person and, reciprocally, that the first person attests to itself only by thinking ("*ego ipse cogitans*," insists Descartes[3]). Thinking implies saying *I* in the first person, and saying *I* implies thinking. But what can I think, I who think by "having the ability to utter the word 'I,' a word that says so much"?[4] Indeed, what does this I say?

Obviously, it says much, or even everything, since it is up to it to say all that can be thought—"mind is in a sense potentially whatever is thinkable (but not in actuality)."[5] If I think, I know things. It is up to *me* to know things by the very fact that thinking is up to *me*. Clearly, even if I do not always know myself with certainty, and most often merely by approximation, I never think without knowing, without a certain science, even if by experience or simply by appearance. For the difficulty of science is not found first of all in its uncertainty or its greater certainty: from one to the other it is only a matter of degrees, following a transition that is always possible provided that a first view opens the field to viewings that are more and more exact. Everything becomes easier after the first error, which imperceptibly transforms science into an approximate truth, assuming that every truth does not remain so—approximate, that is. To know, it is enough to think, at least in order to set in motion the indefinite process of knowledge. And yet, it is precisely here that the real, fundamental difficulty arises: when I think and thus spontaneously know, I know all the more and better that I think that which differs from me. Let it stand forth in front of me: "[O]utside me, besides the extension, shapes and movements of bodies, I also had sensations of their hardness and heat, and of the other tactile qualities. In addition, I had sensations of light, colours, smells, tastes and sounds, the variety of which enabled me to distinguish [among them] the sky, the earth, the seas, and all other bodies,"[6] and thus the trees and the street, the passersby and the shop windows, the cars and the houses, too—I know them because I see them immediately (or almost immediately). But I see them and reconstitute them by differentiation among them only because I conceive them outside of me (*foris*), as objects that, literally (*ob-jecta*), face up to me, appear only by resisting me in the radical and never abolished face-to-face of the "*purae Matheseôs objectum*" ("the object of pure knowledge").[7] What I know "objects itself" to me [*s'objecte à moi*] like an object available to knowledge, but also like an objection to immediacy. This goes also, and all the more so, for all that I have ever seen solely through mediation, that which I have been taught, that of which I have heard tell: writing and reading, languages and their grammars, quantities and measures with their numbers and their figures, the models of the positive sciences, their statistics and their approximations, the objects of the technologies about which I am completely ignorant, and that I nevertheless use; in other words, everything that technoscience alone claims to know. I have undeniable knowledge of all of that: the best proof being that I can doubt it (and I doubt it more than anything in the world). But right away I discover an essential gap here, one that is transcendental and fundamental: if thinking signifies thinking what "objects itself" to me, then the fact that thinking refers back *to me* is not the same as me thinking *myself*, *me*; on the contrary, it excludes it. If I want to know myself, the one who knows, the one who thinks and who is me, or at least the one who comes closest to the *thinking* me, I no longer succeed in thinking anything, neither immediately, nor by mediation. Or rather, I will always think something *thought*, and thus, whatever it may be, something in front of me that will never coincide, by definition, with the *thinking thing* [*le pensant*] that I am, in whatever manner I may be it.

Thus, the first word in philosophy (at least its putative first word, since no one knows the author, and it can be attributed to an indefinite multitude of names)[8]—γνῶθι σεαυτόν ("Know thyself!")—should be heard as a challenge that is impossible to accept, or at best a paradox. On the contrary, I know that I never know myself, because I can know only that which does not coincide with me and allows itself to be an object of my thought [*se laisse objecter à ma pensée*]. I know from the first and without return that I will remain the knower unknown to himself. The philosopher would thus appear as she who preeminently knows that she will never know herself in the manner in which she knows every other thing—precisely because she will never be able to say or think this specific thing, the *I* so full of meaning, like an object seen frontally. She does not know herself, and *must* not: "Be ignorant of thyself" (Levinas).[9]

Kant put forth exactly this "paradox that must have struck everyone": we do not know ourselves, not only because in the external sense (space) we only appear to ourselves as a thing in the world, but likewise in the inner sense (time). Indeed, "[the inner sense] presents even ourselves to consciousness only as we appear to ourselves, not as we are in ourselves, since we intuit ourselves only as we are internally *affected*."[10] We know something that we can of course call ourselves; I thus know myself, but precisely I know myself only as *known*, and never as *knowing*, thus never as I am specifically that one who thinks that which, without him, would remain neither thought nor known. Perhaps man can know himself, but solely and exactly as he knows every other object of experience, which is to say insofar as he is given in sensible intuition:

> But how the I (*Ich*), the *I think*, is to differ from the I (*Ich*) that intuits itself [. . .] and yet be identical with the latter as the same subject (*als dasselbe Subjekt*), how therefore *I* (*Ich*) can, as intelligence and thinking subject, cognize my self *as an object* that is thought (*mich selbst als gedachtes Objekt*), insofar as I am also given to myself in intuition, only, *exactly like other phenomena* (*gleich anderen Phänomen*), not as I am for my understanding

> but rather as I appear to myself, this is no more and no less difficult than [to know] how I can be for myself *in general an object* (*überhaupt ein Objekt*) and indeed one of intuition and inner perceptions.[11]

It cannot be said more clearly: the knowledge of oneself by oneself is not exempt from the conditions of knowledge: yet again, the issue is no more and no less than that *I* know an object, *me*, that gives itself like any other object in intuition, at precisely the distance of the *ob*-ject in front of the mind of the human being who thinks it, *I*. But I can never know this *thinking* I as such, subsistent and permanent: "That I, as a thinking being, *endure* for myself, that naturally I neither arise nor perish—this I can by no means infer [from the concept of substance] [. . .]. So much is lacking for us to be able to infer these properties solely from the pure category of substance, that we must rather ground the persistence of a given object on experience."[12] Here, the external sense (space) recovers its precedence over the inner sense (time). In every other case, the spatial intuition of an object is in the end transcribed into time. *Here*, however, when the issue is that of thinking that which thinks (the thinking thing [*le pensant*]) and not that which is thought (the thought thing [*le pensé*]), paradoxically, this thinker that basically thinks temporally must ground itself and allow itself to be validated by persistence in space—in short, by the nonmoving, or -passing, or -flowing intuition of an object remaining self-identical. In other words, in knowing myself I nevertheless will never know myself insofar as I know (according to the privilege of being the only knower, because I am the only thinker), but always insofar as I am already simply a *known me*, known to the same extent as any other known, that is to say as any other object. Strangely, I thus know myself never as *I* who know, but always only as a known *me*, as an *object* among others. I only know myself as that which I am not, as the me-object.

And yet, I still remain the sole knower, the thinking *I*, who makes possible all the thought things as just so many of its thoughts. How can I think, or rather *not* think, that alone which thinks thoughts and thought things? The most extreme and the most immediate, the most recognizable and the most inalienable property of the being that *I* am, the property of exercising a thinking thought, becomes, by a renewed and even disquieting paradox, "the simple and in content for itself wholly empty representation *I*, of which one cannot even say that it is a concept, but a mere consciousness that accompanies every concept. Through this I, or He, or It (the thing), which thinks, nothing further is represented than a transcendental subject of thoughts = *x* [substratum, *subjectum*, ὑποκείμενον], which is recognized only through the thoughts that are its predicates, and about which, in abstraction, we can never have even the least concept."[13] Just as, according to Descartes, substance (even thinking substance) does not affect us as such but only by its attributes, thinking thought remains for us "unknown" and is "not an experience,"[14] except through the mediation of the representations of real and really intuited objects that it "accompanies" as substratum.[15] I will only ever have knowledge of thinking thought in conformity with the common conditions of knowledge: I will know it as an object, or, in other words, as *thought* thought, and never as such, as thinking thought.

Far from this distinction between the *I* (which is transcendental, an empty form that accompanies every cognition but remains itself unrepresentable and unknowable) and the *me* (which is empirical, belonging to phenomena and thus to objects) giving access to the man that I am, it prevents me from approaching the man that I am and disfigures each man's self.[16] What first appeared as a paradox could thus become *another* "scandal of philosophy and universal human reason,"[17] more detrimental than the first—for it no longer has to do with the existence of the world outside of myself, but with the essence of the *I* that is me. And Kant furnishes the perhaps involuntary index of this scandal when he undertakes the sketching of an anthropology. Here, anthropology can only be understood as the science of man; now, since every science by definition refers back to man (as science *by* and *for* man, as "human science" according to the first meaning of this construction), it can only be a question of a science taught by man *about* man himself. Kant formulates this clearly: "The most important object [*Gegenstand*] in the world to which he [man] can apply them [acquired knowledge and skills] is *man*: because he is his own final end. — Therefore to know him according to his species as an earthly being endowed with reason [*mit Vernunft begabtes Erdwesen*] especially deserves to be called *knowledge of the world*, even though he constitutes only one part of the creatures on earth."[18] A science of man by man, then, which explicitly signifies a science of man as an object, and an object of the world. That man shows himself to be gifted with reason is not an exception to these determinations, but instead completes them as a knowledge that is additionally *thought*. Moreover, it is a matter of a knowledge held by man *over* himself in the most radical sense, and that is deployed, says Kant, "from a pragmatic point of view."[19] This must be understood in opposition to an anthropology from a physiological point of view, which "concerns the investigation of what *nature* makes of man." By contrast, pragmatic anthropology aims at "what *he* as a free-*acting* being [*Wesen*] makes, or can and should make *of himself*."[20] Let us note that this knowledge of man by himself cannot be reduced *to* a simple empirical knowledge, since it involves man's freedom. But right away the question becomes one of knowing if man can apply to himself his own knowledge in order to become his own "object" and, more generally, by what right he can "make of himself" anything at all. What is more, the aporia of this self-objectification is marked out very quickly and clearly by the interpretation of the question of the *ego* (and of the consciousness of the *I* in the child), and by the description of *selfishness* [*l'égoïsme*], which is the moralizing and psychologizing devaluation of the aporia of an access to thinking thought (the only real difficulty). Anthropology leaves the very *question* of the *ego* (not to mention the answer to its paradox, which is here completely lacking) all the more undetermined, seeing as Kant invests it with the almost exorbitant function of concentrating in itself the three questions of the entire system of philosophy (in fact of metaphysics): respectively, "What can I know?" or *metaphysica generalis* reduced to the science of the first principles of human knowledge; then "What ought I to do?" which is to say moral philosophy; and finally "What may I hope?" or religion itself. If, as he often repeats, these three questions "could reckon all of this as anthropology, because the first three questions relate to the last one," and thus if the last question, "What is man?" once again becomes the first,[21] the aporia of knowledge by man of man would recapitulate an aporia of the system of metaphysics itself. Metaphysics would be characterized then as the impossibility of thinking man otherwise than as one of the objects of the world, one of the known things, the evidence of which serves only to dissimulate even more radically the obscurity into which thinking thought sinks itself. The paradox of the *I* therefore stigmatizes the aporia of man for metaphysics, that is, for himself: he knows himself and defines himself only by his objects, and never as such.[22]

The crisis that Kant thus makes manifest does not arise with him: the impossibility of knowing the thinking thought and of thereby reaching the *I* as such does not contradict what is typically attributed to Descartes under the title of the *cogito*; in looking at it more closely, this impossibility on the contrary confirms a caesura, or rather a fracture, that arises with this *cogito* itself as it was rigorously instituted but also minutely delimited. Indeed, as soon as it is noted in the second *Meditatio* that if I say or conceive that "I am, I exist," then this proposition is necessarily validated, and therefore, in fact, I am and I exist "each time" and "for as long as"[23] I think it—in short, no sooner is my existence established, but my essence becomes all the more problematic, for "I do not yet have a sufficient understanding of *who I am* [*quisnam sim*], *this 'I'* [*ego ille*] that I already am necessarily. And once again I must be on my guard against carelessly taking something else instead of and in place of this 'I' [*in locum mei*] and so making a mistake in the very knowledge that I maintain is the most certain and evident of all."[24] The existence of the *ego* as and by way of the *cogito* not only does not open any access to its essence, but on the contrary manifests its aporia.

This is so in several ways. First of all, the definition of existence by the act of thinking invalidates the received definition of man as rational animal, *animal rationale*: not because this definition has no sense at all or does not designate man, but because it does not accomplish what it says in saying it and, thus, does not produce itself, instead still presupposing the concepts that allow it; thus, far from defining the essence of man, it first asks, in order to get to that definition itself, that one define for it its own terms: what is an animated being, what is a rational being? The definition does not define but asks that we define it, such that "one question would lead me down the slope to other harder ones."[25] The essence does not answer the existence like a solution, but becomes in its turn a question, which, with each new proposed response, becomes yet more questionable or aporetic. And what is more, Descartes will in fact never provide a definition of the essence of man. For, contrary to oft-repeated appearances, to invoke a "thinking thing" ("*res cogitans*") does not allow for the definition of the least essence, precisely because *res* indicates preeminent indetermination. Not only does thinking proliferate into a plurality of definitively heterogeneous modes (to doubt, to understand, to will and not to will, also to imagine and even to feel), without allowing for one to be deduced from the other, nor all to be reduced to a single dominant mode; but above all, thinking remains an act, which, as such, produces no definition, and does not even *need* to do so. And nothing changes if we substitute a "thinking substance" ("*substantia cogitans*") for the "thing that thinks": substance applies indifferently to bodies (*substantia extensa*) and to God (*substantia infinita*), so that, if there must be a definition, it would come from the adjective that is in principle qualifying, and not from the substantive, which is neutral and empty. But the qualifiers here added (aside from the infinite, reserved for God) do not bear on individuals, but rather on genres: all material bodies are extended substances, all minds are thinking substances; thus, they do not define man as species or genre, and even less do they define me myself as the agent of my own thought, as *ego*. Descartes, then, will never define the essence of man and will never claim to know the *ego* itself. Kant did not criticize him, but rather confirmed him exactly. The question "*Quisnam sim ego ille, qui jam sum?*" ("Who am I, this *I* that I nevertheless really am?") has no reason to be asked, since, by definition, it will never receive an answer. I am not me, or more precisely *I* is never anything but a *me*, that I am not and which is not *I*, since it is a *me*.

There is, then, a first and chief impossibility in defining the essence of man, an epistemic and directly metaphysical impossibility: when knowledge exerts itself starting from an *I*, it bears only on objects, known with certainty in the exact measure that they allow themselves to be constituted by certainty and submit themselves to its conditions of possibility; as a result, what will eventually be known under the name *I* will always remain an object, strictly speaking a *me*, and thus precisely what is opposed to the *I* (the *ob*-ject), that which never and on principle will say the *I* or show it. If it were necessary to reclaim or contest a supposed human exception (which for that matter does not go without saying), it precisely would not consist in man's knowledge of himself by himself, according to a definition that is more complete than for any other object, but rather in the impossibility of knowing by this name anything but a *known* object, a *thought* thought, and therefore in the inaccessibility of the *thinking* thought itself. If man is an exception to what he knows, he owes it to the impossibility that the thinking thought in him would know itself as a thought object, and that the slightest thought object, even under the name of "man," would coincide with that which thinks it. The thought of thought, if there is one, remains the privilege of the divine, and foreign to me.[26]

§ 3. "*Ipse mihi magna quaestio*"

Having arrived at this point, we could draw a simple, almost inevitable conclusion: since the transcendental *I* remains an empty form, barely a thought, the simple substratum of the thoughts that it accompanies without giving anything to know, and since, consequently, the knowable *I* is reduced to the rank of a simple *me*, the empirical object of anthropology, an object constituted by the knowledge that produces it just like any other object, "man," this recent invention, may very well inevitably have to disappear, like a fragile sand castle that the rising tide obliterates. And in fact, man has already disappeared, and all that remains is to register the end of the human exception. This conclusion ceaselessly comes (and goes), like the waves on the shore, but, again like the waves, without really taking hold, or convincing us.

There is a good reason for this. The aporia we've isolated offers much more than an impasse: it allows a paradox to appear.

The inaccessibility of man to himself and his irreducibility to any definition could indeed also be understood as a describable determination, or even as a privilege that is all the more solid because it offers itself first of all negatively. For if the man that *I am* remains inaccessible (*to me*), or more precisely if that which I am cannot be defined as "man" (nor as any more detailed equivalent), this is not the result of my not knowing it, but on the contrary of my knowing it only too well and too easily, because I know it only as an *object*. Man escapes me to the extent that the very mode of his possible knowledge, which makes him a *thought* object, contradicts and hides his first characteristic, that of a pure *thinking thing* [*un pensant pur*], who thinks without becoming a thought thing [*un pensé*]. Must we conclude from this fundamental impossibility that the *I* itself means nothing? Yet not only does it "say much" (Leibniz), it says itself, it allows itself to be said by my *I*, as an ever-performable act, incontestably performable, because it requires no other condition than precisely this one—that *I* say *I*. If *I* "says much" and says itself, and provided only that it says nothing more, nor anything other than this *I* itself, ought we not to conclude that it would have access to itself as such only to the exact extent that it does not allow itself ever to be confused with a thought object, or in short, to the extent that it gives up the illusion of knowing itself as a *me*, in order to accept *not knowing itself*, at least in the way in which it knows objects? Put otherwise, my access to this *I* that I recognize solely for my own and as *I* would require me to assume no power, nor even any *obligation* to appear to myself as a knowledge (a thought object), but only as a definitive question (a thinking thing without any answering object). For the *I* is experienced and grasped all the better as a thinking thought that the *I* thinks without a thought object, or that it doubts knowing, and questions without any answer.

Before testing this hypothesis, we must conceive it more clearly. Now, as it happens, the impossibility of knowing oneself (as an object) can be described in a precise characterization, albeit negative: Saint Augustine, perhaps more than anyone else, was able to recognize the *I* as a question for himself, and detail its dimensions. For if one is able to observe, as if from the outside, "what a vast deep man is" ("*grande profundum est ipse homo*"), it is necessary above all to sound the depths of the very question that dug that deep: "*Factus eram ipse mihi magna quaestio*." ("I had become to myself a great question.")[27] What we have here is not merely a formula tossed off as if in passing by the rhetorical impetus, since in the three cases that illustrate it we always find a particular form of the same observation: what I think (or think I think) as a *me* does not coincide with that which *I* am, and thus that which I am does not appear in this *me* that *I* think; not only is the *me* not identified with the *I* (since the relation of subject to object opposes them), but I cannot even see clearly any longer if that which thinks remains an *I* in action, or instead proceeds from a more obscure point, from where *that* [*ça*] thinks the objectively thought *me* without my being able to identify myself as an *I* thinking it.

That *I* do not know *me* because their very distinction lacks validity is noted by Saint Augustine on three occasions. — A first time occurs when he experiences the death of a very dear friend, indeed "half [his] soul," or even "a single soul in two bodies"; this loss of another thus becomes at the same time a loss of himself, of the self itself. This is translated by the disappearance of the entire phenomenon of the world for me—the surrounding world, the nearby world, or more precisely this proximity that I open to myself as a world belonging to me and precisely *where* I assure myself of a *me* (*Umwelt*). That which finds itself suspended resides neither in me nor in my friend, nor in such or such being, but in everything and anything (*omnia, quidquid*). "*Oderam omnia*" ("Everything became hateful to me") means that nothing remained available to me anymore, usable for my ends, practicable as a world opened to and by *me*. Thus, the *I* loses its homeland and there is no more paternal home ("*Et erat mihi patria supplicium et paterna domus mira infelicitas*"): no world of his remains for him, whatever he contemplates opposes itself to his intentionality and puts to death his familiar world, and leads him to see nothing but death around him ("*quidquid aspiciebam mors erat*"). The nearby world fades away and a world of objects is substituted, at a distance from and in opposition to the network of referrals that a certain sphere of beings used to arrange for him, or that used to make him *himself*. Reduced to itself, the *I* finds itself without a self, and thus refers itself back to less than itself. *I* no longer knows *where* it is, nor from *whence* it comes. And thus "*mihi quaestio factus sum*."[28]— A second crisis, in appearance much different because this time it follows conversion ("*in primordiis recuperatae fidei meae*"), once again brings about the observation that I am to myself a pure question (*mihi quaestio factus sum*): while listening to the chants sounding in the church, Saint Augustine believes first that the emotion comes to him from the words he is chanting, and not from the chant itself (“*moveor non cantu, sed rebus quae cantantur*”); but quickly, in experiencing the splendor of the liturgy of Saint Ambrose, he starts to suspect that in fact he enjoys the chants themselves more than the prayer of the Psalms (“*me amplius cantus, quam res, quae canitur, moveat*”).[29] Thus, the intention of his prayer would find itself perverted by the mere enjoyment of the means of this prayer, or at least one cannot put aside the permanent suspicion that this is so. This time, the world that is closest is not the issue, but rather the innermost part of his identity, that of a Christian who believes and wills to believe, but who discovers that he does not truly know what he wills when he believes he is believing. His faith, and thus his deepest will, “from which all that he does proceeds” (“*unde facta procedunt*”), escapes him, since it could, without his mastering it, still obey the logic of the world. The *I* no longer coincides with the self, even if it had toiled so hard to meet up again with Christ in itself. It must recognize, once again, that “[i]n your eyes [God] I have become a question to myself.”[30] I become to myself a *quaestio*, indeed an aporia, because I discover that I cannot order my own prayer voluntarily. That which escapes me, when my conversion itself becomes inaccessible, no longer concerns only a theoretical knowledge (that of my essence, of my definition, indeed of my *I*), but the most precise act of my ipseity: what I truly will, what I decide in the final instance. — A final observation removes, or rather confirms, all the ambiguity: the aporia indeed closes access to ipseity because it puts into question that which most irreducibly constitutes it (and which allowed, or rather delayed, conversion itself, and thus had characterized the self of the preceding *quaestio*): the freedom of what is in my power. Indeed, even though while in a waking state I succeed completely, through social reflexes or moral decisions, in avoiding real erotic temptations, on the contrary during my nocturnal dreams it happens that I give in without willing to the impression of erotic images, even to the point of actual enjoyment. How do we explain this suspension of the power of the will from one moment to the other? Why was I on leave from myself at night, even while I was in control of myself during the day? There is only one obvious answer: my alienation from myself, my alienness: “At this moment, *am I indeed not myself*, Lord my God? Yet what a *difference* between myself and myself in a [single] moment.” (“*Numquid tunc ego non sum, Domine Deus meus? Et tamen tantum interest inter me ipsum et me ipsum intra momentum.*”)[31] When my power to decide and to will no longer coincides with my ipseity, not only do I lose all knowledge (and thus every definition) of myself (and of my essence), but the *ego* in me comes undone through a definitive and irreparable splitting from itself (*Ichsplatung*, or schizophrenia, if you will). At issue in this ordeal is the dissolution of ipseity—not only a compromised access to self, but an alienation of self from self. In a single and unique moment, I find myself other than myself: *I* is another, but here it is to *me* that this alienation is happening. Thus, I am no longer anything for myself, and cannot even say *I*. Or, I am only the aporia itself that divides me.

And yet this aporia does not burst forth without reason [*raison*], or rather without a certain folly [*déraison*]. Indeed, it refers back to what Saint Augustine calls *memoria*, and which overlaps only with the edges of what we understand commonly by *memory*, the faculty of making present again at the present instant that which once was present, but no longer is. For, if nothing defines me more intimately than this memory ("*cum ipsum me non dicam praeter illam*"), perhaps this proceeds from the fact that memory first plays another role, otherwise determinant: not that of allowing me to become conscious again (of what I knew and forgot), but that of submitting me to the immemorial and dismissing me from myself, in an original unconsciousness. After all, how is it that not only can I forget, but I can also remember *that* I have forgotten what I have nevertheless forgotten? For if I did not retain in my memory at least the fact *that* I have forgotten that which I nevertheless no longer remember, paradoxically I would forget every memory to come. And in fact, I do not forget *that* I have forgotten, when I forget *that which* I have forgotten ("*mihi certum est meminisse me oblivionem*," "*ipsam oblivionem meminisse me certus sum*"[32]). It would be absurd to claim to dissolve this paradox by distinguishing between a (lost) memory of *that which* I have forgotten, and another (retained) memory of *the fact that* I have forgotten: for I would still have to tie these two memories to each other in order to understand how something forgotten remains sufficiently in my memory so that I do not forget *that* I have forgotten *that which* I have forgotten; and this link in its turn would call for a double *memoria*, ad infinitum. I have only to admit, then, that through the same memory I have retained the image itself of forgetting, without the image of the forgotten object; which forces me to conclude that my memory, what is innermost to my consciousness, doubles itself, since it holds that which overcomes forgetting as well as that which succumbs to it. Thus, when my *memoria* escapes itself, in this escaping, I escape myself, or better: *I* escapes from me, which finds itself as a *me* without itself: "*Factus sum mihi terra difficultatis.*" ("I have become for myself a soil of difficulty.")[33] My difficulty (my aporia) is for me my sole ground, such that I can only ask myself, and ask God: "*Hoc animus est, et hoc ego ipse sum. Quid ergo sum, Deus meus? Quae natura sum?*" ("This is my mind, and I myself am it. What then am I, my God? *What nature am I?*")[34] I am without definition, or essence, or nature other than this aporia to myself. — Thus, to the first impossibility of a definition of the essence of man, we must add a second: no longer is it simply that *I* can only be opposed, by definition, to the *me ob*-ject, but, as such, this I itself divides itself, dissolves itself, and escapes itself.

What significance do we find in such an impossible access of the self to the self? Are we dealing here with a failure of knowledge, or a limitation in self-consciousness, or, in short, a version of the usual critiques of the *cogito*, in the style of Malebranche ("We therefore have no clear idea either of the soul or of its modifications"), or of Spinoza ("the mind does not know itself except insofar as it perceives ideas of affections of the body"), or of Locke, concluding with "this ignorance we are in of the nature of that thinking thing that is in us, and which we look on as our*selves*"?[35] Unquestionably, Saint Augustine had to give up on the ambition of his beginnings, when he believed he was not asking for much in desiring to know nothing other than God and the soul ("*Deum et animam scire cupio. / Nihil ne plus? / Nihil omnino*"), to the point of admitting, after having experienced the permanence of the temptation, that he knew God better than himself ("*Minus mihi in hac re notus sum ipse quam tu*").[36] This purely negative conclusion, which we have little difficulty translating into contemporary language (neuronal or neurotic), has its rightness: *I* has no idea of itself, other than that of a *me* object, and it will on principle never have another. And yet, it still has to be decided whether this very conclusion does not already constitute, in its denial, a knowledge. The aporia as such teaches something—it gives certainty of the paradox of self-unknowing. Pascal ended up literally with this paradox as the negative and certain form of the essence and definition of man as the one who says *I*: "Know then, proud man, what a paradox you are to yourself. Be humble, impotent reason! Be silent, feeble nature! Learn that man infinitely transcends man, hear from your master your true condition, which is unknown to you."[37] A paradox indeed, one that is insufficiently noticed: the humiliation of feebleness isn't supposed to degrade man, but on the contrary stigmatizes the fact that he does not know that he surpasses his own nature (for it does seem to be asking much of the reason of philosophers to recognize indefinable greatness). But the paradox of man becomes a thesis only if one first understands it, starting from Montaigne, as the necessary consequence of a more original paradox, that of the injunction made to man to know himself: "It was a paradoxical command that was given us of old by that god at Delphi: 'Look into yourself, know yourself.'" Why paradoxical? Precisely because we *are unable* to look at ourselves, except by reversing our phenomenon, and because the god in question is therefore not asking us to do what we would not like to do, but rather that which we must not even hope to do, because we never could do it. Self-unknowing constitutes the human exception. "'Except for you, O man [*Sauf toi, ô homme*],' said that god, 'each thing studies itself first, and, according to its needs, has limits to its labors and desires. There is not *a single thing* as empty and needy as you, who embrace the universe: you are the investigator without knowledge, the magistrate without jurisdiction, and all in all, the fool of the farce."[38] It must be understood that every other thing can and must know itself, *except* [*sauf*] *man*. Is this a fault? Probably, since it prevents me from knowing my limits, and leaves me empty of myself. But it's a fairly happy fault, since it forces me to admit the fundamental impossibility of knowing myself and defining myself:

> The advice to everyone to know himself must have an important effect, since the god of learning and light had it planted on the front of his temple, as comprising all the counsel he had to give us. [. . .] The difficulties and obscurity in any science are perceived only by those who have access to it. For a man needs at least some degree of intelligence to be able to notice that he does not know; and we must push against a door to know that it is closed to us. [. . .] Thus in this matter of knowing oneself, the fact that everyone is seen to be so cocksure and self-satisfied, that everyone thinks he understands enough about himself, signifies that everyone understands nothing about it.[39]

Thus, the paradox consists, ironically, in commanding man to know himself, so as to instruct him thoroughly in the impossibility of this conceit; and to make him see that in this farce, the fool may not be who we think it is: for, in not knowing himself, not only can man devote himself as "investigator without knowledge" to knowing all else, but, free like a "magistrate without jurisdiction," he remains, precisely, *safe as an exception* [*il reste sauf*] from every jurisdiction over him exerted by the authority of a knowledge. *Except for man* [*Sauf l'homme*] should be understood as a slogan: everything knows itself, everything is defined, everything judges itself, save man. Man, or the animal safe from definition, the being saved from essence.

§ 4. What It Costs to Know (Oneself)

At this point, we see that the aporia of self-knowledge harbors much more than a failure. For in order for this aporia to be summed up as a mere failure of knowledge, it would first be necessary, beyond this presumed impossibility, for it to be *preferable*, in the case of the *I* of man claimed by me, that I know it by a "clear idea" or, what follows from that, by a concept. Now, such a knowledge raises not only the question of its possibility, but above all that of its legitimacy. Assuming that it is not contradictory to claim to reach the *I*, which alone understands (and produces) concepts, through one of its own concepts, would it be at all *licit* and thus desirable to know this *I* by concept as an object? If such an enterprise finally destroyed the very *I* that it claims to reach, then the *quaestio* would no longer become simply an aporia, but would open a reverse path toward an entirely other mode of conquest of *who* I am. For what good would it do man to know himself by a mode through which he knows everything else—the world and its objects—if in order to get there he would have to know himself as one more object? What does it profit man to know himself through a concept if he has to lose his humanity in doing so? And, inversely, what would man lose if he did not gain himself in the mode of an object, but in the mode—to put it provisionally—of incomprehensibility? Does it indeed go without saying that every knowledge, and even the knowledge of that which has the privilege of exerting knowledge rather than being submitted to it, must be accomplished according to the same and univocal concept that it uses to bring objects to evidence?

To respond to this question, it is first necessary to make clear what should be understood by the verb "to know." No doubt, we understand in the strict sense (that is to say, precisely, *without a doubt*) "to know" as to have or to produce a clear and distinct idea, in the Cartesian sense of the formula; not necessarily because we accept the Cartesian theory of science, but because we share its final intention: knowing doesn't seem worth our while unless, through this idea, we obtain at the very least the equivalent of "a concept so clear and distinct, produced by a pure and attentive mind, such that no doubt remains about what we are understanding."[40] Now, that which therefore can be known (through an idea and a representation) in such a manner that no doubt about it remains is defined as an object. Or, which amounts to the same thing, we may only allow into science that which offers an object that is certain: "We should attend only to those objects of which our minds seem capable of having certain and indubitable cognition."[41] Consequently, what cannot be known as an object, and thus what cannot be according to the mode of being of objects, falls outside of all knowledge and thus of all being in general. A radical consequence indeed, but an inevitable one, drawn explicitly by Clauberg when, in order to found the then new science of *ontologia*, he imposed the strict equivalence between being and the thinkable: "*Ens est quicquid quovis modo est, cogitari ac dici potest*" ("Being is all that which, in whatever manner may be, can be thought and said"), to the point that all beings end, or rather begin, by being identified with the single type of the *ens cogitabile*.[42] The entity, as cognizable, as thought according to its objection to thought, is opposed and apposed as object to that which represents it to itself—namely, the *I*. This absolute thesis, which fixes the first historically documented meaning of *ontologia*, therefore does not separate that which *is* from that which *is thought* (as the real to the idea) but, on the contrary, poses their strict equivalence: the preeminently thinkable is, because the entity first of all is thought. Accordingly, the condition of being of the entity understood as an object is no longer decided in or by this entity itself, but in and by the mind that knows it, because the knowing mind constructs its concept. In Cartesian terms one could say that only that which can satisfy the conditions of possibility fixed by the *mathesis universalis* (namely, order and measure) becomes intelligible, and thus belongs to being *insofar as known*.[43] It follows that the object is never defined in itself nor by itself, but always by the thought that knows it in constructing it. More essential to the entity as object than itself, the *ego* makes of it an *alienated entity*—alienated by the knowledge of another. It falls to the *intuitus* to accomplish concretely this alienation of the object: *in-tuitus* rather than intuition, a gaze that is active and on the lookout, not a neutral vision; a gaze that exercises its view only according to the mode of a guard (*-tueri*), the guard that makes sure and places under security, that keeps an eye on and watches over that which henceforth remains under its dominion, the object. In Kantian terms, it will be said that the object conforms itself to the faculty of knowing, and thus first of all against the intuition: "If intuition (*Anschauung*) has to conform to the constitution of the objects (*Beschaffenheit der Gegenstände*), then I do not see how we can know anything of them *a priori*; but if the object (as an object of the senses—*Gegenstand als Objekt der Sinnen*) conforms to the constitution of our faculty of intuition, then I can very well represent this possibility to myself."[44] Ordering objects to our power to know them does not leave open the inverse possibility (objects that would order our power to know them), but must be understood as a tautology: the object, by its definition, conforms to our power to know it. Otherwise, we would not be dealing with an object, but rather a thing in itself. The object is defined precisely by the disappearance into it of the *self* of the thing (in itself). The object, that is, the alienated object, alienated clearly from its *self*, for the benefit of the only *self* that is still permitted to an entity as thinkable thing thought—the *self* of the *I think*. The object designates that which, of the thing, is left as the prey of the *I think*. "The object is the part of the real that is put forward: it is in front of our eyes like prey; it is placed in front of everyone like booty."[45]

No one has exposed the alienation of the thing in an object by the concept that precedes and constitutes it better than Hegel. In naming a thing, man substitutes for its immediate being and its qualities of sensible representation precisely "a *name*, a *sound* made by [his] voice, something entirely different from what [the thing] is in intuition"; this name does not tell the immediacy of the thing, but that into which the thing "withdraws" and where it becomes "something spiritual, something altogether different." Thus, all of nature, once named, transforms itself into "a realm of names," because "the external object itself was negated in that very synthesis."[46] The object appears henceforth as such—as alienated being, which has lost its being in order to receive it from the *I*: "*[T]he object is not what* it is [. . .], the thing is not what it *is*."[47] The being of the object only consists in receiving its being from man, who alienates it exactly insofar as he names it: "[M]an speaks of the thing as *his*. And this is the *being* of the object."[48] Put another way, "[B]y means of the name [. . .] the object has been born out of the I [and has emerged] as *being*. This is the primal *creative* faculty exercised by Spirit. Adam gave a name to all things."[49] Hegel obviously alludes to the biblical episode in which God gives to man power over the animals by giving him the right to name them: "[He] brought them to the man to see what he would call them" (Gen. 2:19). Adam gives a name and therefore a definition to the animals, which thus become subject to him, because in general all knowledge by concept reduces what is known to the status of object. Adam therefore names in the manner by which the *I* knows—by concepts of objects.

Hegel's reading allows for two remarks. First, the call must not be understood in a univocal manner. It does not always draw out another me by my recognizing in the call a *self* that attests to itself by its response; the call can also just as well amount to *calling the roll*, that is to say lining people up (as *figures*), enumerating names that in fact function like *numbers*, or are even reduced to registration numbers, in which case, the response that replies "Present!" only has the function of validating the registration number, or in other words of *invalidating* the identity of the one called by accepting that he is indeed summed up by this number. Thus, the call here can also reduce to silence, cut speech short, and in this way produce an object even of the other, since it can deny the *self* of any thing. To reach this point of denial, it is enough for the call to impose this name as a definition, minimal but for that very reason exhaustive, of the one called—who henceforth is reduced completely to a figure, to his registration number. From which it follows that Adam has the power to call in this way only whatever can legitimately become for him an object: the animals (and the rest of the world).[50] Significantly, he did not receive the power to call either the angels, or another man,[51] or himself, or of course God, by fixing them with a name. Indeed, in these last three cases, if Adam claimed to name by identifying, he would discover the previous aporia. Either he would name them by identifying them genuinely as such, and then they would only amount to objects, pure and simple *thought things*, at an infinite distance from that to which they nevertheless testify—namely, to the exercising, each irreducibly, of the thought that says *I*, and which even says Adam's *I*. These names, precisely if they identified something, would thus identify something other than these *selves*: more precisely, they would identify things without any *self*, objects; in short, if the names identified something correctly, they would substitute objects for what was to be named, and would name into empty space. Or, Adam's names correctly name what they intend, but to do so, they must name without identifying, or registering, or objectifying; just as the infinity of divine names correctly designates God, because no one of them claims to identify him or define his essence in the least, and just as the proper name that calls the other man (or me myself) evokes him and provokes him only by remaining at a distance from his identity, from his definition and his essence, since such a man will appear as such and in his *self* only to the extent of his response; a response, or a taking up of speech, the overturning of my thought thought about him by a *thinking* thought come from elsewhere, namely, from him, and, as such, from an *I* inaccessible to my objectification.

Having thus posed some characteristics of knowledge by concept, there follows as a consequence the impossibility for man to name—that is, to define—a man except by reducing him to the rank of a simple concept and thereby to know not a man but an object, possibly animated, but always alienated. There is, then, no contradiction between, on the one hand, the knowledge of man as the object of anthropology, and, on the other, the impossibility of this knowledge within a reflexive self-consciousness; for knowing *I, myself* [*le moi*] as an object, constituted by the alienation common to all objects, in no way opens access to the *I*, which alone knows objects precisely because it *opposes* itself to them (*ob*-jects itself to them). Their distinction shows itself simply according to the case where I am (man is) the insurmountable difference between the two sides of the *cogitatio*: the *ego* and the object. From this there necessarily follows another conclusion: if one is unaware of or neglects this distinction, that is to say if one persists in claiming that man can (and therefore must) become an object for man (*homo homini objectum*), one only displaces this very distinction: for that which will be known as an object, even dressed up with the title of "man," will in fact *not be a man* and will not be able to make itself be recognized as one. Indeed, each of us can, in various ways, have this crucial experience for ourselves: *defining a man always eventually amounts to having done with the humanity in him, and thus to having done with him.* Not because he would no longer be conceived, or thought *of*, but precisely because one conceives him by in fact not thinking of him, because one conceives him without *beginning from he himself* but, instead, by beginning from one other than him, namely, from the *I* who defines him by alienating him according to the mode of understanding. Or, put another way, *to classify a man is to downgrade him as human*, because he could not be classified any other way than according to an order and a measure (models and parameters) that come to him from elsewhere—namely, from the workings of *my* rationality.

§ 5. Proscription

This alienation, which degrades the man who is understood, defined, and assigned the rank of an object, can be noticed every time we end up agreeing to dare to formulate the question "What is man?" This simple question, apparently inoffensive in the way it overflows with *humanist* benevolence, contains, disguised within it, an extreme danger: it assumes, as if it went without saying, that the question of man bears a *what*, and that the answer consists in designating the appropriate *that which* or *what*soever. The very formulation of the question thus prejudges the answer by covering over the stakes of man that lie beneath the evidence of the *that which*—namely, that he always says himself in saying this *I* "that says so much"; by saying this simple *I*, he says each time that it is a question of he himself, who says me by saying *I*. By masking this original mineness (*Jemeinigkeit*), the question "What is man?" forbids from the outset an answer using *I*, or *who I am*, and even less *here I am*. It thus accomplishes the eclipse of the *who* by the *what* (quiddity).[52] However, by forbidding an answer with an *I*, the question "What is man?" as a result opens the field to another question, in appearance hardly different, but in fact much more threatening. Indeed, searching for the definition of (the quiddity of) man in general seems, *once this definition is held to have been found* (which in fact is not possible, as we have seen, and shall see again), to authorize another question: "Is this *still* truly a man?" There is nothing easier, or even more tempting, than the taking of this immense step: the mere claim to know man (to define his quiddity), even and above all if it does not accomplish its ambition, in effect has no other objective than to will to make of man its object. Or rather, this claim has *decided* to decide the humanity of a *particular* man according to objectification, that is, according to the object that it assures the power to produce on his occasion and in his place. And it will determine the humanity of this *particular* man precisely by abolishing the irreducible mineness of the *I* in him. The abolition of man begins with his objectification, which itself consists in being able (believing oneself able) to define him without admitting the *who* within him. Defining man by a concept does not always or immediately lead to killing him, but it does fill the first condition required to have done with all that which (all of *he* who, *quis, quisqui*) does *not* fit this definition. This danger—having done with certain men because we have decided to define "man"—fortunately does not haunt the democratic societies today. And yet, these societies are constantly developing, each day a bit further, the ambition to fix tighter and more and more complex quidditative definitions on man, according to all the figures of the objectification in me of the *I*. That these figures display their unfailing "humanism" in no way attenuates the threat: in thus seeking to justify themselves, they admit all the more what they deny. The same devices that reassuringly claim to take into account every man indeed can (and must) also be described as just so many perils to the *I* in each one of us. Among many such perils, I will briefly describe the ambiguity of three.

When I find myself in a *medicalized* situation (admittance to the hospital by filling out registration papers, removal of clothing in order to put on a garment that prevents me from going out into the world of the nonhospitalized, submission to a battery of preliminary tests, prescription of a treatment, experimental adjustment of the treatment, passage to the operating room, anesthesia and postoperative procedure, convalescence protocol, and so on), I become a medical object. I thus allow myself to conform to what the medical gaze sees, or rather, what it wills to see, that which it agrees to retain, among all the characteristics that *I* was carrying, as me myself. More precisely, the hospital technology's inevitable hold of power over me can only eliminate in me anything that will not reduce to a medical object: indeed, it must do so in order to function. Thus, under the gaze of the medical profession, the hospital personnel, and very soon under my own gaze, the suffering of my *flesh* will be transmuted into a disease of my *body*. Now, the treatment of this sick body demands that it be interpreted according to the parameters of physical bodies (dimensions in extension, location, quantification, expectations of duration, the measurement of all parameters that are useful or likely to be useful, and so on). As these physical bodies, which are not me, remain perfectly foreign to the distinction between health and sickness, a distinction that affects only the flesh, the in-hospital interpretation of me as a physical body thus implies the cancellation in me of my own flesh. But, since my flesh alone lives, and life, by definition, implies feeling my flesh and feeling its feeling, or, in short, the undergoing of the self, along with my flesh there is, at least tangentially, my living flesh [*ma chair vivante*], and thus my life itself. Soon I will no longer feel the fact that I feel myself, because I will no longer feel as much as usual, or even at all: analgesics and anesthesia will deliver me not only from my pain, but from my suffering *self*, and thus from my experience of myself, from autoaffection. As a consequence, every nonobjective function will make this self and my flesh disappear, that is to say, what is animated in me will disappear into an animal-machine, something animate reduced to a mechanism (however complex it may be, it will still be a machine), in order to allow for its conceptual understanding. And moreover, only such a clinical definition of my body as a medical object will allow, unquestionably for my own good, the distinction between health and illness in terms of normative standards.[53]

Here there opens the fearsome region where man as doctor must decide if, and when, that which the machine maintains as functioning in this *particular* sick man still deserves consideration as a life, and if this life can still claim to be human. Debates about the beginning and end of life are constantly developing and increasing in complexity only because we have made ourselves both capable and culpable of them, by considering it our domain to have to determine the humanity of birth and death. We have transformed them from the events that they are into regions of objectification, subject to our control and our decision. We have thus constructed our crisis: that of having to decide the normality of the life and death of other men—because we have, for a long time, and insensibly, and without having really wanted it or noticed it, allowed them to become mere human objects, or what are assumed as such. Here the adjective "human" becomes ever more problematic and deprived of an identifiable signification. As a result, the sign of a cure is not found only, nor always first, in the modification of the performance of the animal-machine (for instance, better *numbers* in tests), but in the exit from the process itself of medicalization, in the indifference of *my* flesh toward the medicalized body that has been substituted for it, in the silence of the organs or at least the partial deafness to their noise; in short, in the *transgression* of the rules of health, in the *indifference* to medical prescriptions, in the *resistance* of *my* flesh to the medicalized body. This is the meaning of getting up, of walking around without an aim, of putting on the clothing we're used to, of ceasing to be scrupulous in taking medications, of starting to smoke and drink again, in short, *of no longer paying attention.* Obviously, this demedicalization can present certain dangers, and it should not be recommended without taking precautions. Yet, whether it succeeds or not, only my flesh's reconquest of the animal-machine in me attests to the fact that *I* am alive again. And sometimes, I must go through that demedicalization if I want to live out, to the end, that which ultimately qualifies me as *what I am,* without possible substitution: my death in the first person. For a body (an animal-machine) cannot die. At best, one can have done with it, stop it, unplug it, precisely because, for a long time already, it was no longer living. In order to die a good death, it is necessary to die living, not to survive like an animal-machine, without anyone there anymore at the end of the tubes. — The medicalization of my flesh, of the flesh that *I* am, thus appears as a prescription, which imposes on me a (quidditative) definition of man in general, and thus decrees a proscription of *who I* am.

The same is true when I am defined as an object reduced to the parameters selected by economic theory—when I seemingly become the "economic agent," presumed to be wearing himself out in the calculation of his needs, in their cost analysis, in the balancing of these costs against his purchasing power, and finally in the behaviors of acquisition and sale that correspond to this rationalization of exchange. In order to attain even an approximation of rigor, such a tiered reduction must assume that the choices of acquisition and sale are made according to the laws of an exchange that can itself be calculated with exactitude; and thus that the "economic agent" will proceed strictly according to interest, an interest he can account for quantitatively; in short, it is assumed that *I* know and practice only that which *anyone* (and thus no one in particular, the They) must do in commerce and exchange, and that I do so according to the iron rule of a selfishness that is no longer moral, but epistemological. Of course, these hypotheses cannot be realized perfectly: it is evident that the "economic agent" does not constitute a fact, but rather an economic interpretation of facts; put otherwise, he is a model, allowing for an interpretation that is tangentially verifiable, but never real. At issue, then, is not a description, but a prescription. But, even understood as a prescription, the interpretation of *who* I am as "economic agent" proscribes in me this *I* itself. This is true in at least two senses.

First, the supposed economic analysis doesn't really deserve this title, since it is ignorant of or simply cannot comprehend all that which, in the management of the house, in the real *oikonomia*, escapes from exchange and commerce, but undoubtedly makes them possible, frames them, and overflows them in every direction: the needs, the desires, the groups or individuals that act as partners in the exchanges, the political and juridical conditions that regulate them, beginning with the language that sanctions them, and so on. But the economic interpretation proscribes above all that which excludes itself preeminently from exchange: the gift itself. The gift of course comprises all the gratuitous forms of sociality: services rendered, nonmonetized exchanges in the familial sphere and among friends, and so forth, all of that which the "human services" have not yet integrated into the economy; but it is not summed up in this. Indeed, the gift extends beyond the space not yet rendered economic, to that which can in no way become economic: the events of my death and birth, which, at least for the flesh that *I* find myself to be, remain unforeseeable, unavailable, nonnegotiable, unappreciable, unsubstitutable. Just like pain and pleasure, love and hate, confidence and despair, desire and fear—in short, all that without which I would not experience myself. This is given and happens, but is not exchanged, or shared, and even less so is it fungible.

Whence there follows the other limit that affects the economic interpretation of the *I* that belongs to me. This time it is no longer about what the prescription leaves out of its grip (and thus what it proscribes), but rather what it presupposes for its own functioning, and which nevertheless radically contradicts the rationalization of exchanges. For, in order to subject each *I* to the economy as a simple and reasonable economic agent, the economy itself must appeal to that which straightforwardly contradicts economic calculus: desire, which makes of each of us a consumer, which is to say an "economic agent." Desire, or in other words advertising and all the related techniques (teasing, marketing, merchandising, distribution, credit, fostering of customer loyalty, etc.) that allow for its arousal, orientation, and maintenance. Now, in order to master and, first of all, arouse the desire to consume a desired object, it is necessary to give rein to the reasons that belong to *desiring desire*, which precisely do not respect economic rationality: in order to produce the consumer's desire, advertising must in fact give in to the economic irrationality of that desire—not only give in to it, but exalt it to the point of delirium. For indeed this desire raves, because it does not wish to buy a defined product for its optimal technological performance in exact response to an actual and calculated need (the use value regulating the exchange value), but, on the contrary, it seeks an indefinite product, technologically indeterminable, commercially unforeseeable, often without any real utility, provided that it responds to a need that is itself entirely unreal (recognition, distinction, narcissism, at least presumed enjoyment, etc.), and thus forever provisionally satisfied and endlessly to be satisfied again. In the final instance, economic growth rests on consumption, which itself does not grow with real needs for definable objects, but rather with that which renders them identifiable, modifiable, and producible: desire, which remains limitless, without identifiable support, and, finally, without a defined object. And thus economics, in order to lay out its interpretation of the totality of beings as objects of *value*, must itself contradict its condition of possibility—the interpretation of man as an "economic agent" who is supposedly absolutely rational—and recognize him, at least tacitly, as an actor without an objective goal, obeying a desire without end, because *without definition*. Of course, one can say that the economy economizes on the gift, on the condition that we recognize that, more essentially, the gift economizes on the economy itself by making it possible and, at the same time and under the same relation, by contradicting it. Thus, the economic interpretation of the fact that *I* am remains a limited and contradictory prescription, so that the (quidditative) definition of man in general that it decrees appears all the more like a perfectly illegitimate proscription of *who I* am.

Similar descriptions could bring out comparable processes of objectification in many other fields (for instance, psychiatry, biology, sports, the erotic phenomenon, spirituality, and so forth): it is enough that they simply touch upon the domain of the flesh of the self to threaten, at the very same moment, its proscription. And yet, the most extreme and the most symptomatic case, which completes all of the others, arises out of the definition of man not only as a social animal (a social "living one" [*vivant so-*

cial]), but as a political object, insofar as politics ratifies and completes the "mobilization"[54] without remainder of the humanity of man, *at once both* master and bondsman of itself (for henceforward the clash of master and bondsman plays out inside of each man, alternatively taking now one, now the other role, not only toward the other man, but first and above all toward himself).[55] The political definition of man seizes hold of his socialization only by imposing on him its technological treatment. This process of indefinite technologization of man's definition begins with the determination of his identity, that is to say first of all with the construction of a *name* through a number; the number, in fact always already *several* numbers, appropriates the proper name by disappropriating it from itself through reduction to the paradigmatically improper, the always repeatable, recurrent, and common number. These numbers become the *improper* name, alienated from the assumed proper name (just as, in Hegel's description, the concept as imposed name alienated the thing itself).[56] Such numbers of the name encode the impossible proper name with the digitization of dates (all the possible dates, from birth to death, including diplomas, deeds and certificates, military service, etc.), places (places of residence, places of employment, jobs, moves, etc.), health status (hospitalizations, operations, treatments, etc.), business and financial information (bank accounts, credit cards, funds, settlements, purchases, sales, etc.), local communications (audio and visual recordings, passage through secured entries) or those at a distance (electronic addresses and messages, mobile telephone numbers and messages, etc.), so that a *digitized* identity according to endless parameters sets up a potentially comprehensive definition of the numbered and counted citizen. And inevitably this comprehensive *definition* ends up authorizing, or even requiring, the distinguishing of human beings from one another, by separating those who satisfy all the fixed conditions at a given political moment of this citizenship from those who do not, and who thus find themselves de facto excluded from it, and capable of being excluded de jure. Exclusion, to begin with, of all of those who are "job seekers," "homeless," or "undocumented" (the metaphors and euphemisms serving as the language-ruler for the exclusion), then very quickly of the maladjusted, the delinquents, and finally the mentally ill, or embryos considered (by whom?) as not yet humanized, or supernumerary, and so forth. From the identity card to the list of proscription, the outcome, while neither right nor obligatory, is nonetheless possible, easy, and quick. Between the digitized definition and the description reduced to the registration number and the proscription, from exclusion to physical elimination, the continuity proves to be perfect, the transition easy, the temptation irresistible. This sudden transition becomes the true *digital* fracture: that which separates men from nonmen.

Political wisdom and the demands of democracy clearly lie, albeit with difficulty, in resisting this rational and thus imperceptible inclination. Failing such resistance, there will be no end of ideologies or racisms that produce definitions of man and, through an inverted outcome, proscribe those who do not fit in before moving on to the arrest, or indeed to the extermination of the submen or nonmen thus identified.[57] Crime exploits rationality and invites itself within its parameters and models as a "logical crime."[58] The point, then, is to resist this logic, first by identifying reason reduced to its extreme ideological limits, which supports it and claims to justify it. Such a reduced reason is found in the state of nihilism.

The very problematic in what we call, without really paying it any attention, an *undocumented immigrant* [*un sans-papiers*], a problematic that sums up all the other figures of the identification of man by his numbered definition, deserves our consideration. It amounts to identifying or promulgating an identity. Identifying what with what? Clearly, a man with a collection of information, digitized information, and thus with numbers, themselves of an indefinite number (always *barely sufficient*, always awaiting further additions). The identity of this man in the end is equivalent to his equality with the sum of this digitized information: his identity rests on the identity between him and it, his identity is verified by the identity of himself with some numbers. This is a situation that brings to light several oddities. — First, that the *undocumented* [*sans-papiers*] appears as subject to the principle of identity, in the sense of the first principle of being according to metaphysics: to be, for every entity, implies that it be identical to itself, that it correspond to its essence and not contradict it, or, what amounts to the same thing, that it not contradict itself. The *undocumented* contradicts his essence, by showing himself unable to state it, to reproduce it, to produce it (*Ausweis*, the identity paper, designates what one shows in order to prove that one is well and truly what one says one is, that one is indeed self-identical, thus furnishing a proof, *Beweis*, of self). In contrast, the documented citizen demonstrates his identity and his good faith by exhibiting his identity papers, duly digitized, and proves that he is not someone other than himself, that he is equal to himself. The identity paper thus strictly applies the metaphysical principle of identity to the one who identifies himself by it by identifying himself with it and enforcing its recognition as such.

Next, we must find it astonishing that this identity, attested to by the identity paper and guaranteeing to its bearer her identity with herself, is indeed precisely not identical, or even proper to her, but comes to her from elsewhere, from an exterior authority that assures her her identity, her equality with herself. This exteriority and this distance are so patent that they offer precisely the possibility of forged papers, and call for the constant verification (authentification) of these papers, real or false, by an authority exterior to their bearer. The identity paper provokes, by definition, an inquiry to validate or invalidate it, exactly as the possibility of counterfeit money results directly from the issuing of money. The one and the other derive their ambiguity from their fiduciary status: it is necessary to trust in them, or in other words, to believe that they do indeed come from the administrative or political authority that has issued them. Issued—sent, assigned far away, entrusted to another, the bearer. Thus, the identity paper, which alone assures the identity of its bearer with herself according to the metaphysical principle of identity, functions, by a strange reversal, only on condition that it comes from elsewhere, that it depends precisely on an *other* than itself that nevertheless attests to its *self-identity*. Identity, attested to (or not) by the identity paper, rests on the essential alienation of the essence thus received: I am who I am only through the intermediary of an *other* authority, who tells, in my place and better than me, who I am—or more exactly, who I am supposed and reputed to be: the public records administration, the prefecture of police, and so forth, in short, the state, the prince. My identity comes to me through government action [*le fait du prince*], not from my own action [*mon fait*]. In the case of the identity paper, the identity of self with self comes from elsewhere: it has to do essentially with the identity of the object with itself, which never comes to it from itself, nor from any sort of *in itself*, precisely because the object *is* only with relation to the intentionality that constitutes it—in this case, the gaze of the prince or of the state. Thus, the *undocumented person* contradicts self-identity only by contradicting, or making manifest and denouncing that this identity is identical to itself: the fact of proclaiming that I am *I* equal to *me*, the fact of proclaiming my identity (with myself), has no juridical value, since we expect that this self-identity comes from another. The *undocumented*, deprived of this other, makes manifest the alienation required at the foundation of identity (of self to self), the absolute necessity of which is performed by the identity card, rightly and with total metaphysical coherence. The contradiction of identity by its alienation from the origin does not contradict the principle of identity, but fully *accomplishes,* in the political mode, its metaphysical function.

A third surprise follows. The principle of identity must be completed by another principle in order to surmount (or confirm) the alienation of identity that it inevitably provokes. Thus, following the dispositions of metaphysics toward every entity, here the principle of reason enters in. If an authority (the state, the prince) concedes, attributes, or distributes its identity to the *undocumented,* so that he becomes equal to himself and can guarantee his identity from the outside through an approved alienation, it is fitting that this authority justifies his saying so about himself by providing him the sufficient reasons for this identity. The dead piece of paper (*Ausweis*) that the *undocumented* will present will quickly become the single sufficient reason that will authorize this living one [*ce vivant*] to live in peace, protected by the law, as a citizen, and thus as a man—that is to say, free. But free within the limits of the law, which is to say under the condition of its sufficient reason—the authority that administers to him his (alienated) self-identity. Here, as always in metaphysics, the principle of sufficient reason assures the principle of identity, and not the reverse. The political definition of the identity of *who* I am, that is to say the issuing of identity papers that attest to the digitized definition of my identity, thus puts into operation the two fundamental principles of the entity, in this way sanctioning that man indeed has the status of a being at the end and in the terms of metaphysics—a being as object, that only identifies itself through the loss of any *self,* in the gaze of the other who constitutes it by this very alienation.

The rule that we have set up—that to claim to define what a man is leads to, or at least opens the possibility of leading to, the elimination of that which does not correspond to this definition—now becomes much more intelligible. The definition allows one to pass so easily from prescription to proscription, and then to possible elimination, only because, simply as a definition, it already alienates the man that *I* am by claiming to fix on him an identity. The identification (or not) of man as such in *me* already constitutes a proscription—the most decisive, making all the others possible, because it takes place within theory. For, if it is up to another *I* to *judge* that that which walks hidden in a coat and hat that he sees passing beneath his window must be interpreted not as a mere object, automaton, or animal-machine, but as a man—in the sense in which the *ego cogito* declares that "I judge that they are men" ("*Judico homines esse*")[59]—then the humanity of man falls to the responsibility of the one who speaks and thinks, or to whoever assumes the exclusive right to it as administrator of the transcendental *I*. And in this case, even the philosopher, and perhaps he above all, has the means to confirm and thus also to put into question the humanity of other men: it is enough to establish that man defines himself as Greek, European, Aryan, and so on, to be able *also* and in each case to decide which men are barbarian rather than Greek, which are and are not European, which are not Aryan—thus defining in the end which are not human.[60] Every political proscription, every racial extermination, every ethnic cleansing, every determination of that which does not deserve to live: they all rest on the claim to define (scientifically or ideologically, because in the end the difference is canceled out) the humanity of man, whatever its formulation; without this claimed guarantee, no one would be able to put them into operation. For even the worst of the modern tyrants needs reasons and concepts, and the extent of their murders owes everything to the declared scientificity of their certainties. Here we find a crucial experience of the essential connection between definition and proscription: in order to kill a human being, it is always necessary to have a reason, and a good reason at that; the rationality of the reason sets the extent of the crime. In short, no one kills without having, in one way or another, a *license* to kill; but it seems there is none more liberating than an ideological license to kill, because it alone first authorizes the reasoned denial to this particular human being (the well-named "So and So") of his or her face, and thus of his or her humanity; and one gets there by defining and comprehending the humanity of this particular man through concepts, or by fixing its limits, and in this way discovering the one who cannot make a claim to humanity, and therefore can or must die.

Here a metaphysical proposition, in appearance perfectly neutral, takes on the features of a silent threat: every determination is a negation, or more exactly (because, as it happens, extension alone is at issue), "*figura non aliud, quam determinatio, et determinatio negatio est*" ("figure is nothing but determination, and determination is negation").[61] Determining amounts to denying, and not the inverse, for if determination is sufficient for denial, a negation is not always enough to determine. Determining by definition the humanity of man amounts, then, to seeing the end of him. — What is more, this experience can be confirmed by inverting it: indeed, I can love (the contrary of killing) only another that I *do not* know, at least in the sense of being able to comprehend him or her as an object and define him or her by a concept.[62] I can only love the one who remains for me without definition, and only for as long as he thus remains, which is to say for as long as I have not put an end to him.

Thus, to the two impossibilities running counter to a definition of the essence of man (that of the *ob*-jection of the *me* to the *I*, and that of the split within ipseity itself), is added a third: the impossibility, or more exactly the illegitimacy, of defining the simple limits of humanity, for this has to do not only with the irreducibility of the *I* that I could be, but also with that of the other human being. If defining humanity is enough to make it possible to put an end to certain human beings, then, inversely, the impossibility of such a definition becomes the privilege of man as such—never able, and thus not even *obligated*, to allow himself to be defined.[63]

§ 6. The Fund of Incomprehensibility

Thus, nothing of what I would understand through a definition of essence (of quiddity) reaches the humanity of the other man, nor for that matter my own humanity, because in giving me access to an *ob*-jected *me* [*un moi ob-jecté*] or to an *object* of the other, this very understanding closes off my access to it. If we still wish to maintain the precept that, as a human being, nothing human is or ought to be foreign to me (Terence), it would be necessary to add a corrective: nothing that I know by a (supposedly) comprehensive definition of humanity could reveal the other man as such, any more than it could give me access to myself. On the contrary, I will share the humanity of the other man only by according him the same unknowing [*inconnaissance*] and the same indefinition [*indéfinition*] that I recognize for myself, according to an equal resistance in the one as in the other to the grasp of definition and to the status of object. We vouch for our common humanity by each preserving the indefinition of the other: each safeguards the incomprehensibility of the other by holding back his own gaze from reducing the other to the rank of a clear and distinct object. It follows as a result that here, in the particular case of man, philosophy would not have as its task to correct his self-unknowing [*son inconnaissance de soi*] as a defect to overcome (through the fine-tuning of a definition, an essence, or a quiddity), but instead to *preserve* it as a privilege to reinforce, the privilege of never becoming an object held under a gaze and named by a concept.

And yet, protecting man in this way from his own gaze to the point of erecting his incomprehensibility as the sign and proof of his humanity could end up in pure and simple ignorance. Does a de jure incomprehensibility not always lead in the end to a de facto unknowing? Doesn't this inconstancy demonstrate a poorly formulated question? Isn't it the case that all knowledge must end up with the constitution of an object, so that knowing without knowing an object would make no sense at all? In short, by what right can one maintain and claim the understanding of such a fragile incomprehensibility? In order to reach a solution, it would be necessary to legitimize radically the impossibility of defining and comprehending man starting from a positive case of a knowledge necessarily without comprehension—of a knowledge of incomprehensibility as such. A knowledge that might in fact confirm man's right to his own incomprehensibility, by flowing back over it, so to speak, and protecting it from its shadow.

This positivity—in whatever sense one understands it—can come to philosophy from an argument developed by theology, which here plays a strictly rational role, to assess as such. It is formalized explicitly by Gregory of Nyssa, among other authors:

> The icon (εἰκών) is properly an icon so long as it fails in none of those attributes which we perceive in the archetype; but where it parts from its resemblance to the prototype it ceases in that respect to be an icon; therefore, since one of the attributes we contemplate in the Divine nature is incomprehensibility of essence (τὸ ἀκατάληπτον τῆς οὐσίας), it is clearly necessary that in this point the icon should be able to show its imitation of the archetype. For if, while the archetype transcends comprehension, the nature of the image were comprehended, the contrary character of the attributes we behold in them would prove the defect of the icon; but since the nature of our mind, which is according to the icon of the Creator, evades our knowledge (διαφεύγει τὴν γνῶσιν ἡ κατὰ τὸν νοῦν τὸν ἡμέτερον φύσις, ὅς ἐστι κατ' εἰκόνα τοῦ κτίσαντος), it keeps an accurate resemblance to the superior nature, by keeping the imprint of the incomprehensible [fixed] by the unknown within it (τῷ καθ' ἑαυτὸν ἀγνώστῳ χαρακτηρίζων τὴν ἀκατάληπτον φύσιν).[64]

And this is why Basil of Caesarea, so close to Gregory of Nyssa, will come to the conclusion that man must be understood with reference to the incomprehensibility of God, like him just as "invisible" and "hidden" (ἀόρατον, ὑποκεκρυμμένον).[65] In short, in order to justify positively and in reason the principial impossibility of defining the humanity of man, nothing less is necessary than to refer it back to divine incomprehensibility. Clearly, the issue is not that of *grounding* it, through a principle that would remain exterior and heteronomous to it, but to situate it in its own place, wherein knowledge does not attempt to constitute an *ob*-ject, and where that which appears indeed does not depend on an alienation, but instead comes from itself and shows itself only in its own reserve—beginning from *itself.* Now, from among that which thus appears radically *of itself,* in subjection to no *I* whatsoever, there is to be found, in a time of nihilism, little else than the incomprehensibility of God and, in its shadow, the indefinition of man.

To know man thus requires referring him back to God as the incomprehensible and thus justifying man's indefinition by virtue of his being in the image and likeness of God. John Scot Eriugena begins by taking up almost literally the argument of Gregory of Nyssa: "If in any way man could understand what he is (*quid sit*) he would necessarily deviate from the likeness with God (*a similitudine Creatoris deviaret*). [. . .] And concerning the other things which are to be understood and declared concerning the similitude of the image anyone who desires fuller knowledge may read the book of St. Gregory of Nyssa 'On the Image.'"[66] Drawing on this tradition, he deduces the consequences with unequaled clarity:

> For the human mind (*mens humana*) does know itself, and again does not know itself. For it knows that it is (*quia est*), but does not know what it is (*non [. . .] quid est*). And as we have taught in the earlier books[67] it is this which reveals most clearly the Image of God to be in man. For just as God is comprehensible in the sense that it can be deduced from His creation that he is (*ex creatura colligitur quia est*), and incomprehensible because it cannot be comprehended by any intellect whether human or angelic nor even by Himself what He is (*quid sit*), seeing that He is not a thing but is superessential (*nec a seipso, quia non est quid, quippe superessentialis*): so to the human mind it is given to know one thing only, that it is—but as to what it is no sort of notion is permitted it (*datur nosse, se esse, quid autem sit, nullo modo ei conceditur*); and, a fact which is stranger still and, to those who study God and man, more fair to contemplate, the human mind is more honoured in its ignorance than in its knowledge; for the ignorance in it of what it is is more praiseworthy than the knowledge that it is (*se nescire quid sit, quam scire quia est*), just as negation accords better with the praise of the Divine Nature than affirmation and it shows greater wisdom not to know than to know that Nature of Which ignorance is the true wisdom and Which is known all the better for not being known (*sapientius est ignorare illam quam nosse, cujus ignorantia vera est sapientia, quae melius nesciendo scitur*).[68]

Thus, we pinpoint quite openly the divine likeness in the human mind, in that the mind "knows only that it is, but does not know what it is" ("*solum-*

modo esse scitur, quid autem est, nescitur").[69] And this intensified unknowing clearly leads to the impossibility of defining that which bears the likeness of the infinite, which is itself undefinable: "So the human replica of the Divine Essence is not bound by any fixed limit (*humana substitio nullo certo fine terminatur*) any more than the Divine Essence in Whose Image it is made."[70] The incomprehensibility of God preserves the essence of man from succumbing to a definition, and it alone, not man, can do so.

That what is at issue here is not a grounding, but rather a reference, is something Saint Augustine perfectly conceived and described by putting this relation into operation in the figure of the *confessio*. Or rather, in the constitutive duality of a *confessio* oriented both toward my ignorance of myself and toward the knowledge of myself by an other: "*Confitear ergo quid de me sciam, confitear et quid de me nesciam.*" ("Accordingly, I will confess what I know of myself, and I will confess too what I do not know of myself, since even what I know of myself I know because you grant me light, and what I do not know of myself, I do not know until such time as my *darkness* becomes *like noonday* before your face.")[71] Man differs infinitely from man, but with a difference that he cannot define, that he precisely *must* not define if he wants to safeguard it so as eventually to conceive himself in it. Of course, man knows that he does not know himself, if only because in his innermost depths he comes to discover himself as an unfathomable memory: "*Quid ergo sum, Deus meus? Quae natura sum?*" ("What then am I, my God, what is my nature?")[72] But above all he understands, in this dead end, that the one who nevertheless alone knows him remains an other, God: "*Utrum ita sim, nescio. Minus mihi in hac re notus sum ipse quam tu. Obsecro te, Deus meus, et me ipsum mihi indica.*" ("Whether I am thus I do not know. In this matter I know myself less well than I know you. I beseech you, my God, show me myself.")[73] Finally, and above all, by a strict consequence, only the infinite and the incomprehensible could comprehend man, and thus say him and show him to himself; only God can reveal man to man, since man reveals himself only by revealing, without knowing it, that whose image he bears. Not only "*I* am another," but this other is named God in him—the *speculative* Emmanuel of self-unconsciousness. Consequently, at least with regard to God, man can no longer appear as such, but distorts himself by disfiguring himself under the figure of something other than himself; or rather, by believing himself able to take on the figure of himself, which is in fact inaccessible, and not the figure, alone accessible, of an other. For man resembles nothing, least of all himself, from the moment he resembles nothing less than

God. *A contrario*, sin is defined in this way: man imagines himself attaining to himself by choosing to resemble himself, or put another way, by choosing to resemble something less than God: the dissemblance in the image thus devalues him to something short of God and, as less than God, man loses his *human* face, no longer resembling *anything*. Thus, the soul, "instead of staying still and enjoying these goods [of God] as it ought to, wants to claim them for itself, and rather than be like God through God, it wants to be what He is through its own right. So it turns away from Him (*volens ea sibi tribuere et non ex illo similis illius, sed ex se ipsa esse quod ille est, avertitur ab eo*), and slithers and slides down into less and less (*in minus et minus*) which is imagined to be more and more. For it is not enough for itself, nor is anything else, once it has departed from Him who alone can satisfy it."[74] Two remarks suffice as commentary on this powerful phenomenology of sin. First: sin does not consist in wanting to enjoy the supreme goods, since they have already been given by God without envy, but rather in wanting to enjoy them *through oneself* and not through God, in wanting to appropriate them to oneself in the first person, in short, to deny them the character of a gift—to spurn the given as gift. Second: all of this movement takes place inside the iconic *likeness* of the undefinable toward the incomprehensible ("*non ex illo similis ejus*"). *I* is an other, but an other who, in the final instance, cannot come to be except through the alterity of God, insofar as I resemble God more than I resemble myself, a fact that, paradoxically, alone can define me. I recognize myself only by recognizing myself *as a* "God," just as one recognizes a Cézanne as a "Cézanne."

§ 7. The Indefinite and the Unstable

In order to recognize himself as a "God," man is further required not to allow himself to have any author's name imposed on him, or to give in to the least name imposed on him by another author—even himself! For every other name would deprive him of his indefinition, would define him, and thus would put an end to that within him which remains irreducible to the objectification of a definition—what we call his very humanity. Or rather, what we should call his *in*humanity, since what is proper to man consists in his not having any, and his definition, in not accepting any. Man distinguishes himself from all the other beings in that he is defined by his very resistance to every *definition*—even a definition by finitude. He is distinguished by the fact that he loses his identity if he identifies it—in a word, he loses himself if he finds himself.

One cannot help raising an objection here: if, precisely in order to reach and establish the undefinableness of the essence of man, it is necessary to have recourse to a likeness to God and deduce from it man as a "God" by relation of similitude, have we not already presupposed the answer to the question and, in fact, already assumed what we are claiming to abolish, namely, a definition of the humanity of man? Aren't we indulging in the most elementary of dogmatisms, borrowing the norm for a philosophical discussion from theology (in this case, Christian theology)?[75]

Before examining the objection (and in order to do so), let us first return to Hegel's interpretation of Adam's privilege in the book of Genesis (see above, § 3). There, man enjoys the privilege of being able to name and thus understand things, to the point of substituting their concept for them; but Adam exercises this privilege only on other living things, never on God, and never *on himself*. Why do these two alone escape naming, and thus man's domination? It goes without saying that God escapes: the creator by definition cannot let himself be understood by his creature, who therefore will not be able to name him (and of course the Name cannot be uttered and, besides, it tells no essence whatsoever, but instead annuls all concepts). Man can only adore God, or in other words, name him by invoking him, without defining him—from which there follows the commandment that forbids idolatry, beginning with the most dangerous sort, that which would claim to say the divine essence. But it remains to be understood why man does not name *himself*, since no commandment seems to forbid it—unless no other commandment is necessary than the second, which forbids making "for yourself a graven image, or any likeness of anything that is in heaven above" (Exod. 20:4), anything, therefore, that would claim to represent God through comprehension. But is man not only "below on the earth," but also "in heaven above"? Most certainly—and this is the decisive paradox—because that which is fitting for God (of whom no name, no image, and no concept can claim comprehension) is also fitting for man: man, and he alone among all other living things, was created not "according to [his] kind" (that is, according to a species, following a definition, with an essence), but "in [the] image . . . [and] after [the] likeness" of God (Gen. 1:24, 1:26). This paradox receives a specific commentary, once again, from Saint Augustine: "*[B]e renewed in the newness of your mind*, no longer *according to kind* [*secundum genus*], as if renewal were achieved by imitating a neighbour's example or by living under the authority of a better man [than us]; for you did not say 'Let man be according to his kind' [*secundum genus*], but '*Let us make man according to our image and likeness*,' so we may prove what your will is."[76] Man remains unimaginable, since he is found formed *in the image* of the One who admits none and, rightfully, resembles nothing, since he resembles only the One that incomprehensibility properly characterizes. Put otherwise, man is referred to no species, belongs to no kind, is not comprehended by any definition of (in)humanity, but, delivered from every paradigm, appears immediately in the light of the One who is above every light.

Henceforth it becomes very delicate, even for Heidegger, to lead such an *in*definition through likeness to the *un*imaginable back to the Greek definition of man as depositary of the λόγος, in order then to understand both as uniformly imposing on man the mode of "Being-present-at-hand" ("*im Sinne des Vorhandensein*").[77] The rather brutal arbitrariness of such an equivalency between two traditions (Greek and biblical), the irreducibility of which Heidegger, incidentally, unceasingly emphasizes, is not sufficient to disqualify them, and especially not for the same reasons. Of course, the definition of man by λόγος can eventually suffer reproach: the *animal rationale* tends, indeed, to objectivize that which it conceives in a permanence as a present-at-hand or subsistent essence (οὐσία), and thus determine itself as precisely such a resistant presence, indeed the most resistant of all.[78] But things are entirely otherwise for the definition of man as *in* the image of God, which on the contrary seems to forbid the primacy of presence in that definition, in the sense of "Being-present-at-hand." This is so, for several reasons.

First, it is necessary to exclude, on principle, the notion that we are dealing with God as an object, petrified into present-at-hand or subsistent permanence by a concept that would fix this object's formal definition (despite the temptation that certain modern theologians may have had to do so); such a petrification would point to a pure and simple idolatry masking the One who has no essence, or being; the eternity of God does not consist in enduring in an endless permanence, but is free from enduring presence (παρουσία) to the exact extent that it is free from present-at-hand or subsistent essence (οὐσία). Second, man cannot be lowered to the rank of a present-at-hand or subsistent image of God, not only because God is *not present-at-hand*, but above all because he is invisible ("No one has ever seen God," John 1:18) and thus offers no visibility to reproduce, disqualifying in advance the slightest permanent reproduction: when it comes to God, there is no visibility to state, take up, or work out. If an image there must be, this will always (as first and above all for the Christ) be an icon, and an icon of the invisible (εἰκών τοῦ θεοῦ τοῦ ἀοράτου, Col. 1:15). The icon does not reproduce something visible, or even some*thing* of this visible; it gives to be seen the trace, the *style*, and the rhythm of that which in it remains as invisible as it is in God himself; more precisely, from the icon there comes to us, like a gaze weighing on us and not like an object intended by us, an *impression* rising up from the invisible—the icon gives us the impression of the invisible, without any thing-like intermediary, and thus without the possibility of the least permanence. And third, the biblical text therefore does not say that man is the image of God, but *in* his image: the Hebrew indicates clearly *in* (ב) the image, *like* (כ) the likeness, just as the Septuagint stresses κατ' εἰκόνα, *according to* the icon. Between God and man, the relation (assuming that this metaphysical category has the least bit of pertinence here) subsists no more than it points to a reproduction, or even less, the reproduction of a subsistent or present-at-hand presence. Man *refers* to the invisible and only bears its image to the extent that this transfer marks him with the seal of the invisible itself. Man owes his tangential status as icon (of the invisible) to the invisibility that little by little saturates his created visibility, which he keeps and shares with the other things in the world, just as a light, according to its intensity, can make invisible what it saturates and swallows up. Think of the face of the Resurrected One of the Isenheim altarpiece.

Heidegger's objection can serve as the paradigm for many others, all just as biased, because they aim in the final instance simply to deny to theology, in general and on principle, the right to take up the question of the status of man, on the basis of the denial of any right to respond to the question of creation. And, in order to arrive at their denial, they must first caricature theology: for in order to disqualify the thesis of man *in* the image, or rather, *in* the icon of God, it is first necessary to assume that theology in that thesis anticipates (and then reproduces) the very gesture of metaphysics—fixing a definition of the essence of man and in this way allowing its identification. But this argument presupposes what is supposed to be established: that creation responds to a question as radically metaphysical as that which asks, "Why is there something rather than nothing?" when instead it could be that the creation by God, by its unprecedented facticity, its absolute unconditionality, and its initiative without any *before*, annuls from the very outset the site where the question "Why, for what reason?" could have the slightest meaning and the least legitimacy. It could be that creation does not answer, by taking up a place in the catalog of possible answers, *the* question of metaphysics, but instead radically disqualifies it: "*Where* were you when I laid the foundation of the earth?"

(Job 38:4). The purported answer of theology to the question of man does not fall beneath the blow of the opinions of philosophy and of metaphysics, not only because it does not answer the same questions as they do, but above all because it does not respond dogmatically *to any question*. Or rather, it recognizes in man a question that is on principle without any answer, and which therefore *must* remain that way. The argument drawn from the Scriptures does not intend to furnish any clear and distinct knowledge to answer the metaphysical question of the ground of beings in general and of the definition of the essence of man. On the contrary, it admits and ratifies the indefinition of man, by reading it starting from divine incomprehensibility itself. The believer does not act *as if* he were asking the question, for which he would in fact already have the answer: instead, he receives all of those claims to define man as an idolatrous offense against God himself. The believer alone, or at least he first of all, truly enters into indefinition, rather than acting *as if* the definition of man could serve as the answer to whatever question there may *be*. He alone, or at least he first of all, recognizes that the question without an answer constitutes precisely the locus of man for himself. Without any illusion or allusion, he supports with his gaze man as *magna sibi quaestio*.

On the other hand, one could ask whether those who persist in claiming to be able—one day, close yet indeterminate, announced as all the more imminent the more it is delayed—to answer the supposed question of man are not limited to pretending to conceive of his indescribability. In all this fury to believe that they know, what are they afraid of? Perhaps of sensing in this question the incomprehensibility of God. How do they reassure themselves? Perhaps by believing it possible to hide from themselves the incomprehensibility of God by deleting in themselves the indescribability of man. And in order to arrive at this result, they continue to *hope* in any definition of man whatsoever, provided that it allows for putting an end to him, above all to this "*in* the icon" by which he proves himself to be imprescriptable. If questioning defines the piety of thought, then, because Scripture leaves the aporia of thought forever intact, it may very well be that Scripture also exhibits, above all, the piety of thought.

God alone knows the secret of man, and preserves it in his own secret. But the theological justification for the impossibility (and illegitimacy) of assigning to man any definition whatsoever does not imply that philosophy is unaware that the indefinition of man properly characterizes him and alone guarantees that we will not be done with him. When Nietzsche designates man as "the not yet stabilized animal" ("*das noch nicht festgestellte*

Tier"),[79] the animal that doesn't "hold together" and doesn't know how to "hold itself together," he meets up with Kierkegaard, remarking that "to become subjective" constitutes a task that is "very difficult, indeed, the most difficult of all, because every human being has a strong natural desire and drive to become *something else and more*."[80] But above all, and without any paradox whatsoever, Nietzsche picks up from Pascal. For, if man remains undecided, he owes it to the fact that he rightfully has the status of one who is undecidable: his essence consists in not having any, and his definition, in exceeding every attempted definition, such that in himself he passes beyond himself. Instead of the self, man finds himself only outside of the self, or more exactly in the outside-the-self [*le hors-soi*]: "man infinitely transcends man"[81] and "human being is something that must be overcome" ("*etwas, das überwunden sein soll*").[82] He remains himself only for as long as he remains without distinctive quality, other than that of "an incomprehensible monster" (Nietzsche says "unformed, *Unform*").[83] And, let us not forget, Pascal understands this as a privilege: that of *showing in* oneself [*montrer en soi*] the incomprehensible. The nature of man is characterized by this undecidable issue for man, who will lose himself if he claims to define and stabilize himself. Incomprehensibility imposes the impossibility of its definition, but the latter itself results from the instability of its form, or nonform. But it is necessary to take yet a further step back. "Man [is an] animal of another nature, multiform, variable, and which leaps [from one status to another]" ("*[H]omo variae ac multiformis et desultoriae naturae animae*"),[84] likewise noted Pico della Mirandola. But we owe it to him, as one of the first, if not the only one, to have explained why the nature of man is thus undone by leaping from one form to another, without ever being fixed; this results from the fact that man himself decides his own form by the privilege of his having been created without a kind or species, and thus without a form:

> At last the best of artisans ordained that that creature to whom He had been able to give nothing proper to himself should have joint possession of whatever had been peculiar to each creature. He therefore took man, this work of an indeterminate image (*indiscretae opus imaginis*) and, assigning him a place in the middle of the world, addressed him thus: "Neither a fixed abode nor a face that is thine alone nor any function peculiar to thyself have we given thee, Adam, to the end that according to thy longing and according to thy judgment thou mayest have and possess what abode, what face,

> and what functions thou thyself shalt desire. The defined nature (*definita natura*) of all other beings is limited and constrained within the bounds of laws prescribed by Us. Thou, constrained by no limits (*nullis angustiis*), in accordance with thine own free will, in whose hand We have placed thee, shalt ordain (*praefinies*) for thyself the limits of thy nature. [. . .] We have made thee neither of heaven nor of earth, neither mortal nor immortal, so that with freedom of choice and with honor, as though the maker and molder of thyself, thou mayest fashion thyself in whatever shape thou shalt prefer (*tui ipsius quasi arbitrarius honorariusque plastes et fictor, in quam malueris tute formam effingas*). Thou shalt have the power to degenerate into the lowest forms of life, which are brutish. Thou shalt have the power, out of thy soul's judgment, to be reborn into the higher forms, which are divine."[85]

Man appears then as the unstable, and thus the indefinable, animal because he remains yet to be decided, but above all because he still has to decide *for himself*. Thus, indefinition constitutes him immediately, because it results directly from his free will and is bound up with it as its inverse. In question is an essential paradox that should never cease to astonish us: "[M]an is rightly called and judged a great miracle and a wonderful animal." ("*[M]agnum miraculum et admirandum profecto animal.*")[86] And all of these formulas resound, in the end, like impeccably Augustinian echoes: "*Grande profundum est ipse homo.*" ("Man considered in himself opens like a vast deep.")[87]

Man remains himself for as long as he escapes himself by deciding for himself. And the issue is not only to wonder at this, but to force oneself to *merit* it—so as to avoid the always dangerous ridicule in claiming: "I perfectly understand what man is, without added mysteries. [. . .] Man is not a puzzle."[88] On the contrary, a philosophy remains worthy only to the extent that it keeps open this undecidability that takes the place, for man, of definition, this instability that takes the place of essence. There is perhaps no other criteria of truth or falsehood on this *subject*. Only the divine, says Aristotle, succeeds in thinking its own proper thought, in so very far as it must think nothing other, always in actuality, without matter, eternal. In contrast, man would characterize himself as a thought that never succeeds in thinking its own proper thought, and yet that characterizes him but does not define him entirely. For man, the animal endowed with λόγος, certainly thinks (*homo cogitat*), and even thinks of himself, but in thinking of himself he nevertheless does not think *himself* as such. He does not *think himself* first of all, nor as such (§ 1), because everything that he thinks by defining it becomes for him an object (the epistemological aporia of *objection*). Next (§ 2), man only thinks *himself* by experiencing his division in principle from himself in an *I* that never coincides with a *me* or identifies itself by it (the aporia of splitting). And finally (§ 4), man thinks *himself* only by refraining from delimiting the conditions (of elimination) of the humanity of the other human being (the ethical aporia of alterity). In the end man does not think *himself*, no longer merely in the sense of a prohibition, but as a grace and a privilege (§ 5), because, at least in theology, his indefinition qualifies him as in the image and likeness of incomprehensibility par excellence, that of God. Put another way, man appears to himself only as a phenomenon that he cannot constitute, because he passes by excess beyond the field of every horizon and of every system of categories (§ 6). This can be formulated thus: man appears to himself as a saturated phenomenon; and no concept (quiddity, essence, or definition) can constitute as an object the excess with which the intuition gratifies that phenomenon.

No longer can we avoid considering the claims of that which goes under the imprecise name of *humanism*. The fact that this term does not cover a single concept, and that no real historical continuity links its modern meaning (the autonomy of man, his end and definition) to its Renaissance origins (education in classical letters), might lead us astray, persuading us to believe that it lacks coherence. On the contrary, the difficulty lies in its coherence, which ties together two theses that are stubbornly recurrent, under formulas as variable as can be. These theses claim first of all that man knows himself to the point of defining himself by himself alone; next, that man progresses infinitely in light of this definition. Whoever invokes humanism lays claim to the autonomy of man, and challenges his heteronomy (through any other that there may be, but above all, through that which one understands as "God"); and in order to assure this autonomy he assumes a dogmatic definition (albeit inevitably imprecise) of man's humanity, less in order to think man positively than to implement proscription (§ 4) and master man's essence (§ 5). But immediately the difficulty arises: even assuming that it is permitted and licit to seek a definition of man, what does such a definition require taking on in theory? It implies (§§ 1–2) a knowledge of self by oneself. But, as the knowledge of self cannot be verified by self-consciousness, except by giving up on its project,[89] humanism must complete the unthinkable *cogitatio sui* through an unforeseen *causa sui*—displaced from God onto man.[90] That in fact the autonomy of man winds up laying claim to the *causa sui*—explicitly with Sartre, who, more than anyone else, tried to establish a somewhat precise concept of humanism—confirms the judgment of Heidegger: "Every humanism is either grounded in a metaphysics or is itself made to be the ground of one. [. . .] Accordingly, every humanism remains metaphysical."[91] Humanism, whatever the formulation that it borrows (for the issue is not one of thought, but of ideology, where concepts become a mere packaging), misses (or rather refuses to see) the fact that man does not remain in himself, and finds within himself neither his origin, nor his essence, nor his end. Admittedly it is necessary to "think against humanism," not in order to oppose oneself to man, but rather "because it [humanism] does not think the *humanitas* of man *high enough*." And to think this humanity "enough" requires conceiving that man only remains himself if he remains ecstatically, or put otherwise, *outside* of himself ("*des ekstatischen Innestehens in der Wahrheit des Seins*").[92] Of course, the debate opens immediately over whether standing out ecstatically implies standing out into the truth of *Being*, or into another light. But, *here*, the issue is not this disagreement. The point is to see that man becomes himself only by passing outside of himself—while humanism imagines on the contrary that man becomes himself only by defining himself, in himself and through himself, with the ambition of accomplishing the idol of the self that is fantasized in this way.

Indeed, how could a de*finition* allow (in the double sense of tolerate and uphold) a passage to the *in*finite? And yet, finitude can and even must infinitely repeat the experience of its limit: by endlessly crossing its limit, it experiences it anew a step further on; until it steps beyond that step, to stop for a time; and then does so again. Finitude is assured of itself by surpassing itself, but always provisionally. The indefinable stays himself for as long as he exceeds what he believed he knew of himself, and which, legitimately, held him back *in* himself, that is to say just short of himself—he is the one who meets up with himself only by exceeding himself, outside of himself.

A finality without end can indeed be conceived (and it can even be required in order to conceive certain phenomena, first among them that of the living one [*le vivant*]), but an *end without finality* prohibits conceiving saturated phenomena, even the indefinable. The demand for progress, even indefinite, can only put the humanity of such progress into question, that is to say, put into question its attribution to something that is still worthy of the title of man.

Likewise, humanism does not see that, in spite of this absence of an end, indefinite progress remains human only to the extent that the original indefinition of man does not remain undecided and anonymous, but instead is inscribed and developed within the horizon opened by its assignation and its reference *to* the image and likeness of the invisible.

II. THE IMPOSSIBLE, OR WHAT IS PROPER TO GOD

Certain days, you must not fear naming
the things that are impossible to describe.

—RENÉ CHAR[1]

§ 8. The Impossible Phenomenon

To say, or even to want to say, "God" is already enough to make us notice God's first, radical, and definitive characteristic: inaccessibility.

And it is an inaccessibility of a new sort. It no longer concerns, as it did under metaphysics, the establishment or even the demonstration of the existence of God: that is no longer a concern in this time of nihilism, where not only the "death of God" seems a settled fact, but, above all, where the notion of existence itself becomes generally problematic for every being without exception, precisely because "beings" succumb in general to nihilism. The difficulty, more obscure and also more worrisome, lies in our inability to define the least concept of the essence of God: in wishing to say "God" (well before we've come to the point of seeing him *or not*), we do not even succeed in knowing what we are talking about, or what we are aiming at. This aporia clearly goes beyond the first one. The first one remains metaphysical, since it doubts the existence of God without ever contesting the possibility or the legitimacy of producing God's essence,

Translator's note: Sections of the translation of this chapter follow a translation of an earlier version of this material that appeared in Jean-Luc Marion, "The Impossible for Man—God," trans. Anne Davenport, in *Transcendence and Beyond: A Postmodern Inquiry*, ed. John D. Caputo and Michael J. Scanlon (Bloomington: Indiana University Press, 2007), 17–43.

and thus of inscribing him in a concept; for atheism itself not only never refuses itself a concept of "God," but always presupposes one, precisely in order to be able afterward to exclude God from existence. This is so because essence remains, in metaphysics, the royal and unique road for reaching (God's) inexistence as much as existence (in general). In contrast, the second aporia wrenches itself free from the metaphysical horizon by contesting that one might ever or must always make use of a concept of "God," and therefore make use of it as an essence among others (however privileged it proves to be). Breaking the tie between "God" and its concept, and thus between "God" and an essence in general, it liberates God from his inscription in logic, and thus, possibly, in onto-theo-logy. In this way it meets up with the path of apophasis, and thus with the critical moment that mystical theology forces on every ascent toward the Name which is above every name.

Consequently, not only our (metaphysical) impossibility of demonstrating the existence of God but especially our (nonmetaphysical) impossibility of defining by concept the least essence of God become ambivalent themselves, and therefore problematic. From now on, the evidence of the double impossibility of God trips over a precondition: what does the impossible mean here? And the same question goes for the possible. The impossible and the possible each bear on experience, what it admits and what it excludes, and thus on that which *can* or *cannot* appear: the phenomenon. At issue, then, is the possibility and the impossibility of a phenomenon. And, in turn, how do we define a phenomenon? It seems reasonable here to privilege the answers, convergent in the essentials, advanced by Kant and Husserl, since they almost single-handedly established the only positive concept of the phenomenon ever formulated in modern philosophy. According to this understanding, a phenomenon is defined by the adequacy in it of an intuition (giving and fulfilling) to a concept or a signification (empty and to be validated). Consequently, a thing can appear to me in two ways. Either I determine the intuition received by fixing it (identifying it, subsuming it) with an imposed concept, so that I am no longer dealing with a simple lived experience of consciousness (or a manifold of intuition) but instead precisely with a lived experience assigned to the case of a particular object or being, which then becomes describable; or the concept that I could form on my initiative (through spontaneous understanding or conscious intentionality) ends up finding empirical validation in an intuition, which comes subsequently to fill it and to qualify it as a particular object or being. It matters little from which of these two end points the adequacy is accomplished, since in every case the phenomenon only appears by synthesizing in itself the intuition and the concept.

How does this work when I say "God"? From the outset it seems clear that in this case I have neither an intuition nor a concept at my disposal. — I have no intuition at my disposal, at least if by intuition I mean that which can be experienced according to the forms of space and time. For, by "God" I mean by definition and first of all the eternal, that which endures unceasingly because it never even begins to endure. I also mean by definition what is nonspatial: that which is situated nowhere, occupies no extension, admits of no limit (that the center of which, no less than the circumference, is found nowhere), escapes all measure (the immense, the incommensurable), and thus is not divisible, or capable of increase. Let us note that this twofold impossibility of entering into intuition implies no particular doctrinal choice, or even the least denial; it results from the unavoidable requirements of the mere *possibility* of something like God. The most speculative theology, which itself maintains that "No one has ever seen God" (John 1:18), agrees here with the most unilateral atheism to postulate that, in the case in which one wishes to say "God," what is involved is the transgression of the formal conditions of intuition: if intuition implies space and time, then there cannot be intuition of God. Or, more radically, there *must* not be any such intuition, if God is ever to be considered. Thus, God is distinguished by the impossibility, for us, of ever receiving the least intuition of him.

But there is more (or less). Let us suppose that it so happens that I have a rather exceptional intuition, such that I consider assigning it to something called "God"; in spite of this, I would not know "God," since, without any corresponding concept, I would not *recognize* this intuition as (that of) God. I could recognize it as such only by assigning it a concept that identifies it as the intuition *of* something *as* divine, a god or even "God," or, what amounts to the same thing, a concept that it fills and that in return confers on it a form and signification. Here, let us note, the fundamental inanity of the notion of "natural mysticism" stands out: it can mean, in the best of cases, only a perfectly undifferentiated intuition (more blind than any other) of a divine, of god, or of "God" that is completely indistinct. — And what about this concept? Here too, by definition, I can legitimately assign no concept to God, for every concept implies the delimitation of that the comprehension of which it assures; it thus contradicts the only acceptable definition of God—namely, that he passes beyond all delimitation, and thus every possible definition supplied by a finite mind. Incomprehensibility, which in every other case attests to a weakness of my knowledge or an insufficiency of the thing to be known, here and here alone ranks as an epistemological demand imposed precisely by what must be thought—the infinite, the unconditioned, and thus the inconceivable. "Incomprehensibility is contained in the formal definition of infinity" (Descartes).[2]

But, it will be objected, if no concept that I use to designate God can, by definition, reach him, all of them nonetheless retain a certain pertinence: it is enough to overturn them, to transform their illegitimate affirmations into just so many legitimate negations. For lack of saying of God what he is, the concepts at least say what he is not. In this case, the principle is upheld that the negations always go further than the affirmations. Perhaps. But this gesture, as legitimate as it may be, does not restore any of these concepts' theoretical validity for aiming at "God," even in a solely negative mode. Indeed, if my potential concepts designating "God" in principle say nothing about God, they at best say something about me, insofar as I am confronting the incomprehensible.[3] They say what it is that I am able to consider, at least at a given moment, as an admissible representation of God; they thus articulate the conception of the divine that I make for myself—a conception that occurs to me as the best because it defines precisely the maximal and the optimal conceivable for me. In short, the concepts that I assign to God, like so many invisible mirrors, send back to me the image that I make up for myself of the perfection of the divine, and therefore are images of myself. My concepts of God end up as idols—that is, as always, as idols of myself.[4] Consequently, not only can I not aspire to attain the least concept of God (for in the final analysis such a concept must claim to comprehend and seize the essence of God, which would contradict that essence), but above all I *must* not do so, for in this way I would only reflect (on) myself, me alone.

This unavoidable weakness of the concept in general concerning God leads to a double consequence. — First of all: because the "death of God," in order to identify this "death" as that of a particular "god" or even of "God," must necessarily assume a particular concept of his essence (the "moral God," the "final cause," *causa sui, summum ens*, etc.), it thus disqualifies in each case only that which corresponds to this sole concept, leaving all the others (undefined, but just as inadequate as the first) still to be reviewed and critiqued. In other words, every conceptual atheism remains regional, and thus provisional: it progresses at the slow pace of justice, which investigates, examines, and challenges the ever-repeated concepts that claim, always just as illegitimately, the mastery of the essence of "God," precisely in order to challenge it. But each refutation refutes itself, since it only ever refutes one definition that is by definition *inadequate* of the essence of "God," opening at the same time the path for every new possible definition; which, in turn, will be able to claim to be adequate only for as long as the tribunal of reason leaves it unchallenged. And so on, for atheism refutes itself by having to repeat itself, following the rhythm of the concepts that it assumes and then challenges. It could establish and stabilize itself only if the *same* concept assured it of the adequate essence of "God" and, *at the same time*, its refutation. Atheism is always delayed with regard to itself, or rather it prolongs itself only by retrospectively eliminating each of its provisional assurances. Because this contradiction cannot be conceived in the same instant, atheism, if it wishes to remain rational and, frankly, honest, must renounce the proud title of a definitive and universal dogma in order to accept the more modest, but coherent, name of a trial that is never ended and always limited to specific petitions. But if, against all logic, dogmatic atheism claims to uphold itself, it sinks into ideology and its violence—as history constantly confirms. In short, from the "death of God" there follows immediately the "death of the death of God."

A second consequence results: the difficulty of a concept of "God" applies just as well to every form of theism or deism, for "They imagine that it [the Christian religion] simply consists in worshipping a God considered to be great and mighty and eternal, which is properly speaking deism, almost as remote from the Christian religion as atheism, its complete opposite."[5] Deism, which is to say that which philosophy can say of "God," claims to reach definitive and dogmatic conceptual formulations; thus, it condemns itself of idolatry no less than does atheism; they differ from each other only as a positive idolatry differs from a negative one. Whether we say of "God" that he exists or that he does not would appear to make a difference; but this difference proves in reality to be indifferent as soon as we note that, in the two cases, we come to a conclusion only by presupposing in each case a definition and a concept of the supposed essence of "God," such that the two conclusions sanction the same dogmatic idolatry. In particular, in each case, we presuppose that "being" or "existing" still mean something when we apply them to "God." But nothing is less certain, or betrays more clearly a second idolatry. The impossibility of assigning a concept to God, then, lies in God's very definition—which is that he admits of none. And God also distinguishes himself by the impossibility, for us, of conceptualizing him.

Confronted with this double impossibility, it becomes inevitable to conclude from the common determination of phenomenality the impossibility of any phenomenon of God. And here again, which is to say within the rational theology of metaphysics, theism accepts this result, just as atheism does.

Nevertheless, speculative theology, which thinks from within faith and in view of belief, diverges radically from atheism and theism when it comes to the interpretation of this impossibility of the phenomenon of God. From its point of view, the very impossibility of such a phenomenon could come from a credible, if not indisputable, experience of God, under the figure of a paradox, which allows itself to be formulated in this manner: if God cannot *not* be thought as beyond the conditions of possibility of the phenomenon in general—without intuition and without concept—this very impossibility results directly from his infinity and confirms it under the title of incomprehensibility. What belongs properly to God (that is to say, for philosophy, the infinite) characterizes him as that which by definition surpasses the finite; now, the conditions of phenomenality remain, for us, definitively finite; the sensibility of intuition marks the finitude of our minds and limits the usage of concepts by our finite understanding. And, since we can go so far as to apply finitude to being itself,[6] how can we not conclude that God *must* make an exception to the norms of finitude, and that, above all, this exception itself constitutes a kind of experience—an impracticable experience according to the norms of finitude, which, in this case only, could be worthy of the title of God, and, once retranslated into epistemological terms, would be stated thus: if incomprehensibility certifies the impossibility of phenomenalizing the infinite, it further postulates, certainly in a negative mode, a positive experience of the infinite. Put another way, the epistemological impossibility of the phenomenon of God (that is, his incomprehensibility) is itself experienced as a counter-experience of God.

This inversion—an impossible phenomenon offering the paradoxical possibility of a counter-experience—may be contested, and in fact has often been contested. Indeed, one can argue that incomprehensibility no more offers a formal account of God than it does of the infinite, since it authorizes knowledge of nothing at all, except the general impossibility of all experience generally. Incomprehensibility offers no second degree of experience, but ties every experience of the infinite to the first degree. The fact that I am unable in this case to comprehend anything does not allow me to infer indirectly a purported incomprehensible, yet conceivable, presence of anything whatsoever. On the contrary, and in a more trivial way, the fact that I comprehend nothing confirms straightaway the ontic inconsistency of every object, and the failure of the *ratio cognoscendi* simply reproduces the uselessness of the *ratio essendi*. I do not understand precisely because there is nothing there generally (*überhaupt*) to understand, or even to conceive.[7] Experience as such becomes impossible. Nor is there any question of a noumenon, since some appearance might very well appear (an idol, an illusion) without anything appearing in and of itself. "Strictly speaking, one can elaborate nothing philosophically about divine eternity, because God is not an object of philosophy. What one uncovers with the help of the concept of God is an idol, which philosophically has only the signification of making us see what idea of *summum ens* and of Being is generally directive. Philosophy, when it understands itself correctly, is *without God*. [. . .] If God is, he only lets himself be discovered as little as possible by philosophy. He can be discovered only if he reveals himself. But philosophy has not the least organ for understanding a revelation."[8]

We will conclude, then, that, concerning God, we only encounter a triple impossibility—impossibility of intuition, impossibility of concept, and thus also impossibility of experiencing the slightest phenomenon of him.

§ 9. The Irreducible

Nonetheless, there remains of God something irreducible that never disappears, that nothing can prescribe, that no silence smothers, because the issue is not a statement that one could validate or challenge, but instead a question—a doubt, an indecision, a flaw. At issue is a question that possesses the privilege of imprescriptibility: its dossier is never closed and filed away, one has never finished pleading its cause—that, precisely, of the *causa Dei*. This question, the question of God, is characterized by its always making a comeback, its being repeated despite the refutations incurred, its being reborn from all attempts to put it to death, in theory as in practice, in concept as in history. As we all know, the categorical imperative imposes the moral law on me without any discussion, contestation, or escape, even *and above all* if I leave it be without performing it: the absence of actualization in no way prevents what is at stake from being a fact of reason. In thinking about it, the question of God likewise forces me to recognize irreducible meaning and pertinence in it, even *and above all* if the existence of God remains problematic for me, or even impossible to establish: the absence of a demonstrative answer in no way prevents what is at issue here from being a fact of reason. Not being able or not wanting to answer the question about God remains a rationally acceptable philosophical position, but not *hearing* the question about God betrays philosophy and becomes ideology, or the lifelessness of the concept. It is not enough not to be able or not to want to answer the question about God to go unmarked by it, as a pure and simple question.

The objection that, instead of irreducibility, what is at issue here is merely a transcendental illusion or an ill-framed question changes nothing. Even if we are dealing with an ill-framed question, it still must be admitted that it does not cease to be ill framed; going forward, the very consistency in error becomes a second-degree question, as irreducible as the question of God that it sought to make go away. In order, then, to understand such a lengthy persistence of a supposedly ill-framed question, we must go back to what provoked it: the semantic error or the grammatical mistake that maintains in logical life the question of God. Will we say that what we are dealing with is an illusion of reason, an intellectual effect of perspective, which gives rise to a "transcendental appearance"? We might accept this perfectly intelligible hypothesis, except for the fact that it reinforces the difficulty, rather than diminishing it, since such an illusion, precisely because it has a transcendental rank, proves itself to be "unavoidable" and "natural."[9] Still to be understood is why and how the question of God, even and above all without any answer, remains the nostalgia and the phantom of philosophy at the end of metaphysics. It is *all the more* necessary to understand it, since the very fact that the illusion of God survives the impossibility of both the phenomenon and the experience of God constitutes, in and of itself, a question.

Thus, what we have here is truly a fact of reason—no rational mind, not even the most reticent, can claim that it does not comprehend the question of God, *even and above all* if it comprehends the impossibility of responding to it positively. Descartes had already noted a paradox in the idea of God: "As for those who deny that they have the idea of God, but in its place form some idol etc., although they reject the name, they concede the reality."[10] In other words, in order to be able to deny having an idea of God, it is necessary already to have one. We can take up and radicalize this paradox by applying it to the impossibility of the experience and phenomenon of God (§§ 7–8): we notice right away that we cannot understand the meaning of that the impossibility of which we nevertheless cannot contest—precisely because this very impossibility already offers a perfectly conceivable and thus acceptable meaning. This amounts to saying that we can very well disqualify the knowledge of God (of his essence, of his existence, of his phenomenon), but we cannot eliminate the very question of God, which always remains intelligible *as a question*, and thus remains to be deconstructed again and again each time it makes itself heard, which is to say at all times. — One cannot object that the same goes for other questions without an answer. The questions of the squared circle, of the squaring of the circle, and so on, do not survive the demonstration of the contradiction of their supposed objects, just as the questions bearing on a green virtue, the date of the beginning of time, reincarnation, and so on, disappear as soon as the non-sense of their supposed objects is established, precisely because in each of these cases it is a question of objects that are finite, univocal, and definable. But in this case, because with "God" the issue is that which passes beyond every univocal and finite definition and which therefore encompasses them all without end, there will never be any demonstration of particular impossibility (of contradiction, of non-sense) that would allow for the exclusion of an infinity of other definitions, and thus extinguish the question itself. This unique question seems to enjoy the exorbitant but irreducible privilege of having the ability (and therefore the duty) to pose itself to us in spite of (or because of) the impossibility we encounter of answering it. *The question of God survives the impossibility of God.* Simple reason thus demands that we take into consideration this paradox: either it is necessary to surrender to its reason, or lay down one's arms—that is, admit that it is right, contrary to our evidence. — No longer can the difficulty be reduced by having recourse to the psychology or sociology of a putative "religious need." Indeed, the point is not to guess how the irreducibility of the question *is experienced*, but to take into account the *logical* possibility that it endures in the impossible. Put another way, the point is to conceive why—when in every other case the impossibility of giving an answer to a question ends up extinguishing it by making it, too, impossible, and thus unthinkable—in this case and this case alone, the question of the impossible survives the impossibility of answering it, and the thought of the impossible remains, in the end, still possible. The difficulty lies in the status of this possible impossibility and in its power.

How can we conceive that here the impossibility does not contradict the possibility? What sophism are we missing? To begin with, how do we locate it? The aporia probably comes from the fact that we seek an answer elsewhere than in the question itself. Let's instead stick to the initial fact—the fact that the impossibility of answering the question of (the existence of) God does not annul the very possibility of the question of God. How do we conceive *here* the paradox and the privilege of the impossible? Precisely by recognizing it as God's privilege—for *God, and God alone, lets himself be defined by impossibility itself.* Indeed, we enter the realm where it becomes possible to pose the question of God, and therefore of the incomprehensible, only from the moment we confront the impossible—and then only. God begins, as a question and as his question, only once the point has been crossed where the possible *for us* ends, where what our rationality comprehends as *possible for it* comes to a halt, at the precise border where our thought can no longer advance, or see, or speak—starting from this moment the inaccessible domain of the impossible as such opens up. What is impossible for our reason does not prohibit the question of God, but on the contrary indicates to reason the limit where this question can be posed and actually bear on God, because it genuinely transcends that which does not yet have to do with God, namely, what is possible *for us*. In God's case, and in this case only, impossibility does not abolish the question, but makes it possible.

Now here there is a strange encounter. Three lines of thought, which otherwise are completely opposed, agree with one another to determine explicitly the question of God through the undergoing [*l'épreuve*] of the impossible and of the surpassing of the limits of the possible. — First of all, there is metaphysics: to the extent that it constructs the "God of the philosophers and the scholars," it construes this God as the instance that is precisely capable of every thing, including that which remains impossible for us. Following Homer ("with the gods everything is possible"[11]), pagan philosophy agrees: "There is nothing, they say, that god cannot do" (Cicero).[12] This is a view taken up, moreover, by certain Church Fathers. Tertullian formulates it positively: "For God nothing is impossible, except whatever is against his will," while Gregory of Nyssa is polemical against its denial: "There are [. . .] some who, owing to the feebleness of human reasoning, judging the Divine power by the compass of our own, maintain that what is beyond our capacity is not possible even to God (τὸ ἡμῖν ἀχώρητον οὐδὲ θεῷ δυνατόν)."[13] Which accords with medieval thought: "[A]ll necessity and impossibility are subject to His [God's] will; but His will is not subject to any necessity or to any impossibility" (Anselm).[14] Or: "We must firmly and surely assert that God, just as he is in fact said to be omnipotent, can in truth, without any possible exception, do all things, either in respect to events that have happened or in respect to events that have not happened" (Peter Damian).[15] Or: "God is called omnipotent because he can do all things that are possible absolutely; which is the second way of saying a thing is possible" (Thomas Aquinas).[16]

These two lines of thought continue into modern metaphysics, first of all through the intermediary of Montaigne: "[B]ut reason has taught me that to condemn a thing thus, dogmatically, as false and impossible, is to assume the advantage of knowing the bounds and limits of God's will and of the power of our mother Nature."[17] And next through Descartes, who takes into account such a tradition in order to make valid through his reader the argument for hyperbolic doubt: "[F]irmly rooted in my mind is the long-standing opinion that there is a God capable of everything."[18] But he ratifies it as well on his own behalf: "I do not think that we should ever say of anything that it cannot be brought about by God."[19] This determination is rooted so deeply that not even efforts to marginalize the question of God fail to uphold and privilege divine omnipotence. Thus Locke: "This eternal source then of all being must also be the source and original of all power; and so *this eternal being must be also the most powerful*."[20] The difficulty here does not concern the identification of God, in his opposition to all the other beings in general, with omnipotence and as omnipotence, but instead with the determination of the possible and the impossible (see below, §§ 11–12): wouldn't certain absolute possibles remain still impossible even for divine omnipotence? But this strange contradiction of an omnipotence limited to impossibilities that are still (logically) possible itself marks *a contrario* the point in question: if God must recognize certain absolute impossibilities, then he falls to the rank of a relative idol, and that which the impossible is lacking is also lacking in the divinity of God.

It becomes only more remarkable to notice that, against all expectation, the attempts to "destroy" metaphysics keep intact this determination of God as the one for whom "the extraordinary (*overordentlige*) does not exist at all" (Kierkegaard).[21] Phenomenology not only assumed this position, but privileged it; indeed, to the extent that in the course of Husserl's development teleology (and givenness) submerged and finally deconstructed the transcendental privilege of the *I*, it became simply unavoidable that with Heidegger the Dasein conceives itself, according to the guiding thread of "Being-toward-death," as open to, or rather open *through*, the final possibility because it is radically nonontic, the possibility of impossibility. From this moment, whether the issue is the death of the other (the impossibility of possibility)[22] or the erotic phenomenon (the impossibility of impossibility),[23] the end point and aim of the deconstruction inevitably concern "what appears impossible, more than impossible, the most impossible possible, more impossible than the impossible if the impossible is the simple negative modality of the possible."[24] Of course, the impossible is not, in any of these cases, laid claim to as a name of God. But it nevertheless de-nominates in each case the approach of the abolition, if not already the abolition, of the limits set by metaphysics to experience, such as the delimitation by transcendental definition of the possible and the impossible. The region, or rather the nonregion, of the im-possible extends across the deregionalized and freely decentralized opening of that which already no longer is—the other, the flesh, the erotic phenomenon, the gift and forgiveness, the event. If God ever has to appear to our eyes that have become blind to the twilight of the idols, clearly it will be in this opening, and no longer in the desertlike domain of the possible. To the point that, *a contrario*, if God is defined as the one for whom the impossible remains forever impossible, then, for as long as one speaks of the impossible, one speaks always of God, regardless of what one says. "In place of God, there is only the impossible and not God" (Bataille).[25] And vice versa: once there is the impossible, a place for God is found; it is as if even the caesura traced by the "end of metaphysics" did not put into question but rather radicalized the paradox that God comes to thought only through the possibility of impossibility.

This first agreement, surprising in itself, becomes astounding when we realize that it is augmented by a second agreement, this time between these two philosophical eras, on the one hand, and Revelation (Jewish and therefore Christian), on the other. For here again, here above all, the impossible defines the limit between man and God: however far the possible may extend, it is still and only the domain of man, who governs his profane world within it; but, as soon as the impossible arises, we are dealing with God's own domain, where holiness reigns (in fact, *his* unique holiness)—which transcends what is possible *for us,* and where we therefore cannot and must not set foot. The impossible furnishes man with the only indisputable sign by means of which God himself accepts to allow himself to be recognized: "Nothing is impossible on God's part" (Gen. 18:14). The distance imposes itself so radically that even Christ in agony, during the night of his kenosis, again calls upon his Father in these terms: "Abba, Father, all things are possible to you (πάντα δυνατά σοί)" (Mark 14:36). The border between man and God is described as the climb from the possible *for us* up to the impossible *for us,* and then by the reversal of this impossible *for us* into the possible *for God.* Our impossibility of seeing the phenomenon of God and of knowing the experience of it is radicalized specifically and precisely by the recognition that God alone has power over the possible, without exception, and therefore also over the impossible *for us*; this impossibility for us is part and parcel of his own proper possibility: he appears as the "only potentate (μόνος δυνάστης) [. . .] whom no man can see, whom no man can know" (1 Tim. 6:15–16).

Thus, three points of view, which otherwise diverge in every way (metaphysics, the philosophy that transgresses metaphysics, and Revelation), come together at least on one point—that the impossible, as the concept above all concepts, designates or rather de-nominates "God, the one whom everyone knows, by name."[26] Most likely, impossibility defines the place of the question of God only with variations and at the price of an equivocity that will have to be assessed; yet always according to the same principle: the border between the possible and the impossible *for us* is strictly what unfolds impossibility itself as what is possible *for God*.

It is solely a question of thinking what Nicholas of Cusa formulated in a powerful and simple paradox: "Hence, since nothing is impossible for God, we should look for Him (in whom impossibility is necessity) in those things which are impossible in this world."[27] Or in other words: since possibility for us defines the world exclusively and since God's potential region begins only with impossibility (for us and according to the world), then to proceed toward God means to enter upon the marches of the world, to step beyond the borders of the possible in order to tread at the edge of impossibility. The only possible pathway to God opens in, and passes through, the impossible. Thus, this time following Tertullian, we would come "to know God, belief in whom is conditioned by belief that he can do all things." From which it follows, for example, that one must believe the account of the resurrection of Christ precisely because it is about an impossibility, which it belongs to God and God alone to accomplish—and *here* it is precisely God who is at issue: "It is certain—because it is impossible."[28]

In order to settle this departure definitively, it is enough to return to the texts that impose this paradox; and in order to do that, we must attempt to comprehend with some rigor three verses from the synoptic gospels. Two of them coincide: "With men this [a rich man entering the kingdom of God] is impossible, but with God all things are possible" (Matt. 19:26), and "With men it is impossible, but not with God. For all things are possible with God" (Mark 10:27). A decisive point is in play here: the texts do not limit themselves to opposing certain cases, where there would be impossibilities that would be found on the side of men, against other cases, where there would be possibilities that would be found in turn on God's side, like two exclusive domains, separated by an intangible limit: there are things that are impossible *for us*, for example that a rich man might enter the kingdom of God, that become possible from the point of view of God, and thus pass into actuality, even though they remain impossible *for us*. And, as a verse from the third synoptic gospel makes clear, in general this is true of the same cases, which, impossible for men, become possible for God: "τὰ ἀδύνατα παρὰ ἀνθρώποῖς δυνατὰ παρὰ τῷ θεῷ ἐστίν." ("The impossibles on the side of men are possibles on God's side" [Luke 18:27].) The conversion of the impossible into the possible therefore plays out through the passage of men to God. But this conversion and this passage are made starting from God.

§ 10. Possibility without Conditions

Let's pause to consider for itself the still very abstract determination of God that we have reached: God manifests himself in such a way that nothing remains impossible for him. This determination holds at least two implications.

The first implication concerns precisely the inversion of the impossible into the possible, or more exactly the conversion of the impossible *for us* into the possible *for God*. This conversion puts into operation the principle that the only region that we can reasonably and legitimately attribute to God (whoever God may be, and whether he may be or not) begins to open itself only from the moment at which we encounter an impossibility; in fact, it opens itself only when we stumble over something impossible for us *and* when we attempt to transgress it, in actuality or in thought. We must be more precise: the impossible appears only at the confines of finitude, at the edges of *our* region, the little township of our narrow possible, that the infinite space of an other unknown possible envelops and submerges, one that is perhaps *still possible* but that *we* term the impossible. Under the negative title of the impossible there emerges in fact a residue of the excess of the possible, or rather the trace of a possible without conditions (for example, without the *conditio* of creation) and inaccessible to us, like a remainder left by its excess, when it fades away in the twilight of finitude. Moreover, left to itself, finitude would remain a pure and simple undergoing of self [*épreuve de soi*], and thus an undergoing of what is possible for it. But it is precisely the case that the possible cannot be conceived without first being experienced [*s'éprouver*] in finitude; and the undergoing of finitude already in fact necessitates enduring the border of the impossible, despite all the denials that are simply repeated because they fail to challenge the evidence. The possible already implies the impossible. The resistance of the impossible alone makes the finitude of the possible *for me* thinkable. The possible imposes itself on finitude only as the trace of the impossible. In experiencing myself within the bounds of the possible *for me*, I am only the trace of the impossible. I am not only following the trace of the impossible—I already trace myself with the features of the impossible, I find my bearings by its trace, I discover myself as this very trace. The impossible falls to me: impossible as much *for me* as for its trace, which is the possible *for me*. I experience myself by tracking down this limit—the (im)possible, or the unfolding of the possible in the impossible and the folding of the impossible onto the possible, but without opening onto the impossible, which is God's proper region. From the moment that the possible signifies the possible *for us*, but also when the possible *for us* implies the impossible *for us*, the trace leads a step further: the impossible *for us* harbors and thus reveals [*recèle et donc décèle*] an impossible possible *on the side of* another possibility, that of God. God means: *the side* from which we see the impossible for us as a possible without conditions, without conditions of possibility. Here a remark is necessary: in order to conceive that the impossible *for us* opens onto the possible without limits (*for God*), we have absolutely no need actually to transcribe the border that separates what is possible *for us* from what is impossible *for us* (what sense would that have?). It is simply enough that we conceive, albeit correctly, the possible itself as possible *for us*, or in other words the possible as the trace of the impossible; for the impossible, also inevitably and first of all *for us*, unfolds itself straightaway in its own possibility *from another side*. Thus, the point here is in no way that of actually producing the impossible (an illusory hypothesis), nor even of understanding the impossible *for us* as a new possible *for us* (an absurd hypothesis), but of following the trace of the impossible—the possible—up to its final implications. The point is to think the possible, the trace, up to its limit, the impossible. To the impossible we are held, because the possible ties us essentially to it, and because only through it do we hold together.

Following the possible as the trace of the impossible does not lead to the absurd claim of transgressing the border of the possible *for us* in order to enter into the region of the impossible *for us* and to have a direct experience of it; rather, it leads to the counter-experience of the impossible *for us* (and of the possible *from another side*) starting from the undergoing of the possible *for us* and its finitude. The counter-experience consists, here as always, in experiencing a phenomenon insofar as it refuses the conditions (by definition transcendental) of experience, and contradicts, in its nonstandard phenomenality, the norms of manifestation of the objects of finite experience. The counter-experience thus allows for the only possible trial of phenomena that are impossible, because saturated: paradoxes.[29] We therefore cannot take God's point of view on the impossible becoming possible *from his side*; but we can, and even must, conceive that the possible *for us* remains intelligible for us only for as much as we follow its trace toward the impossible *for us*, and then toward the possibility *for God* of the impossible *for us*; or more exactly, toward the possibility of this possibility *for God* of the impossible *for us*. We could just as well describe this conception as an eidetic variation, a counterfactual, or a thought experiment: it matters little, so long as we follow the trace of the impossible into its last stronghold, the impossible; and provided that the unconditioned possibility, the direct experience of which remains inaccessible to us, becomes manifest to us through a counter-experience.

The same objection can recur in other terms: if the impossible *for us* defines our finitude, and if the possibility (or the possibilization) of this impossible in a possible without conditions or limits designates the infinite, by what right can we claim to transgress the border between them, since it exactly determines what we are and are not, the thinkable and the unthinkable for us? But once again, we have to answer that the question of finitude does not arise from a merely quantitative approximation, no more than the notion of limit plays out *partes extra partes*. Every limit encompasses its outer bound, since without it it would overflow itself, would remain still undetermined, awaiting a border, and would rightly appear in-finite. Just so, in order that finitude be experienced as such, that is, as restrained and limited, as nothing but itself, it is absolutely necessary that the infinite impose on finitude by contraposition, in the experience of resistance, the undergoing of the *beyond-self* [*l'outre-soi*]—that which already no longer confines itself to itself, without yet reaching the nonself. In this sense, and paradoxically, the counterordeal [*contre-épreuve*] of the infinite perhaps alone allows finitude to undergo itself.[30] Thus, we cannot experience our finitude without experiencing the infinite *a contrario*, if only according to the reason of incomprehension. Without the counter-experience of the infinite, the finite would never be experienced as such, and would be missed completely: without the counter-experience of the infinite, the finite would not be experienced as finite, but as in-definite;

that is to say, it would remain without limits for settling itself and, finally without an end, it would, quite simply, not experience itself. And thus, since the counter-experience of the infinite can also be translated into the terms of conversion of the impossible *for us* into the possible *for God*, we must conclude that I would miss myself, I would be lacking to myself, without this counter-experience of the impossible. The transgression of the limits of the impossible—more exactly, the thought of the impossible itself, not understood as a region but as a limit, and thus as the inescapable possibility of a transgression—is therefore not at all imprudent, or illusory, since, short of it, I do not know myself in my very finitude. On the contrary, the illusion and the imprudence would consist in imagining oneself defining oneself without the counterordeal of the infinite, which alone fixes finitude, or without the counter-experience of the impossible, which alone makes the possible appear as ours, as possible *for us*.

And yet, if in order not to miss ourselves we must conceive in thought that which remains incomprehensible to us, we must also do so in order to avoid masking the question of God. For the question that opens onto God only truly begins to operate once the exact limit is reached where the possible folds itself back against the impossible, precisely where the impossible could convert itself into the possible. Which is proved *a contrario*: if ever an impossibility should remain inescapably impossible, both for our logic and in our experience (supposing, of course, that such a hypothesis has a meaning, and that, by definition, its validity remains admissible only provisionally, until proof to the contrary—in short up to the point of looking into it more closely), we should neither answer the question of God, nor close it, but simply recognize that we have not yet reached the appropriate region for the infinite, that we still remain in our region, in short that we do not yet walk on a ground sufficiently holy for posing the question of God—so that the question that we would pose merits that we receive it as *from* God and *about* God. For as long as the question is that of an impossible, it is a question of an impossible *for us*, and thus not yet of God. On principle, God therefore cannot encounter the impossible, since for as long as an impossible remains impossible (for a supposed "God"), for as long as it remains possible that an impossible would stay impossible for him, *we are not dealing with him*, but with a "very attenuated God" (Supervielle),[31] an idol likewise struck by impossibility, by the exact same impossibilities that strike us, we human beings, for whom, alone, the impossible remains properly possible as impossible.

For the place of God, precisely, is defined by the impossible and, short of the impossible, the question (whatever the question may be) could not be that of God. One cannot say, then, that in the place of God there is the impossible, since only the impossible makes room for God. God stays in his place, his only possible place—the impossible. "He who is undoubtedly omnipotent cannot be ruled out on the grounds of impossibility" (Richard of St. Victor).[32] Or even better: he can only enter into play under the sign of impossibility, precisely in order to exercise his mode of omnipotence there.

Here we can develop the second implication of the formal definition of God: if no impossible has a grasp *on* God, then neither can anything make God *himself* impossible. In other words, if there is nothing impossible about God, it becomes impossible that God should remain impossible. And indeed, at the point where we have just arrived, the objection falls apart according to which the intuition, the signification, and thus the phenomenon of God (§ 1), and finally any experience of him (§ 2), prove his impossibility. For even by admitting the impossibility *for us* of experiencing the phenomenon of God, this impossibility clearly concerns only us, and is only valid according to our point of view (*from our side*), precisely the only point of view where the impossible can impose itself and must do so. Paradoxically, the impossibility of God has meaning only for us, we who alone can *a contrario* experience impossibility, above all the impossibility for us of attaining to him; but it has no meaning at all *for him*. On the contrary, this impossibility does *not* concern *him*, he for whom impossibility remains by definition impossible. The impossibility of God can be proved (possible) only for us, and never for God. If we seriously take into consideration that God only allows himself to be thought in the form of the impossibility of impossibility *for him*, then it turns out that it is impossible for God not to turn out to be at the least always possible and thinkable—if only as the impossible *for us* and the possible *for him*.[33] Let there be no objection that, in this case, the impossibility of impossibility for God remains inaccessible to us and teaches us nothing about him; indeed, once again we conceive this gap, certainly irreducible and incomprehensible in the strict sense, inasmuch as we understand why and how God remains impossible *for us*—precisely, that is, *for us*, and not *for him*. "The pre-eminently most [more than] impossible is possible (*das Überunmöglichste ist möglich*)" (Angelus Silesius):[34] the most impossible *for us* proves itself absolutely possible *for him*, because, as the more than impossible, it passes beyond the difference between the possible and the impossible, which indeed has meaning only *for us*. In this way, we conceive God insofar as he is not confused with us, and insofar as this difference is drawn forever. Which is what had to be demonstrated.

This brings us to a revision of the so-called ontological argument, radically transforming it. This argument, in metaphysics and according to Kant's reformulation of it, consists in deducing God's existence from the concept of God's essence, by simple concepts (without recourse to experience). Contrary to what is so constantly repeated, its principal difficulty does not lie in the illegitimacy of passing from a concept to existence as a position external to the concept,[35] but more radically in the impropriety of assuming that just any old concept adequately defines the supposed divine essence; in its "ontological" (metaphysical) version, the argument presupposes this essence and its definition, so as inevitably to wind up forging an idol of "God." How can this aporia be overcome? By renouncing all presumed concepts of God and holding to his incomprehensibility itself. Yet how are we to conceive this incomprehensibility in such a way as still to be able to think of God? By conceiving it not only as the impossibility of every concept (of God), but also as the concept of God's impossibility—in the double sense of an impossibility of thinking God by concept (and intuition), but also the impossibility that God imposes on the concept. In short, by conceiving impossibility as the distinctive hallmark of God's difference with regard to man. Indeed, of God we cannot, without contradiction, assume any concept other than that of impossibility, such that it marks for us his specific difference: God, or what is impossible *for us*. Once we substitute for a comprehensible concept the incomprehensible one of the impossible, the whole argument is turned upside down: it no longer concludes with the existence of God,[36] but with the impossibility of his impossibility, and therefore with his *own, proper* possibility *for him*, not relative to us—an unconditioned, *absolute* possibility. God turns out to be the one for whom possibility remains ever possible, precisely because it turns out to be impossible that anything is impossible for him, above all himself.[37] The necessity of God's possibility without conditions flows from the impossibility of his impossibility.[38]

Such a reversal of the argument into a proof of the absolute (unconditioned) possibility of God based on his concept (as impossible), strange as it may seem, nevertheless has already been formulated in an exemplary way—at least by Nicholas of Cusa. Let our starting point be the thematization according to which Saint Thomas Aquinas framed the difference between God and what is created: in the created case (finite entities), essence always remains really distinct from *esse*, just as potency differs from act; on the contrary, in God, essence is not only always identified in act with *esse* but (at least according to certain passages) disappears into *esse*, to the point that in God the whole essence, which is to say the whole power and potency and thus the whole possibility, is accomplished and abolished in the *actus*, as *actus essendi*. Nicholas of Cusa affirms this distinction, but reverses the application. A finite and created entity can actualize only its potency, which is in itself limited; but by actualizing it, the potency is all the more exhausted qua possibility given that it is abolished in its act, which is also limited; consequently no finite entity attains to the level of an infinite possibility, because both its essence and its act ratify this finitude and close it in on itself. God, on the contrary, is in actuality all that he is potentially, according to a double infinity of act *and of possibility*: "And hence, God alone is what (He) is able to be; but no creature whatsoever [is what (it) is able to be], since potency and act are identical only in the Beginning."[39] God *is* not in actuality, at least there where potency and possibility abolish themselves, but in such a way that possibility is fulfilled *also* in this act even as possibility: "God is what (He) is able to be."[40] God and creature are opposed less by act (relative to essence, as for Saint Thomas Aquinas) than by the privilege in God of possibility; more exactly, God has the exceptional possibility that *his* possibility is put into actuality as such, by remaining this very possibility; God, and He alone, is able to be in actuality (in actuality of being) his possibility as possibility, called *possest*, *Actualized-possibility* [*le pouvoir-être*], or even *being-Actualized-possibility* [*être-le-pouvoir-être*]. While "no created thing is Actualized-possibility,"[41] God transcends created being first and above all by his definitive, irreducible, and eternal possibility; in short, by an uncreated possibility—"uncreated possibility is Actualized-possibility itself."[42] God's omnipotence, which is to say his denomination based on the impossibility for him of impossibility for us, results in a possibility that is eternal and infinite, originary and ultimate. God's omnipotence means here less an unlimited efficient power than the actuality of eternal possibility itself:

> Let us agree that [there is a single] word [which] signifies by a very simple signification as much as [is signified by] the compound expression "Possibility exists" ("*posse est*")—meaning that possibility itself exists. Now, because what exists exists actually: the possibility-to-be exists insofar as the possibility-to-be is actual. Suppose we call this *possest* [i.e., *Actualized-possibility*]. [. . . Such] is a sufficiently approximate name for God, according to our human concept of Him. For it is equally the name of each and every

> name and of no name. And so, when God willed to first reveal knowledge of Himself, He said: "I am God Almighty"—i.e., "I am the actuality of every possibility."[43]

God lets himself be named according to the actuality of the potency itself conceived (and upheld) as possibility, not according to the simple assumption of power in act, even infinite. In God, possibility trumps active efficiency because God's highest efficiency consists in surpassing impossibility (for us) by making it possible (for him)—which he does by virtue of the necessity in him of the impossibility of impossibility. The sole preserver of unconditioned possibility, God safeguards it to the very depths of what is impossible for us.

§ 11. The (Im)possible: From Contradiction to Event

And yet, one might ask oneself: Do the paradoxes that these two terms, "possible" and "impossible," undergo here not render them ambiguous and equivocal, or at the very least foreign to their common logical and metaphysical meanings? Or rather, how could they not have veered sharply from their meanings when, by definition, we have referred them to God in order to indicate the gap between God and us? And in fact, going forward, no longer will the issue be that of the possible or the impossible as they are opposed only *for us*, but rather that of the conversion that, *for God*, makes them pass into each other, running along a single, unique fold, where the one gives the trace of the other. Henceforth, I will mark this conversion and this trace by writing: the (im)possible. Still to be understood is what I mean by writing the word in this way—namely, that the pair possible-impossible does not hold out against the thought of the (im)possible.

At the very least, we know already that this (im)possible can only be understood by opposition to that which it surpasses—by opposition to what metaphysics understands in its way as the relation between the possible and the impossible. Indeed, if it is admitted that the "highest concept with which one is accustomed to begin a transcendental philosophy is usually the division between the possible and the impossible,"[44] then God will be defined once again in terms of his relationship to the impossible, precisely under the figure of omnipotence. But, by a strange reversal, this very omnipotence can deploy itself only by letting itself be bound by the limits of impossibility, not by transgressing them. God can certainly do (actualize) all things, but on the express condition that they be inscribed within the field of the possible and not prove to be contradictory: "God is called omnipotent because he can do all things that are possible absolutely; which is the second way of saying a thing is possible. For a thing is said to be possible or impossible absolutely, according to the relation in which the very terms stand to one another [. . .]. Therefore, everything that does not imply a contradiction in terms is numbered among those possibles in respect of which God is called omnipotent."[45] Divine omnipotence limits itself, metaphysically, to the realm of the possible; it does not concern the impossible, which limits it instead of offering it a site to conquer.

This position will quickly prove itself untenable for obvious reasons. — First of all, because it ends up reducing God to the role of an efficient laborer, working on behalf of a possibility, an essence, or a formula "to which, so to speak, God submits himself."[46] The order of Reason would thus impose itself on God as it does on any creature, law of "all intelligences and of God himself,"[47] such that a logical submission (to the possible) annuls the omnipotence of actualization. The road is open to determining God within the limits of pure and simple reason, at the cost of a disappearance of the difference between the possible and the impossible, and thus also of a disappearance of the conversion of the (im)possible. But there is more: if the possible, which limits divine omnipotence, is defined as the noncontradictory, and if the noncontradictory is understood in turn as the nonimpossible (following Wolff's formulation, "Possible is that which includes no contradiction or which is not impossible"[48]), then this tautology still has to be conceived. How does a concept contradict itself, if not according to the norms, rules, and axioms of a conception? One cannot speak of contradiction that is absolute and without conditions, but only and always of a contradiction in and according to the measure of the concept, "*contradictio in conceptu*."[49] Now, what concept can be at stake here, if not the only one we know, our own, such that it defines our representation? "*Nothing*—which is negative, something that cannot be represented, something impossible, something inconsistent, (an absurdity), something involving or implying a contradiction, something contradictory." In other words: "That which is not nothing is SOMETHING: the representable, whatever does not involve a contradiction, whatever is not both A and not-A, is POSSIBLE."[50] Clearly, the representable and the nonrepresentable come into play only within our concept, within our finite conception, and thus for our finitude. There is, then, no contradiction other than what is conceivable, and nothing is conceivable that is not within a conception of ours, and therefore *quoad nos*, for us, for our finite mind. In this situation, the demand for an omnipotence *unconditioned* with regard to the impossible *for us* no longer makes any sense, since here the possible and the impossible themselves are always already defined in relation to *our* representation, and therefore in relation to *our* understanding, which is finite by definition. We will never know the slightest thing about what is impossible and contradictory from the governing view of God's extraordinary omnipotence: these will remain perfectly undecidable since we will never have access to the very conditions of their question. In fact, as the notion of contradiction as such supposes finitude, if God is God—which is to say infinite—no contradiction, by definition, can apply to him, but only to us. To God, that nothing is impossible means that the possible *for us* (the noncontradictory for our representation) in no way concerns him. God does not limit himself to possible logic, since the metaphysical impossible does not even concern him.[51]

In order to understand what sort of (im)possible God transgresses, beyond the impossible and the possible that are limited by noncontradiction, it is necessary to question the metaphysical distinction between possible and impossible. Once again, Heidegger serves as guide when he takes up anew the question of the possible by freeing it from the domination of the act, and thus of actuality: "Higher than actuality stands *possibility*."[52] This inversion of the possible's relation to actuality, however, is not yet enough to redefine possibility: in order for possibility to free itself as such, it must escape every *condition* of possibility that would come to it externally in order to limit it, to the point that a radical possibility must, in a paradoxical yet perhaps inevitable sense, refuse the least de-*finition*, because any "finition" would contradict it by limiting it. Formally, this possibility would be characterized by the transcendence of all impossibilities—taking its starting point not within some noncontradiction defined by the limits of a positive representation and conception, but negatively in the transgression of these very limits, which is to say, within what remains impossible for every conception and representation. Possibility in the radical sense would take its point of departure in the impossible as it transcends the impossible; that is to say, it would annul it, not by making it possible, but directly, without transition, by making it actual. Radical possibility would start with the impossible and, without passing through the conception of a noncontradictory possible for finite representation, would impose it within actuality. *Radical possibility, or the actualization of the impossible as such.* In contrast to possibility as de-*fined* by metaphysics, radical possibility would not transform possible things into actual things, but impossible things into actual things, directly. — It would actualize (im)possibilities that were hitherto unthinkable.[53]

§ 12. The (Im)possible from My Point of View

How can this happen, since I know no (im)possible of this kind? And how would I know of one, since the (im)possible must in principle characterize God and his domain, which, rightly, remains irreducible and inaccessible to mine? But once again, the fold of the (im)possible unfolds itself between the possible *for me* and the impossible *for me*, and therefore *also* as far as the possible on *God's side*, according to one and the same trace (§ 10), and the conversion of the impossible into the possible manifests the line between the possible and the impossible only by transgressing it. Thus, it is not self-evident that I cannot, and even less that I must not, have some knowledge of the (im)possible.

And moreover, am I really so certain that I know nothing about it? Doubtless, I know of no such (im)possible for as long as I define myself as *ego cogitans* (at least when I am thinking according to my representation and its concept); for in this posture, I screen, so to speak, everything that can happen through my conception and according to the measure of my finitude; henceforth and by definition, causality (whether it starts with me as causal agent, or with some other cause than myself) never brings about anything, except what my concept has foreseen for it as possible in conformity with the principle of noncontradiction, understood according to the measure of my representation. — But I do not always or even primarily define myself as *ego cogitans*, according to a conceptual representation. For, before being, it was necessary for me not to think, but to be born. I emerge, or rather *I have* emerged into my own existence through an entirely different mode than that of being and that of being as thinking—I emerged through the mode of an event in which I myself happened to myself [*j'advins moi-même à moi-même*] without however having predicted it, or understood it, or represented it, precisely because I was not there yet, nor was I already thinking, when this event happened. Strangely, at this event through which I became, or rather, through which I came to become who I am, I was not present, I myself wasn't there: I was not present at the event that made me present. Birth, or rather *my* birth, has preceded every thought of my own: it was mine before my thought, and without it. Consequently, it exceeds every figure of possibility, as defined by concept and representation.[54] For, even if retrospectively I am quite able, based on someone else's testimony, to reconstitute what came before me and even lead it back to a representable possibility, even one that is predictable after the fact, this interpretation in no way retroactively establishes possibility as defined by noncontradiction, such as it ought, according to the metaphysical order, precede the event of my advent; but this interpretation on the contrary relies on the fact (the facticity) of my birth, which nevertheless is itself without cause and is unforeseeable, in order to assign to it, too late and always very partially, a coherence and a conceivability that are supposed to avoid absurdity and render it simply plausible. What is more, all the genealogies and the romanticized memories will come only after the event (*post festum, post factum*), belated not only relative to that which happened without awaiting them, but also frozen in their tracks, suddenly mute before the obscure, silent, and inaccessible moment of birth, gestation, and conception—a period without speech, consciousness, or memory. In short, in front of, or rather behind, the immemorial. Birth, *my* birth, which delivers me, opens me up, and makes me, happens without me, and I will never be able to join up with it. It happened, it made me without me, without my consciousness or my concept, both of which follow after it. Advent of the event, because originarily it happened in the stead and in place of me. Brought about, or rather having happened without me, earlier than me, my birth precedes me starting from itself, without cause or presupposition or concept—in short, without possibility according to common (metaphysical) sense. My birth happens to me as something impossible that is immediately actual, factual from the outset, without precaution, or foresight, or provision.

Therefore, in the case of my birth, I am forced to admit that I experience a radical possibility—namely, the one out of which I arise and which has rendered me actual. Or better: by making itself actual precisely as impossibility, my birth has opened to me possibles without number and perfectly unforeseeable, undefined by my concepts, yet delivered (according to the double meaning of freed and made available) by it—and that therefore unlock for me as many concepts to come in its wake. The impossible, turning actual, imposes possibles and allows for the production of their concepts, according to an order that reverses that of (metaphysical) possibility according to noncontradiction.

But still, based on the (im)possible that is my birth, how is an (im)possible for God to be imagined? Doesn't the disproportion between the two domains (finite and infinite, possible *for me*, possible *from another side*) prevent the transition between them, and, even more, the assimilation of one to the other? Probably, if one clings to the division internal to the horizon of the concept of being. But probably not if we focus on the advent of the (im)possible as such. For what birth discloses for the living one, creation indicates from God's point of view. On the condition, of course, that we understand creation here as a theological concept, and not as a taking to the limit of efficient causality in a factual world. Because *for us*, creation thematizes and brings together the totality of events that happen of themselves, without concepts, without predictions, and therefore without cause—in short, the unconditioned possibles that we not only receive within creation, but from which, first and foremost, we first receive ourselves, as those gifted [*adonnés*] to our gifts. Certainly, for me, creation starts always and only with my birth; yet, by the same token, my birth opens me up to the whole of creation, giving me access to every (im)possible in its primitive, matinal, and native (im)possibility. God, the master of the (im)possible,[55] actualizes creation by making the (im)possibility of each birth actual, starting with my own.

We really do, then, have access, albeit in the realm of counter-experience (or rather *by virtue* of counter-experience), to radical possibility, in the phenomenological paradox of the (im)possibility of our own birth. Moreover, through it, we also have access (by way of an analogy that should be probed further on another occasion) to the radical (im)possibility that God accomplishes in the event that, paradigmatically, happens *for us* from him—creation. God, the one aimed at by an unconditioned transcendence, the one for whom nothing remained impossible, is from now on certified as the one who opens radical possibility, *the opener of the trace*. The master of unconditioned possibles—not the one who actualizes them or predicts them, but the one who makes them burst forth from (im)possibility and gives them to themselves.

§ 13. The (Im)possible from God's Point of View

The whole question now appears in a new light. We remain anchored in God's operational name: *for him*, nothing is impossible that nevertheless remains clearly so *for us* men. As this (im)possible *for God* belongs to radical possibility, unconditioned by either representation or concept (both of which are finite by definition), it can no longer be understood as the outcome of a simple actualization (*Bewirkung*, production); consequently, the relation of God to this radical possibility can no longer be thought in terms of omnipotent actualization: omnipotence has only a metaphysical signification, which corresponds to God's knowledge of eternal possibles, which are independent of him; omnipotence thus *limits* divine power, since it conforms itself to possibility in the metaphysical sense, to noncontradiction as represented by concept (see § 11). It follows that abstract and therefore arbitrary omnipotence no more suits the transcendent God of radical possibility than the representation of eternal possibles defines his primordial opening of the possible. The difficulty is thus to characterize God's posture with regard to the (im)possible without *reducing* it or *degrading* it to the level of omnipotence as it is conceived by metaphysics; put another way, we must conceive of how God chooses his (im)possibles for himself, with regard to which he allows the fold of the impossible *for us* to unfold into the possible *for him*. Indeed, we can assume that, if the master of the (im)possible can do what remains impossible *for us* men, he does not intend to actualize the same possibles that we imagine—because, *for him*, omnipotence is doubtless not exerted on that which provokes it *for us* (power, possession, permanence, substance, in short, being [*l'étant*]). That which, *for him*, calls for the exercise and the unfolding of the (im)possible indeed surpasses our understanding, since it has to do with stakes that we cannot even imagine, or that, if we did imagine them, we could not endure. What is (im)possible for God remains absolutely foreign to us, certainly because of our total lack of power with regard to the impossible *for us*, but above all because of our total lack of intelligence, and even more because of our lack of interest in him. The (im)possible of God remains above all something that is unthinkable for us, since it bears so much upon that which is not important for us and remains unaware of what concerns us. If God can be thought only as "*Is cui nihil impossibile cogitari possit*," he remains no less "*Id quo majus cogitari nequit.*"

This difficulty appears straightforwardly and clearly in the biblical texts: when they expose the unconditioned power of God over the (im)possible, this evocation also always elicits a worried interrogation of the identity of this power, and of its intention, both of which are unthinkable *for us*. — Let us consider the exemplary, yet difficult, narrative of the Annunciation: to the angel who alerts her to the possibility of her maternity, Mary responds first with a factual impossibility *for us*: "I know no man" (Luke 1:24); against this factual impossibility, the angel then asserts the principle of unconditioned possibility (the possible *from God's side*), which unfolds the (im)possible: literally, "οὐκ ἀδυνατήσει παρὰ τοῦ θεοῦ πᾶν ῥῆμα." ("For on God's part, no saying, no word, shall be impossible" [v. 37].)[56] And when Mary then accepts the annunciation that is made to her, she indeed recognizes the "saying" of the angel ("may it be done according to your saying," v. 38), which announced the "saying" of God; in this way, her decision and her faith in the (im)possible are *not* addressed first and foremost directly to the omnipotence of God (which in any case the text never mentions in these terms), but to the "saying" of God. She has faith in the "saying" that God has said, and thus in the commitment that he has in this way made to carry it out; she believes God's word, because she takes God at his word and knows that each of his words commits God definitively. Deep down, the point is not to acknowledge mere omnipotence (which commits to nothing, permitting every reversal and every lie), but to have faith in God's good faith (who holds himself to what he says, who allows himself to be taken at his word, by the letter of his saying). Moreover, it would be useless to have recourse to omnipotence, since it still remains immanent to our finite point of view (like the simple reverse face of possibility according to representable noncontradiction), while the issue is to transcend our finite point of view so as to pass over to God's point of view—or at least to aim at it, to admit it in intention. The difference between the impossible *for us* and the possible *on God's part* plays out elsewhere: not in omnipotence, but in fidelity to the word given. *For us,* to say does not mean to do; *for us,* to say does not commit us to anything (we lie). On the contrary, *on God's part,* to say and to do (what one says) coincide absolutely. More than the power to do all things, God has the power to say all things—not by virtue of his omnipotence but by virtue of his fidelity: God can allow himself to say all things, because anything that he says, he does (ῥῆμα signifies indivisibly both word and fact).[57] In order to face the (im)possible, fidelity transcends and replaces omnipotence in God. God can do all things because he gives his word without return, and he can give it in this way only because he can *give himself* without remainder, and without going back on his word. The one who, in turn, assumes that this word says him absolutely is filial to him, is his Son. God does not unfold the (im)possible according to omnipotence, but according to the gift.

Two details of the text confirm this. To begin with, the question here is not only one of a simple affirmation ("all things are possible"[58]), but of a double negation ("nothing is impossible"): a negation of the possible, which a negation of this negation on God's part doubles: which signifies that nothing will come about to oppose God's word. Second: the verb is conjugated in the future (nothing *shall make* impossibility, ἀδυνατήσει), suggesting that, as soon as Mary gives her consent, God will act, keep his promise, make it his business, and that we will see the effect.[59] The possible, or rather the unfolding of the fold of the (im)possible (which, for the world as it is known by human beings, is translated by the virginal birth), will open up a possible that is proper to God alone—the Incarnation, which allows Redemption (or *that* Redemption allows). Not only is the possible not the same *for us* and *on God's side*, but the (im)possible opens itself only for God.

We see clearly now that with the question of the possible and the impossible, the issue is not simply, or even first of all, or even above all, one of contradicting, by means of an abstract omnipotence, the laws of the world and of being (even though it happens that this must in fact become the case), but rather that of opening and putting into operation a bunch of possibilities that up to that moment are unthinkable and therefore held to be impossible *for us*, such that God alone could see them and will them. The issue is the unfolding of the fold of the (im)possible. Unfolding this fold is done only from the point of view and *from God's side*. But passing from *this side* requires much more than recognizing omnipotence as a proper name of God: "The Lord is a warrior. For Omnipotent is his name" ("*Dominus quasi vir pugnator. Omnipotens nomen ejus*") (Exod. 15:4, according to the Vulgate). This requires that we conceive that in the case of *this* omnipotence, the fold of the (im)possible does not fall out into just any outlandish or ridiculous monstrosity, according to the sort of omnipotence that we human beings dream of. The impossibility of the impossibility that God exercises does not do everything and anything—it does all that it wills, but it does not will just anything, because it wills only in loving.

Moreover, pure and simple divine omnipotence quickly appeared to many from the beginning as a fragile and abstract argument. Celsus already reproached Christians: "As they have nothing to say in reply [regarding the possibility of the resurrection of the body], they escape to a most absurd refuge by saying that 'nothing is impossible to God.'" Origen, in turn, had to specify that "we know that we may not understand the word 'nothing' [referring to Luke 1:37] of things which do not exist or which are inconceivable (ἀδυνατήσει)."[60] This prudent response is once again insufficient, for a finite thought has no right to oppose unthinkables and things that are nonexistent to God if "with him nothing is impossible." More essentially, the question no longer consists in fixing a limit beyond which divine omnipotence would be going too far (relative to what norm?), but in determining what God can will *as his word*, as a word that he commits to keeping, allowing himself to be taken "at his word." Neither logic, nor contradiction, nor the principle of identity, nor efficiency and the principle of sufficient reason retain the least pertinence when the task is to conceive that to which the word of God commits itself and commits God. Obviously, if God is God, he can do whatever he wills—that is not the question.[61] The question asks instead what *God* is able to will, and wills to be able [*peut vouloir et veut pouvoir*]. What power does he will without restriction? That which corresponds to him, and therefore comes from him. That for which he can answer, because he says it. Saint Augustine explicates this remarkably:

> God is all-powerful, and, since He is all-powerful, He cannot die, He cannot be deceived, He cannot lie, and, as the Apostle says, "he cannot contradict himself." Very much He cannot do, yet He is all-powerful; because He cannot do these things, for that very reason is He all-powerful. If He could die, He would not be all-powerful; if He could lie, if He could be deceived, if He could deceive, if it were possible for Him to do an injustice, he would not be omnipotent [. . .]. Absolutely omnipotent, our Father cannot sin. He does whatsoever He wills: that in itself is omnipotence. He does whatever He wishes well, He does whatever He wishes justly, but, whatever is evil, that He does not will.[62]

God does whatever he wills, but above all he wills only what it is fitting for him to will—namely, what comes from him, what one can will only by loving it. God does what befits God, which is to love. Such is the impossible for man: that which befits God.

But is there sense in pushing further to determine what it befits God to will, and then to be able to do, and thus to determine what God alone is able to have the power to do, because he alone is able to will it? Does not such a claim cancel itself in an absolute metaphysical dogmatism or a delirium of insignificant interpretation? But there remains a third way: to go back to the biblical texts, where God reveals himself willing and being able to do the most extreme (im)possible things, (im)possible for us to begin with, but also for all humanity, *including his own*. Let us consider in particular Matthew 19:26: "With men this is impossible [namely, that a rich man enter God's kingdom], but with God all things are possible" ("παρὰ ἀνθρώποις τοῦτο αδύνατόν ἐσειν, παρὰ δὲ θεῷ πάντα δυνατά" [Matt. 19:26]).[63] What (im)possible does Christ here designate as the criterion, under the name of difficulty (or facility), that distinguishes man from God? "It is easier (εὐκοπώτερον) for a camel to go through the eye of a needle than for a rich man to enter the kingdom of God" (v. 24): physical and worldly impossibility serve as a sign to expose an even greater impossibility, but one that does not strike the human eye directly or appear in the world's light. There is a chiasmus here: an impossibility for human beings (but not for God)—entering the Kingdom—precisely does not appear to human beings (but only to Christ, and thus to God). How do we explain it? For men—the spectators of the dialogue as well as the rich young man himself—the youth in question has *already* entered the Kingdom of God, since he has *already* accomplished the commandments ("I have kept them all"). Hence his astonishment at the idea that he is still missing something: "What more is there for me [to do]?" (v. 20). Indeed, what does he lack? Strictly speaking, nothing—except precisely this nothing and this lack. The rich young man lacks, as his last and most perfect treasure, no longer possessing the accomplishment itself of the commandments. He lacks experience of the accomplishment of the commandments as a poverty and a *gift received*, but never possessed. He lacks, precisely, possessing and keeping nothing but Christ alone ("Come, follow me," v. 21); which means becoming one with God through Christ, becoming holy as God is holy ("If you would be perfect . . . ," v. 21), and in this way fulfilling the highest commandment: "You shall be holy because I am holy" (Lev. 11:44 and 19:2)—a commandment that Christ repeats to the letter: "You, therefore, must be perfect, as your heavenly Father is perfect" (Matt. 5:48).[64] What is impossible for man ("the rich young man") lies in the lack of lack (the lack of poverty, of identification with Christ)—and, in the world that sees only that which subsists ("riches"), this lack can of course never appear. The impossible thus remains inaccessible to the one who is powerless to do it [*qui ne le peut pas*], but above all to the one who does not even *see* what he is powerless to do. Only Christ sees it and points it out with a light that is as clear as day to the spectators and to the interlocutor, who, despite (or because of) this light, sees nothing. At least we understand that here the radical impossible *for man* appears only *from the point of view of God*, for it consists in a possibility that men do not truly consider—a genuine conversion of man to God. They hide from themselves this radical impossible behind a mere worldly impossibility (renouncing the possession of wealth). What is impossible according to the world thus has the function of masking the (im)possible.

But, in discovering that the worldly impossibility seems *for us* actually less impossible, or in other words, "easier" (εὐκοπώτερον) than the impossibility of conversion, we catch sight of the fact that by right, *from God's point of view*, the real difficulty—the (im)possible—consists in the conversion to God, which is infinitely more difficult than all the worldly impossibilities *for us* that we recognize.[65] We read this reversal of the possible and the impossible between Christ and men, a reversal that constitutes the very game of the (im)possible, in the story of the healing of the paralytic (Matt. 9:1–9).[66] A paralyzed man is brought before Christ; but strangely, instead of healing him physically (as everyone expected, since he had constantly done so before), he declares the man spiritually healed ("Your sins are forgiven," v. 2). But through this reversal, Christ accomplishes precisely what is possible for God and supremely impossible for men: the forgiveness of sins, which God alone can give (Mark 2:7, presented as an objection), and which only the omnipotence (ἐξουσία, Matt. 28:19) of the Resurrected can confer on his disciples. And some of those present, or at least some "among the scribes," understand the claim to forgive sins as a "blasphemy" (v. 3), since Christ in this way clearly claims the privilege of God. Nor are they wrong in this regard: to claim to do the impossible for men is indeed the same as claiming to be God. How is Christ able to sustain his claim before men? In accomplishing a relative impossibility, one that is physical and mundane—healing the paralytic of his paralysis—he proves the greater by the less. Through this impossibility that is both undeniable and visible *for us* in the world (the less), he attests that nothing is impossible for him in our world—that he holds the rank of God, and thus that nothing is impossible for him *even outside the world* (the greater). By asking the question "Which is easier (εὐκοπώτερον)?" (v. 5), he forces men to make a decision about the real presence of God in him. Since for men nothing seems more difficult in the world than curing a paralytic of his physical paralysis, Christ by healing him accomplishes the impossible *for us*, which is what is proper to God; one must either deny the evidence of the world, which paradoxically manifests that Christ comes from God, or admit the visible evidence in this world that he is indeed God—which implies recognizing in him the actual power of the (im)possible, namely, the forgiveness of sins. Christ thus makes phenomenally manifest what is impossible *for us* by accomplishing it, while also accomplishing what is most difficult *from God's viewpoint*, namely, healing the heart of man.[67]

The impossible for man has the name God, but God *as such*—as the one who alone does what man cannot even *contemplate*: forgive the faults made by man against God. Here we find the fold of the (im)possible, here we find true power in play, of which the world, or metaphysics, or perhaps even philosophy are capable of merely the slightest glimmer.

III. THE UNCONDITIONED, OR THE STRENGTH OF THE GIFT

Donum proprie est datio irredibilis.
(A gift is properly an unreturnable giving.)

—THOMAS AQUINAS[1]

§ 14. The Contradictions of the Gift

We give without counting. In every sense of the word. — First, because we give *without ceasing*: we give in the same way we breathe, at every moment, in every circumstance, from morning until night, and there is no day that passes without, in one way or another, our having given something to someone, or even our having "given it all."[2]— We also give without keeping an account, *without measure*, because giving implies giving at a loss, or at least we give without taking into account our time or our thought, or our efforts, so that we quite simply do not keep an account of our gifts. — Finally, we give without counting because we give most often *without* having a clear *awareness* of doing so, for lack of time and attention, giving almost mechanically, automatically, and without knowing it.

Thus, the attitude of the gift, the posture of giving, seems at first glance obvious enough, because its exercise so often takes place unconsciously, without our thinking about it or preoccupying ourselves with it; the very evidence of the gift would make consciousness of it seem almost super-

Translator's note: The translation of this chapter borrows frequently from an earlier translation of some of the material here. See Jean-Luc Marion, "The Reason of the Gift," trans. Shane Mackinlay and Nicolas de Warren, in *Givenness and God: Questions of Jean-Luc Marion*, ed. Ian Leask and Eoin Cassidy, 101–54 (New York: Fordham University Press, 2005).

fluous. Thus, there would appear to be nothing more to discuss about the gift, and no reason to interrogate its essence; the only concern would be to carry it out; in this view, the gift would not give something to reflect on, something about which to become aware, but would instead directly determine an ethical demand and a social obligation. And if it still presented a difficulty, it would not be the difficulty of its definition, but of its exercise; for, concerning the gift, there would be nothing to say, and instead, as with love, only the question of making it.

And yet, right away this evidence takes back the certainty it seemed to provide us. For these three ways of giving cannot be brought together without contradicting one another: indeed, the third way of giving without counting—giving without being aware of it—manifestly cancels the preceding two ways; after all, if we truly give unceasingly and without measure, how could we not be conscious of it in the end? Reciprocally, if we give without being aware of it, how will we know whether we are giving unceasingly and without measure? Or more exactly, how do we assure ourselves that this "unceasingly and without measure" qualifies our gift as genuine, if we have no consciousness of it? In short, how can we give without counting, if we give without rendering an account[3] of it?

But, beyond this formal contradiction, an incomparably deeper contradiction takes shape, which puts into question the gift itself: this gift, which claims to give without counting, in fact is always keeping account, and even keeps account much too much. The gift gives in such a way that it never loses anything, but instead always benefits [*trouve son compte*], at the least breaking even, equal to where it would have been without ever having given anything. In fact and in principle, the gift does not give without counting, because in the final analysis, the bottom line, in one way or another, proves to be positive; the gift gives cheaply because it remains intact after having given, equal to itself; in short, it does well and always makes some profit. Or at least, one can always interpret a gift in such a way that it seems to collapse inescapably, not because of an exterior obstacle, but due to the simple fact that it occurs spontaneously and is perfectly carried out. It is enough to analyze its three dimensions—those of the giver, the givee, and the given gift—to see how the gift is abolished in favor of its contrary: *exchange*.

Let's begin with the giver. In point of fact, she never gives without receiving in return as much as she has given. If she gives while being recognized as a giver, she receives at least the recipient's, or "givee's" recognition, even if her gift is never returned to her. And even if the givee fails to recognize her, the giver will still receive the esteem of the witnesses of her gift. Supposing that by chance she gives without anyone recognizing her as the giver, either because the gift remains strictly private (without a witness), or because the beneficiary does not know about this gift or rejects it (ingratitude), the giver will still receive from herself an esteem for herself (for having been generous, for having spent gratuitously); and this esteem, in fact perfectly merited, will assure her a "self-contentment" (Descartes), and thus the autarchy of the sage. She will experience herself, moreover rightly, as morally superior to the stingy man, whom she knew not to imitate, and this gain will largely compensate her loss. But, as a result, the giver will have canceled her gift in an exchange—and thus she herself disappears as giver, becoming the buyer of her own esteem. At the price, certainly, of a good that is lost, but found again. A benefit would therefore by definition end up as never lost. The misfortune of the gift would consist precisely in this: the giver never loses anything in the gift, but in exchange, she always finds herself there, making a good deal.

Next, consider the givee. By receiving, he receives not only a good, but especially a debt; he thus becomes obligated to his benefactor, and thus obligated to give back. If he gives back without delay another good for the first good received, he will be even, but precisely because he will have annulled his debt by substituting an exchange for the gift, or in other words, by annulling the gift, which disappears as such. Inversely, if he cannot give back right away, he will remain a debtor into the future, whether provisional or definitive; during the time of his debt, he will have to state his recognition and admit his dependence; thus, he will only be pardoned by reimbursing his debt through his submission as debtor, or even by accepting his status as servant to a master. If, finally, he denies having received a gift, perhaps at the price of a lie and a denial of justice, he will have to argue that it was simply a matter of what was his due, or that he received nothing. Thus, in each of these cases, the givee will erase the gift and reestablish an exchange—whether real or fictive, it matters little, since he will always end up suppressing himself as givee.

Finally, let's look at the given gift: it tends no less inexorably toward erasing in itself every trace and every memory of the gesture that gave it. Indeed, no sooner given, the thing that is the gift, whatever it may be, imposes its massive and immediate presence; inevitably, its actual evidence blots out the act that delivered it: the given gift occupies the entire stage of the giving givenness and turns it back to the inactuality of its concluded past. If (as we drum into little children) it is always necessary to remember to thank the benefactor before taking possession of the present, the fault lies less in bad manners than in a phenomenological necessity: the gift confiscates all the attention and cancels its provenance. As soon as it is offered for possession, as soon as it is received and confirmed, the given gift is detached from its giver, and lets her fade into the background on the stage of givenness. Without return and all at once, the gift loses the status of a given by givenness, no longer to appear except as a pure and bare piece of merchandise—valued according to its price, wiped clean of the intention of its giver, having become once again an autonomous object, assigned its own exchange value, ready to return into the commercial circuit (to be resold, exchanged, "monetized"). As soon as it is given, the gift disappears as given gift, to be solidified into its value as an object available for an exchange that is possible, and therefore almost inevitable.

How, then, can we not conclude that the gift, once accomplished in actuality and appearing in the cold light of experience, must inescapably turn into its opposite, following a triple assimilation to exchange and to commerce? From this self-suppression, how do we not infer the gift's fundamental instability, which makes of it a mere appearance of phenomenon, incapable of constituting itself into an objective phenomenon? The gift contradicts itself with a contradiction in terms—in terms that do not rightly belong to it, because they are the *terms of exchange*. As a result, a simple dilemma arises. Either the gift appears in actuality, but it disappears as gift; or, it remains a pure gift, but it becomes nonapparent, inactual, excluded from the process of things, a pure idea of reason, a mere noumenon, resistant to the conditions of experience. For that which appears according to the conditions of actual experience must, from the gift that it was, be cashed out in an exchange. Either the gift conforms with givenness, but never appears; or it appears, but in the economy of exchange, where it is transformed into its opposite—precisely, exchange, the thing given rendered back (*do, ut des*), the thing given for a thing in return, and the thing in return in order to cancel a thing given; in other words: the business and the management of goods. Exchange imposes itself as the truth of the gift, which it crosses out. In submitting itself to the economy, the gift exchanges its gift essence for an actuality that denies it, precisely in exchange. For the economy economizes on the gift.[4]

§ 15. The Terms of Exchange

But does this critique of the gift, as efficacious as it is abstract, itself escape from critique? To all appearances, it still lies exposed there, because it rests at the least upon an unquestioned assumption: that the gift, in order to appear, implies a perfect and pure gratuity, which it must always give for nothing.

Now, the assumption of gratuity can be debated. — First of all because, for the giver and the givee alike, to receive or to agree to a gain that is moral (esteem, recognition) or symbolic (obligation), and thus unreal (no thing, nothing of value or price), is not equivalent purely and simply to a real reimbursement (a sum, a thing, a good). To confuse the two types of gain received or given implies, indeed, canceling every difference between the real and the unreal, between the thing and the symbol. Hesitating between cynicism (which realizes the unreal) and idealism (which derealizes the thing), the description simplifies the specificity of the phenomena here in play to such a point that it reduces them to nothing. — Next, it is not self-evident that the gift disappears when it is accompanied by the least bit of satisfaction; for satisfaction can result from the gift without its having to precede it as its motive, nor anticipate it as its prerequisite intention. We can just as well find ourselves happy at having given or received, without necessarily having given or received in order to become happy, and done so uniquely with this aim. It could even happen that we receive this satisfaction only because we had precisely *not* looked for it, or projected it, or even foreseen it; in short, it fulfills us because it comes to us as an excess, and catches us unawares. The joy of the gift does not motivate it any more than it precedes it, but instead it adds to it, each time, as an unexpected grace, unforeseeable and, in a sense, unmerited. And thus, while it crowns the gift, it does not disqualify it. — Finally, how can we avoid suspecting that the ever so unyielding purity thus required of the gift would not ultimately imply its independence from every possible other? It would finally lead to a complete autarchy, forbidding not only the exchange and the gift, but alterity in general. And how can we avoid having the sense that such gratuity would not put into question, along with the alterity of the other in the gift, the very ipseity of the *ego*, which I put into play as giver or givee? Would it not be necessary, in the end, to cancel our ipseities or, on the contrary, claim to be a god so as to give with full gratuity, "without desire"? Unless this supposed gratuity reduces to a pure and simple indifference, which, with eyes closed, would give nothing to no one, and receive nothing from nobody?[5]

The aporiae of gratuity seem so patent that we ought never to have been unaware of them: if the gift contradicts itself when gratuity is required of it, why have we required it? Perhaps we have had recourse to the criterion of gratuity for an excellent reason: gratuity seems to erect the best rampart for defending the gift against exchange and economy, its absolute contraries. And yet, why might gratuity, more than every other option, in this way be excluded from economy? To this question it is necessary to add another: why, in passing to gratuity, should the gift immediately disappear, as if excluding itself from exchange were equivalent to excluding itself at the same time from experience in general? What do the requirements of exchange and of economy have in common with the conditions of possibility of experience? For the latter end up by coinciding with the former, provided that we reconstitute several stages on the path of their encounter. — First, economy posits and produces the equality of exchange: "In exchanging, it is necessary that each party is convinced of the quality and quantity of every thing exchanged. In this agreement it is natural that every one should desire to receive as much as he can, and to give as little" (Turgot).[6] Still, where does the power of this equality come from, and how does it extend its empire, as if inevitably? It arises not merely out of a concern for formal rigor, nor even out of a demand for honesty, but rather as a theoretical possibility: "Whatever man can measure, calculate, and systematize, ultimately becomes the object of measurement, calculation, and system. Wherever fixed relations can replace indeterminate ones, the substitution finally takes place. It is thus that the sciences and all human institutions are organized" (A.-A. Cournot). For example, "[A]s the abstract idea of wealth [. . .] constitutes a perfectly determinate relation, like all precise conceptions it can become the object of theoretical deductions."[7] Measure (mathematical quantification) makes equality possible, and thus exchange; in these conditions, the gift becomes, through the exchange that equalizes it, an object—an object of exchange, and thus of commerce, following "the abstract idea of *value in exchange*, which supposes that the objects to which such value is attributed *are in commercial circulation*."[8] And commerce allows the exchange of goods only because it fixes equalities between objects of value; but it fixes these equalities in value only because it first interprets the terms of the gift in terms of exchange; now, these terms of exchange are themselves found to be constituted into objects by the measure, which places them in equality, and thus in equations, and finally in order. In this way, the gift enters into exchange and commerce because it is transcribed into the terms of economic exchange, and there transposes itself in terms of an object. — We understand, then, that the economy can fix the conditions of possibility of experience for the objects of exchange: it unfolds and puts directly to work the exigencies of the *mathesis universalis*, according to its strict Cartesian definition: the order imposes exchange, and measure guarantees equality in the field of the gift, which becomes henceforth as such problematic, or even aporetic, inasmuch as it is converted into its contrary, an exchange. Either the gift complies with its concept—exchange—and satisfies its conditions of possibility; or it remains gratuitous, which is to say without order or measure, and contradicts the conditions of its possibility. The gift can certainly be thought, but only by transposing itself into exchange—according to the properly metaphysical requirements of rationality.[9]

The abolition of the gift, such that it passes into the (measured) equality of exchange, also defines the conditions of possibility of its appearance in experience. For the equality of exchange matters only to the extent that it "renders reason" [*rend raison*] for or justifies its possibility and its actuality in experience. The economy thus claims to measure exchange on the level of reason so as to render reason to it; every exchange shall have its reason, for no longer shall anything be exchanged in vain. In fact, the "economy never consumes without an object," since what is at issue in "political economy," as in every other science (even "moral" sciences), is an "art of connecting cause with effect"—in this case by means of exchange, which alone defines value (J.-B. Say).[10] In an economy, just as elsewhere, to render reason allows one to give an account [*rendre compte*], because reason calculates, restores equality, and provides self-identity—which in this instance is value. Reason renders reason because it identifies the conditions of exchange and therefore assigns its conditions to possibility and justifies wealth, like so many other phenomena, by its effects, by attributing adequate causes to them.

That this equality of exchange renders reason to the economy was moreover confirmed *a contrario* by Marx. When Marx objects to the "jurist's consciousness [that] recognises in this [comparison between exchanges involving labor and all other exchanges], at most, a material difference, expressed in the juridically equivalent formulae: *Do ut des, do ut facias, facio ut des, facio ut facias* [I give so that you will give, I give so that you will act, I act so that you will give, I act so that you will act]" and insists on a contrary view, that "[c]apital, therefore, is not only, as Adam Smith says, the command over labour. It is essentially the command over *unpaid labour* . . . a definite quantity of other people's unpaid labour," he not only unveils the mechanism of "the secret of profit making" but also, by denying the supposed equality in the exchange between wage and labor, destroys the whole "political economy."[11] Thus, the economy as such consists in restoring equality between the terms of exchange so as to provide this phenomenon—the exchange—with the means of satisfying the conditions of its possibility and thereby actually appearing.[12]

In this way, exchange suffices for "rendering reason"—rendering its due to the gift (in the economy) and rendering its cause to the effect (in experience). Reason always suffices, and its sufficiency restores equality, intelligibility, and justice. In principle, nothing has the right to exempt itself from reason's demand—every pronouncement, every action, every event, every fact, every object, and every being[13] must supply an answer to the question that asks them, Why?; διότι; *Cur*? Even the simple idea must comply, and even God[14]—and thus, even and especially the gift. On the contrary, if the gift rests on gratuity, sufficient reason cannot but economize on it, precisely in the name of the economy in which reason carries on. Consequently, sufficient reason owes it to itself to exclude the gift from experience, and therefore from phenomenality: everything for which one cannot render a reason, starting with the gift, must be rendered invisible.

In this way, we can understand the nullification of gratuity by the economy: rendering reason to the gift amounts to demonstrating that no one gives without realizing it [*sans s'en rendre compte*], nor without giving an account of it [*sans en rendre compte*]—that is, without being reimbursed, in either real or symbolic terms. In short, it amounts to demonstrating that one gives only with immediate payment in mind, and for the sake of satisfaction. Indeed, sufficient reason can always seize the gift by assigning a reason of exchange to each of its moments. The gift's self-contradiction, which I have formally sketched above (§ 14), can then be repeated more visibly, in the form of a threefold response to the demand of sufficient reason. To arrive at this interpretation, it is enough to distinguish between external reasons (or causes) and internal reasons (or motives).

The giver does not give gratuitously because, as we have seen, she is always reimbursed, either in real or in symbolic terms. But above all one can cancel out the giver's merit by arguing that she has given only what she was able to give, and thus that she has given from her surplus. Now, since by definition she was able to dispose of this surplus, it therefore did not truly belong to her. By giving it, then, she merely redistributed an excess of property that she had unjustly confiscated. In principle, the duty of justice obliged the giver to distribute that which did not belong to her. In claiming to give, she did nothing more than fulfill the duty of justice. Justice, which is the motive (or internal reason) for the apparent gift, explains it and commands it as a simple duty. Consequently, the giver's claim to gratuity, and even the gift's entitlement to be called a gift, collapse in the face of a simple duty of justice—the duty to render to each her account, her due.

Reciprocally, the givee or recipient can put forward sound motives for receiving a good as part of a simple exchange and deny that he is the beneficiary of a gift. It is enough for him to maintain that this supposed gift has come to him simply as his due. For if I find myself in the situation of a truly needy poor person, I am destitute. This means not only that I am in need, but that I need that which I lack because my condition as a man requires it, necessarily and by right. On the basis of human rights, I have the right (and not simply the need) to feed myself, to clothe myself, to shelter, and even to earn a wage. Therefore, what public or private assistance might give me is delivered as my due, and no longer as a gift. Not only is there no question of gratuity, but gratuity would do me injury and an injustice.[15] I claim my due by right and in the name of the dignity of man, and those who give me my due owe it to me out of a duty that is imposed on them in accordance with an objective right. In fact, if they abandoned me to my misery, they would put at risk not only my life but also my humanity, thus debased to the level of animality. By the same token, they would lose their own humanity by abolishing mine. They must render reason to the humanity that is in me, but also in themselves: if they do not come to my rescue (out of simple solidarity among fellow men), they put at risk their own status as human beings and their ethical dignity as subjects with rights. Thus, by giving me what I need in order to remain a man, others only fulfill their duty—they do not give me a gift, but render to me what is due, which in return assures their own rank. At issue is an exchange, symbolic to be sure, between my humanity and theirs, in which the symbol is infused with the highest possible reality, that which joins us together in the same humanity. In this way, the gift is abolished in what is due, gratuity is abolished in solidarity, and the symbolic exchange of sociality is alone operative as the ultimate economy.

If now, beyond motives (internal reasons), we consider the causes (external reasons), we can likewise lead the given gift (the object itself, the thing) back into the economy. Let us take a banal example: when a "humanitarian" organization (to avoid calling it "charitable") or a local community association "gives" (let us accept this problematic term for the moment) food, clothing, housing, or work ("social" or reserved employment), that organization certainly distributes these goods gratuitously, without payment or an economic transaction. However, this does not mean that these goods have no value for exchange, or market price. On the contrary, to dispense these goods gratuitously, they must be produced and distributed; that is, procured. How? Obviously, by means of gifts: the surplus of individuals, the unsold stock of businesses, or subsidies from community funds. In each case, it is a matter of consumable goods and equipment, with a market value that is calculable with precision and already inscribed within the economic sphere. Quite simply, these goods and values are removed from the economic sphere by those who, having acquired or produced them within the economy, rid themselves of them at an economic loss (pure gratuity, or gratuity mixed with realism—these goods having become useless, unsalable, depreciated in value, and so on). During the period of time in which they are under the control of "humanitarian" organizations—that is, until their redistribution—these goods remain outside the economy, with their exchange value neutralized. However, as soon as they are given, they recover this value; and it is precisely for this reason that they are a real assistance to those in need, in that these people are provided with goods for which they do not have to pay a price, but that nevertheless have an exchange value, a value in the economy. The advantage of the "humanitarian" stage of this process obviously does not lie in a definitive and thus utopian suspension of the exchange cycle, nor in an illusory escape from the economy. On the contrary, the advantage lies in the reinscription, through a certain period of gratuity and approximate neutralization of exchange, of the destitute person into the economy. The short moment of the suspension of exchange (the gift strictly speaking) is aimed solely at finally reinjecting the gift into the economy, and thus making it *disappear* as a gift. Moreover, the provisional moment of the gift lacks the merit of even having suspended the economy—on the contrary, it was the poverty of the poor person that, by preventing her from entering into exchange, canceled the economy by default; the gift has thus merely suspended (through a secondary positivity) the initial suspension (the primary destitution); then, by paying on behalf of the one who is insolvent, it has reinstated her in the cycle of exchange. The gift is therefore not a gift, in two senses: first, because in the end it restores the economy; and second, because it "buys back" (so to speak) poverty by providing the poor with the means for paying, buying, and exchanging anew. The gift, therefore, labors for the economy's reinstatement, and not at all for its suppression. The gift restores the poor person's former unbalanced accounts in order to allow her to render accounts once again—or in short, to render reason for future exchanges. Consequently, regarding these "humanitarian" organizations, we often speak not only of an *economy* of gratuity, but also of business ventures of reintegration (reintegration into what, if not the economy?). The moment of the gift is not only provisional, but appears in the end as an indirect economic agent, a cause or reason; indeed, a reason and cause so powerful that it succeeds in restoring the economy at the very point where it was blocked.

The gift, in its three figures, can and even must (out of a simple care for social functioning) either allow itself to be led back into an exchange (justice between giver and recipient), or work toward reinstating exchange (reintegration through the gift). It must, then, disappear into the economy that it restores, rather than be exempted from it. There is therefore always a motive or cause for submitting the gift to an economic interpretation and rendering it reason according to exchange. Either the gift remains provisional and a mere appearance, or it appears, but as an object and according to an exchange, by satisfying the sufficient reason that assimilates it into the economy. *The economy economizes on the gift because it sufficiently renders it reason.*

§ 16. Reducing the Gift to Givenness

Despite all this, is it possible to understand the gift as it is given and spoken—that is, as a gift—without in the end surrendering it to economic reason or dissipating it in the phantom of an empty gratuity? At the very least, such an understanding would call for preserving the gift from the logic that demands not that it give what it claims to give, but instead that it give *reasons* for giving (or, rather, for *not* giving). In other words: how is it possible to avoid compelling the gift to surrender itself to a reason that authorizes it only by canceling it?

But the gift becomes unthinkable in the economy because the economy always interprets it as necessarily being a quid pro quo relationship, an exchange of gifts, where the first gift is recovered in the gift that is returned for it, and where the returned gift is registered as the return on the initial gift (*do ut des*). Paradoxically, the gift is lost here because it never manages to be given genuinely at a loss—in short, it is lost because it has lost the freedom to be lost. Consequently, how is one to conceive of the gift as such, as a lost gift, a mad gift, a loss without return, and yet not without a thinkable meaning, or even a certain reason adapted to it? Clearly, we will not arrive at an answer to this question for as long as we investigate the gift in terms of exchange and describe it within the economic horizon. We will succeed only if we stop approaching the gift as a concealed exchange that is yet to be interpreted according to economic reason—either as an unconscious exchange or as a supposedly gratuitous exchange (presuming that this is not a contradiction in terms). In short, we will succeed only if we conceive the gift as such, irreducible to exchange and economy. However, if the gift is not related to exchange, even as an exception to it, we would have to be able to think it starting from precisely that which exchange abolishes—that is, excess and loss, which are in fact the same thing. But we can do justice to excess and loss, and therefore to the gift as such, only by leaving the horizon of exchange and economy. Yet is there any other horizon than this one, and if so, how are we to identify it? This other horizon could be discovered—if this were to be done without illusions or arbitrariness—only on the basis of the gift itself, or rather from the point where its phenomenon wells up just before it is dissolved into exchange, during the fragile instant where its three moments have not yet surrendered to the economy's sufficient reason. Thus, we will discover this other horizon only by restraining the phenomenon of the gift from sliding down into an exchange, and by maintaining it in itself; that is, by reducing the gift to itself, and thus to givenness, which is the gift's proper horizon. Givenness is opened as a horizon only to the extent that we reduce the gift to it, in the double sense of leading the gift back to givenness and submitting the gift to a phenomenological reduction.[16]

Yet givenness is not self-evident and, because it always precedes the gift, it seems to us even less accessible than does the gift. Nevertheless, we can assume that if givenness must open a horizon for the gift, it will at least testify to itself by not immediately assigning the gift to a social process or an ethical behavior (even if it eventually does this), but rather by allowing the gift to appear without requiring that it be dissolved into exchange. In order to appear, the gift reduced to givenness would only have to be given—no more and no less—without having to render reason for itself by reverting to revenue and making the least return on investment. This means describing the gift without reconstituting the terms of exchange; that is, without the terms that are the minimum basis for any exchange. For if the giver were to give *without a recipient* to acknowledge it with gratitude, or if the recipient were to receive *without any giver* to honor, or even if both the giver and the recipient (givee) were to exchange *no given thing*, then in each case one of the conditions of possibility of an exchange would be missing, and the gift would be realized absolutely and as such. Let us attempt such a threefold description of a gift that has been freed from the terms of exchange.

First, a gift can be fully realized as gift without any giver being rewarded (in either real or symbolic terms), because it can be realized without any giver at all. To see this, it is enough simply to analyze the hypothesis of a gift received from an anonymous or even nonexistent giver. These two conditions in fact coincide in the case of an inheritance, where death steals away the giver and prevents anything at all from being rendered to him. Indeed, I am so unable to render anything to him that this very impossibility constitutes the condition of the gift that is made to me: since the testator's death alone puts the will into effect, it is necessarily the case that I no longer have anyone to thank for my being able to receive that for which I ought to thank him. The testator will receive from me neither the recognition of gratitude nor the recognition of a debt, since he is no longer here to enjoy it; and if I declare my recognition, this will take place in front of the social group that knew him, yet of which he is precisely no longer a part. It could even happen that I receive the gift of this inheritance without the testator having wanted it, and even against his intentions, because either he was completely unknown to me up until that point, or I to him, and only a genealogical inquiry led his executor to me.[17] In each of these cases, the giver is lacking, and thus recognition and reimbursement are ruled out. Nevertheless, the gift is perfectly accomplished. It thus appears fully, even though unexpected, undeserved, unsettled, without recognition or return. On the contrary, it takes on its full meaning in this very absence of motive and sufficient reason.

Second, the gift can be fully realized as a gift without a givee or recipient of any sort. To establish this, it will be enough to take up the argument from anonymity once again, this time applying it to the recipient. Indeed, in the vast majority of cases, when we contribute to a "humanitarian" organization, we do not know and never will know the individual person who is going to benefit from our help. The organization mediates our gift, such that I remain anonymous to the recipient, who in turn is anonymous to me. The gift is carried out even though no recipient is made known, and as a result, by definition, he or she can never give anything to me in return. However, the argument from anonymity could be contested by arguing that here, in the final instance, there is no gift, because the intermediary (the association)—even if it does its work scrupulously (distributing contributions, helping efficiently)—precisely refuses to make a gift by making the recipients anonymous and merging them into the crowd of those who are helped. We have seen elsewhere (§ 15) that it is more a matter here of solidarity and what is due by right than that of a gift.

But there is still another case where a gift is perfectly realized, with a clearly identified recipient, without, however, any risk that he or she will be able to make a reimbursement and thus transform the gift into an exchange: the case where I give to an enemy. Whether an enemy is private or public matters little, since in either case the hate she bears toward me will make her return my gift, experienced as an insult, as well as every claim to generosity as an additional humiliation. Not only will she not give me a gift in return for mine, not only will she deny that there is even a gift at issue, but she will as a result foster a still greater hatred for me. She will return my favor by inverting the debt a hundredfold—I will deserve to be even more hated by her, because I wanted to make her benefit from my wealth, make her a slave to my protection, overpower her by my generosity, and so on.[18] She will therefore take vengeance on me in order to free herself from the least obligation of recognition: she will kill me rather than acknowledge that she owes me the least recognition. Nevertheless, is my gift thereby compromised? Not at all, for a gift that is spurned and denied, or even transformed into an affront, nonetheless remains perfectly and definitively given.[19] And this very destitution makes the gift appear with a more sovereign strength, for it frees it from reciprocity. A foundational paradox results: if it is only to the enemy that I can make a gift without the risk of finding it taken up in an exchange or trapped in reciprocity, then it is only my enemy who preserves and honors my gift, by guaranteeing that it will not fall into a quid pro quo relationship. *My enemy appears as my gift's best friend.* Whoever gives to his enemy does so without return, without revenue, and without sufficient reason—he gives incontestably.[20] And this is why only he who gives to his enemy gains a hundredfold: not, of course, another gift, a countergift, but the reduction of his gift to givenness itself.

Third, the gift can be fully realized without giving any object susceptible of reverting to an exchange value. Indeed, what can I give that is more precious than such a gift? Nothing, perhaps, other than my attention, my care, my time, my faith, or even my life; and, in the final analysis, the other person expects nothing less and can hope for nothing more. Nor I from him. For in giving these nonobjective and nonobjectifiable gifts, which elude both understanding and possession, supply no gain or assignable return, and really provide *nothing* (*nothing real* [*ne rem*]), I in fact give myself in my most complete ipseity; with this *nothing*, I give all that I have, because I am not giving something that I possess apart from myself, but rather that which I am. Whence comes this other paradox: that I give (myself) more, the more I give nothing—no given gift limited within a substrate or a real predicate. From here on, I am giving outside the horizon of possession (and *also* dispossession) of whatever may *be*, and therefore outside both objectness and the reason that would account for it. It should not be objected that by giving no object, I would give less, or would even exempt myself from giving in earnest; for on the contrary—and here the argument repeats itself—I exempt myself from really giving, that is, from giving *myself*, me in person, when I settle for giving a finite object (even if huge, it remains finite) in the stead and in place of myself. Thus, I give money in order to exempt myself from giving my time and attention. I pay into an annuity in order to be excused from having to love, and so regain my freedom. What happens when, for example, I give a woman a piece of jewelry (even a magnificent one)? Two hypotheses: Either I give her this object alone, but in order to get her to accept that I am leaving her or that I do not really love her (i.e., to settle accounts); or I give it to her, but as the indication that I love her irrevocably, and thus as a simple sign of the true gift, which remains nonobjectifiable and invaluable—the gift of my time, my attention, my faith, my life—in short, the gift of myself. A gift that, at this moment of the gift, I can only give symbolically, since it will require the entire duration of my lifetime to truly accomplish it.[21] In summary, either the object given remains alone and signifies the denial of the full gift (the gift of self), or it is presented as a simple indication and marks the promise of the full gift (this same gift of self), which is ever still unaccomplished. Every gift that is given, insofar as it implies more actuality, must become unreal, nonobjectifiable, and invaluable. Its perfection grows with its nonrealization.

The gift in its three moments, then, can be reduced to the givenness in it. It is bestowed all the better when it lacks one of the terms of reciprocity and is freed from what the economy claimed to downgrade it to in each instance: the quid pro quo relation of exchange. The gift is given more perfectly the more there is ignorance of either the giver compensated by his (good) conscience, or the recipient freed from all consciousness (of debt), or the given thing recoverable as an exchange value by a (commercial) consciousness. The gift is reduced to givenness by being fully realized without any consciousness of giving (*conscience de don*)—without the self-consciousness that would make it reasonably account for itself and multiply reciprocity. The gift reduced to givenness has no consciousness of what it does. The hands to make the gift are not lacking, but the right hand does not know what the left hand is doing—and the gift is made only on this condition.

However, this result may still raise a concern: perhaps it proves too much, and moves too quickly for a rational argument, offering instead merely a rejoinder? Aside from avoiding reciprocal exchange, doesn't the bracketing of each term of the exchange come at the price of the disappearance of all of the gift's real processes? Doesn't suspending the sufficient reason of exchange also entail the abolition of all the rationality of the gift itself, and of its actuality? For we have arrived at an outright contradiction: instead of being defined in relation to her recipient, the giver would give all the better by disappearing (as unknown or deceased) from the recipient's view; the recipient or givee, far from appearing by managing his debt, would better appear by denying it (as anonymous, or an enemy); and that which is given, far from being concretized in a manifest object, would appear all the better by evaporating into the unreal or the symbolic (as an indication). Under the pretext of clarifying the gift in light of its givenness alone, have we not instead dissolved the gift's phenomenality? In short, doesn't the would-be phenomenological reduction of the gift to its givenness in the end prohibit its very dignity as a phenomenon?

This difficulty cannot be dodged, but neither should it be overestimated, for it is, essentially, the result of beginning the examination at the wrong point. We began our inquiry into the gift by starting with its contrary, exchange, and we recovered proper access to it only by disqualifying that which prevented it, reciprocity; having left the economic point of view, and making our way through the debris of exchange, we run the risk of getting entangled there at the very moment when we are doing our best to free ourselves from it. The approach *a contrario* may at any moment overturn everything. We need instead to attempt to describe a phenomenon of the same kind as the gift, no longer *a contrario* but directly and starting from itself, by inscribing it from the outset within the horizon of givenness, so that it never allows itself to be recaptured by the economic horizon—a gift that is always *already* reduced to givenness, free of any degrading fall into economy, born free of sufficient reason. In short, a gift that is *naturally reduced* to givenness, an exceptional case where the difficulty would not, as in Husserlian rhetoric, consist in overcoming the natural attitude so as to carry out the reduction, but rather, in front of a phenomenon that is already (naturally) reduced, would consist in reconstituting (so to speak) that on the basis of which it is found to be reduced. Which phenomenon would be able to satisfy this inverted description of appearing *only as always already reduced*? Let me suggest one: *fatherhood*.

Fatherhood is undeniably a phenomenon, since it appears wherever a man lives; it is a phenomenon that is regularly observable, since it stretches over the entire duration of each life; and finally, it is unchallengeable, since no human can claim not to have experienced it. Indeed, no one can deny it, least of all those who themselves are either fatherless or childless, since this phenomenon manifests itself even more in such absences, as we shall see. Fatherhood (provided that we do not diminish it straightaway to the level of exchange) never unfolds as a mere biological result of procreation, nor as a primary interest group, nor as an elementary political category; it may also be connected to all these things, but only after the fact, once it is subjected to an economic interpretation in terms of exchange, according to which it is a first stage in a series of increasingly complex communities that lead, in principle, up to the state. But this interpretation, no matter how powerful and widely accepted it may be, still belongs to metaphysics; above all, it conceals the determinations of this gift as it appears within the horizon of givenness.

First of all, like every phenomenon, fatherhood appears to the extent that it gives itself; but, unlike most other phenomena, it gives *itself* first *to the extent that it gives*.[22] Fatherhood manifests all the given phenomenon's characteristics, but they are exhibited not only in the mode of the given, but also in the mode of giving; for if fatherhood did not give, neither would it give itself as a phenomenon that shows itself. Thus, it gives, but with a style that is absolutely remarkable and all its own. — Fatherhood does indeed give, but *without being foreseeable*; for the intention to procreate is never enough for procreation to happen, any more than the intention not to procreate is a guarantee against its happening. — Again, fatherhood gives, but *without cause*,[23] and without any univocally assignable reason: demographic science is unable to calculate the developments of the fertility rate or to anticipate long-term population growth or decline, to the point where it must resort to the nonquantifiable consideration of psychological, cultural, and even religious factors that at best allow a simple intelligibility a posteriori without the promise of a serious forecast. Fatherhood brings about, or rather takes place as, an *event* and not as a simple fact, because, welling up from pure possibility, it does not manufacture a finished result, determined and concluded once it is delivered, but rather induces a possible (the child), the future of which, in turn, cannot be foreseen, nor deduced from causes, nor anticipated, but must be awaited. — All these determinations also characterize the phenomenon in general, considered as given,[24] except for one decisive difference: the given phenomenon here *gives* and thus lays claim to an exemplary role among all given phenomena: that of the given that itself gives. That the given not only gives itself, but also gives a given other than itself, implies the opening of an uncontrollable excess, growth, and negentropy, which misery, death, and fear are not enough to extinguish (on the contrary, in fact). Simply put, here the given always and necessarily gives something other than itself, and thus more than itself; it proves to be uncontrollable and inexhaustible, irrepressible and impossible; in other words, without master or god, it makes possible the impossible. But there is more, for here the given gives insofar as it phenomenalizes both itself and that which it gives; this means that the visible itself—in fact, nothing less than the sum of all the phenomena visible up until this point—will also grow, with an irrepressible, incalculable, and inexhaustible excess that nothing will conquer. By giving itself and showing itself, fatherhood on principle gives and manifests more than itself; the event of its arrival in the visible thus provokes a phenomenal event that is in principle endless. Nowhere else does the character of being given (*Gegebenheit*)—in other words, the character of appearing in the mode of the given, which would almost deserve the neologism "given-ness" [*donnéité*]—announce itself as clearly as here, thus conferring on fatherhood an exceptional phenomenological privilege.

But this exceptional privilege of the highest form of givenness is echoed or balanced by another characteristic, which can only be conceived negatively, at least initially. This very phenomenon that gives itself in giving cannot, for its part, give itself without first having been given to itself—that is, received from elsewhere; namely, from a(nother) father. But the gift given by the father accomplishes anew the threefold paradox of the gift reduced to givenness. — First, the giver here remains essentially absent and bracketed. For *the father is missing.* To start with, the father is missing because he procreates only at the moment and then, having become superfluous, withdraws immediately, in contrast to the mother, who remains, and in whom the child remains. The mother's happy immanence to the child by contrast stigmatizes the father's miserable transcendence. The father is also missing later, because he leaves (must leave), and attracts the child's attention by letting her down, on principle no less. Not that he leaves always like a thief in reverse, necessarily abandoning mother and child. Rather, he is lacking because he can never merge with the given child (in contrast to the mother, who can and even must do so, if only for a time), since he can only remain united with the child by taking leave—precisely so as to bestow his help, as extroverted provider, as hunter, warrior, or traveler; in short, as the one who constantly returns, coming back to the hearth from which he must distance himself if he wants to maintain it. In order to remain, the father must shine by his absence. He appears to the extent that he disappears.[25] Finally, and most of all, the father is missing because, due to his previous two shortcomings, his fatherhood can never count on an immediate empirical confirmation; even a genetic identification is mediated (it requires time, instruments, and study), and results further in a juridical process of recognition (or denial) of paternity: the father remains inevitably putative. This does not mean that he conceals or disavows himself as father, but rather that he can declare himself only by recognizing, necessarily after the fact, the child whom he was never, by definition, able to know from the outset; he can only claim the child as his (and therefore also deny him) after a delay, through a mediate word and a juridical declaration. He can genuinely give a father to his child only by *regiving to her*, after biological life in its randomness, a status and a name: in short, an identity, a symbolic identity that he must ceaselessly give again, in every moment, without end, and that he can make secure only by repeating it to the child until the end. The father must spend his whole lifetime giving and regiving to the child her identity, her status as gift without return, but also without certainty. Fatherhood, or the regiving [*redondance*] of the flawed gift (see § 24). For these three reasons—withdrawal, departure, and regiving—the father appears as the giver who is perfectly reduced to givenness, the bracketed giver.

Second, the gift reduced to givenness is further confirmed in the phenomenon of fatherhood in that the child, however much he appears to be a givee or recipient (and paradigmatically so, since he receives not only a gift but also himself as the gift of a possibility), by definition cannot make good on the least consciousness of a debt. Indeed, no matter how deeply he is moved by the feeling of indebtedness, nor how earnestly filial piety is sometimes at work in him, nor how seriously he strives to correspond to the father's gift, an obstacle always stands in the way. It is not a question here of subjective ingratitude or of empirical hate, though these are always possible threats. The question is the more radical one of a fundamental impossibility. Whether he wants to or not, whether he feels bound to it or not, the child can never "give back [*rendre*]," and will remain ungrateful, inadequate, and inconsiderate, because it will never be given to him to render to his father what he has received from him—namely, life. The child can render him time, care, and attention (watching over his advanced years, ensuring that he is lacking nothing, surrounding him with affection, and so forth), possibly until the very end; but the child will never be able to give him life in return at the hour of his death. At best, the child will render to his father a peaceful death, but he will never give back or render him life. That the child will be able to give life in turn is not an objection. True, the child may be able to do this, but whoever he may give it to, it will not be to his father. For he, too, will give it to those who, by the same principle, will be able to give it only to their own children, and never to their father. These children will, in turn, be exposed as recipients who are absent and, in turn, installed as givers who are missing. This is how the arrow of time is pointed, with a genuinely original *différance* (from which is also derived even the *différance* of the delay of intuition). The child responds adequately, even justly, to the father—the giver who is missing—only by avowing himself to be a recipient who defaults. Genealogy extends onward in accordance with these ineluctable impossibilities of rendering the gift, of closing the gift that is reduced to givenness back into the loop of exchange.[26]

As for the gift that is given in fatherhood, at this point it goes without saying that it can in no way be converted into an object or a being (whether subsistent or ready-to-hand, it doesn't matter). The father gives nothing to the child other than life (and a name that sanctions it). The given gift is reduced here precisely to life, which, because it renders possible and potentially actual every being and every object, itself belongs neither to beingness nor to objectness. Life is not, since all that is is through it, and nothing is without it; no one sees it, defines it, or grasps it as something real, as one thing among others. A corpse, after all, lacks nothing real that would allow it to be distinguished from the living—one says of someone who has just died: "She almost looks as if she could talk." But speech is not one real thing among others; it triggers things by naming them and, while making them appear, it never itself appears as a thing. Life that is given does not appear, is not, and thus is not possessed. In life, the gift is perfectly reduced to givenness, to that nothing which tears everything away from nothingness.

Fatherhood thus lays out, in fact and by right, the whole phenomenality of a gift reduced to pure givenness. With fatherhood, the giver is manifested even insofar as he is absent, the recipient insofar as he defaults, and the gift in direct proportion to its unreality. Not only do the phenomenological requirements of a reduction of the given to givenness not contradict the description of the gift as a full-fledged phenomenon; not only are these demands fulfilled, here at least, almost perfectly; but above all, fatherhood appears as a full-fledged phenomenon (given), and even one that is privileged (the given that itself gives), only if the phenomenological view interprets it as always already naturally reduced, by reconstituting (so to speak) that on the basis of which it is discovered as reduced, and in the face of which the modes of exchange, procreation, and production definitively show themselves to be powerless and inadequate. The contemporary difficulty with conceiving fatherhood follows directly from a powerlessness to reduce the gift to the givenness within it.

§ 17. Without the Principle of Identity

Once reduced without remainder to givenness, the given and giving phenomenon of fatherhood opens new domains to the phenomenality of givenness in general. We cannot explore them here in detail, but we can at least emphasize a characteristic of the gift's phenomenality in the strict sense, which is here brought fully to light.

Fatherhood clearly distinguishes itself in that it unfolds on the one hand without reciprocity and on the other with excess. What importance should we attach to these two particularities? Fatherhood unfolds without reciprocity because the father can give (life) as father only on the express condition of never being able to receive it in return from the one to whom he has given it. The father cannot give in order to receive in return—and is singled out precisely by this apparently negative privilege. The privilege becomes paradoxical only if one persists in considering it within the economic horizon, where it seems a lost exchange and a thwarted reciprocity; but this privilege is perfectly justified, on the contrary, as soon as analysis transgresses the economic horizon for good and enters into the horizon of givenness. The father appears without contest as he for whom I, as the child, can do nothing, as he to whom I can render nothing, as he whom I will allow to die alone. However, the dereliction to which I must finally abandon him, regardless of what may happen and what my filial sentiments may be, has nothing to do with a bitter impotence or a harsh injustice. For, before all else, it marks the sole indisputable transcendence that all human life can and must recognize in its own immanence; if we ever have to name God with a name, it is thus very appropriate to call Him

"Father"—and Him alone: "Call no one on earth your father, for you have only one Father, and He is in heaven" (Matt. 23:9). The father is distinguished as he to whom we can render nothing, precisely because we owe him our inscription in the given. He makes evident the son as he who could not give to himself that which he has nonetheless received as most his own—and vice versa. For, as sons, we do not experience ourselves solely as given, like every other phenomenon, but as gifted [*adonnés*]—as those who receive themselves in the reception of the given, far from waiting for this given in the position of a receiver who is already available and secure in himself. To what extent does the undergoing of oneself [*l'épreuve de soi*] as one who is gifted also imply the recognition of filiation in myself? The response to this question perhaps (and no more than perhaps) exceeds the scope of philosophy and touches possibly on a domain that is already theological; but the phenomenology of the reduced gift leads one at least inevitably to pose it as a question.[27]

Beyond the transcendence that fatherhood imposes within the gifted's immanence, it also and especially unveils its essential phenomenal determination: the invalidation of reciprocity. For if the reduced gift proves itself irreducible to exchange, this results, as has just been seen, from the fact that it no longer depends on the terms of exchange; it can give its all, without security, and receive without being able to return anything, and be realized without transferring any reality susceptible of being possessed. Consequently, not only can fatherhood, like every other reduced gift, exempt itself from reciprocity, but it cannot even tolerate it, nor leave it with the least authorization. The reduced gift gives and receives without return or revenue, even on condition of having nothing in common with these. What does this abandonment of reciprocity signify? This question does not concern ethics, whose operations (altruism, justice, generosity, disinterestedness, etc.) themselves become intelligible and determinant only once reciprocity is overcome, and on the basis of this overcoming. This overcoming, anterior to ethics, goes back to the fundamental determination of metaphysics, putting one of its radical principles in question: the principle of identity. This principle supposes that nothing can be, at the same moment and in the same respect, other than itself; in other words, possibility is founded on logical noncontradiction: "We judge to be false that which contains contradiction, and to be true that which is opposed or contradictory to the false."[28] Logical noncontradiction, which founds the formal possibility of each thing on its thinkability, hence on its essence, is accomplished in self-equality. In consequence, reciprocity in exchange reproduces between two entities and their two (or more) essences the single requirement of noncontradiction; the economy extends and applies this requirement to the relations of production, possession, and consumption of objects that are woven by societies, and that support their cohesion; inversely, not to respect this requirement provokes contradiction, and therefore sooner or later is prohibitive of exchanges and societies. The political ideals of equality and solidarity take up the same requirement at a higher level of complexity. Reciprocity generalizes under all these figures the same principle of identity and the same requirement of noncontradiction.

Consequently, if the reduced gift attests to itself only by subverting reciprocity and thus the self-equality of things, not only does it contradict the economy and its conditions of possibility for experience, but it also and especially contradicts the principle of noncontradiction itself. As the case of fatherhood proves, the reduced gift allows for a thing not to be equal to itself, but to become (or, rather, give) more than itself, or as much as it loses in the exchange of being fully realized as gift. The reduced gift always gives (or receives) more (or less) than itself, for if the balance stayed equal, the gift would not actually take place, but instead an exchange would occur. For exchange respects the principle of identity, offering only an elementary variant of it in the case of a relation between two terms. The father, for example, loses himself in giving a life, which will never be returned to him; and he contradicts himself by renouncing an equal exchange, precisely to fulfill the office of father; but one could also say that he gives much more than he possesses in giving a life that in one sense he does not have (in nor of) himself, because it is not identified with him, since every father himself remains the son of another father. Fatherhood manifests the nonidentity of each self with itself, this contradiction of self to self then unfolding itself in all the figures of inequality. In general, the gift takes place only by provoking this nonidentity with itself, and then by releasing an inequality without end: that of the giver with the gift, of the recipient with the giver, of the recipient with the gift, and of the gift with itself. These inequalities, which are moreover nonidentical with one another, can be described successively and even alternatively as a loss, as an excess, or as an equivocation; but they can never be understood on the model of self-identity.

This essential and polysemous nonidentity, which the gift liberates everywhere it operates, in the end imposes nothing less than a new definition of possibility. Henceforth, it must no longer be conceived as mere noncontradiction—namely, the self-identity of an essence, which attests to its rationality by posing no contradiction for the understanding (the finite understanding)—but as the excess (or, just as well, the deficit) of the self over the self, which, in giving itself without return, gives more than itself and provokes an other different from the first self (and hence itself also different from itself). Here, possibility no longer consists in self-identity with self, but in the self's excess over itself (§ 11). Following the paradoxical logic of the gift, which excludes exchange and reciprocity, everything always ends up as much more (or less) than itself, without any impossibility being opposed to this; for the impossibility that would have to be opposed to this would remain a simple nonpossibility, in the sense of non-self-identity and the principle of identity, the contradiction of which defines *precisely* the new acceptance of possibility that the gift puts into operation. Far from perishing from its nonidentity and its inequality with itself, the gift wells up only if these are unfolded completely. This means that no impossibility can prevent the new possibility of the gift, since it feeds on impossibility and on the very contradiction of self-identity, self-equality, and the reciprocity of exchange. To that which gains itself only in losing itself—namely, the gift, which gives itself in abandoning itself—nothing is impossible any longer. Not only does that which does not give itself lose itself, but nothing can ruin [*perdre*, lose] the gift, since it consists in the contradiction even of its possibility.

§ 18. Without the Principle of Sufficient Reason

The phenomenon of the gift, such as we have just reduced it to itself under the figure of fatherhood, unfolds, once again, only by bracketing the terms of exchange, to the point of contradicting the principle of noncontradiction. And yet, this result, far from solidly establishing the phenomenality of the gift and illuminating its logic, could reinforce the difficulty. First, because the exception made to the principle of identity seems to marginalize the gift all the more, turning it into an extreme case of phenomenality by contrast with the common regularity of exchange, which is left conforming to identity and noncontradiction. After all, if the gift in general is exemplified above all by the case of fatherhood, would it not be necessary to confine to this indisputable phenomenal exception (that of a gift naturally reduced to givenness) the possibility of contradicting noncontradiction, or in other words the possibility of impossibility? Only the exemplary gift, fatherhood (and hence also the gifted, *l'adonné*), could be an exception to the principle of identity, which would continue to be the rule for the remainder of phenomena and even for all other gifts.

But this side step fixes nothing. — First, because in fact *all* gifts without exception are fully realized by contradicting self-identity within themselves, since they must abolish equality, or better, establish an inequality between their terms, the giver and the recipient; fatherhood offers an example only because it manifests this contradiction of identity not merely in itself but in all gifts, which it alone makes possible. — Next, because the gift as such (in other words, all gifts) exempts itself not only from the first principle of metaphysics (the principle of identity and noncontradiction) but also from the second: "that of Sufficient Reason, in virtue of which we consider that no fact can be real or actual, and no proposition true, without there being a sufficient reason for its being so and not otherwise."[29] This principle posits that every fact, proposition, and therefore phenomenon too must have a reason that justifies its actuality; in other words, for a phenomenon to be fully realized, it is not sufficient that the possibility of its essence (noncontradiction) be certified; it is also necessary to justify the actuality of its existence, and this can happen only if a term other than it comes, as cause or reason, to make intelligible this transition. But can we always assign a reason or a cause other than it to that which gives *itself*? I have shown elsewhere the phenomenological fragility of this claim: the phenomenon, in the strict sense, has the essential property of showing itself in itself and on the basis of itself, and therefore of not entering into manifestation under the figure of an effect entering into actuality—that is, by means of a cause or a reason other than itself. A phenomenon shows *itself* all the more as itself, in that it gives *itself* on the basis of itself.[30] Must we imagine that, in the particular case where the given phenomenon takes the figure of the gift, we could find an exception and assign to its phenomenalization another *self* than itself? Merely formulating the question is sufficient to see that the gift, even less than any other phenomenon, does not allow another instance to preside at its phenomenalization. Indeed, the gift shows itself on the basis of itself in a double capacity: first of all, because, like every other phenomenon, it gives *itself* on the basis of itself; next, because, more radically than every other phenomenon, it gives its *self* on the basis of *itself*. The gift that gives (itself) gives only on the basis of itself, and therefore without owing anything to another reason (or cause) than itself. One need only return to the precise description of the gift to verify that this phenomenon manifests itself as it gives—*of itself*, on the basis of itself alone, without any other reason than itself.

Let us take the simple illustrative case where a gift appears, as a phenomenon in the world, to its giver before she gives it (the recipient or givee remaining bracketed here). How does the reduced gift happen to this giver so that it becomes an actual gift? Let's first consider the conventional and uncritical answer (the one that would be posited outside of the reduction): the gift passes into actuality when the giver *decides* voluntarily to give it and lays claim to establishing herself as its efficient cause and final reason. But this response is clearly insufficient, for this voluntary decision offers only an apparent solution; in fact, it itself remains a difficulty, since we must more essentially understand how the giver comes to the decision of actually giving this gift, and thus how the decision of making the decision comes upon her. And responding to this question proves to be harder than one might expect. — For the giver does not decide to give some gift because of the object that she is giving. First, because an object as such can decide nothing; in particular, it cannot decide between itself and all the other objects susceptible of being considered as what one might give. Next, because the reasons for preferring to give one object rather than another could not result only from calculations, which in any case the object would suffer, without producing them or justifying them. — Nor does the giver decide on giving a certain gift because of some potential beneficiary, who might have begged for it more than the others: the number of the needy discourages, and the impudence of the claims disgusts, without allowing one to decide. — Therefore, it must be that the giver alone decides to give, by herself; she still must decide *to give* and not only to part with an available object following rules that include a benefit for her, nor only to share it out by calculation (even by justice, which is itself an equality), nor to distribute it following economic laws (an exchange). Here it must be that a gift purely reduced to the givenness in it gives itself.

And that can happen only if the gift wells up from itself and imposes itself as such on its giver, and therefore only if it occurs to this giver as something *to give*, which, so to speak, demands that one give it (*donandum est*), or which appears among many other objects or beings as the one upon which the gift imposes itself. The gift to give can impose *itself* as so useful for a distress close to its actual (and provisional) owner that henceforth he or she must become the leaseholder whose time has expired, and finally the giver; or as so beautiful that it is only fitting for a beauty greater than that of its possessor, who is obliged to pay homage with it; or finally, as so rare that the one who found it feels forced to convey it to a jewel box more exceptional than himself. The examples of this silent constraint—political (devolutions: Lear to his daughters), moral (renunciations: the princess of Clèves), religious (consecrations: the stripping of Francis of Assisi), or others—abound to the point of exempting us from having to describe them further. The gift that *has to be given* happens here so clearly on the basis of itself, on the basis of a *self*, that it imposes itself in two senses. First, it imposes itself as that which must be given—a phenomenon distinguished among other phenomena by a prominence such that no one can legitimately proclaim himself its possessor, as a phenomenon that burns the fingers, and the very excellence of which demands that one be rid of it. Next, the gift imposes itself by obliging its initial possessor to let it go toward an addressee who is always other; for the gift determines the self of its possessor, and it therefore demands of this possessor that he make himself its giver and dispossess himself of it (in this order, and not the reverse). In this way the gift reduced to givenness is fully realized by virtue of nothing other than its own *givability*: in appearing as givable, it transforms its reality as being or object and thus convinces its possessor to be rid of it, in order to be able to appear itself in perfect givability. The gift decides its givenness by itself and decides its giver by itself, by appearing indisputably as givable and by making itself be given. This phenomenality comes to it from nothing other than itself. It has recourse to no cause, nor to any reason, other than the pure demand of showing itself as it gives itself—namely, in itself and of itself. It occurs on the basis of its own possibility, such that it gives this possibility originarily to itself.

Let us suppose the inverse case, where a gift appears as a phenomenon to its givee, who receives it (the giver remaining bracketed here). How does the reduced gift happen to this recipient as an actual gift? Is it because this same recipient decides to receive it and lays claim to establishing herself as its final cause and initial reason? It certainly could be understood in this way, outside of the reduction. But this response remains an appearance, because it does not yet allow us to understand how the recipient comes to accept this gift as such, as something to be received, nor, therefore, how she makes the decision to accept it. Now the difficulties mount up. — First, the potential beneficiary has to accept to receive a gift; but this acceptance implies her consenting to a prior difficult renunciation: that of abandoning the posture of self-sufficiency and of calm possession of self and of her world; in short, the renunciation of the most powerful of fantasies, which grounds the whole economy and every calculation of interest in exchange: that of the self-identity of the "I." In short, it is a matter of contradicting the principle of identity. Before accepting a gift (which would nevertheless seem easy, since it appears to be a matter of gain, pure and simple), it is first necessary to accept to accept it, which implies recognizing that one no longer increases oneself by oneself, but rather by a dependence on that which I am not, or more exactly on that which the "I" in me is not. And this acknowledgment supposes that one has abandoned self-equality—not only that which morality would label egoism, but above all that which the reduction to givenness has stigmatized as exchange and economy. At issue is nothing less than abandoning one logic for another, which sufficient reason no longer governs and no cause controls. — Next, it is necessary to distinguish between that which it is appropriate to accept and that which one should not accept; for not every good is offered as a gift that is to be received. Either it remains the possession of an absent or unknown proprietor (and if I take it, I simply give in to the desire for an object that was lost, abandoned, and found, and which belongs by right to another); or it can in no way become an appropriable good for the enjoyment of anyone (such as environmental goods, which belong to no one, or like the human body, which is unavailable on principle); or the appearance of a gift ends up proving in reality to be an evil (the horse abandoned to the Trojans by the Greeks); and so on. There follows this conclusion: in order to discern if and when it is a matter of a gift, it is first of all necessary that this gift itself appear as such, namely, as given to be received. — These two requirements, accepting to accept and knowing what to accept, cannot be satisfied by the beneficiary alone, since she herself will become a recipient only at the moment when they are satisfied in her eyes, and hence *before* her.

Thus, there remains only one hypothesis: the gift itself must make it acceptable to accept it, and it must impose itself as something to receive. And the gift succeeds in this precisely when, from the innumerable crowd of beings and objects that are available but undistinguished or ruled by possession, there is one that detaches itself and imposes itself by appearing as the one that I must accept (*accipiendum est*). It will appear, then, as a phenomenon that has burst forth under the aspect of *acceptability*. It will appear in designating itself as to be received, and in making itself accepted by the one who, at first and most of the time, neither saw it as a gift nor intended himself as the recipient. Such an acceptability exerts itself on the one who would not recognize himself as a recipient without it. It is not exerted solely, nor at first, as a moral pressure or a sensual seduction, but by virtue of a privileged aspect of phenomenality—the phenomenality of that which gives itself to be received in itself and by itself. The gift phenomenalizes itself of itself insofar as it shows itself as it gives itself: as that which no one can begin to *see* if he has not already begun to *receive* it. In order to appear in its own right, the gift thus received refers back to no cause, nor to any reason, other than its pure givenness. Presupposing neither its recipient nor its giver, it happens on the basis of its own possibility, such that it gives this possibility originarily to itself: it shows itself in itself because it gives itself in itself.[31]

At the end of this still inchoate description, we arrive at the outline of a result: if one seriously undertakes to reduce the gift to givenness, the gift gives itself on the basis of itself alone; not only can it be described by bracketing its recipient, its giver, or its objectness (§ 16), but above all it gives rise to them all under the two aspects of its own phenomenality: givability and acceptability. The reduced gift thus happens with no cause or reason that would suffice for taking account of it, other than itself; not that it renders an account to itself, but because it renders itself (gives its reason) inasmuch as it gives itself in and by itself. Actually, it renders itself in multiple senses. It renders itself in that it abandons itself to its recipient, to allow him the act of acceptance. It also renders itself to its giver, in that it puts itself at her disposal to allow her the act of giving. Finally, it renders itself to itself in that it is perfectly accomplished by dissipating itself without return, as a pure abandoned gift, possible in all impossibility. Thus, the reduced gift accomplishes the self of the full phenomenon: that which appears, appears as that which shows itself (Heidegger). But that which shows itself can in turn show itself only in itself, and thus first of all on the basis of itself. And once again, it can do this showing of itself on the basis of itself only if, in showing itself, it puts its self in play; that is, if it gives itself in itself. A phenomenon shows itself in itself only if it gives itself of its *self*.[32] And giving itself here signifies giving itself in the visible without reserve or retreat, and thus without condition or measure, and thus without cause or reason. Or we could say that the real reason for appearing, like that for givenness, consists in not having a reason. The gift gives itself of itself without borrowing anything from a possibility that comes from elsewhere, such as the parsimonious calculation of sufficient reason—in short, without any other possibility than its own. The gift reduced to givenness requires no rights or special favors in order to give itself or show itself as it gives itself. It requires no possibility from anything, but gives possibility to all, on the basis of that which it opens by itself.

Consequently, by exceeding the requirement for a cause and a reason, not only does the gift not condemn itself to a lack of rationality but, completely to the contrary, it might impose a "greater reason" than the narrow *ratio reddenda* of metaphysics. Or again: Might not the gift provide the preeminent nonmetaphysical figure of possibility, and might not the possibility that is "higher than actuality" be able to open itself first of all as gift? In other words, if the phenomenon in the strict sense shows itself in itself and on the basis of itself, welling up from a possibility that is absolutely its own, then might not the gift offer itself as the privileged phenomenon, or more exactly, as the paradigm of all phenomenality?[33]

That the reduced gift and the phenomenon as pure given arise from no other cause or reason than themselves in no way implies that they lack rationality or that they have a conceptual deficiency, for nothing proves that the highest rationality of a phenomenon is defined by the requirement to justify its phenomenality [*rendre raison de sa phénoménalité*] by an instance other than itself. On the contrary, it could be that such a figure of reason—the metaphysical figure of heteronomous reason—compromises and even censures the phenomenality of all phenomena, to the point that, in these nihilistic times, only phenomena whose intuitive saturation frees them from the grasp of the principle of reason can still burst forth into broad daylight. To contest the primacy of the principle of reason over the phenomenon or, what here amounts to the same, the primacy of the economy over the gift, in no way constitutes a misguided undertaking, since the one and the other, in their respective formulations, spell out a fundamental contradiction precisely from the point of view of givenness. — Let's look at the economy first. It is founded on exchange, requiring its equality and its justice, since it is defined in those terms: "The proper act of justice is to *render* (*reddere*) to each his own."[34] But what does *reddere* signify here, if not "to render," that is, "to regive," and thus first of all "to give"? Justice would therefore consist in giving to each, possibly (but not necessarily) in return and by reaction, what is due to him; but then justice is no longer based on exchange, since exchange itself is understood here as a particular (moreover, devalued) mode of the gift! Justice, like exchange, would on the contrary presume an original, albeit concealed, intervention of the gift itself. Could the gift hold the reason of exchange and justice, and not the inverse? To be sure, the economy would no more reduce the gift than be reduced to it, but it would certainly result from it by simplification and neutralization. In short, the economy would require the gift as its genuine reason.

Does the same go for the principle of reason? We can assume so, since Leibniz constantly bases this supposed "great metaphysical principle" on a similar surrender to *reddere*: "The great axiom. / Nothing is without reason. / Or, what amounts to the same: Nothing exists without it being possible (at least for [a mind that is] omniscient) to *render* (*reddi*) some reason why it is rather than is not and why it is so rather than otherwise."[35] One can render a reason for everything—but how is one to render a reason for its being necessary also to *render* this very reason? If the evidence for the principle of reason has nothing to fear from attempts to submit it, for example, to the principles of contradiction or identity, and if it can resist the quietist pretensions of gratuity or the empiricist suspicions of indeterminism, it nevertheless wavers before the immanence of *reddere* within it. For to ensure sufficient reason, it is necessary that a mind (an omniscient mind, as it turns out, for contingent statements) render it. But rendering it (*re-dare*) implies that one regives it, that one gives it in return, and thus, essentially, that one gives it. For the French *rendre* (to render) derives from the colloquial Latin *rendere*, formed from *reddere* in relation to *prendre* (to take).[36] In the end, maybe "*rendre raison*" ("render reason") can be translated by a "re-presentation" (Heidegger); but this re-presentation does not replace givenness, from which it arises, and that allows it as one of its derived operations. That even and especially (sufficient) reason, which is so foreign to the gift, must be given is plainly no longer justified by the principle of rendering reason, which in this instance is helpless. If it is even necessary to render reason, then reason rests on the gift, and not at all on itself. This other "reason" in the second degree, required in order to render reason in the first degree, is something that reason in the first degree, which does not know how to give, is therefore never sufficiently able to *give*—and so only a gift can give it. Reason becomes genuinely sufficient only if a gift (reduced to givenness) gives it (and renders it) to itself. Reason no more suffices for thinking itself than it succeeded in thinking the gift. In short, if it is necessary to regive reason, this implies that the *ratio* remains, in itself, secondary and derivative from a more originary instance—the givenness that puts it in the position of operating as a final reason. Givenness governs the *ratio reddenda* more intimately than exchange rules the gift, because no reason can be exempted from being rendered, that is to say, from a gift putting it onstage and preceding it. The gift alone renders reason to itself, for only the gift suffices for giving it. This time the gift no longer awaits its justification from reason, but on the contrary justifies reason, because it precedes reason as a "greater reason" than reason.

The gift alone gives reason and renders reason to itself. It thus challenges the second principle of metaphysics, just as it contradicted the first. How, precisely, do we understand this privilege of the gift's metaphysical extraterritoriality, and how do we extend it to phenomenality in general?

The gift gives reason, and gives it to reason itself; in other words, it renders to reason its full validity, because it gives itself reason, without any condition or exception. In fact, what is proper to a gift consists in its never being wrong and always being right (literally, having reason[37]): just as it depends on no due or duty, so too it never appears as owing or in debt. Having no presupposition (not even the justice of equality or the equality of exchange), no prior condition, and no requisite, the gift gives (itself) with absolute freedom. Just as it always comes upon us unhoped-for and unexpectedly, in excess and without being weighed on a balance, so too it can never be refused or declined; or, if it is refused (and we have clearly seen how often it can be refused), it can never be refused with reason, nor above all can it be refused the right to give itself, since it gives itself without price, without salary, without requirement or condition. Always coming upon us in excess, it demands nothing, removes nothing, and takes nothing from anybody. The gift never does wrong, because it never is wrong. Never being wrong, it is always right: literally, it has reason. Therefore, it delivers its reason at the same time as itself—the reason that it gives in giving itself and without asking any other authority than its own happening. The gift coincides with its reason, because its mere givenness is sufficient for it as reason. Reason sufficing for itself: the gift gives itself reason—proves itself right—in giving itself.

But isn't it the same for the phenomenon in general—at least provided that it truly shows itself in and on the basis of itself—because it gives itself of itself in a fully realized givenness (according to anamorphosis, the unpredictable landing, the fait accompli, the incident, and eventness)?[38] Isn't it clearer still if we consider saturated phenomena (the event, the idol, the flesh, and the icon or the face)?[39] When the phenomenon shows itself on the basis of itself and in itself, it comes to pass only in giving itself, hence in happening without any other condition than its sovereign possibility. It shows itself in that it imposes itself in visibility, without cause or principle that would precede it (for if they are found, they will come only after its coming, reconstituted a posteriori). Moreover, the phenomenon does not simply show itself in the visible that its horizon defines *ne varietur*; it adds itself there because it adds a new visible that until then had remained unseen and that would have remained so without this unexpected event. Thus, the phenomenon redefines the horizon according to the measure of its own new dimensions, pushing back its limits. The phenomenon is never wrong, but always right, or literally, always has reason, a reason that appears with its gift—its sole and intrinsic reason.

IV. THE UNCONDITIONED AND THE VARIATIONS OF THE GIFT

§ 19. Sacrifice According to the Terms of Exchange

Properly speaking, we should not begin with sacrifice, at least in the sense of a noun or of a substantive, because sacrifice (*sacrificium*) always results from the action of a verb, of the verb "to make" (*sacrum facere*): a sacrifice appears once an agent has rendered something sacred, has set it apart from the profane and thereby consecrated it. Moreover, *sacrum facere* gave us *sacrifiement* in Old French, which more clearly states the process of rendering something sacred than its result. The question of sacrifice concerns, then, first and above all the act of making something sacred and of wresting it from the profane (the act opposed to that of profanation), an act of which sacrifice is only a result that it limits itself to recording, without explaining it. This clarification raises a difficulty: how can we conceive the transition between two terms, the profane and the sacred, while their very distinction becomes, in the era of nihilism in which we live, indistinct and confused, if not completely obscured? Indeed, it is as if the "death of God," and above all what has provoked it—the realization that the highest values consist only in the valuation that confirms them, and thus are only worth what our valuations are worth—had canceled at the level of principle any difference between the sacred and the profane, and thereby any possibility of crossing over it by a *sacrifiement* (or on the contrary, by a profanation). Would not sacrifice disappear along with the sacred that is disappearing, just as blasphemy becomes fuzzy when one no longer even knows what a blessing means?

However, this is not the whole story. We still have a common, if not entirely vernacular, sense of sacrifice: sacrificing is equivalent to destroying; or, more precisely, to destroying what should not be destroyed, at least according to the normal practices of daily life, namely, the useful and the functional. In effect, beings understood as that which I make use of (*zuhanden* beings according to Heidegger's distinction) are defined by the finality that links them not only to other ready-to-hand beings but ultimately to my own intention, which gathers the subordinated finalities of these beings into a network of finalities, all oriented toward myself as the center of a surrounding world (*Bewandtnis*). This being, not only useful but ready-to-hand (*usuel, zuhanden*), refers to me, and, in so doing, becomes me: it is good insofar as it is mine, it is a good insofar as it is my good. As a result, doing away with it would amount to my doing away with myself; and if, taking a step further in the negation, I were to destroy it, then I would also destroy myself. Such destruction of property as such, and even as my property—thus this destruction of myself—has not disappeared in our own time, and is still designated as "sacrifice." Even daily, we are subject to its paroxysm in the form of *terrorism*. Both common usage and the media rely on the semantics of sacrifice in order to qualify terrorist acts: the terrorist, it is said, "sacrifices himself" for his cause, or else he "sacrifices" along with his own life the lives of his random victims in order to draw attention to this very cause. Such terms, as approximate as they may be, nevertheless retain some relevance because pure violence, without any moral or even political justification, in its stupidity and its barbarism, in fact elicits a paralyzing dread before an act that in principle is alien to the world of living beings or the community of reasonable people and obeys the logic, absurd to us, of another world that moreover denies and annihilates our own. Terrorism abolishes property, innocent people, and the terrorist himself, because it accomplishes first and radically the destruction of all beings as useful and functional (*zuhanden*), and the destruction for us of the organization of the world itself in terms of ends and accomplishment. Thus destroyed, the everyday, ready-to-hand thing becomes the sacred insofar as it no longer belongs to the world in which we can live, and in which it is our purpose or intention to live in the normality of the profane. Now, if we grant that terror (*terrorism*) under its polymorphous though faceless figures remains today our ultimate experience of the sacred, and that this figure of the sacred, as debased as it proves to be, nevertheless allows us a common concept of sacrifice, then what makes a profane thing sacred, the *sacrifiement*, consists in its destruction. The terrorist produces the sacred (under the figure of absurd horror) by *destroying* life, including his own.[1] The process that makes the profane sacred entails the destruction of the thing thus sacrificed.[2] One access to sacrifice thus remains available to us, since the experience of terrorism guarantees us the experience of the destruction of property as such, and thus of the world as ours.

Nevertheless, this first result, by providing us with an indisputable because perfectly negative access to the sacred and to the *sacrifiement*, only reinforces the aporia. The point is not merely to deplore the fact that destruction is the only remaining figure of sacrifice, but above all to contest its intelligibility. How, indeed, does destroying something contribute to making it sacred? What does sacrifice do if all it does is undo? What can it consecrate if it limits itself to annihilating? To what or to whom can it give, since it nullifies the content of any gift and nullifies itself as possible giver? The definition of sacrifice as the destruction of a good as such not only explains nothing of sacrifice but could actually explain its opposite—the self-appropriation of autarchy. Indeed, the wise and the strong want to rid themselves of a possession by destroying it and thereby becoming free of it; they alone can do this, and they prove it to themselves because they survive what they destroy in themselves: in making a sacrifice of other goods (by ascesis, renunciation, mutilation, and so forth), they demonstrate their autarchy to others; or rather they prove at least to themselves their autonomy and ataraxy. Sacrifice thus becomes the autocelebration of the ascetic ideal, in which the *ego* attains a kind of *causa sui* by no longer owing anything to anyone in the world, not even his own person. Sacrifice, understood as the destruction of a good, can be inverted into a construction of the self, which sacrifices nothing of its own, and only the world to itself.

We must then give up on defining sacrifice only by the destruction of a possession. In fact, it becomes possible to speak of sacrifice only if one introduces a third term, beyond the destroyer and the good destroyed—precisely the third, the other. Even in the most banal understanding of sacrifice—for example, the sacrifice of a pawn or a piece in chess—the other already appears, even if only in the most basic guise of the mimetic rival, the alter ego, my opponent: even if, in making this supposed gift to my opponent, my purpose is simply to strengthen *my* position, it is my position vis-à-vis *him*, and I sacrifice this piece *to him*. In short, my sacrifice always assumes the other as its horizon of possibility. Thus, it is the other that determines the destruction of a good, either because he benefits from it as its new recipient (I transfer it to him while mourning its loss), or because he shares its loss with me as my rival (I give it up in order to deprive him of it) in order to strengthen my position.

Following this new sense, where it occurs within the horizon of the other, does sacrifice become more intelligible than in the previous case, that of pure and simple destruction of a good? Undoubtedly, because we notice immediately that it is in fact no longer simply a matter of destruction, but also of privation (with, but also sometimes without, destruction). And this obtains on both sides of the alternative. — On the one hand, I deprive myself of a good, because I can do without it, and in this way assure my autonomy (autarchy, ataraxy, etc.); in other words, I deprive myself of a good precisely in order to prove to myself that it has only a minor importance and that I remain myself even without it; hence by losing a possession that is other than me, I gain a more perfect possession of myself. — On the other hand, I deprive myself of a good, not because I would simply destroy it, but because by destroying it or by making it unavailable to me, I want to divest myself of it to the point that, by this definitive loss, another might possibly appropriate it in my stead; in fact, I display the good I have renounced so that it may become available for the other to appropriate it. — Nevertheless, these two situations clearly differ. In the first case, it is enough for me to deprive myself of a good (to the extent that I myself survive), in order to prove its dispensable character and in this way demonstrate my autarchy: the sacrifice is accomplished perfectly by itself. The second case is rather different: admittedly, I manage to deprive myself of a good (I indeed sacrifice it), but this renunciation as such is not sufficient for some other to take possession of that of which I have nevertheless deprived myself; the sacrifice remains unfinished: my renunciation only allowed for the display of the good, which, though made available, still remains in escheat at this point in the process. For even when I divest myself of a good, whether or not the other takes possession of it is not up to me; that depends only on the other. By my decision alone, the sacrifice is thus only accomplished halfway; its realization does not derive from my simple act of dispossession, but awaits the other's acceptance, and thus depends upon another decision, on an *other* decision, come from elsewhere. I can at best act *as if* my dispossession alone were equivalent to a taking possession by the other, but I can neither assure that nor assume it. Dispossession cannot anticipate reception because the other's acceptance can come only from the other herself, and thus by definition it escapes me. Sacrifice involves my dispossession, but my dispossession is not sufficient for a sacrifice, which only acceptance by the other can ratify. If we assume that giving up is enough to begin the sacrifice as a loss, accomplishing it as a gift is contingent upon its acceptance by the other. There is nothing optional or secondary about this discrepancy between the loss and the acceptance, which marks the irreducible distance between me and the other, such that neither I nor the other can abolish it. Even when offered (or rather: precisely *because* offered), it is part of the definition of sacrifice that it can nevertheless be refused and disdained by the other—the other's role lies specifically in this. Thus, even defined within the horizon of the other, the destruction, the loss, or the disappropriation of a good is not enough to account fully for the possibility of sacrifice.

Yet it happens that the most current explanation of sacrifice, produced by sociology and the sociology of religion in particular, presupposes exactly the opposite: that my dispossession of a good is enough for the effective accomplishment of a sacrifice. Sacrifice would consist in effecting the loss of a good (by destruction or by devolution) for the benefit of an other (divine or mortal, most often superior hierarchically), such that he accepts it and consequently renders a countergift to the one who initiated the sacrifice—with this reciprocity constituting the decisive presupposition.[3] Obviously, the realization of the sacrifice by its initiator does not imply and does not at all guarantee the acceptance of the good that has been ceded, and still less, the reciprocity of a countergift. Nevertheless, this interpretation of sacrifice imposes itself, perpetuates itself, and prevails, even today. How does it manage to do so? By assuming what it cannot prove, to wit, that the acceptance and the countergift always (or at least in the majority of cases, as the standard situation) follow from the dispossession (or the destruction). But, once again, how does this presupposition legitimate itself? By implicitly basing the entire explanation of sacrifice on the model of exchange.[4] Moreover, in the majority of cases, we find the three terms "gift," "exchange," and "sacrifice" equated, or even substituted without distinction for one another. Just as the gift consists in giving up a possession in order to obligate the other to give back a countergift (*do ut des*), and just as exchange implies that every good that passes from the one to the other is compensated by a good (or a sum of money) passing from the other to the one, in like fashion, the sacrificer (the sacrificing agent) abandons a good (by dispossession, of exposure or destruction), so that the supposedly superior other (divine or mortal) will accept it, and in so doing, enter into a contractual relation, and, by contract, return a good (real or symbolic). In the three cases, under the imprecise terms of "gift," "exchange," and "sacrifice," the same economy of contract obtains: I bind myself to you by abandoning a possession, *therefore* you bind yourself to me by accepting it, *therefore* you owe me an equivalent item in return (*do ut des, da ut dem*). Henceforth, sacrifice does not destroy any more than the gift gives up, because both work to establish or reestablish exchange; or rather, where sacrifice destroys and the gift gives up, both operate thereby precisely to uphold the economy of reciprocity.

We must conclude that destruction or dispossession and the horizon of the other still do not allow us to determine a concept of sacrifice, but only lead us to assimilate it with exchange in the same confusion that undermines the notion of the gift. In this context, at best, one would call sacrifice the imprudence of an incomplete exchange where a gift is given up without knowing whether an acceptance ratifies it, while at worst, sacrifice is the illusion of a contractual arrangement that no one would ever have entered into with the one who is making the sacrifice. Unless it were a matter of a deception, of the other or of oneself, claiming to give up unconditionally, hoping all the while, secretly or unconsciously, to receive a hundredfold what one loses only once. It would then be necessary instead to consider the very term "sacrifice" an impropriety: an empty or contradictory concept, and apply to sacrifice the contradiction that Derrida deplored in the gift: "The truth of the gift [. . .] suffices to annul the gift. The truth of the gift is equivalent to the non-gift or to the non-truth of the gift."[5] The truth of sacrifice culminates in exchange, that is to say, in the nontruth of sacrifice, since it should consist precisely of a relinquishing without return; it also ends in the truth of the nongift par excellence, that is to say, the confirmation that whenever one believes he speaks of, and makes, a sacrifice, one still hopes for an exchange and a return that would be all the more profitable, since one claimed to have lost everything.

§ 20. Regiving, Beginning from the Recipient

Nevertheless, a way could be opened through, and thanks to, the aporia itself. More precisely, the extension of the aporia of the gift to sacrifice might already indicate another path—provided only that it lead us to think sacrifice precisely in its relation to the *gift*, forgotten up to this point. We would then no longer only think of sacrifice beginning from exchange—for example, as the dispossession (or even the destruction) of a good within the horizon of the other—but also as a moment of the more comprehensive phenomenon of the gift, and of the giving up [*l'abandon*]. — Now, the phenomenon of the gift at the outset manifests much more than exchange: as we have begun to describe it (§ 16), the gift can and thus must be separated from exchange, by letting its natural meaning reduce to givenness. For, while the economy (of exchange) denatures the gift, the gift reduced to givenness on the contrary excepts itself from the economy, by freeing itself from the rules of exchange. The gift in effect proves able to accomplish itself, even and especially by reducing each of the terms of exchange: without a giver, or indeed without a recipient or givee (thus freeing itself without reciprocity) and even without a thing given (thus freeing itself from a logic of equality).[6] As reduced to the givenness in it, the gift is fully realized in an unconditioned immanence, which not only owes nothing to exchange, but dissolves its conditions of possibility. The gift so reduced accomplishes itself with an *unconditioned* freedom—it never lacks anything that would prohibit it from giving itself, because, even without the terms of the exchange, it still shows itself, even all the more so (§§ 17–18). Henceforth, if the gift proves *unconditioned* in this way, would it not also offer sacrifice its most appropriate site, since sacrifice claims precisely (though without having at this juncture justified its claim) to give and to give up without conditions? The issue would be to think sacrifice as a variation of the gift, which one might rightly call the *giving up* [*l'abandon*]. In this hypothesis, the solution to the aporia of sacrifice would come from the answer to the aporia of the gift—from the reduction of the gift to givenness. We will need to proceed to a reduction of sacrifice to givenness, in order to formulate the giving up in terms of the phenomenon of the reduced gift.

Where, then, does the most evident aporia arise when the phenomenon of a gift unfolds? Precisely at the moment when the given gift *appears*. For when what the giver gives (a thing, a being, a piece of information [*une donnée*], a present, and so forth) comes into full light, the gift as such inevitably starts to become obscured, and then to disappear. Indeed, the gift given, which takes on the consistency of the thing and of a being, cannot but occupy the center of the phenomenal stage, so as to conceal or even exclude everything else. Everything else, that is to say first of all the giver—for the giver disappears in her own gift: on the one hand, she must indeed give *something*, whatever may be the actual status of this something (a simple sign of goodwill or a real gift in itself, useful or useless, precious or trivial, inaugural or reciprocal, etc.); otherwise, she would not appear at all as a genuinely giving giver. But, precisely to the extent that she gives truly and irrevocably, the giver allows her given gift to separate itself from her, and assert itself as such, autonomous and thus available so that the recipient can use and appropriate it. The gift not only becomes a phenomenon independent of the phenomenon of the giver, but it excludes her, either by consigning her to the phenomenal background, or by obscuring her completely. This disappearance of the giver does not result from any maliciousness on the part of the recipient, but from the very definition of the gift given: it is not ingratitude that causes the exclusion of the giver, yet this exclusion ultimately results by virtue of the very phenomenality of the gift given, in itself exclusive and appropriating. The giver must disappear (or at least her obviousness [*évidence*] must diminish and her presence withdraw) in order for the gift given to appear (or at least for its presence [*évidence*] to increase and for it to announce itself in the foreground). Otherwise, the gift given would not only not appear as such; it would not be truly given at all: its recipient would not dare to approach it or extend his hand, or even claim himself the recipient, because the tutelary and overhanging presence of the giver would still cast a shadow of possession over it. The recipient cannot take the gift given for his own, so long as he still *sees* in it the face and the power of its previous owner. The owner must withdraw from the giver, so that the gift can start to appear as given; but ultimately, the giver must disappear completely for the gift to appear as given definitively, that is to say, given up, *abandoned* without return.

For there is more. Indeed, just as the gift appears only if the giver disappears, the gift thus abandoned ends by masking in itself not only the giver but the very process of the gift. If a gift appears as truly given only from the moment the giver yields it, the abandoning is reversed: the gift given appears because *it*, in turn, abandons its giver. But a gift without relation to any giver no longer bears the mark of any process of givenness, and thus appears as alien to what is given in it. Paradoxically, a gift truly given, by erasing its giver, ends up disappearing *as given*, too. Or rather, it appears henceforth only as a *found* object: a thing, a being or an object, that is found there, in front of me, by chance and without reason, such that I may wonder what status I should grant it: is it here in its own right (like a piece of fruit fallen from its tree); by the voluntary intention of an other (like an installation in a museum, a sign on the side of the road, etc.); by involuntary accident (like a possession lost by its distracted owner, or stolen from him); or even possibly placed here by an anonymous giver, either for the benefit of some unspecified beneficiary, or for the benefit of an identified recipient, in which case it could be intended for an other, or for me? The gift-character of the found object is thus no longer self-evident; it is only one hypothesis among others, and not the least plausible. In the extreme, if my hermeneutic does not allow me (or does not wish) to recognize the gift as given, the gift as such disappears completely. What is specific to the gift, once we grant that it implies relinquishment in order to appear, thus consists in disappearing as given, and in allowing nothing more to appear than the neutral and anonymous presence, left without any origin, of a thing, of a being, or of an object, coming only from itself, never from elsewhere—nor originating from a giver or from a process of giving. The major aporia of the gift derives from this paradox: the gift given can appear only by erasing in its phenomenon its giver, the process of its gift, and, ultimately, its entire gift-character.

Two examples unambiguously confirm this paradox. First, the one in which Saint Augustine analyzes the case of

> a fiancé who gives a ring to his betrothed; but she loves the ring thus received more than the fiancé who gave it to her. Wouldn't we consider her adulterous in the very gift made to her by her fiancé, even while she loves what her fiancé has given her? Certainly, she loved what her fiancé gave her, but if she were to say: "This ring is enough for me, now I don't want to see his face again," what would she be? Who would not detest this lunacy? Who would not accuse her of adultery? You love gold instead of your husband, you love the ring instead of your fiancé; if you truly have in mind to love the ring in place of your fiancé and have no intention of seeing him, the deposit that he gave you as the token of his love would become the sign of your loathing.[7]

Of course, in the case of this caricatured ingratitude, the issue for the theologian is to condemn sin in general, as the attitude that leads us to love the gifts of God while rejecting God himself, who gives them to us. But the phenomenological description of the gift remains no less pertinent here: the betrothed first sees the fiancé, the giver, then the gift, the ring; the fiancé of course intended that, by seeing the gift (the ring), the betrothed would not stop seeing his face, the face of the giver. He reckoned to benefit from a phenomenal structure of reference (of *Hinweis*): the phenomenon of the ring offering its own visibility and, moreover, conferring it through transparency upon the (absent) visibility of the giver, who, by this indication or transparency, would benefit from a second-degree visibility, by association. In this way, in a well-understood exchange, the giver, invisible as such, gives being to the visible gift, but in return the visible gift would give him a visibility by proxy. Yet this apparently simple exchange (the gift of being for the given thing exchanged for the gift of appearing for the giver) is not phenomenally valid: in fact, the betrothed sees and wants to see only the ring, and not, by indication, reference, or transparency, the *facies sponsi*, the face of the giver. The gift given, as such and at the outset (the ring), monopolizes all of the visibility and condemns the giver to disappear from the visible stage. Henceforth, not only does the fiancé/giver no longer enter the phenomenon of the gift, but the gift-character of the given is erased: the ring becomes the possession of the betrothed, who sees nothing more than herself in it, possessing it. Along with the giver, the gift itself disappears.

In fact, every being masks that of which it bears the mark: Being [*l'être*]. What Saint Augustine describes in a particular case and in a restricted view Heidegger makes manifest for all entities. Indeed, in describing the *es gibt*, such that it determines the appearance of time and Being (for neither one nor the other *are*, so that with respect to them it is necessary to say *es gibt*, "it gives"), Heidegger insists on the phenomenal characteristic of the gift, which gives (itself) in this *it gives*: "The latter [*es gibt*] withdraws in favor of the gift [*zugünsten der Gabe*] which It gives [. . .]. A giving [*Geben*] which gives only its gift [*nur seine Gabe gibt*], but in the giving holds itself back and withdraws [*zurückhält und entzieht*], such a giving we call sending [*das Schicken*]."[8] We understand that the giving can precisely *not* give *itself*, precisely because it gives its gift (the gift given), makes it appear as such, and in order to arrive at this, must not only remain in the background but must withdraw itself from visibility. The *es gibt*, because it gives (and dispenses) Being as much as time, neither can nor should give itself. The giv*ing* gives only the giv*en*, it never gives *itself*. The giving cannot return on itself in a *donum sui*, as *causa sui* in metaphysics claims to do. Can we advance in the understanding of this fundamental impossibility? Possibly, by considering difference as such, namely, the difference that Heidegger in this case no longer calls ontological (*ontologische Differenz*), but the different from the same, the differentiation (*der Unterschieden aus dem Selben, der Unter-Schied*). What differs here is called the unique *Austrag*, the accord, which unfolds at once as Being and as a being, which are both given in the same gesture, but precisely not in a similar posture: "Being shows itself as the unconcealing coming-over [*zeigt sich als die entbergende Überkommnis*]. Beings as such appear in the manner of the arrival that keeps itself concealed in unconcealedness [*erscheint in der Weise* *der in die Unverborgenheit sich bergenden Ankunft*]. [. . .] The difference of being and beings, as the differentiation of coming-over and arrival [*Unterschied von Überkommnis und Ankunft*], is the accord [*Austrag*] of the two in *unconcealing keeping in concealment*."[9] In fact, nothing is clearer than this phenomenological description of the *es gibt*: when it is given, or more precisely when *it gives*,[10] the being arrives in visibility because it occupies and seizes visibility entirely (just as the arrival, *Ankunft*, of a train, precisely in the banal sense of the term, fills the station and focuses every gaze upon it). But beings can neither unleash nor prompt the visibility that they appropriate in this way: only Being can open and uncover it, because it alone consists precisely in this display, because it alone comes from a coming-over (*Überkommnis*), opening the site that the arrival (*Ankunft*) of a being will eventually occupy. This arrival receives its site in the coming-over, but by occupying it, it masks it and also renders invisible the opening from whence it proceeds. By occupying the entire stage, beings make this very scene invisible. Being thus disappears in the visibility [*l'évidence*] of the being whose arrival covers up its unconcealing coming-over. The being hides Being from view by a phenomenological necessity that attests that Being never shows itself *without* a being nor, moreover, *as* a being (as *Sein und Zeit* had already repeated with insistence). The process of the givenness of the giving thus reproduces, here ontologically, in the agreement of Being and the being according to the *es gibt*, the aporia of the gift in general, which Saint Augustine had described in theological terms.

It is characteristic of the gift given that it spontaneously conceals the givenness in it; thus, a characteristic of the phenomenon of the gift is that it masks itself. Is it possible to locate the phenomenon of sacrifice within the essential aporia of the phenomenality of the gift? And, in being articulated there, might the phenomenon of sacrifice even allow us to solve the aporia of the gift?

By virtue of its visibility, the given constitutes an obstacle to that which makes this very visibility possible. What, then, makes the visibility of the gift possible, if not the very process of givenness, whereby the giver turns the gift over as given, by handing it over in its autonomous visibility?

Yet we should note carefully here that the gift given does not mask only (or first of all) the giver, as an effect is detached from its efficient cause, or as the beneficiary of a favor refuses out of ingratitude to recognize it. The gift given masks the very process of giving givenness, a process in which the giver participates without however constituting it intrinsically, since she can even recuse herself without the process of giving being suspended. For, as we noted above, a gift (reduced) can remain perfectly possible and complete even with an anonymous or uncertain giver, or indeed without any confirmed giver. In fact, at issue here is one of the cardinal figures of the reduction of the gift to givenness. The question thus does not consist in reverting from the given to the giver, but in letting appear even in the gift ultimately given (in a being arrived in its arrival [*arrivage, Ankunft*]) the advancing process of its coming-over, which delivers its visibility by giving it to the gift, or, more generally, the very coming-over that delivers the gift phenomenally (the *Überkommnis* that unconceals the visible). At issue is the suspending of the gift given, so that it would allow the process of its givenness, namely, the given character of the gift (its given-ness [*donnéité*], to translate *Gegebenheit* literally), to appear in its own mode, instead of crushing it in the fall from the given into a pure and simple found object. So it is not a question of suppressing the gift given, for the benefit of the giver, but of making this gift transparent anew in its process of givenness by letting its giver eventually appear there, and, first and always, by allowing to appear the coming-over that delivers the gift into the visible. At stake here is the phenomenality of this very return: to return to the gift given the phenomenality of its return, of the return that inscribes it through givenness in its visibility as gift coming from somewhere other than itself. The gift appears as such—in other words, as arriving from somewhere other than itself—only if it appears in such a way that it ceaselessly refers to this elsewhere that gives it, and from which it finds itself given to view.

That the gift given allows the return from which it proceeds to appear, and gives itself up for that reason: this defines the signification and the phenomenological function of sacrifice. To sacrifice does not signify to relinquish a good (by destruction or dispossession), even if this relinquishing were possibly for the other's benefit; rather, it makes appear the referral from which it proceeds, by reversing it (by making it return) toward the elsewhere, whose intrinsic, irrevocable, and permanent mark it bears insofar as it is a gift given.[11] Henceforth, sacrifice supposes a gift already given, the point of which is neither destruction, nor its refusal, nor even its transfer to another owner, but, instead, its return to the givenness from which it proceeds, and whose mark it should always bear. Sacrifice gives the gift back to the givenness from which it proceeds, by returning it to the very return that originally constitutes it. Sacrifice does not separate itself from the gift but dwells in it totally: it maintains the gift in its status as given, by reproducing it in an abandon. Sacrifice, this abandon, manifests itself by returning to the gift its givenness because it repeats the gift on the basis of its origin. The formula that perfectly captures the conditions of possibility of the gift is found in a verse from the Septuagint: "ὅτι σὰ τὰ πάντα καὶ ἐκ τῶν σῶν δεδώκαμέν σοι" ("[A]ll things are yours and it is by taking from among what is yours that we have given you gifts") (1 Chron. 29:14). To make a gift by taking from among gifts already given in order to regive it; to "second" a gift from the first gift itself, to make a gift by reversing the first gift toward the one who gives it, and thus to make it appear through and through as a gift given up [*abandonné*] arising from elsewhere—this is what accurately defines sacrifice, which consists in making visible the gift as given according to the coming-over of givenness. At issue is absolutely not a countergift, as if the giver needed either to recover his due (in the manner of an exchange), or to receive a supplementary tribute (gratitude as a symbolic compensation); rather, the point is the recognition of the gift as such, by repeating in reverse the process of givenness, and by reintegrating the gift to it, wresting it from its factual fall back to the rank (without givenness) of found object, nongiven, *ungiven*, so as in the end to make visible not only the given but the process of givenness itself (as coming-over, *Überkommnis*), which would otherwise be left unnoticed, as if excluded from all phenomenality.

Sacrifice does not return the given to the giver by depriving the givee or recipient of the gift, for thus the point would be only an annulment of the first gift. Sacrifice renders givenness visible by regiving the gift, as a gift given up, an abandonment of which no possession any longer masks the provenance and hides the status as given. *Sacrifice effects the redounding* [*la redondance*] *of the gift in the giving up.* As a result, sacrifice loses nothing, above all not the gift that it regives; on the contrary, it wins—it wins the gift, which it keeps all the more that it makes it appear for the first time as such, as a gift given, given up, and thus finally safeguarded in its givenness (given-ness, *Gegebenheit*). Sacrifice wins, but without even having to play the game of "loser wins" (as in the so-called pure love of God), as if it were necessary to lose much in order to win even more by retribution. Sacrifice wins by regiving [*redondance*]: it conquers the true phenomenon of the gift by restoring to it, through the act of regiving it in the giving up, the phenomenality of givenness. Sacrifice regives (gives up) the gift starting with the recipient and makes the gift appear as such in the light of its givenness and, sometimes, for the glory of the giver.

§ 21. The Confirmation of Abraham

Thus, we have determined sacrifice according to its phenomenality by inscribing it within the framework of a phenomenology of the gift: its function is to make appear what the gift, once given, never fails to cover over and hide—the process of givenness itself—such that on the basis of *the giving up of the gift*, this process reappears, to the point that the giver eventually becomes visible again as well. Can we confirm this determination of sacrifice by a significant example? Probably, if we consider the episode of the sacrifice of Abraham, or rather of the *non*sacrifice of Isaac by Abraham, related in Genesis 22:1–19. Without glossing over its radically theological status (indeed, how could one do so?), we shall sketch an interpretation of it according to the principle of the phenomenality of the giving up [*l'abandon*].

Certainly, there is a sacrifice involved, specified as such: "[O]ffer [your son Isaac . . .] as a burnt offering upon one of the mountains of which I shall tell you" (22:2)—but it is a sacrifice that precisely does not take place, at least if one confines oneself to the common determination of sacrifice as a destruction or dispossession guaranteeing an exchange within the framework of a contract. Understanding this sacrifice presupposes, paradoxically, understanding why Isaac has *not* been sacrificed ("Abraham went and took the ram, and offered it up as a burnt offering instead of his son," 22:13). Or more precisely, it involves understanding why, while there was no sacrifice following the common understanding (no destruction of Isaac), there was indeed, according to the biblical account, fulfillment of the obligation toward God, since God acknowledges: "[N]ow I know that you fear God" (22:12). This is possible only because this account does not follow this common determination of sacrifice, but instead follows a phenomenological concept—that of a sacrifice conceived as abandonment on the basis of the gift, and of the gift reduced to givenness. Here is where we must locate the concept. — A first moment seems evident: God demands of Abraham a sacrifice, and even a consuming sacrifice (where the victim is consumed in fire, leaving nothing to share between God, the priest, and the one offering, in contrast to other forms of sacrifice). This demand of sacrifice falls upon Isaac, the one and only son of Abraham. Do we have here a sacrifice according to the common concept? Precisely not, because God asks nothing out of the ordinary of Abraham, nor does he enter into any contractual agreement with him; he simply and justifiably takes back Isaac, who already belongs to him, and even doubly so. First, quite obviously, because all firstborns belong to God by right: "The first-born of your sons you shall give to me. You shall do likewise with your oxen and with your sheep; seven days it shall be with its dam; on the eighth day you shall give it to me" (Exod. 22:29–30). Or again: "Consecrate to me all the first-born; whatever is the first to open the womb among the people of Israel, both of man and of beast, is mine" (Exod. 13:2). The question consists only in knowing what this belonging and this consecration really imply. The answer varies, from actual putting to death (in the case of the plague on the firstborn of Egypt, Exod. 12:29–30), to the ritual sacrifice of animals in the Temple, right up to the redemption of the firstborn of Israel, prescribed explicitly by God (Exod. 13:11–15, 34:19; Num. 18:14), who forbids human sacrifices.[12] In this sense, Isaac belongs first to God, before belonging to his father (Abraham), in the same way as any other firstborn, of Israel or of any other people.

God has nevertheless another right of possession over Isaac, radical in another way: Isaac in effect does *not* belong to Abraham, who could not—neither he, nor his wife—engender him ("Now Abraham and Sarah were old, advanced in age; and it had ceased to be with Sarah after the manner of women," Gen. 18:11). Thus, Isaac belongs from the beginning and as a miracle to God alone: "Nothing, neither word nor deed, remains impossible for God. At the same season next year, I will return to your home and Sarah will have a son."[13] And in fact, "The Lord visited Sarah as he had said, and the Lord did to Sarah as he had promised. And Sarah conceived, and bore Abraham a son in his old age at the time of which God had spoken to him" (21:1–2). Thus, by right, Isaac, child of the promise through divine omnipotence, comes to Abraham only as a pure gift, unexpected because beyond every hope, incommensurate with what Abraham would have possessed or engendered himself. But this gift nevertheless disappears very quickly, indeed, as soon as Isaac appears as such, that is to say, as the son of Abraham, or more precisely, as the one whom Abraham claims as his son: "Abraham called the name of his son who was born to him, whom Sarah bore to him, Isaac. [. . .] And the child grew, and was weaned; and Abraham made a great feast on the day that Isaac was weaned" (21:3, 21:8). And for her part, Sarah, too, appropriates Isaac, since she brags of him as *her* son ("*I* have borne him a son in his old age!" 21:7), and since she drives out as a competitor the other son, natural born, whom Abraham had had with Hagar (21:9–14). As a consequence, the call that God addresses to Abraham aims only to reestablish the truth by denouncing explicitly this improper appropriation: "Take your son, your only son Isaac, whom you cherish"—because Isaac precisely *is not* the possession of Abraham, who therefore must not cherish him as such. To this illegitimate appropriation, which cancels the gift given in a possession, the demand for a sacrifice opposes the most original right of the giver to have his gift acknowledged as a gift given, which is to say, simply acknowledged as an always provisional, transferable, and alienable usufruct: "Go to the land of Moriah, and offer him there as a burnt offering" (22:2). Abraham hears himself asked not so much to kill his son, to lose him and return possession of him to God (according to the common concept of the gift), as, first and foremost, to give back to him his status as gift, precisely to return him to his status as gift given by reducing him (leading him back) to givenness. Strictly speaking, to abandon him in order to assure the regiving [*la redondance*] of the first gift.

And Abraham accomplishes this reduction in the most explicit and clear manner imaginable. Isaac, who spontaneously reasons according to the common concept of the gift, of course notices that his father does not have (that is to say, does not *possess*) any possession available to sacrifice (to destroy and to exchange in the framework of a contract): "[W]here is the lamb for a burnt offering?" (22:7). Abraham, who already reasons according to the phenomenological concept of sacrifice, as gift given up to givenness, answers that "God will provide himself the lamb for a burnt offering" (22:8)—which means that God decides everything, including what one will offer him, and thus that neither Abraham, nor even Isaac, will be able to give anything to God, except what God, himself and in the first place, has already given to them; in a word, this means that every gift made to God comes first from God as a gift given to us. The place of sacrifice is thus called "God provides" (22:14). It should be pointed out here that the Hebrew says יִרְאֶה *yir'eh* (from the root ראה *r'h*, to see, to foresee, to provide); but that the Septuagint first understands, for the name Abraham attaches to the mountain, *God saw*, εἶδεν (second aorist of ὁράω), and then, for the name that it later retains, ὤφθη, *God appears* (passive aorist of ὁράω). Thus, it is as if the fact that God sees and provides, and therefore quite clearly *gives* the (substitute) offering of the sacrifice, or put another way, *gives the gift to give*—that is, makes the gift appear as such (given by the giver)—were equivalent to the appearing of the giver, to the fact that God *gives himself to seeing*. So God gives himself to be seen as he gives originally, as he shows that every gift comes from him. God appears as the giver that the gifts, finally abandoned by Abraham, manifest to the extent that they refer to him. The gifts *refer* to God, in the double sense in which they return to him from whom they proceed, and belong to him in the final instance.

Abraham, and he alone (the text does not say that Isaac sees anything), sees in this way that God alone gives the gift of the burnt offering, such that God subsequently continues to appear to him. But he had already recognized God as the giver of gifts from the moment that he had finally agreed to recognize Isaac as for him the principal among the gifts given by God, and thus due to God. Abraham's giving up of the gift of Isaac, an abandoning that renders him to his giver and recognizes him as given, accomplished all that God was expecting in terms of sacrifice. So it is no longer important that Abraham kill, eliminate, and exchange his son for God's benefit in order to accomplish the sacrifice demanded (according to the common concept of sacrifice); rather, it matters exclusively (according to the phenomenological concept of the gift) that he acknowledge his son as a gift given and that he acknowledge as such this gift by rendering it (giving it up, abandoning it) to its giver, and, thus, that he let God appear through his gift, rightly recognized *as a gift given*. God clearly understands it as such, since he ratifies this regiving of the gift by sparing Isaac. It is important to note that to the extent that he restrains Abraham from killing Isaac, God does not refuse Abraham's sacrifice (as he did refuse that of Cain, Gen. 4:5), but nullifies only the putting to death, since the putting to death does not belong to the essence of sacrifice. The actual death of Isaac would have ratified only sacrifice in its common concept (destruction, dispossession, exchange, and contract). In fact, God does not interrupt Abraham; he lets him go right to the end of sacrifice, but understood in the sense of its phenomenological concept: the recognition of Isaac as a gift received from God and given up or abandoned to God. And in order to recognize it, one need only acknowledge Abraham's giving up of Isaac, a recognition accomplished perfectly without his being put to death, and from the moment he is accepted as a boundless gift: "The angel said, 'Do not lay your hand on the lad or do anything to him; for now I know that you fear God, seeing you have not withheld your son, your only son, from me'" (22:12). By refusing to let Isaac be put to death, God does not thereby refuse to acknowledge the gift offered by Abraham; he accepts the sacrifice all the more, understood this time in the strict phenomenological sense of abandonment. By sparing Isaac, henceforth recognized (by Abraham) as a gift (from God), God regives Isaac to Abraham, gives him a second time, presenting a gift by a redounding [*don par une redondance*], which consecrates it definitively as a gift henceforth shared and, ultimately, transparent between the giver and the recipient. The abandonment redoubles the gift and consecrates it as such for the first time.[14]

In this way we can conceive, as Levinas puts it, an "approach of the Infinite through sacrifice,"[15] because "to sacrifice is not to kill, but to abandon and to give," as Bataille notes with precision.[16] Or, in a more direct relation with the phenomenological aporia of *it gives* as Heidegger would describe it, we can, following Jan Patočka, conceive an approach to appearing through sacrifice: "In sacrifice, *es gibt* being: here Being already 'gives' itself to us, not in a refusal but explicitly. To be sure, only a man capable of experiencing, in something so apparently negative, the coming of Being, only as he begins to sense that this lack opens access to what is richest, to that which bestows everything and presents all as gift to all, only then can he begin to experience this favor."[17] In each of these cases, however, it is a phenomenological concept of sacrifice that is at issue—as that which abandons the gift in order to make appear the given reduced in it and, eventually, its giver. Reverence for the giver through reference to the gift—Thomas Aquinas spoke for everyone in linking the one to the other: "Every virtuous deed is said to be a sacrifice, *in so far as it is done out of* reverence of God."[18]

§ 22. Forgiveness According to the Terms of Exchange

In this way the abandonment or giving up allows the gift as given to reappear by sending it back to its giver through the renunciation of the obstinate presence that was masking it. But in this case, the case of sacrifice, the regiving of the gift restores the process of givenness only from the point of view of the givee or recipient: the one who receives the gift renounces its possession in pure and simple presence, thus abandoning it and in this way rendering it transparent anew to its recipient. The abandonment takes place, in sacrifice, in the heart of reception, which is then dispossessed of the given and returns it to the giver. But couldn't we go further? Indeed, we would go further if we succeeded in locating the process of givenness a second time, on the basis of the giver. The giver would accomplish in turn the redounding [*la redondance*] of the gift by regiving it as given, even as it had disappeared as such by being solidified into a possession. To regive a gift that has become invisible and canceled out through possession means, from the point of view of the giver, *to forgive*.

Passing in this way from sacrifice to forgiveness is not obvious. In particular, sacrifice and forgiveness differ essentially from each other if one compares their respective gifts (and modes) to the closest countermodel that they have in common: exchange. The difference stands out clearly. — Sacrifice assumes that the exchange has taken place and that it was equal: the recipient can make a sacrifice only if he has already received the gift, has already accepted it and thus ratified it as right and just; it is only against the backdrop of this justice that the recipient can accomplish a sacrifice by abandonment of the gift; if he gave back the gift as insufficient, or too great, or as obtained under constraint, he would not make a sacrifice, but would instead simply reestablish the equality of exchange. Thus, the sacrifice can begin only once the equality of the exchange has been established; the sacrifice adds *through excess to justice.* — It is completely otherwise in the case of forgiveness, since forgiveness assumes that, if the exchange has taken place, it was unequal, or even that its inequality prevented its taking place: the giver can envision forgiving only if the exchange has not reached equality, or even has passed beyond the tolerable threshold of injustice; it is only against the backdrop of this injustice (the recipient took possession of a greater good than that which the giver had imparted, or he took possession of a good that had not been conceded to him at all, or he took it without the promised counterpart, etc.) that the recipient has annulled the gift in the terms of exchange, and thus the giver must (or at least may) give the first gift anew, this time without condition, in the mode of a giving up [*un abandon*], which definitively seals its status as gift given and nevermore possessed. Thus, forgiveness can begin only on the condition that the exchange did *not* take place, or at least that its patent inequality broke it; forgiveness follows on the gift through a *flaw in justice.*

The same opposition can be formulated in other words. Sacrifice passes beyond exchange, but it presupposes it: the recipient renders up the gift, not at all because this gift would not have been given (it truly was), but because this gift becomes the object of a possession in persistent presence; the gift does not suffer or commit any injustice, but its simple ontic determination (remaining in itself) inevitably conducts it (without committing any fault) to mask phenomenologically in itself both the giver and the givenness. The sacrifice passes beyond exchange, because it *adds* a new phenomenality to it. Forgiveness, on the contrary, passes beyond exchange because it *compensates* it, by establishing that which it had always already lacked: that the gift is found received as such, through a recipient who recognizes it as *given*, and thus accepts herself first of all as gifted: forgiveness thus assumes the fault (the moral injustice) of the recipient, in order to then be able, through regiving, to establish the gift in its (phenomenological) status as *given* gift. Sacrifice is described starting from a gift that has taken place, while forgiveness can appear only on the basis of a gift that *has not taken place*.

It is necessary, then, to take up the question of the phenomenality of forgiveness starting from the injustice that is within it. Indeed, the inequality of the exchange appears as unjust only because, as we have seen (§ 15), the model of exchange already determines the gift and misrecognizes it as such (namely, reduced to givenness) (§ 16). The refusal of the gift as such unfolds against the ground of its misrecognition in general in a simple exchange. At the end, the refusal of the gift and its economic misrecognition join up to offer the field of the conflict, starting from which the question of forgiveness could be posited. For injustice is not limited here to mere inequality in the commerce of things, but installs itself in the duel between consciousnesses. Indeed, when I give, I do not necessarily give in order to receive in return, in a simple economic exchange; often, even in this commerce of things, I give in order to be recognized for having given, for having given first and freely, and thus in order to be recognized as the giver. And in being recognized as giver, I find myself recognized as such as a consciousness. The logic of the gift in this way links up with the dialectic of the recognition of consciousnesses: I give, and in this sense I lose the gift that I abandon, only in order to obtain from the beneficiary of this gift his recognition of me as giver. The giver in effect manifests himself through the strength that he shows in abandoning a gift, without himself disappearing, but, instead, appearing all the more as such, so that he remains as the giver even without the gift that he has just abandoned: whatever he gives, this giver remains equal to himself, loses nothing of himself, and attests to his power. In short, the more the giver gives, the less he loses; the more he abandons, the more he affirms himself as a consciousness irreducible to its gifts—a consciousness that *is* all the more because it is *nothing* of what it loses. This game of loss and gain, where the loss of gifts allows not only for a gain in self-consciousness (with a clear conscience), but is identified with such self-consciousness, nevertheless assumes a condition: that an other recognizes the giver as such, as the one who never loses (himself) when he abandons something. Now, if the recognition of the gift abandoned by the recipient often proves itself in fact difficult, this results from an even more insurmountable difficulty: the impossibility in principle of the recognition of one consciousness (that of the giver) by another (that of the recipient). The dialectic of the recognition of consciousnesses[19] is indeed repeated, with only a few necessary corrections, in the figures of the recognition of the abandoned gift.

At each stage, the impossibility of the recognition of consciousnesses, or in other words the recognition of the giver by the recipient, is manifested, with the inequality of the exchange being marked each time as well. — First, I am myself for myself, as giver, only if I renounce possessing an in-itself other than me, or at least if I take the risk of doing so—only if I give this in-itself, in order to test whether I am something other than what I give up. This means taking the risk of dying: this is the first unequal exchange, in which I risk losing myself in order to prove myself. — A second moment follows: this unequal exchange nevertheless refers to an other, since I can take the risk of giving only if I give to a recipient who alone will be able to sanction the abandonment; but the other of this recognition herself does not risk (herself) (in) the gift, but prefers keeping the in-itself (giving nothing in itself), even if, in order to do so, she must renounce experiencing herself for herself (as the giver beyond all her gifts): thus, we have a second unequal exchange, where the one who risks the essential (consciousness of self for self as giver) in order to free himself from the inessential (self-possession) depends on the one who renounces risking the essential in order to continue possessing the inessential. — Third, the recipient, who remains in herself and possesses without abandoning anything, nevertheless retains an essential function in front of the giver, who abandons everything for himself: the recipient alone sanctions the gift, manifests it, and recognizes it, since she alone can accept it. The one who is ignorant of the logic of the gift given up becomes, paradoxically, the ultimate condition of its realization, because she alone can recognize it: this is the third unequal exchange, where the recognition of the gift and the recognition of the giver each depend on the one who refuses abandonment.

The exchange, thus unequal at several points, reaches its fundamental aporia: the judge of the gift (risked by the giver) finally proves to be the one who knows nothing about the gift (the recipient), because she refuses abandonment. It will not do to object that the recipient herself could render the gift, and, risking herself as well in the ordeal of abandonment (as the giver does), validate the gift and recognize the giver as such: indeed, by *rendering* the gift (even completely, assuming that she succeeds in doing so, which is not to be assumed), the recipient would only consecrate a quid pro quo *exchange*, and in no way a gift in return. Just as, in the dialectic of the recognition of consciousnesses, the servant cannot recognize the master within himself because the servant only experiences himself in himself, likewise the recipient can only render what she knows, one possession for another possession. Thus, the definitive inequality of exchange is characterized: the gift, above all the absolutely given gift, can receive, in the best of cases, only an exchange in return [*un échange rendu*], a return of possession, a repossession.

But this acknowledged inequality regarding acknowledgment is twice overturned. First, because consciousness without self-consciousness (without the for-itself) cannot, strictly speaking, recognize another consciousness, itself gifted with this self-consciousness (for-itself), since it *knows nothing* of either the one or the other. Thus, the inequality that subjects the servant to the master is turned against the master, who finds himself in principle unrecognized by the servant. The master had left life in itself to the servant (sparing him death in the struggle) only in order to receive, in exchange, the recognition of his own for-itself (at the risk of losing his in-itself); but the servant, by definition deprived of self-consciousness (of consciousness for-itself), can no longer recognize in another that of which he is ignorant in himself (this for-itself). At issue, then, is an unequal exchange, in which the master does not receive the recognition in view of which he nevertheless allowed the servant to live. This inequality manifests itself nowhere better than in the erotic phenomenon, at least for as long as it remains caught in the figure of exchange:[20] I can never know if my gift (loving a particular other) is recognized as such, that is to say, if I am loved in return; in the best of cases, I may believe that the other enters into a relation of exchange with me, and that, because I love him or her, the other returns the love; but I know that, if I ceased to love the other, he would immediately do the same; I know it all the better because I myself will cease loving the other as soon as he stops loving me. As a result, wisdom counsels putting myself in the situation of always being able to stop loving first, in order not to have to suffer the ordeal of loving without being loved; this logic leads even to my not loving at all at the moment in which I permit myself to love, that is to say, to establishing the unequal exchange in my favor, in order not to have to undergo it myself. In this way, the aporia of the abandoned gift leads me to rely on the hatred of the other, which appears as the final truth of exchange. The unequal exchange does not return what was first given: it thus exerts a violence by instituting an injustice.

How do we face up to this injustice? It provokes two nonexclusive but most often successive reactions: tolerance, which becomes more and more intolerable and finally untenable, and then violence in return, counterviolence, which tries to reestablish justice, that is, the equality of exchange, or at least claims to do so. In fact, often, the counterviolence limits itself to overturning the meaning of the inequality and provokes the pure and simple resurgence of the same conflict. In fact, the conflict can be stopped, if it must be stopped, only at the moment when the one who suffers from inequality in the exchange, the giver who has gone unrecognized in return, renounces the demand for justice. Either because he has obtained it—and this is the rarest case, for who can think highly of wrongs, reparations, indemnities, and prejudice?—or because the one who was harmed, that is to say the one who gave more than he received, the giver, accepts leaving the unreturned (or insufficiently, unequally returned) gift to the one who received it (writing-off of debt, negotiated compromise, confirmation of a privilege, granting of a charter, etc.). In fact, these two attitudes almost amount to the same thing: for, in order to accept a compromise or a final judgment, it is necessary to have already renounced counterviolence, almost as much (formally as much) as if one abandoned all claims without conditions. In both cases, it is necessary for the injured giver, the one who has given without receiving as much as was lost, to accept the loss of his gift, to abandon it definitively, to give up counting on any sort of return. Such unconditioned recognition of one's gift by the giver without expectation or demand for reparation—namely, the cancellation of debt in the gift and thus the *cancellation of the gift* due to its abandonment—receives in common (and even philosophical) usage the name of *forgiveness*. In the logic of exchange, and as it happens in the logic of unequal exchange, *forgiveness sanctions the abandonment without return of the gift* that was lost.

But a major difficulty arises: there is no forgiveness without injustice. Fundamentally, forgiveness justifies injustice [*le pardon donne raison à l'injustice*], first of all because the gift, even negotiated and sanctioned by a legal agreement, is well and truly lost. Next, there is injustice because the gift turns out not to be lost for everyone, since its recipient keeps it without paying for it, or at least without paying the just price; the new owner appropriates it for himself unjustly, the negotiation serving only to fix the limits of this injustice and make everyone content with them. How far must the giver concede loss? Up to what point must he give in to the inequality of the exchange? Will the unjust recipient also, in response, *concede* something so as to diminish the injustice, by a less unequal return? Forgiveness is thus displaced toward the negotiation of a compromise—an unequal exchange that is nevertheless reciprocally accepted by the two parties: the point will be to establish a reasonably justifiable injustice. The negotiation thus bears upon the fixing of the limit between the negotiable and the nonnegotiable (what the giver will give up of his gift, and what of the initial gift he will agree not to see returned to him). Or, the negotiation bears once again on the line dividing the recuperable goods from those that will be given up as irrecuperable (written off), between reconcilable and irreconcilable enemies (the passage from the principle "whoever is not with us is against us" to the principle "whoever is not against us is or *may* be with us"). From limit to limit, the negotiation succeeds in extending the compromise to the point of equilibrium, where the advantage of suspending violence compensates the abandonment of the gift that is due, and, therefore, where the unequal exchange is reimbursed by suspension of the fear of the other.

Here, however, there appears the real difficulty of a definition of forgiveness as the abandonment of the gift's debt (in unequal exchange): with such a forgiveness inscribing itself within a negotiation, it imposes its conditions, the conditions without which it could never be carried out. Indeed, there are at least two conditions. — First of all, the one who is indebted, the unjust beneficiary of the unequal exchange, must ask for the abandonment (under conditions) of the gift, of the debt of the gift; in short, the unjust and guilty ones must ask for forgiveness; without this asking, there is no reason whatsoever to enter into a discussion; there is no motive for opening negotiations, since the violence of the injustice would be perpetuated without the author of this violence asking that it cease. The first condition, then, is *the asking of forgiveness*. — Next comes a second condition: the forgiveness must be asked of the one who suffers the injustice, of the giver or, at least (a decisive departure), it must be *asked* of the victim of the unequal exchange; for no one other than the one who was injured can relieve the debt; forgiveness can come only from the one concerned with the injustice made against the gift. Without these two conditions—the asking of forgiveness by the guilty party, and the request made to the victim or the giver of the gift that has not been returned—forgiveness, at least in the sense of the abandonment of the gift lost in the unequal exchange so that violence, and thus the fear of the other, is suspended, becomes unthinkable, and thus impossible. Of course, there are cases where these conditions are fulfilled; but there is at least one case, analyzed by Vladimir Jankélévitch, where they are not—the extermination of the Jews by the Nazis during the Second World War. The Nazis never asked for forgiveness: "Forgiveness! Did they ever ask forgiveness of us? Only the distress and the dereliction of the guilty would give meaning and justification to forgiveness." Concerning the victims—for "it is up to the victims to forgive"—strictly speaking one cannot ask them anything, above all to forgive, since they have disappeared, having been assassinated and incinerated (the survivors, in a certain sense, remain as substitutes for the authentic victims, victims under conditions, who have of course not fully known the experience of being put to death precisely because they have survived).[21] In this case, and certainly in several others, forgiveness, understood as the abandonment of the debt of the gift in unequal exchange, proves impossible, because without any *place* for being. Consequently, it is necessary to admit the unforgivable. To make it clear, Vladimir Jankélévitch does not hesitate to formulate a sort of pedagogical blasphemy: he corrects, to the point of inversion, the prayer of Christ on the Cross, who asks his Father to forgive his executioners: "Thus I would readily say, *reversing* the terms of the prayer that Jesus addresses to God in the gospel of St. Luke: 'Father, *do not forgive them*, for they know what they are doing.'"[22] As violent as the rhetoric seems (and is), the conclusion remains no less conceptually impeccable: forgiveness, understood as a negotiation of a debt payment and of the abandonment of a gift due in exchange for the suspension of violence, cannot be applied in every case of unequal exchange. In certain cases, it leaves behind it an indefeasible field of injustice, unforgivable, because no guilty party wants to ask for forgiveness and no victim remains who could grant it.

Admittedly, we could reverse the argument: if forgiveness truly presupposed asking for it with contrition, or even attrition, as the precondition for its possibility, then it would become almost useless to call for it from the victim or giver, since the negotiation would be so advanced, or even *almost* already concluded by this unilateral approach of the guilty party and unjust beneficiary (according to the dictum "a fault confessed is half redressed"). Indeed, ought we not instead say that, in order to remain as such, forgiveness should be extended precisely to the unforgivable and free itself from its own conditions of possibility? In short, forgiveness ought to become possible only at the moment in which it is practiced in the realm of the impossible. Derrida did not hesitate in front of this conclusion: "Forgiveness gets its meaning—if it must retain a meaning, which is not certain—it finds its possibility of forgiveness only where it is called upon to do the impossible and forgive the unforgivable."[23] But by bearing (or aspiring to bear) in this way on the unforgivable, forgiveness would pass beyond its mere possibility—limited, by the compromise of a negotiation, to *suspending* the violence imposed by the unequal exchange—and seek to *cancel* the debt contracted through an enormous injustice, and thereby leave it forever nonreimbursed, thus sanctioning irremediable evil. In wanting too much to forgive, forgiveness would no longer forgive anything, but instead confirm the debt, and impose it as definitively unpaid to its victim or its giver. In short, forgiveness would justify injustice. As a result, suspicion is extended over forgiveness in general. Does it not produce injustice in the most banal manner by confirming it? Why should the victim ratify unequal exchange and accept its violence? Doesn't the duty of truth require on the contrary that we never compromise justice with violence, that we never give in to the *facility* of so-called *impossible* forgiveness?

§ 23. Regiving, Beginning from the Giver

These are indeed the very terms of the aporia in which the definition of the gift as the cancellation of debt or as the abandonment of the gift that is due results; in other words, these are the very terms of exchange which henceforth must become problematic for us. For if forgiveness becomes immobilized in (im)possible possibility (Derrida), this is due to its injustice—to its impotence in repairing the injustice of the unequal exchange that confiscates the giver's gift, or deprives him of his due (Jankélévitch). But if forgiveness disqualifies itself because it ends up either in the impossibility of exchange or in the injustice of exchange, must we come to the conclusion that it is inadequate, or even deceptive? Might it not instead be the case that we are dealing *here* with something other than forgiveness, namely, a mere exchange, or as it happens an unjust variation of exchange? Wouldn't it be necessary to conceive of forgiveness on the basis of another point of view than that of exchange (whether equal or unequal)? That forgiveness forgives the unjust perhaps does not mean that it is (just another unjust) exchange, but simply that it has absolutely nothing to do with exchange, nor with its equality, nor with its justice, and even less with the distributive logic that, in certain cases, puts it into operation. For as long as we can still reproach (or congratulate) forgiveness for its injustice, it will be necessary to conclude that we are not yet in fact speaking of forgiveness, but still of exchange: for only an exchange can be said to be just or unjust. Between forgiveness and justice there lies the same gulf that exists between justice and exchange.

The incommensurability of these two systems of alterity has been perfectly demonstrated by Shakespeare in the example of King Lear. Lear's first movement, which initiates the plot and the tragedy, appears to him as a gift—more precisely, as the giving up of his possessions: "Since now we will *divest us* both of rule, / Interest of territory, cares of state—" (*The Tragedy of King Lear*, 1.1.47–48, emphasis added; references are to act, scene, and line[s]). But it is merely a divestment, an *appearance* of a gift; in fact, it is yet another exchange: an exchange of the weight of the government for the quiet of retirement, of course; but above all, as his explicit demand to his three daughters immediately proves, an exchange of a declaration of exclusive love, in each of their cases, for a third of his kingdom: Lear proposes to exchange love for power. This is an exchange that is already unjust in itself, because love is not measured by power. And, it is an exchange that cannot be realized, because the already-married daughters (as Cordelia, the one who is not yet married, points out) cannot give *all* their love to their father, engaged as they are by love for their husbands (which, incidentally, they will not maintain in the course of the play): "Why have my sisters husbands if they say / They love *you all*?" (1.1.97–98, emphasis added). Lear does not give, but buys, and moreover in vain, through an exchange the injustice and impossibility of which he alone seems not to recognize.[24] The rather exemplary ingratitude that his two elder daughters will immediately demonstrate is thus in no way surprising, nor, in a sense, is it unjust: love, notes Cordelia, cannot be translated into words, and even less can it be sold in speech: "Love, and be silent. [. . .] I am sure my love's / More richer than my tongue" (*The History of King Lear*, scene 1.54, 69–70). This blindness leads Lear to plunge into misinterpretation: by virtue of an unjust and impracticable exchange, he will demand justice, or more precisely, reparation for an injustice, one that was nevertheless provoked by him alone. As his loss is fully realized, he will stubbornly call for a trial and a decision, in this way confirming the fact that his claimed gift originates in a pure and simple exchange: "I'll see their *trial* first" (scene 13.29, emphasis added). More markedly still, he demands vengeance: "I will have such *revenges* on you both / That all the world shall—I will do such things— / What they are, yet I know not" (scene 7.432–34). And this impossible revenge becomes so irrational that he even loses his reason by evoking it. But, at this very instant, and inversely, with a logic this time as sure as it is involuntary, he pronounces, in order to *impugn* it, the very word that reveals what he has been lacking since the beginning: forgiveness. "Ask her *forgiveness*?" (scene 7.304, emphasis added). Would it be necessary, he cries out, to ask forgiveness of his daughter for the evil that she has done him? Lear is the last, at this moment at least, to understand this paradox, or even to admit it. And yet, he will end up stating it and assuming it in the course of the drama. Not by according forgiveness to his daughters (who in fact ask for none, remain firmly encamped in exchange, and deepen the paternal injustice to the point of returning it on themselves and against their husbands), but by receiving Cordelia's forgiveness: "When thou dost ask me blessing, I'll kneel down / And ask of thee *forgiveness*; so we'll live" (scene 24.10–11, emphasis added). How is this displacement of forgiveness to be understood?

By renouncing the recovery of his kingdom and his power, by renouncing revenge, and thus by renouncing the repair of the injustice of the exchange, Lear frees himself from the very logic of exchange, which had obsessed him for so long and so deeply; now, all at once, he can conceive the logic of the gift, which Cordelia had followed from the beginning without Lear's understanding a word of it: she loved him without cause or conditions, and this love already constituted, in its unconditional silence, a total gift, responding to no price (neither a third of the kingdom, nor a "third of the stars"). She remakes this gift without exchange at the end of the drama, by asking it of him over again—precisely, by asking Lear to regive her his blessing ("thou dost ask me *blessing*"), which he had taken away from her ("Here I disclaim all my paternal care") (scene 1.103, emphasis added). Lear knows that he failed to acknowledge this sudden gift, and thus that it falls to him—to him and no longer to his other daughters—to ask pardon of Cordelia: this time, he asks forgiveness; that is to say, he asks Cordelia to reappear to him as he could have and should have seen her before he entered into the madness of an exchange: to appear as the one who loved him, and whom he loved the most. For Lear will never get to reestablish the equality of exchange with his other daughters, not only because they do not ask for any forgiveness whatsoever, but because love cannot be exchanged for a kingdom. And he himself will never forgive them, but by contrast he will succeed in having *himself* forgiven by Cordelia.

Why is forgiveness fully realized in one case (Cordelia forgiving Lear) and not in the other (Lear never forgiving his other daughters, and perhaps not having to forgive them the injustice of the exchange)? Because between Lear and Goneril or Regan, there was never any gift, neither on his behalf, nor on theirs; rather, there was an exchange calculated on the basis of a third of his lands and a certain number of his knights, haggled over almost down to the item, always unjust and never practicable; while between Lear and Cordelia, there was from the outset a gift, the love of

Cordelia for Lear, and thus the possibility of a pardon from Cordelia, regiving the gift to Lear, which he finally recognizes. Here, with extreme discretion but perfect rigor, the decisive point shines forth: *no forgiveness can take place except on the basis of a prior gift*. Forgiveness does not erase or make up for the injustice of an exchange, at the risk of sanctioning injustice. It always repeats an initial gift, which might have disappeared; and by regiving it, it makes it appear all the more clearly. Forgiveness has only one condition of possibility: a prior gift, even if it has disappeared, is unrecognized, or was rejected. And it has only one power: to make the glory of this gift reappear (or appear for the first time) by regiving it with superfluity [*en le re-donnant avec redondance*]. Forgiveness does not correct a deficit of justice in the exchange, but a deficit of visibility in the first gift. Forgiveness thus labors for the phenomenality of the gift.

We still need to conceive the phenomenality of forgiveness more clearly. This cannot be done without once again starting from the gift as it appears. Now, the gift appears most of the time and to begin with only obscurely, in the shadow of exchange, which conceals it as such. What we saw in the case of *King Lear* is true more generally, even among the greatest thinkers: the gift seems to inscribe itself within the logic of the three terms of exchange: the giver, the given gift (the object of the transfer of property), and the givee or recipient. In fact, as we saw earlier (§ 16), the gift is irreducible to the terms of exchange, because it *can only* be described by bracketing one of these three terms. There is a gift only if one of these terms of exchange is *missing*. Either the giver, as in the case of the anonymous gift, the inheritance, and so forth; or the recipient, as in the case of the gift made to an unknown person, one who is absent, or, preeminently, an enemy; or, finally and above all, the given gift, so that one gives nothing real (no thing), but something unreal and therefore something all the more meaningful: so it is that one can give nothing more than unrealities—one's time, one's attention, one's love, one's life, which is to say one's death, and so on. The gift, thus reduced in multiple ways to givenness, can no longer be confused with exchange, since it successively challenges each of its terms, and therefore its entire apparatus.

And yet, the threat of this confusion with exchange still weighs on the gift, because we are able, first of all and most of the time, to remain within the natural attitude, which makes exchange visible and available and conceals from us the gift for at least as long as we do not subject it to its reduction to givenness. The threat that exchange causes to weigh on the phenomenality of the gift can also be pointed out in another way. Indeed, the gift given, insofar as it remains first of all something real—that is to say, most often an independent, material, and subsistent (ready-to-hand) object—appears as such at the center of the phenomenal stage of the gift, especially if this gift is confused with exchange: indeed, when the gift appears, it concentrates on itself the total attention of the recipient (whether that recipient is direct or indirect, individual or collective), precisely because it is found given here and now, in presence; the given gift becomes the present, which occupies all presence, and hoards it, to the detriment of the giver. And thus, the act of giving and giving up the given gift is effaced behind this very gift. We are not speaking here of a subjective disposition of the giver (her discretion, modesty, etc.), but of a strictly phenomenological rule: the *better* the giver has given, or in other words, definitively abandoned the given gift, the *more* she disappears into the background; if she still appeared through her gift, if this gift still remained visibly hers, if she still held it as her possession, then she would not have truly accomplished this gift. The giver must disappear from the gift in order for the gift to appear as such, as given radically under the figure of the abandoned gift, absolutely independent of its former possessor so as to become absolutely available to a new owner—to the point that the gift does not even present itself as a gift (or as the result of an act of giving [*d'une donation*]), but instead is simply found *there*, a pure fact without any meaning, or status, or origin, completely neutral. In this way, the given gift, essentially and in proportion to its completeness, conceals its giver, and thus the very process of givenness [*la donation*]. The phenomenality of the gift implies the possibility or even the unavoidable necessity of a contradiction: the given manifests itself to the extent that it better conceals the giver and the giving [*la donation*] that is in her (see § 19).

This phenomenological contradiction can be considered from the recipient's point of view as well as from the giver's point of view. And it can be resolved from either point of view through two symmetrical operations: sacrifice and forgiveness, each of which consists in a repetition of the reduction of the gift to givenness. — In sacrifice, the recipient once again brackets the given gift, so as to raise the obstacle that its reified, permanent, and subsistent presence sets up between him, the recipient, and the giver, in this way reestablishing the event of giving in all its manifestation. The suspension of the given being (the thing, the object) opens to the recipient's eyes not only the manifestation of the giver of this gift, but above all the manifestation of the course of the gift's event (see above, §§ 20–21). — I do not have to develop the point about sacrifice here, because the issue in this situation is that of reestablishing the phenomenality of givenness no longer from the point of view of the recipient, but instead of the giver. Put another way, the issue is that of resolving the following aporia: how can the giver and, beginning from him, the whole process or course of the event of giving come or return to visibility when the very realization of the given gift implies that it fade away into an essential visibility? How might the given gift prevent its own visibility from screening out the visibility of the event of the gift, and in it, of the giver? Clearly, everything depends on what the gaze of the recipient is able to perceive; now, this gaze only perceives the given gift because its mere presence is enough to blot out and swallow up those of the giver and the process of givenness. Only reinforced evidence of this giver and of the process of givenness would be able to pierce through the all too real presence of the given gift.

How, then, is the evidence of givenness and, within it, that of the giver redoubled if not by repeating the very process of giving the gift, by redoubling the givenness of the gift, so that this *redounding* [*redondance*] of the giving event submerges its own result and becomes more visible than what it gives in the eyes of the recipient himself? Such a redoubling and such a repetition can be accomplished only through the regiving of the given gift, or, put otherwise, and from the point of view of the recipient, through forgiveness. *Forgiveness regives the gift from the recipient's side.* Forgiveness, by elevating to power the process of givenness of the same and prior gift, submerges the given gift and the gaze of the recipient through the evident glory of this remade, repeated, restated, and *redounding* act of giving. While the recipient had not, up to this point and spontaneously, seen the gift as anything other than an object of exchange, something merely passed from one possession to another, keeping no trace of its giver or the least vestige of its gift quality, the forgiveness that the recipient puts into operation by regiving (by redounding) the gift and saturating it with givenness constrains, or at the least leads (for it does not force), the recipient to recognize, most often *for the first time*, this gift as such, as given. And, in finally seeing the gift as given, the recipient *for the first time* sees in the gift, as if backlit, its giver, because he sees him in the glory of the event of giving in operation.

Two consequences follow that are directly tied to each other. — First, no forgiveness can be fully realized if there is not, to begin with, a gift to repeat by the giver in order to make it seen and received as such by its recipient. To claim to accomplish forgiveness where no gift has come first leads to absurdity and injustice—to absurdity because forgiveness has no grasp or hold if there is no gift, even and especially a gift that has been erased or spurned, to offer it a firm ground for its display. Without the screen of the prior gift, the regiving cannot make the glory of the forgiveness burst out. And this illusion of forgiveness can only compromise the functioning of exchange, reinforce its possible inequality, and, in any event, cause forgiveness to be confused with exchange (thus, we return to Derrida's objection). The claim to accomplish forgiveness where no gift has come leads next to injustice, since without a gift to reestablish, and thus without a recipient to enlighten, forgiveness winds up recognizing and consecrating a state of exchange; then, by confusing the redounding of the gift with the inequality of an exchange, it takes as a generosity that which ends up only as an injustice (once again, the objection made by Jankélévitch). *Forgiveness assumes the gift, because it consists in its redounding.*

Next, since forgiveness is extended only as far as a prior gift renders it *a contrario* possible in the mode of redounding, the question of the unforgivable finds an answer, at least a formal one: hypothetically, the only one who could forgive everything would be the one for whom everything already has the status of a gift, and thus the one for whom a redounding proves itself always possible. Now, for whom does everything have the status of a gift, if not the one who would have given everything, and thus who would have created everything in the mode of givenness? Only God, therefore, can forgive everything, precisely because he has created everything. Paradoxically, he appears as the merciful one to the exact extent of his transcendence. God alone can forgive absolutely, with a forgiveness that is impossible for us, because "[f]or human beings this [for a rich man to enter the kingdom of heaven] is impossible, but for God all things are possible" (Matt. 19:26). Thus, we find again the conclusions reached earlier (§ 13): what is impossible *for us* culminates in what God himself recognizes as "the most difficult": to remit sins, to forgive the scorn of the gift given and not received; for "who but God alone can remit sins?" (Mark 2:7). God alone can remit sins, no matter what sin, because he alone satisfies the conditions of forgiveness: every fault against any man proves to be a fault as well against God ("[W]hatever you did for one of these least brothers of mine, you did for me," Matt. 26:40); and next because by "making himself to be sin who did not know sin" (2 Cor. 5:21), he solicits forgiveness for us, who do not ask for it. But God satisfies these two conditions because, more radically, for him alone everything proceeds from a gift (creation) and appears without ceasing as a *given* gift, precisely because God endlessly regives this gift.

He can forgive everything because for him alone everything appears as a gift. He alone saves forgiveness from its injustice, because he alone can regive it, not according to exchange, but *according to the redounding of the gift*. He alone saves it from being tangled up in the impossible *for us*, because he alone can unfold the fold of the (im)possible as far as the possible *on God's side*, meaning the omnipotence of the gift without condition (§ 13), which allows in advance forgiveness without limit.[25] The power of God, which can do anything, even forgive, thus consists only in his goodness. For, indeed, "[T]here is only One who is good" (Matt. 19:17), "No one is good but God alone" (Mark 10:19 = Luke 18:19). Only one is good, and it is not me. This impossibility must be extended as a certainty—a negative certainty.

§ 24. The Return of the Prodigal Son

Henceforth, the logic of forgiveness can be unfolded in all its fullness and rigor: forgiveness is distinguished from a pure and simple unjust exchange by a hermeneutics that conceives of it on the basis of the gift (§ 23). Clearly, in order to arrive at thinking forgiveness on the basis of the gift, this hermeneutics must, first of all, reduce the gift itself to givenness (§ 16). Now, and this is a decisive point, in order to operate such a hermeneutics (from the exchange to the gift, and then to forgiveness), nothing less than a conversion of the hermeneutist himself is necessary. And the accomplishment of this conversion, or rather the delay or even the incapacity to accomplish it, becomes the very stake of forgiveness: what is to be forgiven can—and in the final instance *must*—consist in ignorance of the gift itself, or more exactly, in the refusal to receive the gift as such, preferring instead to interpret it as a mere exchange. Forgiveness then comes to bear on the flaw in its very interpretation as forgiveness, a flaw that masks it in exchange; or more exactly, forgiveness bears on the failure of conversion, which alone had made the hermeneutics of the gift as gift feasible. The hermeneutics of the gift as such makes forgiveness thinkable, but on the condition that a conversion to the gift allows it; and, for as much as this conversion to the gift remains problematic first of all and most of the time, the failure of conversion calls for forgiveness. It would be necessary, then, to describe the circle, itself hermeneutic, that leads from forgiveness to the gift, passing from hermeneutics to conversion, and then returns from (failed) conversion to forgiveness—a forgiveness that is always sought for, but also always already presupposed.

This circle is in fact described in a classic parable about forgiveness: the story of the prodigal son in Luke 15:11–32. In fact, this story proceeds in two stages, each corresponding to the "two sons" (v. 11) of a father and to the two unfoldings of the single fold of the gift as forgiveness, which must not be separated from each other at any cost. Two sons, then, who lead their father to divide the paternal inheritance into two: how can we avoid recognizing an inverted paradigm of *King Lear*, where three daughters (in fact, two and one) face a similar division of an inheritance? Of course, the initiative for this division here passes from the father to the children, or rather to one of the two sons: "[T]he younger of them said to his father, 'Father, give me the share of the property that falls to me'" (v. 12). Here, the son, not the father, provokes the division. Nevertheless, the question remains manifestly the same in Luke as in *King Lear*: are we dealing with a gift (which the request "give me" seems to assume), or an exchange (what seems to be implied by the taking of possession in the name of justice: "the share [. . .] that falls to me")? The hermeneutics of the initial gesture, whether understood as exchange or as gift, constitutes the stake of the story—and gives its stake to the forgiveness that is to come, as well as to the conversion required. From the point of view of the father, who understands himself and behaves (contrary to Lear) perfectly as a father, the reduction of the gift to givenness is assured, precisely because fatherhood consists of a naturally reduced gift (§ 16). The same is not true for the two sons, who cannot see the gift as a gift, but only as an exchange that is probably unjust; and the two parts of the story correspond to the two responses that are successively delivered to this hermeneutics by the "younger son" (vv. 12–24) and by the "elder son" (vv. 25–32), respectively. These two responses converge into a same description of the gift as forgiveness.

The first response (and thus the first hermeneutics) proceeds in four moments. — The son begins by challenging the gift at the same moment in which he asks his father to "give," precisely because he claims from the outset that what is apparently to be given falls to him by right and belongs to him as his part of the paternal property, which is *owed* to him as an inheritance ("τὸ ἐπιβάλλον μέρος," v. 12). A property is indeed what is at issue, as the very use of the term "οὐσία" confirms, which designates both the substance (the Vulgate reads *substantia*) that remains, allowing for its possession (as opposed to the accident, which disappears in the end), as well as the real property, the equity, the funds.[26] In short, the younger son demands his funds, that which is at his disposal according to the right of inheritance; from this point of view, the father gives him only his due, or to state it otherwise, he does not *give* him anything of what he remits and transmits to him: he only does him justice in an equal exchange.[27] And indeed, the father renders him full possession of his "living" (v. 12), renouncing every paternal right over what he distributes to him henceforth without return. In this way, the request for the funds is equivalent to a denial of the gift, or even more, to a denial of the very fatherhood of the father. What was formerly a gift becomes a possession that one gathers, totalizes, and carries off ("συναγαγὼν πάντα ἀπεδήμησεν," v. 13). The son *realizes* the gift, in a permanent possession (οὐσία). After that, the given gift (life) becomes invisible at the same time that the father disappears, he whose presence and even memory fade away in the "far country" (v. 13). The gift disappears in the "far country," the χώρα.[28]

A second stage follows. The denial of fatherhood and thus of the gift leaves the son in possession of his funds (his οὐσία). But possession has its logic: the enjoyment lasts only as long as his *possession* lasts; now, strangely, the οὐσία does not subsist, at least not absolutely, or constantly. Not only can it disappear just as it has arisen (philosophy knows well these two processes: genesis and corruption, φθορὰ); but above all, the funds, to the very extent that they are offered for possession, are consumed, and thus cannot avoid being dissipated (διεσκόρπιζεῖν, v. 13), and end up lacking (ὑστερεῖσθαι, v. 14)—not out of negligence, misfortune, or miscalculation, but by definition: that which is possessed is exchanged, spent, and thus lost. In the strict sense, possession, following the strict logic of exchange, engenders "famine" (vv. 14, 17), simply because from that point on "no one gave" (οὐδεὶς ἐδίδου, v. 16); therefore, the son not only no longer has a father, but he also lacks fellow citizens, since he no longer has a city, or a site (v. 15), or even the social rank of an animal, which for its part at least retains a commercial value.[29] Possession (of the οὐσία) ends in its loss. What remains of the son *who is no longer a son*? No longer able to hope for the status of son, he at least seeks to fulfill a function in the economy of exchange. But he can only envision obtaining this function from his father, since he has no other social assurance in the "far country"; he thus dreams of having himself hired as one of his "father's hired hands" (v. 17). Here we find a formula that is literally contradictory: either he will become an employee, hired by an employer who clearly will not behave like a father to him, or, if the employer is the father, he will not look upon him as a hired hand; or, if miraculously the son recovers his father, he will not be his hired hand; but the son, as totally unconscious of his filiation as he is totally deprived of the gift, no longer even sees clearly the difference between a gift and a possession, or the incompatibility between a son and a hired hand. In fact, and in the final instance, the son well knows that he has lost his filiation by losing the call, that he lost the call by refusing to respond to it, and even that he *is no longer*—for it is in these three senses that one may understand the formula "I am no longer (οὐκετι εἰμὶ) / worthy to be called / your son" (vv. 19, 21). What is more, the father understands it this way when he says that his son was "dead" (vv. 24, 32).

But here, even in the emptiest and most faraway χώρα, or rather perhaps because of this desert, the son begins to pass from one interpretation to the other by starting once again to consider the father. Indeed, he sees the absent father in the very absence of any gift (v. 16), which returns to him, in a sense, his initial refusal of the father's gift (v. 12). His father emerges anew in the lack of the father. Or put otherwise, the father appears as the one against whom the son "[has] sinned" (vv. 18, 21), as the father who was challenged, refused, and lost [*manqué*]. The fault toward the father (the sin) transforms the lack [*le manque*] of the father into the absence *of the father*. And at the same time, in the avowal *to himself* of this shortcoming [*manquement*] (toward the father), the son begins again (or rather begins for the first time) to see *himself* as a son, who can call *his* father (the vocative of vv. 18 and 21 overturns that of v. 12) and return the call (ἐρῶ, v. 18)—even if he does not yet imagine that this father might call him anew as a son. At the least, the son rises up (vv. 18, 20)[30] enough to be able to walk to the father, under the figure of his lack [*manque*], in the double sense of the missing and the lost father [*du père manquant et manqué*]. — Then we come to the final stage: the father, "seeing [the lost son] at a distance" (v. 20), receives him, not only as what the prodigal hoped for at best, in terms of exchange, but right away as a son (the father doesn't even let the son finish his sentence and propose himself as a "hired hand" ["μισθός"], for the words foreseen at v. 18 are not found at v. 21).[31] The father gives to the son what the son no longer asked for, filiation, without even hearing what the son was asking of him: exchange. The father responds to the request to reestablish exchange with the gift, or rather, he responds with the redounding of the gift, with the repetition of filiation, with forgiveness giving over again the initial and lost gift. The son had made the gift (filiation) invisible by appropriating it for himself as a fund (οὐσία). Through forgiveness, the gift given over again, the father does not *render* to the son what exchange had lost (possession), but reestablishes him in the movement of the given gift, and thus appears to him in this way for the first time as father-giver, and makes the son appear himself for the first time as son-recipient. Forgiveness brings to light, for the first time, the complete phenomenon of the gift. The unveiling of the father as father coincides with the unveiling of the son as son. Nothing attests to this better than the formula used by the parable ("This is my son," v. 24): indeed, it reproduces literally that used at the baptism of Christ (Matt. 3:17 and Mark 1:11), when the Father proclaims, "This is my son."[32] The redounding of the gift, forgiveness, thus here takes on nothing less than a trinitarian status. In this way the gift is regiven in forgiveness, to the extent that the son resees the father in the gift, instead of denying him by appropriating the gift to himself. Which cannot be done, except by passing from one interpretation to another, a passage that, in its turn, assumes the conversion of the gaze (in this case, the gaze of the son).

This passage and this conversion are confirmed in the second response and the hermeneutics of the elder son. In appearance (in reality, even), the elder son did not demand his share of the inheritance, and thus did not disperse it. He stayed with his father. And yet, has he *seen* the phenomenon of the gift between him and his father? The part of the story that concerns him answers this question, in three moments. — The elder son, curiously, also finds himself distant from the paternal home and must come back to it (v. 25, ἤγγισεν), not of course because he had renounced it, but because he was working the fields. Nonetheless, in coming back, he no longer recognizes his father's home, because a party has replaced the daily chores; thus, the question arises and, once the explanation has been given, his refusal to enter the house (v. 28, "οὐκ ἤθελεν εἰσελθεῖν"), out of anger: thus, the elder son hates the paternal home in returning to it, exactly as the younger son hated it when leaving it. This similarity is reinforced by the same movement that the father must make in each case: to go out to the son ("[H]is father went out to call him," v. 28 = v. 20). But does the motive for the elder son's anger, which holds him back at the threshold of the paternal home, correspond to that which chased the younger son out of this same home (the latter wanted to leave, the former does not wish to return)? — A second moment shows this to be the case, despite first appearances. For the elder complains at not having had a good to possess ("You never gave anything to me" ["ἐμοὶ οὐδέποτε ἔδωκας"], v. 29), while the father had indeed "given" (δός, v. 12) one to the younger son! The elder son in fact sees the gift no better than the younger son saw it: like him at the beginning, he sees only the possession of the good; the only difference lies in time:

the younger son has already experienced possession, while the elder has not (and he is furious only at the delay in possession, which he dreams of as a completion). The younger son's privilege results: having experienced possession as such (as a shortcoming [*manquement*] and above all as that which provokes lack [*le manque*]), he ended up by experiencing, in its redounding, the gift given and accepted as such.

This is confirmed by two points. First: the elder son understands himself as a "servant" (δουλεύω, v. 29) to his father, just as the younger son saw himself, at best, as a "hired hand" (vv. 17, 19).[33] Next, the elder son would like to possess something for the same reason as his brother: so as to celebrate by spending it. To which he adds a greater insult against his father (likewise revealing the first thought of the younger son): he wants a possession in order to celebrate with those who he considers his friends (v. 29, μετά τῶν φίλων μου). How much more clearly could he show that he does not count his father among his friends, or literally, that he *does not love his father*? In fact, the two points amount to the same thing: the elder son does not see the distinction between the friend and the servant, while the father of the parable never ceases, silently, to warn, like Christ, that "[y]ou are my friends (φίλοι) [. . .]. No longer do I call you servants (δούλους), for the servant does not know what his master is doing; but I call you friends (φίλους), for all that I have heard from my Father I have made known to you" (John 15:14–15). In this way the elder son remains within the horizon of exchange and of possession, exactly like his brother, with the added frustration of not having fully realized it. But unlike his brother, he does not know it: he has not had the experience of possession that leads to dispossession ("famine"), nor has he experienced the lack of the father, nor *a fortiori* the redounding of the gift in exchange for the rerequested exchange. The elder son, "the oldest," in fact finds himself *behind* the younger, "the newest."

At the end of the story, the father teaches the son about the gap between gift and exchange, as it is manifested by the act of forgiveness. The act of forgiveness given to the younger son signifies the gift itself according to its own logic—namely, that the giver and the process of the gift always remain as the horizon of the given gift, contrary to what the refusal of the gift produces: the invisibility of the giver and of the process of the gift, obscured by the possessed, anonymous, opaque gift. In fact, the father (in Luke) twice states the same redounding gift, by twice quoting (so to speak) the words of Jesus (in John). First: "You are always with me"

(v. 31), or in other words, "even as thou, Father, art in me, and I in thee" (John 17:21). Next: "[A]nd all that is mine is yours" ("πάντα τὰ ἐμὰ σὰ ἐστίν") (v. 31), or put otherwise: "[A]ll mine are thine, and thine are mine" ("τὰ ἐμὰ πάντα σὰ ἐστίν, τὰ σὰ ἐμὰ") (John 17:10). The mine comes from the yours, and the yours refers to the mine, so that the gift is ceaselessly being regiven, crossing over, and, in this redounding, appears without end as such. The father *regives* to the elder son his title as son by insisting: "Son" ("τέκνον") (v. 31), which is stronger than the simple υἱὸς used to designate the younger son (v. 30).[34] The trinitarian status of the redounding of the gift is not in doubt here, either. Which does not mean that the redounding fails to make the gift appear everywhere else as a full-fledged phenomenon. In fact, forgiveness reaches into the misery of the everyday as regularly and as powerfully as within the Trinity. Everything depends on the response of the elder son to the teaching of the father: for nothing proves that he has understood it, or that, having understood it, he has accepted it. Each of us can decide what the son will or would respond, since each of us *is* this son.

Forgiveness, then, regives the gift, and, in this irresistible redounding, it re-places the giver and the process of the gift in their primordial visibility, which the refusal of the given gift had obscured in a possession that had become opaque. Forgiveness regives its visibility to the given gift and to its giver from the point of view of the giver, in an exact parallel to sacrifice, which regives the given gift its visibility from the point of view of the recipient or givee (§§ 20–21). In this way, forgiveness and sacrifice answer to each other, making the phenomenality of givenness appear through the double redounding of the gift, whether starting from the recipient, or from the giver. The two biblical narratives insist, in the two cases, on the single condition posed for its actualization by the hermeneutics of the gift as such, that is to say, as the whole process of givenness (and not only as its result): the recipient must renounce possessing the gift (or put otherwise, renounce obscuring it as gift, denying it as such), so as to see it as such and, with the same gaze, see the giver through it, or more exactly, see the whole process of givenness. *The gift cannot at the same time be possessed and manifest itself.* If it allows itself to be possessed, it must, in order to persist in permanent presence, abolish in itself the process of its givenness. But if it succeeds in appearing as gift *insofar as given in the process* of givenness, then it must renounce being possessed in permanence, because the process of givenness must pass, since it *passes of itself* [*il se passe*].[35] The whole process of givenness does not last; it happens in the event of its passing. Renouncing possession of the gift in order to see the process of givenness, or more exactly, in order to allow givenness to show itself as its own process: what is implied in this requirement is less an ethical conversion (to which in any case the two biblical texts analyzed in §§ 21 and 24 are not limited), than first and foremost the thinking of the gift, of the given, and of givenness in their process, and therefore according to the radical character of the event.

V. THE UNFORESEEABLE, OR THE EVENT

Tall, slim, in mourning, in majestic grief,
A woman passed.

—BAUDELAIRE[1]

§ 25. What the Object Excludes

The given rises toward us, in a continuous, multiple, and uncontrollable flow, a pure (or rather impure?) manifold of intuition. Within this given, for a portion, sometimes, and for a period of time that is always eventually counted, we distinguish certain islands of provisional stability, which we constitute or at least believe we constitute (for they can also constitute themselves by themselves) into so many phenomena. These phenomena register perhaps only a small part of the given that happens to us; no doubt we let the greater part pass, without being able to retain or keep any of it as phenomena, or it passes in phenomena that are lost in the instant in which they are given, without ever managing to show themselves. And yet, among those that our attention does have the power to keep in full view, we do not even manage to look at all of them, nor at each in the same way. Or more precisely, we only look at those phenomena that we recognize as having the status of objects. Sight here becomes a guardian's gaze—guarding by keeping watch (*intueri*) every time that it effectively institutes in front of it something that can remain (*ob-jectum*) stable, determined,

Translator's note: This translation draws at times on a translation of parts of this chapter that appeared in Jean-Luc Marion, "Phenomenon and Event," trans. Ella Brians and Elizabeth Lawler, *Graduate Faculty Philosophy Journal* 26, no. 1 (2005): 147–59.

and thus invariable enough, at least for a period of time, so as to offer the conditions for a knowledge that is certain, at least provisionally. As for the rest, this remainder of the given that our sight cannot look upon as an object because it cannot guard it in permanence, common usage (that is, our naturally metaphysical vocabulary) in contrast designates it as "subjective." Thus, we routinely accept that phenomena, at least to the extent that they appear to us, are distinguished as objects or objective phenomena, on the one hand, and as subjective phenomena, on the other, according to a difference that is apparently descriptive, evident, and therefore unquestionable. This difference separates the domain of the sciences, indeed of *science* itself (for science remains essentially single), which consists of objects, from the domain of strictly nonscientific knowledge, which remains subjective.

The vagueness of this term "subjective" in its opposition to the objectness of the object actually suits rather well with what is being characterized when we use it: precisely the imprecision of that which does not reach the status of an object, its contingency, its mutability, its reluctance to be quantified—in a word, its incomprehensibility. By contrast, the object is defined precisely and allows for a stable comprehension. As a phenomenon, it appears according to no less than four fundamental, categorical features. First, it allows itself to be quantified according to dimension, that is to say, according to parameters, which determine all the characteristics of its essence (or of its "concept"), in principle without any remainder; as a result, it can be predicted, since its totality consists only in the sum of its parts and its characteristic quantifications. Second, the foreseeability of the object allows for the deduction of its existence from its essence, that is to say, either to foresee its existence, or to produce it; and, by virtue of the permanence of its characteristics, to reproduce it is no more difficult than to produce it. Third, its passage to actuality results from a cause, to which it is by principle tied as an effect, able in its turn to take up the function of cause with regard to another object. Finally, and summing up the first three features, the object is actual only because it is possible, it is possible only by not contradicting itself, and it does not contradict itself in its definition because it remains always comprehensible for a finite rationality (ours). In short, the object proves itself to be always comprehensible only because, as object of experience, it submits itself by definition to the conditions of possibility of this very experience (ours). The object allows itself to be known exactly, because its definition consists precisely in allowing itself to be known exactly—the remainder, which cannot be led back to exactitude and to its permanence, is sent away to the indeterminate domain of "subjectivity."

The border thus traced between the object and that which does not succeed in satisfying the criteria of objectness can be formulated in different ways, depending on which era of metaphysics one privileges, but it always remains legible and identifiable. Even for Aristotle, who is still unaware of the strict meaning of the *object* (the independence of οὐσία from the knowing mind protects him from it), the border is established between this οὐσία and the accident; or more exactly, between, on the one hand, the enduring presence (up to a certain point, it is true) of οὐσία, which for this very reason will quickly allow itself to name not only essence, but above all substance (*substantia*, which holds and maintains) and, on the other hand, the accident, understood as that which comports to comport itself otherwise than what it had begun to be. Descartes and Kant, by transforming the categories of the entity (still guaranteed by οὐσία) into very simple natures (*naturae simplicissimae*), and then squarely into categories of understanding (henceforth leased out to the knowing mind, that is to say, transcendental), radicalize the distinction: that which cannot become an object falls outside the sphere of the knowable.[2] Ever since then, confirmed in various modes by Hegel, Nietzsche, and Husserl, and thematized by Dilthey and hermeneutics, this opposition seems to raise hardly any difficulty for us any longer.

Indeed, on the contrary, it seems to allow us to distinguish, for the sake of greater clarity and method, between, on the one hand, the phenomena that serve as objects of the exact, or "hard," sciences, or more elegantly but less precisely (since we substitute a difference from the ontic region for the true, methodological difference), the "natural" sciences (*Naturwissenschaften*), and, on the other hand, those that are addressed by the sciences called "human" (and which are in fact so little "human," since man enters into them only as a problematic object), or more exactly "social" (in short, *Geisteswissenschaften*)—the phenomena that are not worthy of the title of object except in a derivative, attenuated, and probably abusive sense. This opposition simply represents a redistribution of roles, and a differentiation between requirements, from which we choose according to inclination, talent, or opportunity. We can easily and offhandedly agree that phenomena of the object type much more readily satisfy the demands of method, and thus more often supply the clarity and distinction of evident knowledge, which is why they produce more certain, proven, and recordable knowledge than phenomena of the other type. Since the latter can only objectify themselves poorly (if at all), they will not allow themselves to be quantified, nor, therefore, preceded by a foreseen essence; nor produced and reproduced, and therefore not repeated, either; nor led back to a cause and, consequently, made to function as one; so that, in the end, they comply only imperfectly with the conditions of possibility for experience understood in the strict sense. In the case of the phenomena of this type, then, it would be necessary to soften the rules for clear and distinct knowledge, or even accept a residual approximation, which can never be eliminated, and therefore give up on their constitution (and thus their production and reproduction), in order to limit ourselves to interpreting them according to their very imprecision (whence the recourse to hermeneutics). After all, the "mind" deserves some exceptions and concessions; all the more so since we must either treat its study as optional, or abandon it to the arts (which is clearly not a compliment)—to "metaphysicians," those "musicians without musical ability" (Carnap).[3] At issue, then, would be merely the division of domains, with gains and losses on both sides, from among which one could make a choice according to one's sensibility, or in other words one's ideology. At stake above all, in fact, is a phenomenological decision: we accept two ontic (in fact, methodological) domains that are independent, autonomous, and in the end antagonistic, and they face up to each other, each accomplishing a mode of phenomenality—either the phenomenality of the object (natural sciences), or the phenomenality of nonobjects in the strict sense (human sciences).

But this division into fields, if it guarantees an armed peace between the disciplines, in no way justifies the heterogeneity of the two modes of phenomenality: it simply presupposes it. Nevertheless, how do we explain that the world admits two modes of parallel and irreducible phenomenalizations? At the least, it would be necessary to ask questions about phenomenality in general, before assuring its equivocity, but, at this stage, phenomenality remains absolutely unquestioned. We will indeed have to question it, for this compromise, seemingly viable and civil, will not hold up for very long; under scrutiny, the two types of phenomena are not opposed as equal to each other, each assured of an autonomous phenomenality; rather, they contradict each other. Each marginalizes the other mercilessly, each ravages the other with its own criterion. — The phenomenon of the object type asserts itself according to its own mode of knowing: it alone succeeds in satisfying the demands of a rigorous science through clear and distinct ideas. It does so first by constituting an essence (a model, a definition, a "concept"), which is known in advance and foreseeable before the production of the object within existence. Next, it does so because this essence allows for the object to be repeated and reproduced, precisely because said essence can produce the object at will as an effect, thanks to the causal relationship. Consequently, the possibility of the object coincides with the conditions for experience—that is, it coincides with the very conditions of scientific knowledge by definition for a finite understanding. According to its mode of knowledge, its *ratio cognoscendi*, the phenomenon of the object type prevails indisputably over the nonobjective phenomenon, which it devalues as uncertain, imprecise, and confused—in short, as being at the margins of knowledge and quasi-irrational: subjective.

And yet, the nonobjective phenomenon unquestionably wins out if its mode of being, its *ratio essendi*, is taken into account. For since it does not depend on the understanding to constitute it but arises from itself, without any warning to prepare us, and without any repetition to accustom us to it, it imposes itself as an actuality without cause, autonomous, spontaneous, fully realized of itself and always in advance of any knowledge we might later glean from it. The phenomenon that does not take on the figure of an object fully realizes itself without announcing itself, but has also already finished realizing itself before we have even begun to wonder what is happening (to us). Furthermore, not only does its happening impose itself on us through its effect of surprise and its advance, but it remains for us an enigma, unlike the object, which stays ever controllable to the very extent that we foresee, produce, and reproduce it—controllable, and thus finite and, so to speak, transparent. In fact, the nonobjective phenomenon, precisely because it cannot be assured of any permanence (as is claimed by οὐσία by itself and the object by the understanding), does not remain, does not persist, does not perdure, but comes about and passes; thus, it always imposes itself, to an extent that is unquestionable but that remains to be determined, as an event. In the case of the event, comprehension always arrives late, but above all comprehension itself *constitutes* this delay, producing it and provoking it. And therefore, as if its intuitive surplus were always calling for a meaning still in reserve and a concept yet to be conquered, or in short, a semantic excess that hangs over us, the event always leaves comprehension behind it, with an "*original delay* of all understanding."[4] Put otherwise: "The greatest events and thoughts—but the greatest thoughts are the greatest events—are the last to be comprehended: generations that are their contemporaries do not *experience* (*erleben*) these sorts of events,—they live right past them (*leben daran vorbei*)" (Nietzsche).[5]

With the event of the nonobjective phenomenon, we find ourselves in fact always and from the outset *after* its event; for intrinsic to the event is precisely that it *happens* [*se passer*], that from the outset it has *already passed*, and thus has always *passed us by*; therefore, we find ourselves still asking after the fact, when it is already too late, "What happened?" ["*Que s'est-il passé?*"][6] It is precisely because it accomplishes its actuality more perfectly than the object, with more autonomy, clarity, and better results, and because it proves itself to be infinitely more actual than the object, that the event of the nonobjective phenomenon also remains infinitely less comprehensible, or more exactly, less rationalizable than the object.

Thus, it would appear that the distinction between the region of phenomena having the status of objects (permanent phenomena) and the region of phenomena having the status of events (nonobjective phenomena), which metaphysics would like to establish as self-evident, proves to be untenable. In fact, this distinction completely overturns the ultimate principle of metaphysics itself: if, for the object, all that is actual proves itself to be rational (and vice versa), then for the nonobjective, that is, for that which happens and passes, the more its actuality is accomplished, the less it satisfies—at first glance—the criterion of rationality. That is not to say that the nonobjective event lacks reason, since, on the contrary, it harbors within itself more than we could ever discover; but, because our efforts to rationalize it always come after the fact, *post eventum*, at dusk when the owl takes flight, and because our progressive effort will remain not only always a step behind, but above all lacking in reason, in the irremediable uncertainty of never being able to reach the meaning of what nevertheless was, in the moment, in the moment that has always already passed, perfectly visible. Right away we suspect that objectivity and its conditions of establishment, if they do indeed define a mode of rationality, only define *one* such mode, and do not exhaust all the figures of this rationality. The object confines the rationality of that the presence of which *persists*—at least for a certain period—by itself into οὐσία, or through the gaze of the mind into *intuitus*. The nonobjective, as it happens and passes, does not avoid all rationality, as if we were dealing with a pure and simple absurdity; rather, it suggests the rationality of that which does not persist in presence, or more exactly, of a nonpersistent, noninsistent presence, because it happens and passes. Clearly, that which happens and passes in presence cannot become rationally intelligible in the same light as that which persists (for at least a period of time) in presence. The gaze does not see two manners of presence that are so temporally different in the same way, or in the same light.

In fact, the two primacies (the primacy of the persistent object according to the *ratio essendi*, and the primacy of the happening and passing nonobject according to the *ratio cognoscendi*) that hold up the two manners of temporalization only seem to directly oppose each other because the distinction between the two phenomenalities that is supposed to determine them has gone unexamined until now. And this distinction remains unexamined because the very ground of the distinction of phenomena into objects and nonobjects remains so as well. For metaphysics, this ground resides in the supposed equivocity of two modes of appearance that are absolutely distinct, cut off from each other by a clear separation that cannot even be questioned. But why couldn't the object and the nonobject instead be registered within a same phenomenality, where they would diverge only by the variations that they introduce into it? If in metaphysics we presuppose that entities may be *divided* into objects and nonobjects according to two absolutely heterogeneous modes of phenomenality, couldn't we instead try to suture this unjustified distinction by considering the contrary hypothesis: that starting with a single and univocal phenomenality, the phenomena end up by *diverging* into objects or nonobjects according to the variations that they introduce into the dimensions of the same, unique phenomenality, so that they are not opposed as two irrationally foreign phenomenalities, but instead diverge as by degrees, according to the extent of these variations? If the hypothesis of the equivocity of the two phenomenalities results in the contradiction of two primacies between objects and nonobjects, would it not be better to test the hypothesis of a univocal phenomenality that allows us to pass by gradations from the object to the nonobject, and back?

This hypothesis may even be stated formally: since the apparent evidence for the radical distinction between two phenomenalities was fed by the fact that we are able to characterize nonobjective happening and passage by the negation (or even denial) of the categories, while on the contrary these are validated in the case of the object, it might therefore seem that the inaptitude and the indigence of the nonobject with regard to the categories attests to its absolute foreignness when faced by the exactitude of the object. But then what would happen if we succeeded in overturning the opposition, by showing, this time, that the indigence and the inaptitude characterize the object as well, albeit in a different way? Or further, that the object, far from accomplishing without cost the positivity of a clear and distinct apparition, on the contrary pays for its evident certainty with a *different* indigence and a different inaptitude, that of a poor, deficient, and diminished phenomenon? It may be that the object, far from setting the model of reference for the phenomenon and establishing the norms of general rationality, offers only a figure that is impoverished, restricted, and, *for this very reason*, more convenient, more practical, and easier for us to manipulate. And even so, if the object could just as easily be read as a poor variation of the nonobject as the nonobject is read as a failure of the features of the object, would it not be necessary to infer that these two variations (indigence and failure) come from the same, univocal phenomenality? The ground of their distinction would then reside, precisely, in their common phenomenality, which alone makes possible the variations that it grants them.

Before getting to this point, it will first be necessary to show that the object is defined in the final instance as a poor and conditional phenomenon, unlike the nonobject, the phenomenality of which is still to be examined. And in fact, the object still appears, but only in the condition of a phenomenon of the second order, one that has undergone a *diminutio capitis*—more precisely, a *diminutio phenomenalitatis*.

§ 26. The Condition of the Object

The object of course appears and, in a sense, appears massively, by occupying the phenomenal scene with its enduring, persistent presence, which monopolizes presence to the extent that it succeeds in maintaining itself, to the point of seizing presence and expelling the nonobjective phenomena from the space of manifestation. The object *occupies* phenomenality, because it invades it and imposes itself there. This occupation nevertheless does not suppress a different modality, quantitatively and qualitatively irreducible to objectivity, of this unique phenomenality: it is limited to covering it over. In fact, the nonobjects always continue to appear, next to, behind, and beneath the scene colonized by the objects. Or indeed, more often than we notice, they appear across and in the very midst of the objects' scene, suddenly and briefly transfixed by the flash of an event, which no sooner happened than it disappeared, all the more quickly completed as it darkened and blinded the phenomena of objects more profoundly. But before describing the extreme phenomenality of that which happens, passes, exceeds the gaze, and disappears in this way (see §§ 27–28), and in order to prepare ourselves for such a description, we must start by describing the flat and middling phenomenality of that which remains and persists under the gaze: the object.

The phenomenality of the object occupies the entire phenomenal scene because it covers it over, but without penetrating it entirely, or completely seizing hold of it. Why this holding back? Because the object appears, despite or even by virtue of its persistence in presence, only in the mode of a poor, diminished phenomenon. And this impoverishment is in no way optional, since on the contrary it assures the object its chief privilege: certainty. The phenomenal impoverishment of the object lies in the fact that it must in this way satisfy the conditions of possibility, which of course guarantee its appearing in the mode of a certainty, but which, in return, exclude from this appearing as uncertain and nonobjective all that which cannot (or must not) submit to those conditions. The object manifests itself, then, as that which *remains* of the phenomenal flow once it has been regulated by "the standards of reason,"[7] screened through the filter of the concepts of the understanding, in short, judged by the norms of the a priori. Descartes was probably the first to have thematized this object determined by subtraction when he submitted the Greek question "What do I know?" to a second question, which limited the first question's scope and disqualified it: "What can I know with certainty?" The requirement of certainty indeed forces us to assign knowledge not to the truth as such—with the movement of its disclosure, the time of its manifestation, perhaps also the moment of its decline, in short with all of its *event*—but to the truly certain or to the certainly true: "We should attend only to those objects (*illa tantum objecta*) of which our minds seem capable of having certain and indubitable cognition (*certam et indubitatam cognitionem*)."[8] In this way, we obtain the object: a thing, but reduced to that which the face-to-face (*ob-*) sees and grasps of it as subjected (*-jectum*) to it, to the view and the knowledge (*certum*, from *cerno*) of everyone, or rather of every gaze (*intuitus*), provided that it knows how to keep it in view (*tueri*) and thus to certify it (take it into certainty, as one takes a prisoner). The object is defined as that which remains of the thing once it has been subjected to the requirements of certainty: "so that what is left at the end [of the process of subtraction] may be exactly and only what is certain and unshakeable—*ita tandem* praecise remaneat, *illud* tantum, quod certum *est et inconcussum*."[9]

Descartes sets the paradigm for this reduction in his analysis of the piece of wax: once its customary sensible qualities have been eliminated (*remotis*) by the modification of the ambient surroundings (when put by the fire, the form, the color, the hardness, the smell, even the taste of the wax all change), that is to say once the wax has been reduced to what the pure *cogitatio* (without the senses) can grasp of it, the wax ceases to appear as a thing that is complex, multiple, with undefined properties, ever changing, never stable, in short, a thing in and of itself, in order to become "nothing other than some extended, flexible, and changeable *x—nihil aliud quam extensum quid, flexibile, mutabile*."[10] I am careful here to avoid translating this *quid* by the usual "*something*," precisely because it is no longer a thing that is at issue, in whatever sense that is understood, but a reduced, diminished, and residual end, a pure and simple *quid*, what Kant will call an object = x. All that remains of the wax and its sensible (and thus intelligible) splendor is the minimum required to assign extension and its modes to a place. This minimum results from a reduction—the formula "nothing other than" counts here as the generic definition of the object, which only is as *nihil aliud quam*, is never other than that which the gaze keeps under its guard, is not authorized to change without permission, so as not to *trick* the gaze's attention, and is to *remain* always that which it must be authorized to be, to *persist* in its definition, as it was registered by the *cogitatio*.[11] The object results from this reduction, because it is merely one with it. The reduction objectivizes, and thus the object appears as a reduction of the thing, like a thing reduced to the gaze.

This reduction, as it happens by itself, of the thing to the rank of the object, which congeals beneath the certifying gaze, literally demands the limitation of knowledge to a simplicity and a purity that experience will no longer disturb: "They alone [arithmetic and geometry] are concerned with an object so pure and simple (*objectum ita purum et simplex*) that they make no assumptions that experience might render uncertain (*quod experientia reddiderit incertum*)."[12] In order to attain and keep [*garder*] certainty, it is necessary to know how to restrict and sometimes even annul the experience itself of the thing. The privilege of mathematics flows from this restriction, rather than imposing it: indeed, mathematics alone proposes clear and practicable criteria for discriminating between the certain and the uncertain, in particular the abstraction of matter. For what is proper to matter, or rather, what is proper to that which the Greeks understood by ὕλη, consists as much in the *play* of its material, its looseness and variation, as in this material itself;[13] the difficulty in knowing matter lies in its imprecision, in its power to *render* imprecise, to blur contours. Mathematics frees itself from this imprecision by wholly reducing ὕλη. But we can also read this imprecision as an ontic privilege, and not only as an epistemological handicap. For only this imprecision allows the thing to become other than itself, to be unceasingly what it was not or what it will no longer be; and the issue here is not only that of contingency and uncertainty (indeed, these qualifications already presuppose the privileging of the point of view of knowledge), but that of the mode of temporality of that which, contrary to the object, does not claim to persist in presence, but presents itself according to a happening that passes on and passes beyond. What the obsession with certainty apprehends solely as an imprecision of ὕλη must in fact be understood, from the point of view of the manner of being and its temporality, as that which allows for the radical eventness of the thing. The thing happens, while the object (the thing reduced to certainty) persists.

The privilege of mathematics in the constitution of objects, or put another way, in the restriction of things to certainty, thus itself has nothing mathematical about it: it derives entirely from the aptitude of mathematics to eliminate the least residue of eventness from things—to constitute them into objects by demoting them [*les destituant*] as events. As a matter of fact, Descartes did not remain at the level of the criteria offered by the two mathematical sciences already available to him (criteria that were badly deduced and ambiguous, and moreover misunderstood by the mathematicians themselves, who were unable to see further than their disciplinary practice), but undertook to draw out from them and formalize two fundamentals in order to establish them as absolute criteria of the "universal science," or *mathesis universalis*. This science can be practiced only (*tantum*) where models and/or parameters are identified: "all [the x] exclusively (*illa omnia tantum*) where a certain order and measure (*aliquis ordo et mensura*) can be examined are related to *Mathesis*."[14] The formulation "all [the x] exclusively" ("*illa omnia tantum*") could seem surprising: if we are talking about *all*, why restrict it to certain "x" in opposition to others? But on the contrary, it becomes completely clear if we note that the focus is on *all those x which* satisfy the restrictive criteria of being submitted to order and measure, and *they alone*. Things become objects through the elimination of those things, or more precisely, through the elimination of that in those things which does not allow itself to be abstracted according to order and measure. This *exclusively* (*tantum*) designates the operation of the reduction of the thing into an object, the subtraction required by the passage from truth to certainty, the shortage of eventness that alone makes the object possible.[15] And this subtraction, which makes the thing into a (certain) object, can be accomplished only through submission to the *mathesis* and its two criteria. The formula "*objectum purae Matheseôs*" ("object of pure science")[16] must be understood as a pleonasm, for there is no object except for and through the certain and certifying science.

We shouldn't be surprised that Kant's definition of the object carries out fully the decisions made by Descartes: it is limited to removing the ambiguities that the notion of *mathesis* (whether it be *universalis* or *pura*) could not avoid. The object does not result from a reduction to the sole criteria of certainty used in mathematics or even those generalized from mathematics, but in general from a submission (and thus a restriction) to the laws of experience: "[R]epresentations, [. . .] which, *insofar as* they are connected and determinable in these relations (in space and time) according to laws of the unity of experience, are called *objects*."[17] The object does not proceed from the thing, but from representations; and not from all representations, but only those which are inscribed within the double condition of, first, pure forms of space and time, and then of a priori laws of experience. The object is defined as the *conditioned* representation of the thing, as the thing *conditionally*: "[T]here are two conditions under which alone the cognition of an object is possible: first, *intuition*, through which it is given, but only as phenomenon; second, *concept*, through which an object is thought that corresponds to this intuition."[18] The object does not depend indistinctly on *mathesis*, but precisely on two *conditions* (intuition and concept), and thus appears as reduced (led back and submitted) to them as its conditions. The object appears from the outset conditionally (like a prisoner freed conditionally), conditioned by intuition and the concept, that is to say, by what Descartes gathered under the single rubric of simple material natures.[19] But, just as the simple material natures draw their simplicity only from a relation to the *ego* ("*in ordine ad cognitionem nostram*" [in the order that corresponds to our knowledge of them] or "*respectu intellectus nostri*" [with respect to our intellect]),[20] so too do the intuition and the concept (the forms and the categories) draw their unity and their power to unify representations from the *I*, or more exactly from the "I think," as transcendental apperception: "The synthetic unity of consciousness is therefore an objective *condition* of all cognition, not merely something I myself need in order to cognize an object but rather something under which every intuition must stand (*unter [. . .] stehen*) *in order to become an object for me* (*für mich Objekt zu werden*)."[21] Being constituted as an object thus consists in losing the phenomenal autonomy and spontaneity of a thing showing itself from itself, that is to say, by its own event, and instead appearing no longer except conditionally, a condition that, in the end, leads back to the rule of the "I think" over the object itself. The object begins when the *diminutio phenomenalitatis* of the thing suppresses its right to the event. There is no object that is not poor in phenomenality.

Henceforth we can clarify the condition of the object (in the double sense of *conditio*: its rank in phenomenality and its grounding) by taking up in greater detail the four rubrics under which Kant grouped the pure concepts of the understanding, otherwise known as the categories that organize the sensible given, already submitted to the pure forms of space and of time, into objects (see § 25). These four rubrics (quantity, quality, relation, and modality) define the phenomenon as object, and yet they already sketch, through counterposition, the phenomenon as event. — The object first appears in terms of *quantity*, for its visibility always results from a sum of already quantifiable elementary visibilities, such that the whole of its phenomenon is obtained by the addition of its finite parts. Reciprocally, the phenomenon of the object can always be divided into as many parts as one would like—for example, in order better to know it by knowing each of the parts of which it always remains the sum. The global apparition that results is therefore always finite, and thus foreseeable. The object appears in such a way that before it even comes to pass, I can know precisely how far it will go and where it will stop. I can see it, then, without yet having seen it; literally, I can *fore*see it. It appears under the mode of pre-vision, according to a phenomenality that is restricted and alienated in and through my gaze.

The object also appears according to *quality*. This has to do with what Kant terms as well the intensive magnitude, the intensity of the quality that is marked by graduated degrees. In the object, in order for it to be defined, its quality requires that we expose it according to a degree; each degree must in turn be measured, and it is understood as it is composed—on the basis of the preceding degrees, with which it remains homogeneous, despite its difference. Thus, each degree reached by the intensity of quality fixes that intensity and determines it clearly and distinctly. In order to find the object (or retrieve it from among others), it is enough to locate this degree in the scale that unites it to and distinguishes it from the other degrees. Whence there follows this other characteristic of every object: it can be repeated in the same way; or more exactly, there is no object unless I can repeat it at my convenience. Yet, I can only repeat it if I assume that it can be repeated identically on different occasions. But the fact is that nothing, not even the simplest object, can be reproduced identically. This is so because, first, there is always the possibility of variation in the figure or in the process of its production, such that, at the least, the form varies.[22] Also, the material used in the manufacture differs by definition and, because the aim is the production of a series of multiple objects, the individuation of objects by matter is enough to prevent their identity. Finally, even if we were to admit that the perfect homogeneity of materials used in the duplication of a form (itself assumed to be absolutely intangible) would allow for the maintenance of a perfect likeness between the objects of a production in series (which in reality cannot be), the irreducible game of succession in time (the date and the hour of production, "traceability") would still be there to distinguish in principle the first object from its reproduction, and this one from all the others. Strictly speaking, then, I will never be able to speak of two objects as the "same." And yet, I claim to be able to say it, and for good reason: I can in effect always replace a technological object that is defective with another one that is as closely identical to it that the second one will "work"; and I will even watch over the substitution to make sure it is as exact as possible (by choosing a "genuine part" with the same characteristics, etc.). But how, then, can I say that two objects are "the same thing," when at the moment when I am saying it, I have in front of my own eyes two objects, produced on different dates and actually juxtaposed in space? I say it because I very consciously decide *not to take into account* their material distinctions, nor their spatial and temporal differences, in order to retain only their formal identity. I make them identical because I abstract in them the form (supposedly unique) from the matter, from space, and from time. Therefore, the technological object is reproduced only because in it I neutralize matter, space, and time; these become indifferent, and thus invisible. This is possible precisely because in the manufacture, matter was eliminated, as were space and time. Paradoxically, the technological object in this way appears as a *dematerialized* and *formalized* phenomenon, or rather one that is radically idealized because reduced to form—and subsequently referred to using equivalent names such as "concept," standard, administrative norm, technical specifications, patent, "product," brand, and so on. As a consequence, the object, always reproducible and available (there are always *more*, for as long as and every time we wish), no longer has any need for the least bit of eventness. Reduced to form, or rather to my concept of it, the phenomenon takes on the condition of the object, according to a phenomenality that is once again alienated in my gaze.

The object appears next according to *relation*, whether that of the substance to its accidents (inherence), or that of a substance interacting with another substance (community), or that of cause to effect (causality). I will privilege this last relation because it offers much more than just one relation among others: it allows one "to advance to metaphysics," to the "great principle [. . .] which teaches that *nothing happens without a sufficient reason*; that is to say, that nothing happens without its being possible for him who should sufficiently understand things, to give a reason sufficient to determine why it is so and not otherwise."[23] For the relation of cause and effect benefits from a massive privilege over the other two: it suffers no exception, and nothing is phenomenalized unless it takes on the condition either of an effect, or of a cause, or, most often, that of an effect of a cause that, in turn, becomes the cause of a subsequent effect. Put otherwise, "*Everything* is either a source or derived from a source" ("ἅπαντα γὰρ ἤ ἀρχὴ ἤ ἔξ ἀρχῆς") (Aristotle);[24] or "*No* thing is a being that is neither a cause nor an effect" ("*Nullum autem est ens, quod non sit vel effectus, vel causa*") (Suárez);[25] or "*No* thing exists of which it is not possible to ask what is the cause of its existence" ("*Nulla res existit de qua non possit quaeri quaenam sit causa cur existat*") (Descartes);[26] "all things are both caused or causing" (Pascal);[27] and further, "[E]verything that happens has its cause" ("*[A]lles was geschieht hat seine Ursache*") (Kant).[28] This principle admittedly is not self-evident, so restrictive does it seem in its conditions and imperialist in its universality; yet the decision that imposes it, for its part, does go without saying: the principle of sufficient reason justifies the cause as the privileged (but not the sole) operator of reason—of reason in the precise sense of explaining the phenomenon, rendering reason to it [*rendre raison du phénomène*], reframing it according to "the level of reason," submitting it to the condition of its intelligibility. In what sense, then, must the phenomenon be reframed? In what sense must it absolutely be rendered a reason? What is it missing such that it needs in this way a reason (re)given, as if from outside? Leibniz responds quite directly to these questions: the phenomenon is missing a reason to happen, according to the principle that "*nothing happens* without its being possible [. . .] to give a reason sufficient to determine why it is *so and not otherwise*."[29] In other words, reason itself results from the principle that requires the transformation of an event (that which *happens*) into that which "is so and not otherwise," and therefore into that which cannot not be such as it is, namely, an object. Reason, and the cause when it requires one, has as its function, its privilege, and its sole ambition the reduction of that which seems at first approach to be an event (that which "happens") into an object, which after the fact will no longer be able to be other than "so and not otherwise." The essential contingency of the event must give way to the absolutely necessary identity of the object. And the cause enters in here only to the extent that it works to put into operation the principle that every event can be reduced to the condition of the object.

But this condition of the object must (or should) be imposed on the event only for the benefit of my knowledge and to the detriment of the thing itself, the phenomenality of which starting from itself is ordered to surrender itself to reason—and thus to let reason render it to *me* as an object at the disposal of knowledge. Still to be justified is this overturning of the thing, which disappears as an event showing itself from itself in order to appear only as an object constituted by me, and thus as an *alienated thing*. By what right can we declare that "when we consider things in the order that corresponds to our knowledge of them (*in ordine ad cognitionem nostram*), our view of them must be different from what it would be if we were speaking of them in accordance with how they exist in reality (*aliter [. . .] quam si de iisdem loquamur prout revera existunt*)"?[30] What does it mean that it is necessary to know objects otherwise than as things truly are—that is, as they arrive and pass away? Metaphysics never explicitly asks itself this question, not even in Descartes and Kant; at best its silence suggests that the power of knowing objects is justified by itself—everything that can be done has the right to be done; the reason rendered can (in principle) reduce events to the rank of objects, and so this reduction will in fact be carried out, whatever the phenomenal or ontological price may be. But, strangely, even from the point of view of knowledge (against that of the thing itself), even in accepting the privilege (lacking reason) of the principle of reason, putting it into operation through the universal search for a cause turns out most of the time to be impracticable.

To begin with, the principle of reason allows for two presuppositions, each of which is contestable. — First: that the cause precedes the effect. Yet, in the order of discovery, the effect comes first and the cause only appears after the fact, *ex eventu*, to help explain the effect. The cause, *if* it appears, appears (or at least makes itself known, is inferred or simply supposed) under the condition of the effect, which is present first, first accomplished, because it arises not first of all as an effect lacking a cause, but straightaway from itself, autonomous and solitary, surprising me precisely because I do not understand it. Thus, according to existence and actuality themselves, the cause depends on the effect, even if it claims to precede it according to knowledge. Only once it is inferred from the fact of the effect (or more exactly, once the fact is interpreted as an effect, and then the cause sought for) can the cause, after validation of the theory through repeated experiments, seem to precede it: its late epistemological anteriority will always result from its originary ontic delay.[31] In fact and in principle, understanding phenomenality consists inversely in conceiving the advance of the visible over my gaze, or in short in awakening with the least delay possible to the sudden arising of the event; the cause and its delay (even if we suppose its epistemological validity for objects) can thus in no way help us to see the phenomenon appear in and through itself, in its primordial glory as event.

Next, and more important, the principle leaves open another question: what status should we grant a phenomenon if its manifestation in fact is not accompanied (or not yet accompanied) by one or several causes? Must we keep it in reserve from phenomenality and exclude it from the realm of knowledge while we await better days (progress in research on causes, broadening of the field of investigation)? But if this *interim* lasts, if its strict causal interpretation finally proves inaccessible, must we definitively eliminate this phenomenon by excluding it from already objectivized territory? To where do we exile it, and by what right? Does the *fact* that a phenomenon happens without an assignable cause, that is to say, without a certain form of rationality—for us, with our finite understandings—justify by *right* its expulsion outside the bounds of phenomenality? If a phenomenon refuses to submit itself to the conditions of our intelligibility (itself supposedly univocal and limited)—in short, if it refuses its alienation in our gaze—does this authorize us to make it a refugee, cast out from the visible? There will be no answer to these questions for as long as we fail to hear them in their phenomenological sense: if objects result from the disappearance of the phenomenality of the event, and then by their being placed in conformity with rendered reason [*la raison rendue*], then they must also be understood as phenomena, but phenomena that have been abstracted from their cause, and thus made destitute of their variations of apparition. This destitution, this reduction, or this impoverishment are registered on the single horizon of univocal phenomenality. Metaphysics can no more exile events from the phenomenality of things than their reduction to the rank of objects can deprive them, according to phenomenology, of phenomenality. It remains for us to question the transition from one region to the other, or rather from one realm of phenomenality to the other.

Finally, the object always appears under postulates of empirical thought in general, defined on the basis of categories of modality. At issue are the *conditions* that phenomena are compelled to take on in order to become, in connection with the "power of knowing," objects. These conditions are formulated in three pairs: possibility-impossibility, existence-nothingness, necessity-contingency. And yet, these pairs do not stand on equal footing: the first, which puts into play possibility, defines preeminently not only the possibility of the other two, but the possibility of every condition, the very condition (foundation) of objectivity. For, if we ask on what condition a phenomenon deserves the title of object, we must answer that it is on the condition (transcendental, not merely logical) that it be *possible*, which is to say that it "agree with the formal conditions (*Bedingungen*) of experience (in accordance with intuition and concepts)."[32] Its possibility of appearing therefore does not lie in its autonomous power of phenomenalization as an event, but in the rules of experience for us, for "empirical thinking in general." Kant thus arrives, following Descartes, at the stupefying equivalence between the principles (of objects) and the "postulates" of our (empirical) thinking. The conditions of our thinking (experience) are at the same time the conditions of the phenomenality of things, and no longer the inverse—and thus the *objects* either do not appear, or they become the *subjects* of our conditions of thinking. And if it is necessary to choose between the phenomenon in the proper sense (the event) and our thinking, then we will take as "conditions" those of thinking, and not those of phenomena. Consequently, the phenomenon must end up being reduced to the impoverished condition of the *conditioned*. We know the quite famous definition of the conditions of the object, and especially of the condition in general: "The *a priori* conditions of a possible experience in general are at the same time (*zugleich*) conditions of the possibility of the objects (*Gegenstände*) of experience."[33] It is customary, and rightly so, to draw from this the conclusion that the objects of experience allow for the same conditions as experience itself, without attaching great attention to another, more essential consequence: if the conditions of phenomenality of the objects of experience are one and the same with the conditions of this experience itself (our own), then our experience defined as the condition of the objects concerns *only objects* and remains the *condition of objects alone*. If objects share the same a priori conditions as our experience, then our experience is limited a priori to objects. Thus, our experience does not reach the entire field of the experience of phenomenality, and in particular leaves totally open the question of the phenomenality of the event.

Moreover, in what does the possibility consist that the a priori conditions of experience govern, or claim to govern? We call possible that which takes on quantity, quality, and relation according to our time and our space, and thus ultimately that which does not contradict our minds; or we call possible everything that does not contradict itself—that is, that does not contradict itself *in our* concept, and thus does not contradict our concept. The noncontradiction of our concept assures the object, this diminished phenomenon, a possibility, and therefore an essence—on one condition: our own. Endowed with this possible essence, to what other existence can this diminished phenomenon lay claim? To an existence that simply "completes the possibility," itself restricted to our conception;[34] to exist therefore means simply to place outside of thought (or *extra causas*) that which thought had already validated as possible, since it did not contradict itself by not contradicting thought. Existence becomes, then, the result of production: the final step in the constitution of the object through the diminution of the phenomenon and the submission of its phenomenality to my gaze. To exist no longer implies any bursting forth into the world of that which shows itself in itself, to the point of being truly through itself, but simply brings to an end, through a simple position administered technically (a production), the making available of the object through and for the concept. Existence is limited to validating the essence, but adds nothing to it and, especially, never contests or surpasses it. The possibility no longer defines only the essence, but in the end governs existence itself. In the world there exists only that which was already thinkable and possible for me, and never a phenomenon that bursts forth from within itself. Nothing happens, and the existence of the object simply serves to name the ban on the event.

§ 27. Concerning the Distinction of Phenomena into Objects and Events

In front of this evidence, in front of the "evidence" (in the common sense) of the evidence (in the Cartesian sense), we cannot avoid a question: *must* every phenomenon take the shape of an object, a thing alienated in the knowing subject, a phenomenon diminished by the measure of the limits of experience for us? Discussing the supposed obviousness [*évidence*] of the pair subject-object in Rickert (and in fact in all of neo-Kantianism), Heidegger raised the inevitable objection: "However, is every being necessarily an object? [. . .] Plainly not."[35] A being, insofar as it appears, may also not take the figure of an object, because objectness, understood precisely in its obviousness, only appears following upon a weak phenomenality:

weak, not strong, as assumed by metaphysics since Descartes. Weak, because the object appears according to a phenomenality that has been imposed on it, following upon conditions other than its own, or which become its own only based on a point of view that is not its own, but that of the gaze that guards it and puts itself on guard *against* it, now become the *ob*-ject. For the conditions of possibility of the *object* (of experience) never refer back to the thing itself, but instead to that which the conditions of possibility of experience promulgate concerning the object. That is to say, ultimately what is retained by the two criteria of the *mathesis universalis*: order (of models) and measure (of parameters), or numbers and figures. Consequently, or rather by contrast, we can and must consider, at least as a possibility, a phenomenality that would free the phenomenon from its status of object by freeing it from these numbers and figures. Here Novalis speaks with perfect exactitude:

> When numbers and figures no longer
> Are keys to everything created,
> When those who sing or kiss
> Know more than the learned scholars,
> When the world returns to a free life
> And to the world,
> [. . .] Then at a single secret word
> This whole inverted mode of being (*Das ganze verkehrte Wesen*) will fly away.[36]

What inverted mode of being is Novalis speaking of here? Without a doubt he is speaking of the mode of being of what Nietzsche will challenge as an "upside-down world,"[37] the world where nothing appears unless transcribed in terms of objects by submission to the conditions of experience, as defined by the *mathesis universalis*: "Our knowledge has become scientific to the degree that it can apply number and measure,"[38] namely, the order and measure that are referred to the world. To free that which is (*Wesen*) from that which inverts it into so many objects, in order once again to allow things, henceforth free of the *mathesis universalis*, to appear as they give themselves and no longer according to the conditions of my reception: this is perhaps the whole program, the sole *end*, of what we call the "end of metaphysics." But we still must describe this overturning of the "upside-down world," or rather the overturning of its "inverted mode of being" ("*verkehrte Wesen*").

But can this liberation announced by Novalis in fact be accomplished?

What example does experience furnish us with of a reestablishment of the inverted mode of being of things? What experience do we have of a phenomenon that passes from the status of object to that of a free thing? It turns out that Kandinsky has described, in a famous account and with the precision of a phenomenologist, just such a liberation of the object in a thing appearing from itself:

> It was the hour when dusk draws in. I returned home with my painting box having finished a study, [. . .] and *suddenly* saw an *indescribably* beautiful picture, pervaded by an *inner glow*. At first, I *stopped short* and then quickly approached this mysterious picture, on which I could discern only forms and colors and whose content was *incomprehensible*. At once, I discovered the key to the puzzle: it was a picture I had painted, standing on its side against the wall. The next day, I tried to *rediscover* my impression of the picture from the previous evening by daylight. I only half succeeded, however; even on its side, I constantly recognized objects, and the fine bloom of dusk was missing. Now I could see clearly that *objects harmed* my pictures.[39]

Let's go over these elements. At issue is the appearance of "an indescribably beautiful picture" as opposed to a mere "object," or in other words, the bursting forth of an exceptional phenomenon instead of and in the place of an object, or, conversely, the disappearance of an object allowing the bursting forth of a matchless phenomenon. This passage (the overturning of the inverted world) must be understood on the basis of its end point: it proves to be impossible to *rediscover* the effect of the painting (its indescribable beauty) because we cannot repeat the light of dusk, and no longer can we see the initial bursting forth; in its place, we always "recognize" only "objects." The object can only be repeated, and thus what constituted its privilege (the power solely to be repeated, because it can solely be [re]produced) becomes a handicap: it can never "produce itself," in the sense of putting itself forward and into the light by itself alone. If it can always be "cognized," it owes this as well to the fact that it can only be *re*cognized, while on the contrary the painting owes its "indescribable beauty" solely to the fact that it bursts forth on the basis of itself, without production, or *re*production. And it bursts forth because it bursts forth *on the basis of itself*, following its own "inner glow," when the light of dusk allows it, without even taking the precaution of making itself *comprehensible*: yes, it makes colors appear and even forms, but I nevertheless see them without *recognizing them, or understanding them.*

Why do they remain "incomprehensible" to me, even though I see them perfectly well? Because I do not foresee them and because they answer to no expectation, strategic foresight, or project that I could have conceived for them in advance; I see them at a delay, without already having a concept of them, without being able to describe them by anticipation—that is, without being able to delimit them and organize them in a model according to the parameters that frame it and constrain them. The painting, overturned and put out of perspective by its leaning sideways against the wall, bursts forth without warning, because it obeys its own *inner glow*, shows itself in itself because it gives itself on the basis of itself. It stops me short, stunned and disoriented, prohibiting access, because the bursting forth of the painting in its indescribable beauty prohibits my at-will entry into an abode that it inhabits in the first person. This initiative of appearing, with the unrepeatable unforeseeability of a spontaneous autonomy, attests to a realm of phenomenality that challenges the object and to which the object forms an obstacle—the phenomenality of the *event*. Kandinsky here records the major turning point in his career: it is not a matter of passing from figuration to abstraction, but, far more radically, of ceasing to paint by (re)producing objects and, crossing a border of what he henceforth looks upon as past, of starting to paint by letting the thing itself happen as an event. The painting imposes, with a primordial clarity [*une première évidence*], the possibility of inverting the "inverted world" of objects into the free world of events.

Thus, events can, in fact, occur and surprise, by inverting objects of the "inverted world" and by serenely contradicting the conditions of possibility (of the objects) of experience—attesting that these are only the conditions of possibility of *objects* and of them alone, defined by subtraction from full phenomenality. Events also and especially contradict the conditions of possibility of experience itself—of *our* conditional experience. For another modality of experience, experience without condition, defies the prohibitions and the limits that metaphysics imposes: experience crosses the limit of its supposed conditions of possibility. Nietzsche shows this perfectly by analyzing the phenomenon of lightning: "If I say: 'Lightning flashes,' I have posited the flashing once as activity and once as subject, and have thus added on to the event (*Geschehen*) a being that is not identical with the event but that *remains, is,* and does not '*become*' (*nicht wird*). —*To posit the event as effecting* (*Wirken*), and *effect* (*Wirkung*) *as being*: that is the *twofold* error, or *interpretation,* of which we are guilty. Thus, e.g., 'The lightning flashes'—'to flash' is a state of ourselves; but we don't take it to be an effect (*Wirkung*) on us. Instead we say: 'Something flashing' as an 'in-itself,' and then look for an author for it—the 'lightning.'"[40] What "error" is he talking about? An error of interpretation, where one attempts to apply to an event (*Geschehen*) that which only fits an object, as it happens in the first two analogies of perception established by Kant: to begin with, the principle of the permanence of substance, according to which: "In all change of phenomena substance persists"; and then: "All alterations occur (*geschehen*) in accordance with the law of the connection of cause and effect."[41] From this, one concludes that, since the lightning happens as a change, the issue is that of a change *of* the lightning, a change that implies, as its condition of possibility, a change *in* the lightning, and thus a persisting substratum (the lightning itself). And, since one interprets this change in the substratum (the lightning) as the effect of a cause, one infers a different cause, another substratum.

Thus, in order to respect the conditions of possibility of an *object* of experience, we construct an inexact description of the phenomenon of the lightning, immediately doubled by an invariable substratum and a variable accident, and then by an effect and a cause, resulting in completely missing the essential character of this event—its *event*-character. The objective interpretation of the phenomenon masks and misses its eventness. For the lightning, like every event of which it offers an elementary type, happens without a substratum, not because it would lack permanence, but because it has no need of any; or rather, because the concept of permanence has no pertinence for its description as the effect of a cause; and it happens without a cause, not because it would lack one (like a chance occurrence or an accident), nor even because it would dispense with any by some sort of grace (like the rose "without a why"), but because it can never be understood as an effect (nor as a cause), since its atomic and (literally) *fulgurant* uniqueness arranges no place, nor perhaps any time (according to its "vulgar concept") to the least ontic difference between two terms of a relation (causal or otherwise). The lightning, as pure event, remains without analogy to an other object of experience—precisely because it happens as an event that, at the instant of its occurrence, happens *alone*, without sharing the phenomenal stage with anything else, and thus without ever being solidified as a relative object, tied and analogous to others. Like every other event, the phenomenon of lightning coincides perfectly with its own bursting forth and consists only in its passage. It passes, without ever (contrary to the picture bursting into Kandinsky's view) having even to free itself from the object that it never was—except in the confusion of its metaphysical interpretation.

The event does not allow itself, then, to be reduced to the status of a dropout from phenomenality, nor to that of an outcast from objectivity, which it would be incapable of bringing about in itself. In the freedom of its bursting forth, the event on the contrary stigmatizes the phenomenal diminution of the object by freeing itself from it; the event deplores the object's enslavement to the gaze that delimits it and the alienation of every manifestation of and by itself. The event does not limit phenomenality—it opens and safeguards it. The object does not realize phenomenality—it restricts and, in the end, masks it. We have to admit as a matter of fact, even if we comprehend only objects because they alone accept the conditions that we impose on them, that that in which we have being and life, that which we breathe as the air around us, is given to us by events alone. If we do not comprehend them, we must not conclude that they do not occur or appear, and even less that we do not know them, but only that they comprehend us, because they exceed the condition of an object enveloped by a gaze. Not all phenomena are reduced to objects; certain phenomena happen as events. Phenomena manifest themselves according to their distinction as objects (of a phenomenality restricted to the conditions of possibility of our experience) and as events (of a phenomenality without any restriction other than that of the mode of showing *itself* by itself).

But, by posing this distinction, we oppose ourselves to what Kant established in order to assure "the completeness of the system" of the critique of pure reason: the distinguishing of all objects into phenomena and noumena, which in effect assumes, beyond the opposition between the possible and the impossible (the final opposition in classical metaphysics) and responsible for grounding it, "a still higher concept," namely, that of "an object in general" ("*Gegenstand überhaupt*").[42] Indeed, the object dominates pure reason in all its uses, from the beginning to the end. From the beginning, since the "Aesthetic" describes the privilege of the intuition as "the art and the way for cognition to relate to objects" ("*auf Gegenstände beziehen*"), but clarifies the condition right away: intuition "takes place only insofar as the object is given."[43] Intuition is limited to the object, which conditions it. And at the end, since the "Transcendental Analytic," when it concludes by defining the four senses of nothingness by the deficiency of intuition, maintains even this absent intuition within the field of the object: nothingness itself is always thought of as an object, whether under the name of a concept *without object*, or of an *object* empty of concept, or of empty intuition without an *object*, or finally of an empty *object* without concept.[44] The table of nothingness, in complete conformity with the initial allocation of every intuition within the by definition limited horizon of the object, thus consecrates the triumph of objectness over phenomenality. Therefore, aside from directly contradicting Kant, contesting the primacy of the object as the "still higher concept" seems inconceivable.

Nevertheless, it may be that Kant himself weakened this primacy of the object, or at least pointed toward a surpassing of objectness. Fundamentally, the position seems to leave no ambiguity: "Appearances, to the extent that as objects they are thought in accordance with the unity of the categories, are called *phaenomena*. If, however, I suppose there to be things that are merely objects of the understanding [. . .], then such things would be called *noumena* (*intelligibilia*)."[45] And yet the parallelism between the two variants of the object is not maintained to the end, because "the transcendental use of a concept [. . .] consists in its being related to things *in general* and *in themselves*; its empirical use, however, in its being related merely to *phenomena*, i.e., objects of a possible *experience*." In other words, only the phenomenon benefits from a "relation to possible experience" or from "the general sensible condition under which objects can relate themselves to" the concept,[46] but not the thing in itself. The thing in itself remains an object, but an object without relation to possible experience, an object without relation to the knowing mind, and thus an object that does not conform to the very definition of the objectness of the object. In a word, only the phenomenon remains an object in the strict sense, while the thing in itself or the noumenon seem to be precisely *nonobjects*.

That the noumenon, in Kant's eyes, remains not only an object without giving intuition but finally a *nonobject* is confirmed in the distinction that he introduces between the noumenon in the positive sense and in the negative sense. The former (noumenon in the positive sense) remains an object, the "*object* of a *non-sensible intuition*, [. . .] namely [an] intellectual intuition, which, however, is not our own"; it indeed offers, then, a genuine object, although its objectness functions only for a nonfinite mind. On the contrary, the latter (in the negative sense) "is not an object of our sensible intuition," for "that which is not appearance (*Erscheinung*) cannot be an object of experience" and "cannot determine any object."[47] This type of negative noumenon is not an object *not* because we could not put it into operation as an object (this is how the noumenon in the *positive* sense is defined), but because it does not appear as an object *in general*. The point is first of all and essentially one of privilege: if the concept of a noumenon in the negative sense "is not at all contradictory," and is even "necessary," this is because it keeps open the possibility of "a thing that is not to be thought of as an object of the senses but rather as a thing in itself."[48] Kant expresses this another way, by recognizing that in the case of the noumenon (in the negative as well as the positive senses), "the entire use, indeed even all significance of the categories completely ceases,"[49] including, with them, the object.

Thus, Kant himself has admitted an exception to the empire of the objectness of the object. Never does he recognize it in a clearer way than when he makes recourse to the ever so strange and ambiguous notion of the object = x. Indeed, the question remains that of determining what makes possible the apparition of the phenomenon as object, "[f]or otherwise there would follow the absurd proposition that there is an appearance (*Erscheinung*) without *some thing* that appears (*etwas wäre, was da erscheint*)."[50] How do we define this "some thing" that appears? Clearly, it is not to be mistaken for the phenomenon itself, since it designates "the ground of this appearance (*Grund der Erscheinung*)," or even the "cause of appearance (*Ursache der Erscheinung*) (thus not itself appearance)," which remains more originary than the phenomenal sensible object that it makes possible, having therefore the status of "non-sensible cause (*nichtsinnliche Ursache*)."[51] In fact, this instance prior to the sensible apparition—that is, in Kantian terms, prior to the phenomenon reduced to the object—ought to remain knowable to us *without being subjected* to the conditions of objectness. These two petitions remain contradictory for Kant, but, like every great thinker, he does not shrink from the contradiction, which he attempts to assume by evoking the transcendental object as a (knowable) object that does not satisfy the conditions of experience. He thus terms it an "object in itself" ("*Gegenstand an sich selbst*"),[52] with a formula that is clearly contradictory, since an object is defined precisely as being for us, and thus no longer in itself or for itself, while the thing remains in itself only because it does not enter into objectness. Therefore, this object "signifies [. . .] a something = *X*," but "of which we know nothing at all (*wovon wir gar nichts wissen*), [. . .] as a correlate of [. . .] apperception." The transcendental object would be like an object that is resistant to knowledge, which is limited to making it possible, to arranging it, without being subject to it: it constitutes "no object of cognition" ("*kein Gegenstand der Erkenntnis*"), but only "the entirely undetermined thought of something in general."[53] In not shrinking back from this contradiction of objectness, the transcendental object testifies that Kant himself saw quite clearly that the concept of the object *does not constitute* the "still higher concept," which would dominate the whole of phenomenality (in its sharing with the noumenon); on the contrary, next to the phenomenon reduced to the object there emerges a nonobject phenomenon, made possible, behind objectness, by the "something in general" of which we know nothing, other than that it holds the possibility of a nonobjectifiable appearance. As a consequence, it becomes licit and at the least noncontradictory to substitute for the distinction of objects into phenomena and noumena another distinction: that of all phenomena into objects (diminished phenomena) and events (saturated phenomena).

§ 28. Without Cause

It is a matter, then, of conceiving the object starting from the phenomenon, and no longer the phenomenon starting from the object. But, in order to succeed in doing so, or at least in order to resist the unavowed primacy of the object, it is fitting to think through the contrasting figure of the phenomenon: the event. The object and the event contrast each other as two figures of phenomenality, one in terms of that which I can actively constitute, the other in terms of that which I can only receive: "In the first place, I note that whatever *takes place of itself* [*se fait*] or *occurs* [*arrive de nouveau*] is generally called by philosophers a 'passion' with regard to the subject to which it happens and an 'action' with regard to that which makes it happen" (Descartes).[54] The difficulty that we experience in recognizing the event in the phenomenal flow lies in the ordeal that "whatever *takes place of itself*" and "*occurs*" imposes on our passivity.

For the event happens: which means that it happens by itself, takes place and passes *of itself*, and thus that it imposes *itself* with an irresistible sovereignty that resists the alleged "spontaneity" of apperception and refutes its alleged originality. The refusal to think the passivity of the event, for the benefit of the object, provokes the birth of the cause. Recognizing the event implies acknowledging its irreducible, originary spontaneity—in short, its sovereignty; following Péguy, it is all about seeing "[w]hat the event is. And then, that it is sovereign," and taking note of the effect: "Isn't it evident that the event is in no way homogeneous?"[55] Indeed, it isn't homogeneous because it does not happen as the effect of our intention, of our intentionality, nor of our activity, but breaks the course of things, at least as we will and see them. The event happens despite us and without us, like an effect the cause of which we do not know, or which we do not ensure. Without a known cause, the event ceases even to appear as an effect.

It makes a mark on us all the more because it is not made by us, is not of our making. Moreover, it always appears to us at bottom as impossible, or even as *the* impossible, since it does not belong to the domain of the possible, of that of which we are able. It transgresses the possible and imposes itself as the realized impossible, precisely because it expects from us neither any possibility nor any actuality, solicits neither any solution nor any resolution in order to pass *of itself* and happen: "It is instead of receiving a solution—something ordinary, a solution—that we find that this problem, this difficulty, this impossibility has just passed through a point of resolution that is, so to speak, physical."[56] A point of physical resolution—this must be understood here as a resolution of fact, by the fait accompli of the happening [*l'advenue*] that asks nothing of anyone in order to be accomplished. The event has no cause and pleads no cause, especially not its own. It needs only itself to be accomplished: *it passes and passes of itself [il passe et se passe], and therefore it does without [se passe de] that which is not itself.* From now on, it becomes clear that we cannot recognize the event, or more precisely the original eventness of the phenomenon, for as long as we think according to metaphysics, since metaphysics always speaks in the name of the cause. Metaphysics knows nothing but the cause, and knows nothing except through the cause, either as cause or as effect; it sees "all things [. . .] caused or causing" (see § 26). But if, when the thing appears as event, it happens without a cause, then one will render its reason, or rather, respect its rationality, only by *not* subjecting it to causality: "*There are neither causes nor effects* (*weder Ursachen, noch Wirkungen*). [. . .] In sum: an event neither is effected nor itself effects (*ein Geschehen ist weder bewirkt, noch bewirkend*)" (Nietzsche).[57] The event thus accomplishes the essential property of the phenomenon: to show *itself* in itself, insofar as it gives *itself* by itself alone.

This happening by itself is of course verified for the collective (or "historical") event, but also for the individual event (which we don't dare call private, since by definition, deprived of nothing, it is accomplished in the absolute opening of its possibility).[58] For the individual event signals even more clearly the powerlessness of every causal explanation, because it offers a place of inquiry that is more restricted and thus in principle more easily mastered by the observer; therefore, especially in its case, the characteristics of the object lose their sharpness and fade away.[59] Consider an example as banal as can be: a sudden encounter brings about the crossing of as few as two gazes, and already within this simple scenario, eventness is freed from causality. Baudelaire saw this and showed it in a classic poem:

Around me roared the nearly deafening street.
Tall, slim, in mourning, in majestic grief,
A woman passed.

Given the event of this woman's passage, what meaning and what rationality would we introduce here by demanding a cause? Not only would the description gain nothing, but it would completely lose its basis; Baudelaire instead manifests the meaning of this passage by suggesting the paradox of an encounter that took place only by not being able to take place, an encounter that only took place in the mode of that which did not take place, precisely because it was lacking any cause or reason: "I know not where you flee, you don't know where I'm going."[60] What is to be seen in this phenomenon lies exactly in this: an event happens by the simple fact that this woman passes and I cross her path without having the least cause to render a reason for her presence or for my own. If I wish to give some reason [*rendre quelque raison*] for this event (this passage of a passing woman who passes *of herself*) without rendering it absurd, I must not only leave it without a cause, but leave it to appear *as uncaused and uncausable*. The passage has the status of an event only by remaining resistant to the demand for a cause and the obligation to have to render a reason.

Of course, I could always carry out an inquiry (perhaps using a private detective) in order to find this woman and establish the causal network lacking in this failed encounter, and thus reconstitute an objective encounter by stripping it of its evental character [*caractère événementiel*], so as to repeat the encounter that did not take place (to see this woman again, to get her back). But in doing this (all risk of indiscretion or wasted time aside), I would not attain a better view of this phenomenon. For either I would substitute for it another phenomenon, one causally determined and that, if it were to be repeated, would perhaps produce an encounter that would be socialized, regulated, and actual; but, aside from probably not gaining anything by it, I would have quite simply destroyed an event that happened *of itself* [*s'est passé*], in order to constitute an unreal object of the past—a pure fantasy, since this event, even if after the fact I found a causal frame for it, could no longer, as an actual event that happened, repeat itself exactly. Or I truly wish to experience anew and as such the passage of the passing woman, that is, as a pure event happening *of itself* [*comme un pur événement se passant*]; but then I would have to relive an event that is by definition without cause, and that will only be so by *not* being the same as this one that I am investigating—another, also without reason.[61] Only a new event, never an object, can give me access to an event; and, since it belongs to the definition of the event that it cannot be exactly repeated (because it lacks a cause and a condition of possibility), it must be concluded that as such only a first event can enable me to find again another event different from it, but with the same mode of phenomenality. This gap allows for history, an ever-deferred repetition.

In order to render this event its rationality, how must I see it? Precisely as something I will never be able to reproduce. We pay attention to "a passerby" exactly to the extent that "[a] woman passed [. . .], with a splendid hand / Lifting and swinging her festoon and hem." That is enough: the event is accomplished, since it passes *of itself*; it only happens to the extent that she, this woman, passes—and thus disappears, without subsisting, enduring, or persisting. The event passes, not because a deficiency of presence would prevent it from enduring, but because its mode of presence implies that it arrives, happens to me, crosses my path, passes ahead of me and thus passes away [*trépasse*] before my eyes—or implies that I pass away for it. This passage is insofar as it has its own time, a time that does not wait for my attention; nor does it tarry long enough for me to take *my time* to inspect it and form an idea of it. It entertains no other idea than its own—its intrinsic appearing, which gives *itself* by itself. In front of this passage, and in order to see it, only a single time is available to me: not my time (which would last), but its time (which passes). The time it takes is its own, decided by it and carried out according to its measure; the time of the passage and thus the time that passes, before my very eyes. The event of the passage arrives when the passage itself wishes, according to its own rhythm, when it decides and sets itself to it.

At issue here is an *unexpected arrival* [*arrivage*], rather than a mere scheduled appearance [*arrivée*]; indeed, the latter arrives most often at a moment that has been predicted and programmed by those awaiting it, and according to their needs; in short, the scheduled arrival arrives "on time," which is to say, at my time. The unexpected arrival, in contrast, arrives at a time fixed by its own constraints, under its own impetus and pressure (like the arrival of the catch, which depends on the tide and the sea more than on the fishermen and the wholesalers). What happens, even if I can expect it, arrives without my being able to expect it at a precise moment. The event arrives, or rather it happens *to me* [*il m'arrive*], by surprising me all of a sudden, unexpectedly. "A woman passed," but suddenly she passes me by, passes away before my eyes: "One lightning flash . . . then night! Sweet fugitive / Whose glance has made me suddenly reborn, / Will we meet again this side of eternity? // Far from this place! too late! *never* perhaps!"[62] Such an incident affects me more than I am able to constitute it; first of all, because its power to regard me is greater than my ability to keep it in my sight; second, because it imposes itself on me as a fact that gives itself, determines itself, and retires at will. For these two reasons, right away I find myself again under its domination, several steps behind its facticity—it begins before me, arrives without me, anticipating my expectation, and disappears from my sight, no sooner done than gone. To say "too late!" *always* means already too late: as soon as it began to burst forth, the event had finished beginning and begun to finish. The time of the event therefore presents itself as perfectly unavailable. Only the time of the object can persist in presence, like the object itself; but this persistence has a price: in the two cases, it costs the abstraction of the passage, the genesis and the defeat of the passage itself. That is, the very transition in which temporality consists, or rather in which it precisely does *not* con*sist*. Consequently, I must receive it unforeseen in order to lose it right away and irremediably. It comes out of the unexpected to return without delay into the irrevocable. Its instantaneousness sends it into eternity. The event gives itself only in abandoning me. It comes too early for me, and I wake up too late for it. Time alone gives the event, but what it gives it does not keep for me, nor is it concerned with me.

But, once again, the gift and the abandonment [*l'abandon*] of the event do not stem from a flaw in its presence, which would leave my intuition lacking. I saw the passing woman perfectly well, with my own eyes, since, in a single moment, I had the time to notice her, describe her, wonder about her, want to love her, and suspect that she knew it—in short, I had the time to see her appear *and disappear* clearly and distinctly. Nothing intuitive in this phenomenon escaped me. And yet, what was lacking, and what prevented me from seeing it as my gazed-upon object comes from my inability to master it with a concept: I was not expecting the passing woman, I did not know her, I wasn't able to say anything to her, and, in the end, I understood nothing of what was happening to me. In fact, the terribly complex intuition that I received of her by far surpassed the concept that I should have mobilized for this encounter (the proper questions to pose in order to gain useful information: place, date, hour, identity, the goal of her movement, etc.). Lacking concepts, I was thus unable to constitute this phenomenon into the calm and intelligible evidence of a certain object. From now on, we are dealing with a saturated phenomenon, in which the intuition overflows the capacity of the concept, which is always lacking and late. And thus, by definition, it is not so much that I understand it as that it understands me, that I reach it as that it reaches me first.

The phenomenon of the passing reached me and, so to speak, constituted me as not constituting it—to the point that all I have to do is recognize myself as the mere witness (the one who certainly saw what he has seen, but does not understand what he has seen), and I renounce my claim to be its transcendental subject. I was not the one who set my sights on the passing woman starting from my own point of view, and by deploying an intentionality reaching from me to her. Rather, from the outset, I was, without even having decided to be so, spontaneously taken into view by her inattentive yet imperious intentionality. I saw myself from her point of view, and I did not see her from mine. I assumed the point of view that she was imposing on me without knowing it or wanting it. I reversed my intentionality in her anamorphosis: "I, shaking like an addict, from her eye, / Black sky, spawner of hurricanes, drank in / Sweetness that fascinates, pleasure that kills." She passed without seeing me, and yet she was only passing for me, and happened only for me; in the crowd, she remained invisible to all other passersby, appearing only for me; she burst forth in her event only for me. The proof lies in the fact that she disappeared only for me, and is lost only for me—because she only left an impression on me. The event, by challenging all constitution and by constituting me as its witness, thus only gives itself to me. And it gives itself to me at the moment when it gives me to myself. Within the event, "Whose glance has made me suddenly reborn," I become the one who is gifted [*l'adonné*].

As a phenomenon, the event thus competes with the object. Their opposition, which numerous criteria can, as we have seen, clarify, is in the end rooted in foreseeability. For if every phenomenon by definition allows itself to be seen, the temporality of this vision can differ radically. The object proceeds from vision, while the event precedes it. — The object *proceeds* from the vision that foresees it to the extent that its essence, its possibility (whether logical or transcendental) is known before its existence, and allows for it; thus, the foreseen object *is* before being, taking the posture of a strictly intentional object, of the objective of an intention that sees it before it appears and knows it without its even existing, or without its ever coming into existence. — By contrast, the event *precedes* the vision that is awakened with it, or most often after it, inasmuch as the fact happens against every expectation, imposing an intuition in the instant that is still innocent of every concept. In fact, the event appears only by already disappearing, since it becomes visible only with, and thus after, its bursting forth: we only discover the event as having always already happened, *ex eventu*, when it is already too late to catch sight of its bursting forth. Consequently, possibility, which does not precede the event in our intentionality toward it, comes as a result of the event's effect on us: even when it is still incomprehensible (although known, or rather precisely because clearly and distinctly known and seen), the event decides sovereignly the possibles that will henceforth be imposed on us. The impossible and the unforeseeable for us open our only and unforeseen possibles: their facticity possibilizes us.

At the moment of disappearing, in an inevitable and necessary disappearance since it passes *of itself*, the event abandons to us the possibles that we couldn't even have imagined prior to its passage into actuality—before the actuality of its passage. Thus, when "the passing woman" had passed, her passage leaves the "I" that saw her coming in front of an unexpected possibility, one that is perfectly new: What am I going to do? Do I try to forget her? Do I try to see her again? Search for another who is passing by? Or dive into the memory of her, as if it were the cenotaph of her absence? Or on the contrary do I pretend that nothing ever happened? I cannot not decide in front of the appearance and especially the disappearance of this passage. While the object appears in order to respond to a question ("What do I know?" "What may I know?"), the event is constituted as a phenomenon that demands a response. In this individual event, what is at stake is an erotic decision ("Could I have loved her? Can I still? Would she love me?"). And if we consider a collective event, the issue would be a political decision.[63] But each time, the event issues a summons and demands a response; it makes itself visible by posing a question, by making itself heard—sometimes silently, but always clearly. The event happens as a call.

An objection to this result seems obvious. The object, one might say, is not opposed to the event as one type of phenomenon to another, but as two uses of the same phenomenon, sometimes known by pure theoretical reason (as an object), sometimes recognized by practical reason (as event). If I know the phenomenon, I apprehend it in theory as an object, but if I receive this same phenomenon, I respond to it (I decide with regard to it) in practice as an event. We should not induce from two uses of the same phenomenon (foreseeing or responding) two types of phenomenality (object, event): on the very same type of phenomenon, namely, an object, there are brought to bear simply two dispositions of the same reason, theoretical or practical. — For the moment let us postpone (until § 29) the examination of the objection claiming that every event, in order to appear, must first of all be, and be in the mode of the object; for now let us consider only the objection of the two dispositions of reason producing two uses of the same phenomenon. Let us note to begin with that this objection presupposes, as if it goes without saying, that reason can be exerted either according to theory or according to practice; now, even in admitting this distinction as self-evident (which, even if we were only considering Aristotle, is in no way obvious), it would still be necessary to justify it in the thing itself—for example, by relying on the distinction between two types of phenomena, one that offers an intentional object, the other that provokes a response of decision—and in this way we would redraw the split that we were claiming to erase. But above all, even by assigning the event to practical reason, we must admit that practical reason itself still *knows*. The fact of reason (*Faktum rationis*), namely, the principle of the moral law, affects practical reason (radically, to the point of provoking respect) only because practical reason knows it and sees it; put simply, to see the fact of reason implies obeying it (or being able to disobey it) and, especially, obeying (or disobeying) it is reciprocally equivalent to knowing it. Relating practically to the moral law amounts to knowing it, and one can know it theoretically only by relating to it practically. Descartes argues no differently regarding the idea of the infinite (and thus of God): I can know it in theory only by confronting it in practice: "*intueri, admirari, adorare*" ("to gaze, to wonder at, to adore") go together, and the first (the theoretical gaze of mathematical objects) passes into the second (which elsewhere names the first of all the passions) and ends up without a solution of continuity in the last (properly practical). For, when the question is that of events, one cannot "so much comprehend them as find oneself comprehended by them" ("*non tam capere quam ab ipsis capi*").[64] When we are dealing with a phenomenon of the event type, its theoretical knowledge itself supposes that one responds to it with practical reason. There are phenomena that one sees only by first responding to them, just as, according to Saint Augustine and Pascal (and Heidegger!), there are truths that one knows only if one loves them first.

§ 29. The Original Unknown

There remains one simple objection, as routine as it is at first sight convincing: ought not a phenomenon of the event type, even if its difference from a phenomenon of the object type is accepted, in every case first of all *be*, and, in order to be, be as an object? The event character does not exempt it from the status of object, but instead adds to it and presupposes it, for in order to happen, it must first of all be, and in order genuinely to be, it must be as an object: subsistent.

It is enough to formulate the objection to see its patent fragility, for it presupposes too much and too quickly what, indeed, does not hold. — First, it is not self-evident that in order to be, a being must subsist in permanence: indeed, what is proper to the event, by definition, is not to be insofar as it subsists in permanence, but insofar as it passes; for the event, to pass does not mean to disappear, but to pass *of itself* [se *passer*], in the double sense of to unfold *of itself* [se *dérouler*] and to surpass *itself* (through the advance of itself over itself, which puts it forward in disequilibrium and allows it to surpass itself endlessly). The subsistent permanence constitutes only a possible temporal mode, not the only one, nor the most radical; it offers only one of the possible modes of presence, probably not the most powerful. Its presumed privilege remains unattackable only against the background of a complete blindness to the temporality of being. — Next, the object only very partially realizes subsistence in permanence. This is true first of all because the object does not endure long in self-identity (as substance, it must admit the variation of its accidents); next, the object by definition is referred to the gaze that constitutes it, produces it, and reproduces it, following the essential dependence of an alienated thing: epistemologically, the object exemplifies to the maximum the impotence of being through itself, and thus that of remaining equal to itself in presence. — Finally, and above all, the objection presupposes that the event, in order to appear, must still *be*, which may be doubted, if at the least one means by *to be* being and being knowable according to the categories of beings and thus of the object. Indeed, as we have seen, an event contradicts these categories all the more since it is accomplished as that which happens on the basis of itself, and which passes (*of*) *itself*. To the point that a radically evential event could (and should) no longer be described according to such categories. But then, can one encounter such an event—such that it could be conceived as a pure happening passing (*of*) *itself* [*un pur avènement* se *passant*], without any support from an object, or better, such that it could be described as a phenomenon only by retaining *none* of the features of the object, that is to say, so that it would disappear if one wanted to see it as an object? That would be possible, if we identified (as in response to the phenomenon of paternity, a gift naturally reduced to givenness; see chapter III, § 16) a phenomenon naturally reduced to eventness, because all objectness in it would already be naturally bracketed; in short, a phenomenon that would appear only as a pure event, without a trace of objectness. And it would be necessary that this phenomenon impose itself inevitably on everyone always, so that one could not be unaware of it or marginalize it as a nonsignificant exception. Now, in the case of *birth*, we find at least one such phenomenon that appears as a pure event.

Birth is described by a series of paradoxes, at least if we persist in thinking about it in terms of the features of the object, features that, precisely and constantly, it contradicts. The first paradox: my birth, the event from which I come and that gives me to myself, the event that concerns no one as much as me alone and that remains inaccessible to anyone: this event nevertheless occurred essentially without me. "Pure chance, *without us*, rules our birth" (Corneille).[65] I result from it like no one else, but I am there as an absent person. "My birth is not my own, for I do not attend it."[66] At the moment of my birth (and in fact during a fairly long lapse of time), I remain unconscious of myself, and retain no memory of my birth; in short, *there* I am not where I am, nor who I am. From stage to stage, from mirrors to memories, I will wind up identifying myself after the fact with what I already was for a rather long period of time, but without ever canceling out this delay, or becoming identical with myself. In this sense, that which is born at my birth is not yet me, or at least, not yet that which says "me, I." I am born *after* my birth and, for a period of time, I am born *stillborn*. At the time of my birth, other living ones can see it, attend it, witness to it (as in the case of the public births of kings, in order to avoid any substitution); I alone do not see it, do not experience it, do not remember it. It belongs to everyone, except me. And if I want to know it after the fact, I must inquire about it—that is, get information about it from others, who in part will take away my innocence: I will obtain only a *certificate* of my birth, and nothing more. Thus, that which rendered me to myself, my original event, remains unknown to me. My birth gives me to myself, but neither does it appear to me or show itself to me. *I am the only one to result from it, but on the condition of being the only one not to see it.* Nothing about this phenomenon is an object, since it is—if, properly speaking, it is, which remains to be determined—by passing (*of*) *itself*, by surpassing me, by passing always already having passed.

Whence there follows a second paradox: I begin from the outset lagging behind my beginning. Thus, at its root, my birth "*cannot be taken over*," it becomes "im-memorial in a rigorous sense,"[67] since it has to do with the memory of that which was never present, at least to me, and to me in particular. The original contradicts the originary, and my origin is defined by an originary inaccessibility at the origin: "[B]irth is the complex phenomenon according to which an *advenant* is not originarily what he nevertheless is originally. To be born is to be a self originally but not originarily."[68] Original, but not originary, the one being born lacks his principle from the first. Not only does my birth remain without a cause, or a reason (just like paternity), but it radically contradicts the very principle that every phenomenon must recognize a principle for itself—birth evidences anarchy, and imposes it. Birth conserves only one single thing: the inaccessibility of the principle, anarchy itself. Not only do I not have a principle to which I might, against the current of time, return, but, more essentially, there is no sense in claiming to establish myself as my own principle: birth definitively refutes every claim to self-equality (A = A), whether we understand it in terms of self-consciousness, the authenticity of a ruling, or some sort of self-belonging we might wish to dream up. The only thing that belongs to me originally is my in-appropriation, my status as the tenant of my place, of my condition that was assigned to me, never chosen or possessed.

As a consequence, there is an absolute *facticity*. As preeminent event, my birth proves to be completely unforeseeable: "*Nullus quando vult nascitur*" ("No one is born when he wills it").[69] What distinguishes birth from death, my birth from my death, consists precisely in the fact that I can always foresee (medically) my natural death (thus the existential analytic on the basis of being-toward-death), or even decide on a brutal death (the suicide of the free Stoic, or the soldier's or the martyr's risk), but I can never foresee my birth—no more than my parents, even once they had decided on having children, could do. If metaphysics and even phenomenology have had no difficulty in treating of death and understanding finite being within it, but have largely ignored birth, this is no doubt because death is still appropriable as a reverse origin, admittedly under the figure of a counterorigin, but one that I can decide on and even, perhaps, experience in the first person, and it is therefore an assumable possibility, while birth escapes me, from the origin and ever after. Death authorizes suicide, the *auto-* or *self*-death, this final appropriation, while birth remains definitively a birth from outside, a *hetero*-birth.

This delay against my birth and the unknowing that it brings me leads us to a third paradox. Indeed, only one who is living [*un vivant*] can be born: "*Being born* does not mean coming into the world. Things are what appear for an instant in the world's light before vanishing in it; things are not 'born.' Being born concerns only living ones [*les vivants*]. [. . .] It is only because we have *come into life* that we can then *come into the world*" (Henry).[70] Things, and thus beings (and *a fortiori* objects), cannot be born, even if they appear visible in the world's light: their genesis and their corruption (to take up Aristotle's terms) obey causes, knowable apart from them, that allow for the foreseeing of these two moments. But can we say, of the living one who is born without a cause, that, in appearing, it sees the light *of day*, and that this day is in a world? Of course it sees it in the end, but does the world's light see the life in it? Without a doubt no, because the world gives the visible to be seen to the extent that it is, and nothing more. That which it is, and how it is, its *mode* of appearing (its phenomenal *how*): these remain inaccessible to the world's light. For this reason, much more than this light is necessary to define the mode of appearing of that which appears: the hermeneutics and the phenomenology of the inapparent are necessary; they alone are qualified to approach those phenomena that, at first sight and most of the time, do not show themselves. In particular, the distinction between the quick and the dead, the living being and the cadaver, requires much more than the world's light to appear: it requires also that which is not seen there, such as speech, freedom, recognition between the living, and so on.

The question in general arises: to what point can we determine a concept of "life" in ontological or even merely ontic terms? It may be that in metaphysics, "life" is only a not-so-lively metaphor for what beings [*l'étant*] fail to allow us to understand. Another confirmation adds to this paradox: if birth takes place before the world, or more exactly, if it introduces the living one [*le vivant*] into a field that the world's light does not illuminate as it illuminates other natural beings and nonnatural objects, then birth remains as invisible as the living one that it delivers. *My* birth not only remains and will remain invisible, because *I* was not its witness, but it in fact was invisible for the witnesses who were there. There is no doubt that they saw something that was moving, crying out, whimpering, and so forth, but they did not see the life in it and did not see it otherwise than as an operating machine. And, for my entire life, this life as such will remain immediately invisible; complex mediations of speech and language, kinestheses, and intersubjective plots will be necessary in order that it may be *mediately* recognized—moreover, only to certain people, and not to others, for a certain period of time each time, provisionally and unequally. The invisibility of my birth will follow me for as long as the event of this birth is prolonged in my life, which itself is invisible. Thus, my birth truly gives me to myself, but only to the extent that it gives *itself* without, however, showing itself. In relation to the definition of the phenomenon (that which shows itself in itself because it gives itself by itself), the phenomenon of my birth accomplishes the paradox of a givenness without monstration. Must we conclude from this that it does not have the status of a phenomenon? On the contrary, we must infer from it that it instead assures the possibility of every other phenomenon, since, by rising through the unseen, it certifies the originary and invisible eventness (giving *itself*) that precedes the visible manifestation (showing *itself*) where, in the end, every phenomenon winds up. In this sense, too, birth constitutes the arch-phenomenon, the one that institutes the anarchy of every phenomenon appearing as an event.

Thus, birth offers the paradigmatic features of the event. Indeed, it proves itself *unforeseeable* (without cause, without conditions of possibility, etc.); it always provokes an *excessiveness* (my life itself, which develops without common or foreseeable measure) that is capable of more than it is able (the im-possible); it happens *once* for *everyone*, and is therefore perfectly unrepeatable, irremediable, and irreversible, thus justifying what metaphysics never explains about time: its irreversible orientation. For the arrow of time comes from my original lag behind my birth.[71] More than one event among others, more than the paradigmatic event, more even than the first among all events that affect me, birth puts into operation the *eventness* that sustains and triggers every phenomenon as an event that passes (*of*) *itself*.

Just as completely, birth presents the characteristics of the gift—that is, of the gift reduced to givenness.[72] Indeed, the giver shines by his absence, since paternity remains by definition absent from the outside, and maternity can be denied (through "anonymous birth" and the like), while, from the inside (so to speak), the one being born remains without a clear consciousness. For his part, the recipient or givee, initially unconscious of the event when it passes (*of*) *itself* in the moment, afterward remains ever lagging behind it, in a *différance* crossed by the call and the response, with which he will never catch up. As far as that which finds itself given as (reduced) gift goes, it never takes on the status of a being, for life itself is not some thing, and even less is it an object: we can even doubt that it is. Nothing is given: life is nothing, it is not. Consequently, more than a gift among others or even the preeminent gift, birth marks the pure and simple *giving* [*donation*], itself invisible, that all phenomena put into operation when, in order to show *themselves*, they must first give *themselves*.

In this way we have available a phenomenon that is purely evential, that not only can be interpreted without borrowing anything from the reduced phenomenality of the object, but that can only be interpreted without it and would disappear with it. The reduction of birth to the phenomenality of the event thus belongs to birth by nature, and, when it is not interpreted according to this reduction, birth vanishes by being lowered to the rank of a production—incoherent and imperfect—of a failed object. As is so easily seen today.

§ 30. The Double Interpretation

We come to the conclusion that a phenomenon does not always have to be defined exclusively as an object, this "*res sibi objecta*" ("thing that sets itself as object to it [the understanding]").[73] Its objectification is the result of a phenomenal restriction, and this *diminutio phenomenalitatis* assures it certainty only by masking, or even by almost suppressing in it its originary event-characteristic: objectification only produces, then, an apparent appearance, a phenomenon by default, suffering from a shortage of happening. In this way, the singular phenomenality put forward earlier (§ 29) is verified, with the pure event (if there is one) and the pure object (if there is one) setting forth its two extreme poles, between which there extends the prism of all the other phenomena, however degraded or mixed. Therefore, object and event no longer oppose each other as two regions separated by an insurmountable wall, each retaining a pure and exclusive nature: all in all, they vary by as many transitions as possible.

Nevertheless, one might object, doesn't this conclusion threaten the clear distinction made earlier between the object (§ 26) and the event (§ 27), and, reciprocally, doesn't the distinction between their territories contradict the oneness of their phenomenological description? In order to take this objection seriously, we must consider two questions: (1) Does the distinction really have a grounding, or does it dissolve in the gradual variation of the object and the event, each passing into the other? (2) What phenomenological status should we give to such variation, so that it does not fade into a pure and simple confusion but instead maintains a status of hermeneutic variation, interpreting a phenomenon *as* object or *as* event? These two questions refer us to Kant and to Heidegger, respectively.

On the first point, Kant is decisive. For the separation of all phenomena into objects and events is grounded in the variations of intuition, in the same way, formally, that the Kantian separation of all objects into phenomena and noumena is grounded in the "form of intuition [*Art der An-*

schauung]."[74] Indeed, Kant insists on the grounding of this distinction in the difference between the forms of their intuition: "Appearances [*Erscheinungen*], to the extent that as objects they are thought in accordance with the unity of the categories, are called phenomena [*Phaenomena*]. If, however, I suppose there to be things that are merely objects [*Gegenstände*] of the understanding and that, nevertheless, can be given to an intuition, although not to sensible intuition (as *coram intuitu intellectuali*), then such things would be called noumena (*intelligibilia*)."[75] The objects appear as phenomena if their subjection to the unity of the categories is made according to a sensible intuition; they appear (or rather, *stricto sensu*, do *not* appear) as noumena when they require an intellectual intuition that is in fact unavailable to us. The distinction between noumena and phenomena is thus based on the difference of intuitions.

And yet, despite, or rather because of, this similitude, the oppositions arise all the more clearly, since, when we pass to the separation of phenomena into objects and events, the distinction between intuitions is inverted. — It is fitting first to underscore that, for Kant, the phenomenon depends on a limited intuition, the sensible intuition, while the noumenon would require a broadened intuition, an intellectual intuition; as a consequence the privilege of the phenomenon over its competition, the noumenon, lies in the poverty of its intuition (in accordance with the decision of Descartes). For the separation of phenomena into objects and events, the inverse is true: the event and the object each require an intuition, but without differentiating as brutally between two intuitions, sensible *or* intellectual; a single intuition (for it implies in the two cases an unrepeatable and irreversible temporality), at once much finer and more ample, varies; either (1) it can let itself be overdetermined by the concept (poor phenomena), or be regulated adequately by it (common-law phenomena) and, in the two cases, it gives objects to be seen; or (2) the intuition overflows the concept (or concepts) available (saturated phenomena), or even combines several saturated phenomena into one.[76] The object thus does not constitute the depth of every phenomenon, nor does the phenomenon constitute an object endowed with a true (and greater) intuition (than the noumena), but, on the contrary, the object constitutes the impoverished figure of phenomenality, impoverished because diminished in intuition, contrary to the event, which is a phenomenon saturated with intuition.

Next (supposing that we take a pass on the Kantian use of "object" and its unjustifiable privilege), our distinction between event and object cannot coincide with that of Kant between noumenon and phenomenon.

On the one hand, what we understand by event clearly is not the same as the Kantian phenomenon, because its incompatibility with intuition that is restricted (to the sensible) would, on the contrary, bring it closer to the noumenon. And yet, instead of the noumenon, what is in question, strangely, with the event is a *noumenon that would appear*, and even with more evidence (an evidence that is freer) than any object. Moreover, this paradox is in no way a contradiction, since it belongs to the definition of the event to be able to appear only by *contradicting* the conditions of experience (at least, of *our* experience of objects). Obviously, and by contrast, what we understand by object would correspond instead to the Kantian phenomenon, with which it shares restricted intuition (restricted to that which, of the sensible, can be reduced to order and measure, to models and parameters) and dependence on the categories: the Kantian *phenomenon* shares with the object the characteristic of a *diminished phenomenality*. Nevertheless, while the distinction of objects into phenomena and noumena remains definitively incompatible with the distinction of phenomena into objects and events, the *ground* of these two distinctions consists equally in the intuition, or more exactly in the distinct figures of the intuition—in the case of Kant, either sensible or intellectual; in our case, either poor or saturated. Thus, by this return to Kant, the distinction between phenomenon and event finds a ground or rather a site for establishing its strictly phenomenological justification.

But Kant proves to be decisive a second time, when he underscores that between the two terms of the alternative (between phenomena and noumena), the distinction results from an interpretation (from an *insofar as*): "[T]he noumenon in the negative sense, i.e., of things that the understanding must think [. . .] not merely *as* [*als*] *phenomena* but *as* [*als*] *things in themselves*." Or again, "The concept of a *noumenon*, i.e., of a thing that is not to be thought of *as* [*als*] an object of the senses but rather *as* [*als*] a thing in itself (solely through a pure understanding)."[77] What's more, this hermeneutical and nonreal distinction is found exactly in practical reason, when the question is that of comprehending the (noumenal) freedom of man, who is, moreover, acting in the (phenomenal) world. Indeed, the "Critical Examination of the Analytic of Pure Practical Reason" (the exact parallel in the *Critique of Practical Reason* to "On the ground of the distinction of all objects in general into phenomena and noumena" in the *Critique of Pure Reason*) underscores that in "one and the same action [*in ein und derselben Handlung*]" where he finds himself first of all "considered *as* [*als*] phenomenon," the "very same subject [*ebendasselbe Subjekt*], being on the other side conscious of himself *as* [*als*] *a thing in itself*, also views his existence *insofar* [*so fern*] *as it does not stand under conditions of time* and himself *as* [*als*] determinable only through laws that he gives himself by reason."[78] The difficulty of a free action in the world is indeed "resolved briefly and clearly" by noting well that causality (and the other categories) necessarily determines only "the natural mechanism of actions *as* [*als*] phenomena," but "does not apply to them *as* [*als*] things in themselves."[79] Moral freedom and natural necessity are reconciled in one and the same "object," man, only by a variation of their modes of phenomenality, a variation that in its turn is made possible by a variation of the interpretation of this same "object" *as phenomenon* or *as noumenon*. The Kantian solution is thus defined clearly: phenomenality varies by hermeneutical variation. But this solution has to be validated: by what right can a hermeneutical variation legitimately decide a phenomenal variation?

The answer to this question can come only from a phenomenological consideration, which we will borrow from Heidegger's analysis of the tool. Take, for example, a hammer. We can wield it in order to hammer by taking it in hand and orienting it toward the nail or the board that mobilizes all our attention so that we are no longer looking at the hammer itself, but at what it is striking. Or rather, what *we* are striking, for this hammer itself disappears in favor either of our body that uses it, and that we feel (its position, its fatigue, etc.), or in favor of the thing being made (its material, its form, its usage, etc.). In this situation, the hammer, become invisible *as object*, nevertheless remains perfectly present and in this sense manifest, since I watch over its "working," its being well adapted to the work—for example, its not being too heavy (so that I am not uselessly made tired), nor too light (so that the nail is driven in by one or two blows). *As* what, then, does it remain visible? In order to respond, let's go back to what we just said: "The hammer is heavy." What do we mean? In other words, what difference is there between saying "This hammer is *too* heavy" and "This hammer is heavy"? Clearly, in the first case, the weight in question defines the hammer at work, insofar as I use it with an intention, or in short, *as* a piece of equipment (*das Zuhandene*), which disappears in its usage (if the hammer is not too heavy, it will not give me any problems, I will no longer have to consider it in itself, and I will absorb myself in my task). In the other case, the weight of the hammer indicates something entirely different: a piece of information about the hammer derived independently of its usage (according to the worker, it becomes too heavy or insufficiently heavy, but in itself this weight does not vary, whether the hammer is left hanging on its hook or is being used); this weight merely figures alongside other objective pieces of information (the size, the types of wood and steel used in its construction, the shape, the date of manufacture, the price, etc.); in short, the weight defines the hammer *as* an object that subsists even outside of its usage (*das Vorhandene*). Thus, the same phenomenon (in this instance the hammer) can vary from the status of a subsistent object to that of a piece of equipment according to the variation in my phenomenological gaze. My gaze, depending on whether it takes the viewpoint of a historian of technology or a craftsman at work, is enough to transfigure the subsistent object into a piece of equipment, and vice versa.

What, then, is happening with the modification of my gaze so that it also modifies the status of the thing? "Why is it that [. . .] the heavy hammer shows itself differently? Not because we are keeping our distance from manipulation, nor because we are just looking *away* [*absehen*] from the equipmental character of this entity, but rather because we are looking *at* [*ansehen*] the ready-to-hand thing which we encounter, and looking at it 'in a new way' as something present-at-hand [*das begegnende Zuhandene 'neu' ansehen als Vorhandenes*]. *The understanding of Being [. . .] has changed over*."[80] The variation proper to my gaze makes the phenomenality of the thing vary (from a piece of equipment to an object and back again) only because in it there is accomplished a changing over of the modes of Being. Thus, the variation of the gaze must have an ontological status, or, put another way, the "as-structure . . . (*die Als-Struktur*)" is inscribed within the rank of the existentialia of Dasein.[81] This is indeed the case because understanding allows phenomenal variation; indeed, if the piece of equipment (the hammer) oriented toward that on which I will use it (and disappearing there), or in short the piece of equipment (*das Zuhandene*) as such, is understood as and in an assertion, it turns right away and inevitably into the object of the assertion, that about which, because it remains, one speaks (*das Vorhandene*): "Something *ready-to-hand with which* we have to do or perform something, turns into something '*about which*' the assertion that points it out is made. Our fore-sight (*Vorsicht*) is aimed at something present-at-hand (*Vorhandene*) in what is ready-to-hand (*Zuhandene*)." The assertion transforms, as such, the piece of equipment (which *is* only in the making) into a subsistent or present-at-hand object, because the assertion can only say that which remains. Thus, it says the one *as* (if it were) the other. This changing over is called the hermeneutical *as* (*als*): "The primordial 'as' of an interpretation (ἑρμηνεία) which understands circumspectively we call the 'existential-*hermeneutical* "as"' in distinction from the '*apophantical* "as"' of the assertion."[82] The variation of the modes of appearing and of being thus is played out in the one and only instance of the existential hermeneutic that the unique Dasein puts into operation.

This confirmation of the variation of the one and only phenomenality by the existential "as" clearly in no way implies that the distinction of phenomena into pieces of equipment (*Zuhandene*) and present-at-hand or subsistent objects (*Vorhandene*) coincides with my distinction between event and object. Certainly, the object corresponds essentially to the subsistent or present-at-hand object, but the same is not the case for the event and the piece of equipment. This is so first of all because every event is not summed up in a piece of equipment, especially because the piece of equipment implies my aim, my intention, and what it is about for me (*Bewandnis*), while the event happens without my aim, most often against my intention, and in every case exiles me outside of what it could have been about for me. Next, because every piece of equipment does not have the rank of an event, since the work that puts the equipment into operation (and on stage) implies know-how, and thus habit, that is, resuming and repeating, foreseeing and causal ties, the measure of the possible and of the impossible—exactly what the event subverts.

But the essential remains: the distinction between the modes of phenomenality (for us, between object and event) can be joined to the hermeneutical variations that, as existentialia of Dasein, have (ontological) authority over the phenomenality of entities. That even a stone could sometimes appear as an event depends only upon my gaze (for example, if my foot stumbled on an uneven paving stone in the courtyard of an *hôtel particulier* in the Faubourg Saint-Germain)—or, inversely, that even God might sometimes appear as an object (for example, in idolatry and its political instrumentalization).[83] The distinction of phenomena into objects and events thus finds a grounding in the variations of intuition. The more a phenomenon appears as an event (is eventialized), the more it proves itself to be saturated with intuition. The more it appears as an object (is objectivized), the more it proves itself to be poor in intuition. Or we could say: eventness fixes the degree of saturation, and saturation varies according to eventness. This distinction thus has a strictly phenomenological status.[84] But then it is immediately necessary to note that eventness does not characterize only one of the types of the saturated phenomenon (the event in the strict sense, as opposed to the idol, the flesh, and the icon): not only does it determine each of these types, which each put it into operation, but it already defined the phenomenon as given in general.[85] For all phenomena, to one degree or another, appear as they happen—since even technological objects cannot completely erase in themselves the vestiges of something that happened, however obscured it may be. If nothing appears without happening, that is the result of the fact that nothing shows itself if it does not give itself and confirm it. But nothing can give itself by procuration or by proxy: everything that gives itself gives itself by itself, happens in itself. The phenomenon appears only to the extent that it happens.

CONCLUSION

§ 31. In Praise of Paradox

The broadening of rationality comes first of all from the *horizon* that we assign to phenomenality (or that it assigns to itself). Now, when it comes to the horizon, what appears does not always result from its transcendental constitution as an object: it can also appear as an entity, which shows itself as such and on the basis of itself. The phenomenon signifies, then, following Heidegger, among others, "*that which shows itself in itself*, the manifest" ("*das Sich-an-ihm-selbst-zeigende, das Offenbare*").[1] Thus, only nonobjectifiable entities can be manifested, above all Dasein or the world of "being-in-the-world," in a horizon no longer objectifying, but ontological—at least in the sense of the repetition of the question of Being by the analytic of Dasein, precisely running counter to the metaphysical interpretation of the *ens* as a *cogitabile*, as an object for the *ego* of the *cogito*. Nevertheless, this broadening itself assumes that what shows itself shows itself on the basis of itself, instead of alienating itself in a constitution come from elsewhere, from the *ego*. But how could a phenomenon dispose of itself, if it does not have in itself any *self* to dispose of? How do we understand the *self* of a phenomenon that is not already an *ego*? To respond to this question, we have to leave not only the horizon of the object, but also the horizon of Being, and pass to that of givenness: indeed, a phenomenon can appear in itself (as a thing) only if it comes into the visible on the basis of itself (as an event); and it comes on the basis of *itself* only if it first gives itself. Everything that shows itself (in the strict sense of showing itself on the basis of itself) must first of all give itself from *itself.* Only the given makes use of itself and has a self at its disposal. Heidegger himself witnesses to this surpassing of the horizon of Being when he insists that neither time nor Being *are* (for only entities are), and thus that it is necessary to say of them "it gives" ("*es gibt*"), that they happen in giving themselves. In fact, Husserl without a doubt had already taken the step toward givenness, in his own way, directly on the basis of the objectness of the object and, so to speak, without passing through Being, when he formulated the "principle of principles": "that *everything that offers itself* to us *in originary 'intuition'* (so to speak, in its fleshly actuality) *must be received exactly as it gives itself out to be [als was es sich (da) gibt]*, though *only within the limits in which it gives itself there [nur in den Schranken in denen es sich gibt].*"[2] All phenomena without exception, before being "objected to" an *I*, before being entities in front of nothingness, happen on the basis of themselves as self-giving, which is to say: as events happening on the basis of their *self.* This is true precisely of the event (collective and historical, but also individual), of the idol, of my flesh, and of the face of the other, which appear on their own initiative, never on mine, and thus escape objectification; but which also *are* not, at least in the sense of a subsistence, or even of a piece of equipment, since I cannot always—in fact, can almost never—see them as stable, permanent, neutral, and public entities. This determination of phenomena as given could prove itself so original that even strict objects would also reach the point of letting themselves be led, in the final analysis, back to *self*-giving givens. Indeed, models and parameters, even reproduced identically, cannot be totally abstracted from their irremediably unique, and thus contingent and nonreproducible, inscription within space and time: in the final analysis, they ever and still remain events, assigned to a *here* and *now* in which they must *give themselves.* A hermeneutics becomes possible here: it tends to retranscribe all the phenomena initially considered as objects or entities into primordially given phenomena, because they are *giving themselves in themselves.* This hermeneutics of the horizons puts into operation the first broadening of phenomenality.

Once the horizon of givenness is identified, we can take a second step toward the broadening of phenomenality. If every phenomenon shows itself, and if, in order to do so, it is necessary that it first give itself, the operator of givenness thus first of all remains intuition. The description of the *saturation* of phenomena by their excess of intuition puts into operation the second broadening of phenomenality. Indeed, nothing gives itself if not in and through intuition, so that every phenomenon assumes the at least partial fulfillment of its concept (or its signification) by the giving intuition. For the intuition does not merely result from a donation [*donation*], but operates this donation; the intuition is not so much given, as first of all giving: "Without sensibility no object would be given to us (*kein Gegenstand gegeben wurde*), and without understanding none would be thought."[3] Or: "[T]hrough the former [the receptivity of sensibility, intuition] an object is *given* to us (*ein Gegenstand gegeben wird*), through the latter [the spontaneity of the understanding, concept] it is *thought*."[4] These two terms allow Kant and Husserl, among others, to maintain the classic definition of truth as *adequatio*, no longer between the thing and the mind, but between the intuition and the concept. When, in certain exceptional cases, the intuition fills the concept without remainder, we will speak of evidence, of subjective experience full of truth; in the majority of the other cases, we will allow for a merely partial fulfillment of the concept by intuition to be sufficient for validating knowledge, according to a common regime of phenomenality.

But both Kant and Husserl seem to omit a third figure from the relation between intuition and the concept: the just as possible and thinkable case in which the intuition would overflow the explicative capacity of the concept, instead of being equal or inferior to it. In this case, it would no longer be necessary to speak of a formal phenomenon, nor of a phenomenon poor in intuition (a *dematerialized* object), nor of a common phenomenon (partially validated by a deficit of intuition), but rather of a phenomenon *saturated* with intuition. Now, such phenomena, even if their phenomenality is characterized by an exceptional excess (the intuition *exceeds* the limits of the concept), are nothing if not banal and frequent in our experience. We can distinguish at least four types. — First, the event, which happens in the superabundant intuition of history, without any concept having foreseen its possibility and conceivability, to the point that it can remain, well after its actual arrival, inconceivable, unthinkable, and, in the strict metaphysical sense of the term, impossible (as a consequence, it calls for the infinite hermeneutics of historians and novelists). — Second, the idol or the excess of sensible quality, which overflows what the organs of perception can receive and handle, provoking visual or auditory bedazzlement (or that of any of the other five senses—here painting and music are of particular concern). — Third, the flesh, or more precisely *my* flesh, insofar as in it I undergo the experience of feeling feeling itself; that is, no longer am I dealing with a physical body (which I feel without its feeling me, and which therefore remains external to me), but instead with auto-affection (where I feel myself feeling myself, and even feel myself feeling myself feel), which provokes the undergoing of self, the experience *of the self.* My flesh no longer assumes any concept, nor does it enter in relation with anything other than itself, because it is identified with and through itself alone (in play here are the phenomena that have assimilated my flesh with "life," and therefore with death and with suffering, with individuality, and thus with the unconsciousness of self). — Finally, the face of the other (or the icon), as it escapes from the inert visibility of a subsistent object in the world, and even from the utilizable presence of an entity available for my ends; that is to say, as it becomes invisible (offering nothing to see to my intentional gaze), but in return speaks to me, since it provokes and convokes me through a reversed intentionality, which henceforth goes from it toward me. In this way the icon opens the space of ethics, but probably other sites as well—all those in which I do not have at my disposal a concept to govern the phenomenon, but, in the best of cases, receive it as an imperative.

Here, this broadening no longer consists only in a hermeneutics of already visible and received phenomena (transcribing them from objectivity to eventness), but in the *discovery* of saturated phenomena, up to this point misunderstood precisely by virtue of their excess of evidence. Strangely, what makes saturated phenomena hard to acknowledge comes not from any difficulty in experiencing them (for who has not experienced an event, her own flesh, idols, and the speaking face of another?), but on the contrary from the superabundance of intuition that renders their concept ineffectual, revealing its delimitation and its finite rationality. These phenomena hide themselves inside the bedazzlement that their excess of intuition provokes. By bedazzlement, I mean not only the pain felt by eyes that can no longer look at the excessive light, but also the ordeal of no longer being able to assign a concept, nor even an identity, to the giving intuition that in fact gives nothing more than itself (like in a painting by Turner, where the light dissolves the contour of things and absorbs all the forms in its submerging obscurity), without leaving behind, when it finally draws back, any definite figure that there may *be.* So much so that the saturated phenomenon does not offer itself to any direct experience, because it furnishes no *object* of experience (as in the case of the icon or of the face), nor, often, even any *entity* present in permanence (in particular in the cases of the event or of my flesh): at best, it allows for a *counter-experience.*

Counter-experience means an experience, but an indirect one: the experience of the flowing back of intuition onto me, masking in this very ebbing the identity and the form of that which withdraws itself and makes itself no longer known except by the resistance that it imposes on me, and on my intentional gaze, which is henceforth deprived of every intentional object and of every intended signification. And yet, counter-experience attests to the actual presence of the saturated phenomenon so forcefully that it makes its concept inaccessible: it is never possible for us to question the fact of a saturated phenomenon, precisely because it is never possible for us not to question its signification. And these paradoxes take place with even more strength when we combine the four types of saturated phenomena in order to approach the phenomenality of the phenomena of revelation (and thus take up again, no longer in a metaphysical but in a *phenomenological* sense that is new, the question of the manifestation of the divine, or indeed of God).

Last, beyond a hermeneutics and the discovery of saturation, we can consider a third broadening of phenomenality: the domain of *negative certainties*. Indeed, the fundamental motive of the limitation of knowledge to the field of objects consists, as we have seen, in the privileging of certainty. But this privilege would impose no limitation whatsoever on the field of knowledge if, more originally, the concern were not that of a finite knowledge, namely, our own. Because it is finite, our knowledge only reaches certainty on the condition of being able to produce objects, instead and in place of things; now, because such production cannot be achieved everywhere, nor in every case, in particular when derealization (dematerialization) proves unfeasible (for example, in the case of the excess of intuition of a saturated phenomenon), the field of certainty is also found to be limited. The finitude of knowledge, or more exactly, of the knower, leads to the delimiting of certainty. Or rather, there is certainty, whatever sort it may be—positive or negative, ample or limited—only to the extent that finitude itself makes it possible.

In this situation, two questions can be posed. — We could begin by asking if it goes without saying that every knowledge must strive to become a *certain* knowledge, and whether, on the contrary, a good number of instances of knowledge not only cannot reach certainty, but *must* not, since such a certainty would contradict what is to be known: this is the case each time that it is a question of knowing that which, as such, implies an essential determination. For example, the knowledge of the other, in the end, should never claim certainty, since every other implies the indetermination of his freedom, precisely without which he could no longer fill the role of my *other* other (and this is why we speak, wrongly but constantly, of an aporia of intersubjectivity, when, on the contrary, this is precisely the royal road to every access to the other than myself). Moreover, the same is true for self-knowledge (by definition man escapes every definition and would lose his humanity if, by defining it, he were exposed to seeing it denied to him, the individual man), or even for the knowledge of God (which by definition implies incomprehensibility, to the point that a comprehensible God would immediately sink down to the rank of a plain idol). Such kinds of knowledge can indeed be described as noncertain, but should not be considered as *un*certain, because the indetermination here plays the role of a *positive* qualification of that which is to be known, and does not sink down into a disqualification of its mode of knowledge. In a word, certitude sometimes constitutes an *obstacle* to the true knowledge of certain phenomena.

Even assuming that the demand for certainty were to admit no exception or contestation, a second question would nevertheless pose itself: in order to know with certainty, is it always necessary to assert an affirmative judgment? Couldn't we also find certainties in negative knowledge? Indeed, there is at least one excellent reason to introduce the concept of *negative certainty* into philosophy: the transcendental status of knowledge itself. For if finite knowledge defines all at once the finite conditions of the possibility (and thus of the impossibility) of the objects of knowledge, it becomes not only thinkable, but inevitable as well, to determine a priori that which can be known and that which cannot, and even the questions that cannot and, a priori, never will be able to receive an answer. Questions *necessarily* without an answer must not (and moreover cannot) always be disqualified as badly posed; on the contrary, it happens that they are posed quite correctly, and that in this very way they make the fundamental impossibility of the slightest affirmative response appear; the tendency to consider always as bereft of meaning any questions for which we have no answers not only testifies, frequently, to bad faith pure and simple, but also brings about a denial of finitude that contradicts the apparent claim to modesty and skepticism. Every (in principle) impossibility of answering a well-conceived question bears witness, for finite reason, to a negative certainty. And, since this negation itself depends on a priori certainty, it constitutes a *negative and real* broadening of the limits of knowledge. The noting and analyzing of negative certainties essentially remains still to be done, but there is no doubt that many are waiting to be found.

Thus, precisely by virtue of the indefinite broadenings of rationality, finitude will prove itself to be indefinite, or more precisely, positively infinite. Shining light on such an *infinite finitude* constitutes a priority for philosophy if it wishes to surmount the nihilism within it.

Clearly, all these broadenings of phenomenality force us to consider paradoxical manifestations as phenomena—at least for as long as we hold up the object as the indisputable paradigm of the phenomenon; but not any longer if we direct our attention starting from a basis in the eventness of the phenomenon. It is still the case that recognizing the horizon of givenness as the most original, and admitting the banality of saturation, and noting negative certainties inevitably gives rise to paradox. But can thought truly avoid paradox? It is a question here not only of the paradoxes of logic, which can still be distinguished into fallacious, truthful, and antinomical, and thus can always disappear straight back into the limits of a rationality left unquestioned.[5] At issue are paradoxes that must no longer be brought back, through elucidation, to an objective or even metaphysically ontic regime of manifestation, because in them I experience phenomena that happen (for first they happen as events) only by *contra*dicting the finite conditions of my experience, only by imposing a *counter*-experience. "This seems a paradox. But one must not think ill of the paradox, for the paradox is the passion of thought, and the thinker without the paradox is like the lover without passion: a mediocre fellow. [. . .] This, then, is the ultimate paradox of thought: to want to discover something that thought itself cannot think."[6] The paradox does not prohibit the knowledge of phenomena, but on the contrary defines the figure that phenomena must take in order to manifest themselves, when they contradict the conditions that finitude cannot not impose upon them. A way of thinking is measured precisely according to the paradoxes that it endures, and that it calls for.

BIBLIOGRAPHICAL NOTE

This book is entirely new and unpublished, but the arguments developed in each of its chapters have a history, and appeared previously in shorter versions. Thus, today they bear the mark of and have benefited widely from the objections and commentaries that they elicited. Here I would like to thank the first readers and listeners who discussed them.

For Chapter I

"*Mihi magna quaestio factus sum*: The Privilege of Unknowing," trans. Stephen E. Lewis, *Journal of Religion*, 85, no. 1 (January 2005), text of the inaugural lecture for the John Nuveen Chair at the Divinity School of the University of Chicago, 29 March 2004.

French original: "'Mihi magna quaestio factus sum': Le privilège d'inconnaissance," *Conférence*, no. 20 (Spring 2005).

For Chapter II

"L'impossible pour l'homme—Dieu," *Conférence*, no. 18 (Spring 2004).

First delivered, in 2003, as "The Impossible for Man—God," subsequently published in *Transcendence and Beyond: A Postmodern Inquiry*, ed. John D. Caputo and Michael J. Scanlon (Bloomington: Indiana University Press, 2007), 17–43, translated by Anne Davenport.

For an abbreviated form, see "L'irréductible," *Critique*, nos. 704–5 (2006).

For Chapter III

Preparatory versions were delivered at Boston University ("The Consciousness of the Gift," 28 April 2001, at the invitation of Dr. Nicolas de Warren); at the University of Paris VII ("Conférences Roland-Barthes," 27 February 2002, at the invitation of Professor Julia Kristeva); at the University of Macerata ("La coscienza del dono," 10 May 2002, at the invitation of Professor G. Ferretti); and at the University of Erfurt, Max-Weber Kolleg ("Sättigung und Erscheinung," 10–12 December 2004, at the invitation of Professor Hans Joas).

Different versions appeared as "La raison du don," *Philosophie*, no. 78 (June 2003), and then, in a corrected form, in *Donner à penser* (in collaboration with J. Starobinski, P. Quignard, et al.), Centre Roland-Barthes, Institut de la pensée contemporaine, ed. (Paris: Seuil, 2005); and in translation: "The Reason of the Gift," trans. Shane Mackinlay and Nicolas de Warren, in *Givenness and God: Questions of Jean-Luc Marion*, ed. Ian Leask and Eoin Cassidy, 101–34 (New York: Fordham University Press, 2005); and "La ragione del dono," *Studia Patavina* 15, no. 1 (2008).

Further development appeared in "La conscience du don," in *Le don: Théologie, philosophie, psychologie, sociologie*, ed. Jean-Noël Dumont, Colloque interdisciplinaire sous la direction de Jean-Luc Marion (Lyon: Le Collège Supérieur, 2001). Revised and modified in *Die Normativität des Wirklichen. Robert Spaemann, zum 75. Geburtstag*, ed. T. Buchheim, R. Schönberger, and W. Schweidler (Stuttgart: Klett-Cotta Verlag, 2002), 458–82.

For Chapter IV

"Esquisse d'un concept phénoménologique du sacrifice," in *Archivio di filosofia* 76, nos. 1–2 (2008), Rome-Pisa, 2009.

For Chapter V

First delivered as a lecture at the New School for Social Research (Professor R. Bernstein), New York, 19 April 2002, and published as "Phenomenology and Event," trans. Ella Brians and Elizabeth Lawler, *Graduate Faculty Philosophy Journal* 26, no. 1 (2005): 147–59. First appearance in French: "Notes sur le phénomène et son événement," *Iris: Annales de philosophie de l'Université Saint-Joseph de Beyrouth*, vol. 23 (Beirut: Université Saint-Joseph, Faculté des lettres et des sciences humaines, 2002); further revised and developed under the title "Le phénomène et l'événement," in *Quaestio 3: L'esistenza. L'existence. Die Existenz. Existence*, ed. C. Esposito and V. Carraud (Turnhout-Bari: Brepols-Pagina, 2003).

NOTES

Abbreviations for Frequently Cited Works

AA Immanuel Kant, *Gesammelte Schriften* (1907–; repr., Berlin: Walter de Gruyter, 1968). The abbreviation "AA" is followed by the volume number.

AT René Descartes, *Oeuvres de Descartes*, ed. Ch. Adam and P. Tannery (1908; repr., Paris: Vrin/CNRS, 1966). The abbreviation "AT" is followed by the volume number in Roman numerals and, in Arabic numerals, the page number and, in some cases, the line number(s).

GA Martin Heidegger, *Gesamtausgabe* (Frankfurt am Main: Vittorio Klostermann, 1975–). The abbreviation "*GA*" is followed by the volume number.

HUA. Edmund Husserl, *Gesammelte Werke (Husserliana)*, ed. Walter Biemel (The Hague: Martinus Nijhoff, 1954–). The abbreviation "*Hua.*" is followed by the volume number in Roman numerals and, in Arabic numerals, the page number.

PG *Patrologiae cursus completus, Series Graeca*, ed. Jacques-Paul Migne, 161 vols. (Paris: Migne, 1857–66). The abbreviation "*PG*" is followed by the volume number and column number in Arabic numerals.

PL *Patrologiae cursus completus, Series Latina,* ed. Jacques-Paul Migne, 217 vols. (Paris: Migne, 1841–55). The abbreviation "*PL*" is followed by the volume number and column number in Arabic numerals.

Epigraph

1. Novalis, *Fragmente oder Denkaufgaben,* § 203: "*Der Philosoph lebt von Problemen, wie der Mensch von Speisen: Ein unauflösliches Problem ist eine unverdauliche Speise,*" in *Novalis Schriften,* ed. Paul Kluckhohn and Richard H. Samuel, vol. 2 (Stuttgart: W. Kohlhammer Verlag, 1960), 565. English translation: Novalis, *Philosophical Writings,* trans. and ed. Margaret Mahony Stoljar (Albany: State University of New York Press, 1997), 68 (translation modified).

Introduction

1. René Descartes, *Regula VIII,* in AT, X:399–400, quoted according to Jean-Luc Marion, in René Descartes, *Règles utiles et claires pour la direction de l'esprit dans la recherche de la vérité,* trans. and annotated by Jean-Luc Marion, with mathematical notes by Pierre Costabel (The Hague: Martinus Nijhoff, 1977), 31–32. English translation: René Descartes, *The Philosophical Writings of Descartes,* trans. John Cottingham, Robert Stoothoff, and Dugald Murdoch, vol. 1 (Cambridge: Cambridge University Press, 1985), 32–33 (translation modified).

2. Descartes, *Regula VIII,* in AT, X:393; Descartes, *Règles,* 27; and Descartes, *Philosophical Writings,* 1:28.

3. Descartes, *Regula VIII,* in AT, X:398; and Descartes, *Philosophical Writings,* 1:31.

4. Immanuel Kant, *Critique of Pure Reason,* A758/B786, trans. and ed. Paul Guyer and Allen W. Wood (Cambridge: Cambridge University Press, 1998), 652–53 (translation modified).

5. Ibid., 653 (translation modified).

6. Ibid. (translation modified).

7. We could also gain support from Saint Augustine, who asks, when the issue is a problem of incomprehensibility: "*An et inventus forte quaerendus est? Sic enim sunt incomprehensibilia requirenda ne se existimet nihil invenisse qui quam sit incomprehensibile quod quaerebat potuerit invenire. Cur ergo sic quaerit si incomprehensibile comprehendit esse quod quaerit nisi quia cessandum non est quamdiu in ipsa incomprehensibilium rerum inquisitione proficitur, et melior meliorque fit quaerens tam magnum bonum quod et inveniendum quaeritur et quaerendum invenitur? Nam et quaeritur ut inveniatur dulcius et invenitur ut quaeritur avidius.*" ("Does he perhaps have to be sought even when he has been found? That is indeed how incomprehensible things have to be searched for, in case the man who has been able to find out how incomprehensible what he is looking for is should reckon that he has found nothing. Why then look for something when you have comprehended

the incomprehensibility of what you are looking for, if not because you should not give up the search as long as you are making progress in your inquiry into things incomprehensible, and because you become better and better by looking for so great a good which is both sought in order to be found and found in order to be sought? It is sought in order to be found all the more delightfully, and it is found in order to be sought all the more avidly.") Saint Augustine, *De Trinitate*, XV, 2, 2, in *Corpus Christianorum, Series Latina*, vol. 50A, *Sancti Aurelii Augustini, De Trinitate Libri XV (Libri XIII–XV)*, ed. W. J. Mountain and F. Glorie (Turnhout, Belgium: Brepols, 1968), 461; English translation: Saint Augustine, *The Trinity*, trans. Edmund Hill, OP (Brooklyn, NY: New City Press, 1991), 395–96.

8. John Duns Scotus, *Ordinatio*, I, d. 3, q. 1–2, n. 10, in *Opera omnia*, ed. C. Balic, vol. 3 (Rome: Vatican Polyglot, 1952), 5.

9. Immanuel Kant, "Attempt to Introduce the Concept of Negative Magnitudes into Philosophy," in AA, 2:171ff. English translation in Immanuel Kant, *Theoretical Philosophy, 1755–1770*, trans. David Walford and Ralf Meerbofe (Cambridge: Cambridge University Press, 1992), 211.

10. See Jean-Luc Marion, *Étant donné: Essai d'une phénoménologie de la donation*, I, § 5 (Paris: Presses Universitaires de France, 1998), 80; and Jean-Luc Marion, *Being Given: Toward a Phenomenology of Givenness*, trans. Jeffrey L. Kosky (Stanford, CA: Stanford University Press, 2002), 54.

Chapter I

1. François Villon, "Ballade des menus propos," in *Poètes et Romanciers du Moyen Age*, ed. A. Pauphilet (Paris: Gallimard, Pléiade, 1952), 1028; English translation: François Villon, "Ballade," in *The Poems of François Villon*, trans. Galway Kinnell (Hanover, NH: University Press of New England, 1982), 167.

2. Baruch Spinoza, *Ethica* II, axiom 2, in *Opera*, ed. Carl Gebhart (Heidelberg: Carl Winter-Verlag, 1925), 2:102. The laconicism of this acknowledgment perplexes as much as its late appearance in the course of the demonstrations: does man alone think, and who then was thinking in *Ethics* I, and besides, what is a *man*, if we must not admit the least of the universals?

3. René Descartes, *Meditatio II*, in AT, VII:33, line 13.

4. G. W. Leibniz, *Discours de métaphysique*, § 34, in *Die philosophischen Schriften von Gottfried Wilhelm Leibniz*, ed. C. I. Gerhardt, 7 vols. (Berlin: Weidmann, 1875–90), 4:459; English translation in *G. W. Leibniz: Philosophical Essays*, ed. and trans. Roger Ariew and Daniel Garber (Indianapolis: Hackett, 1989), 65 (translation modified).

5. Aristotle, *De anima* III, 4, 430a, trans. J. A. Smith, in *The Basic Works of Aristotle*, ed. Richard McKeon (New York: Modern Library, 2001), 591 (translation modified).

6. René Descartes, *Meditatio VI*, in AT, VII: p. 74, line 27–p. 75, line 4; English

translation in René Descartes, *The Philosophical Writings of Descartes*, trans. John Cottingham, Robert Stoothoff, and Dugald Murdoch, vol. 2 (Cambridge: Cambridge University Press, 1984), 52.

7. René Descartes, *Meditatio V*, in AT, VII:71, lines 8–9, 15. We shall not, despite the Duc de Luynes's translations and the majority of modern readers, confuse this *objectum* with the mathematical object, precisely since it includes the whole world of objects insofar as they are knowable, not according to arithmetic and geometry, but, more originally, according to that which assures to mathematics its certainty (the *ordo et mensura* of the *Regula IV*, in AT, X:378, lines 1–2), that is, "*illa omnia in iis sunt, quae clare et distincte intelligo, id est omnia generaliter spectata, quae in purae Matheseôs objecto comprehenduntur*" (in AT, VII:80, lines 8–10).

8. "From antiquity the name of this author has been unknown," states Pierre Courcelle at the outset of the huge dossier that he compiled in *Connais-toi toi-même, de Socrate à saint Bernard*, 3 vols. (Paris: Études augustiniennes, 1974–75), 1:11.

9. Emmanuel Levinas, *Notes philosophiques diverses*, in *Carnets de captivité et autres inédits, Oeuvres I*, ed. Rodolphe Calin (Paris: Grasset, 2009), 279: "Ignore-toi—toi-même."

10. Immanuel Kant, *Critique of Pure Reason*, B152–53, trans. and ed. Paul Guyer and Allen W. Wood (Cambridge: Cambridge University Press, 1998), 257.

11. Ibid., "Transcendental Deduction of Pure Concepts of Understanding," § 24, B155, pp. 258–59 (translation modified; emphasis added).

12. Kant, *Critique of Pure Reason*, A349, p. 416. One cannot take too seriously the surprising equivalence "*dieses Ich, oder Er, oder Es (das Ding), welches denket*" ("this I, or He, or It [the thing], which thinks") (ibid., A346/B404, p. 414): the event and the process that makes it so that thought thinks becomes so unthinkable from the point of view of the thought thought (and thought according to objectness), that it becomes almost problematic to attribute it to an *ego*: as Nietzsche and Freud will soon have it, an *id* could be enough; at the very least a nonindividualized *it* (a "They," *das Man*) would do the job just as well, and at a lower price.

13. Kant, *Critique of Pure Reason*, A346/B404, p. 414, which continues by emphasizing that this "consciousness in itself is not even a representation distinguishing a particular object, but rather a form of representation in general" (ibid.). The fact that the *I* can just as well be understood as neuter (*Es*) confirms that the "transcendental subject" must first be understood in the Aristotelian (and also Cartesian) sense of the substratum (and the *subjectum*) of a predication, the substratum that, as such (and for the same reasons as prime matter), remains always invisible and unknown.

14. Ibid., A372 (p. 428) and A354 (p. 419), respectively.

15. Ibid., § 16, B132, p. 246.

16. Such an application to the *I* of the processes of knowledge suited to objects alone (as empirical *me*) is often found elsewhere, for example, even in Hus-

serl, where "there is no longer any difficulty" in knowing that which thinks from any other object, precisely because this *I* again becomes "the same" as an object: "Here, as everywhere else, 'the Same' signifies therefore an *identical intentional object of separate conscious processes*, hence an object immanent in them only as something *non-really* inherent." Edmund Husserl, *Cartesianische Meditationen*, V, in *Hua.*, I, 154, 155; and Edmund Husserl, *Cartesian Meditations*, trans. Dorion Cairns (Dordrecht, Netherlands: Kluwer Academic Publishers, 1993), 126, 127.

17. Kant, *Critique of Pure Reason*, preface to the 2nd ed., BXXXIX, 121.

18. Immanuel Kant, preface to *Anthropology from a Pragmatic Point of View* (AA, 7:119), trans. Robert B. Louden (Cambridge: Cambridge University Press, 2006), 3 (translation modified; emphasis added).

19. Ibid.

20. Ibid.

21. Immanuel Kant, *Lectures on Logic* (AA, 9:25), trans. J. Michael Young (Cambridge: Cambridge University Press, 1992), 538. See the parallels in Kant, *Critique of Pure Reason*, A804/B832; Immanuel Kant, *Vorlesungen über Metaphysik und Rationaltheologie (Pölitz)*, AA, 28:2, 28:1 (Berlin: Walter de Gruyter, 1970), 534 (*Lectures on Metaphysics*, trans. Karl Ameriks and Steve Naragon [Cambridge: Cambridge University Press, 1997], 301–2); and Immanuel Kant, "Letter to Stäudlin," May 4, 1793 (AA, 11:429), in *Correspondence*, trans. and ed. Arnulf Zweig (Cambridge: Cambridge University Press, 1999), 458. Martin Heidegger's commentary reads: "The Kantian laying of the foundation yields this conclusion: The establishment of metaphysics is an interrogation of man, i.e., it is anthropology." Martin Heidegger, *Kant and the Problem of Metaphysics* (§ 36, in *GA*, 3:205), trans. James S. Churchill (Bloomington: Indiana University Press, 1962), 213. If man's interrogation of man necessarily ends in the paradox of *thinking* thought's inaccessibility to itself, then metaphysics itself becomes aporetic, at the least, but above all in its modern principle.

22. A point that Feuerbach avows, *a contrario* but all the more clearly: "In the object [*am Gegenstand*] which he contemplates, therefore, man becomes *conscious of himself*; consciousness of the objective is *the self-consciousness* of man. We know the man by the object, by his conception of what is external to himself; in it his essence [*Wesen*] *becomes evident*; this object is his manifested nature, his true objective *ego*. And this is true not merely of spiritual objects [*Gegenstände*], but also of *sensuous* objects. Even the objects which are the most remote from man, *because* they are objects to him, and *to the extent* that they are so, are revelations of human essence. Even the moon, the sun, the stars call [*rufen*] to man the γνῶθι σεαυτόν, Know thyself!" Ludwig Feuerbach, *Das Wesen des Christentums* (Stuttgart: Reclam, 1969), 43; and Ludwig Feuerbach, *The Essence of Christianity*, trans. Marian Evans (London: Trübner, 1881), 5 (translation modified). The final sentence inverts to the letter the famous formula of Saint Augustine: "*Dicunt haec omnia: 'Non ipsa nos fecimus sed fecit nos qui manet in aeternum.'*" *Confessiones*, IX.10.25; see also

X.6.9, and "*Ecce sunt caelum et terra*," crying "*quod facta sint*," XI.4.6 (Citations of the Latin text of the *Confessions* are from *Oeuvres de Saint Augustine*, vol. 13, *Les Confessions, Livres I–VII*, and vol. 14, *Les Confessions, Livres VIII–XIII*, 2nd ed., ed. M. Skutella and A. Solignac, French trans. E. Tréhorel and G. Bouissou (Paris: Institut d'Études augustiniennes, 1998 [vol. 13], 1996 [vol. 14]).

23. René Descartes, *Meditatio II*, in AT, VII:25, line 12, and VII:27, line 10, respectively; English translation in Descartes, *Philosophical Writings*, 2:17, 2:18.

24. Descartes, *Meditatio II*, in AT, VII:25, lines 14–18 (my retranslation). Note that Descartes anticipates Kant's hesitation in the *Critique of Pure Reason*, A346/B404 (quoted above, n. 13): the *ego* can and in fact must be said just as well as such, *Ich*, as in the neuter, *Es*, and at the distance of the third person, *Er*. For the demonstrative *ille* places it in the third person, just as the *in locum mei* vouches for it in the neuter. See Montaigne, *Essais* II, 12: "But what was he [Plato] dreaming of when he defined man as a two-legged animal without feathers, furnishing those who wanted to laugh at him with a comical opportunity? For having plucked a live capon, they went around calling it 'Plato's man,'" and III, 13: "We exchange one word for another word, often more unknown. I know better what is man than I know what is animal, or mortal, or rational. To satisfy one doubt, they give me three; it is the Hydra's head." Michel de Montaigne, *Essais*, ed. Pierre Villey (Paris: Presses Universitaires de France, 1965), 544, 1069; and Michel de Montaigne, *The Complete Essays of Montaigne*, trans. Donald M. Frame (Stanford, CA: Stanford University Press, 1958), 407, 819.

25. Descartes, *Meditatio II*, in AT, VII:25, lines 28–29; and Descartes, *Philosophical Writings*, 2:17.

26. Aristotle, *Metaphysics*, Λ, 9, 1074b34, in Aristotle, *Metaphysics, Books X–XIV*, with an English translation by Hugh Tredennick (Cambridge, MA: Harvard University Press, 1962), 164.

27. Saint Augustine, *Confessiones*, IV.14.22 and IV.4.9, respectively. English translation in Saint Augustine, *Confessions*, trans. Henry Chadwick (Oxford: Oxford University Press, 1998), 66, 57 (translation modified).

28. Saint Augustine, *Confessiones*, IV.14.22. The alienation from the *Umwelt* is also reinforced by the fact that the dying friend was baptized in extremis and, returning at the last moment to consciousness, not only did not deny this unconscious sacrament, but claimed it for his own, to the incomprehension of Augustine, who would have wanted to laugh about it with him ("*temtavi apud illum inridere*"). The relation to the other (*Mitsein*) here is erased *with* and probably *before* the opening to the world (*In-der-Welt-sein*).

29. Saint Augustine, *Confessiones*, X.33.50; and Saint Augustine, *Confessions*, 208 (translation modified).

30. Saint Augustine, *Confessiones*, X.33.50; and Saint Augustine, *Confessions*, 208 (translation modified). This gap between me and myself even serves as a conclusion to bk. 2: "*Et factus sum mihi regio egestatis*" (II.10.18), where this "region of

destitution" (Saint Augustine, *Confessions*, 34) defines my alienation from myself (at the time of the first theft) under the influence of the group of wicked friends.

31. Saint Augustine, *Confessions*, 203 (translation modified); and Saint Augustine, *Confessiones*, X.30.41.

32. Saint Augustine, *Confessiones*, X.16.25. See "*Intravi ad ipsius animi mei sedem, quae illi est in memoria mea, quoniam sui quoque meminit animus.*" ("I entered into the very seat of my mind, which is located in my memory, since the mind also *remembers itself.*") Saint Augustine, *Confessiones*, X.25.36; English translation: Saint Augustine, *Confessions*, 200 (emphasis added).

33. Saint Augustine, *Confessiones*, X.16.25; English translation: Saint Augustine, *Confessions*, 193 (translation modified).

34. Saint Augustine, *Confessiones*, X.17.26; English translation: Saint Augustine, *Confessions*, 194 (translation modified and emphasis added).

35. Respectively: Nicolas Malebranche, *Recherche de la vérité*, XIième Eclaircissement, in *Oeuvres complètes*, ed. André Robinet (Paris: Vrin, 1964), 3:168; English translation in Nicolas Malebranche, *The Search after Truth*, trans. and ed. Thomas M. Lennon and Paul J. Olscamp (Cambridge: Cambridge University Press, 1997), 636; Baruch Spinoza, *Ethica* II, propositio 23, in Spinoza, *Opera*, ed. Carl Gebhart (Heidelberg: Carl Winter-Verlag, 1925), 2:154; English translation in Baruch Spinoza, *Complete Works*, ed. Michael L. Morgan, trans. Samuel Shirley (Indianapolis: Hackett Publishing Company, 2002), 260; and John Locke, *An Essay Concerning Human Understanding*, II, 27, § 27, ed. Roger Woolhouse (London: Penguin, 2004), 313.

36. Respectively: Saint Augustine, *Soliloques* I, 2, 7 ("I desire to know [what are] the soul and God. / Nothing else? / Absolutely nothing else"—quoted in Jean-Luc Marion, *In the Self's Place: The Approach of Saint Augustine*, trans. Jeffrey L. Kosky [Stanford, CA: Stanford University Press, 2012], 56); and Saint Augustine, *Confessiones*, X.37.62 (English translation: Saint Augustine, *Confessions*, 216: "In this matter I know myself less well than I know you").

37. Blaise Pascal, *Pensées*, § 131, in *Oeuvres complètes*, ed. Louis Lafuma (Paris: Seuil, 1963), 515; English translation in Blaise Pascal, *Pensées*, trans. A. J. Krailsheimer (London: Penguin, 1995), 35.

38. Montaigne, *Essais*, III, 9, p. 1001; Montaigne, *Complete Essays*, 766. This thesis (that the first knowledge, which decides everything, is that of the self) is also found elsewhere in the *Essais*: "When Thales thinks that the knowledge of man is very difficult for man, he teaches him that the knowledge of any other thing is impossible for him"; or: "Now it is likely that if the soul knew anything, it would first of all know itself" (II, 12, Montaigne, *Essais*, respectively, 557 and 561; Montaigne, *Complete Essays*, 418, 421).

39. Montaigne, *Essais*, III, 13, p. 1075 (I quote only from the text of the 1588 edition); and Montaigne, *Complete Essays*, 823.

40. René Descartes, *Regulae ad directionem ingenii*, III: "*Mentis purae et atten-*

tae tam facilem distinctumque conceptum, ut de eo, quod intelligimus, nulla prorsus dubitatio relinquatur," in AT, X:368, lines 15–17; English translation in Descartes, *Philosophical Writings*, 1:14 (translation modified). Which continues: "*seseu, quod idem est, mentis purae et attentae non dubium conceptum, qui a sola rationis luce nascitur*" (AT, X:368, lines 17–19).

41. Descartes, *Regulae ad directionem ingenii*, II: "*Circa illa tantum objecta oportet versari, ad quorum certam et indubitatem cognitionem nostra ingenia videntur sufficere,*" in AT, X:362, lines 2–4; Descartes, *Philosophical Writings*, 1:10. (This *Regula* title can be compared with that of *Regula III*, in AT, X:366, lines 11–14.)

42. Johannes Clauberg, *Metaphysica de Ente, quae rectius ontosophia [dicitur] . . .*, respectively § 6 and § 4, in *Opera omnia philosophica* (Amsterdam, 1691; repr., Hildesheim, Germany: Olms Verlag, 1968), 1:283. Berkeley will simply radicalize this decision (assuming that it can be further radicalized).

43. See Descartes, *Regulae ad directionem ingenii*, IV: "*illa omnia tantum, in quibus aliquis ordo vel mensura examinatur, ad Mathesim* [sc. *Universalem*] *referri, nec interesse utrum in numeris, vel figuris, vel astris, vel sonis, aliove quovis objecto talis mensura quaerenda sit.*" In AT, X: p. 377, line 23–p. 378, line 4. "I came to see that the exclusive concern of mathematics is with questions of order or measure and that it is irrelevant whether the measure in question involves numbers, shapes, stars, sounds, or any other object whatever." In Descartes, *Philosophical Writings*, 1:19.

44. Kant, *Critique of Pure Reason*, BXVII, 110. This can be read as a commentary on the Cartesian rule that "*hic de rebus non agentes, nisi quantum ab intellectu percipiuntur,*" Descartes, *Regulae ad directionem ingenii*, XII, in AT, X:418, lines 13–14; Descartes, *Philosophical Writings*, 1:44: "[W]e are concerned here with things only in so far as they are perceived by the intellect."

45. Pascal Quignard, *Petits traités* (Paris: Maeght, 1990), 1:224. Or: "Often the forms present themselves to us. These forms are thrown (*objiciuntur*). The object is this dead man in front of our eyes opening his mouth in hunger." Pascal Quignard, *Sordissimes* (Paris: Grasset, 2005), 129. See the study by Vincent Giraud, "L'invisible et la proie: Une lecture de Pascal Quignard," *Studia phaenomenologica* 8 (2008).

46. G. W. F. Hegel, *Hegel and the Human Spirit: A Translation of the Jena Lectures on the Philosophy of Spirit (1805–6), with Commentary*, trans. and ed. Leo Rauch (Detroit: Wayne State University Press, 1983), 89–90 (translation modified).

47. Ibid., 88.

48. Ibid., 90.

49. Ibid., 89. See as well: "The first act, by which Adam established his lordship over the animals, is this, that he gave them a name, i.e., he nullified them as beings on their own account, and made them into ideal [entities] [. . .]. In the name the *self*-subsisting reality of the sign is nullified." In G. W. F. Hegel, *Gesammelte Werke*,

ed. H. Kimmerle and K. Düsing (Hamburg: F. Meiner, 1975), 6:288; English translation: G. W. F. Hegel, *System of Ethical Life (1802–3) and First Philosophy of Spirit (Part II of the System of Speculative Philosophy, 1803–4)*, trans. and ed. H. S. Harris and T. M. Knox (Albany: State University of New York, 1979), 221–22.

50. I hope I will be allowed to avoid entering here into the doubtless important but often biased debate on the phenomenological status of animality.

51. Indeed, the name given to Eve remains of the same order as that of Adam, since she appears to him as "flesh of [his] flesh"; moreover, he does not so much give her her name as take note of it as similar to his own, and thus as proper: "[S]he shall be called 'woman,' because she was taken out of man" (Gen. 2:23).

52. What Heidegger qualifies more simply by *Werheit*: the question of *Who?* corresponding to the mode of being of Dasein, by opposition to that of an innerworldly present-at-hand entity (*vorhanden*), who indeed arises from the question *Was?* Martin Heidegger, *Sein und Zeit*, 19th ed. (1927; repr., Tübingen, Germany: Max Niemeyer, 2006), § 25, pp. 114–17, § 54, p. 267, lines 30–35; English translation in Martin Heidegger, *Being and Time*, trans. John Macquarrie and Edward Robinson (New York: Harper and Row, 1962), 150–53, 312. The confusion, according to Heidegger, was, in a supposedly exemplary way, the work of Descartes, a view that can be disputed, since Descartes explicitly asks himself, "*[Q]uisnam sim ego ille qui jam necessario sum?*" Descartes, *Meditatio II*, in AT, VII:25, lines 14–15. On this complex relation, see Jean-Luc Marion, *Sur le prisme métaphysique de Descartes: Constitution et limites de l'onto-théo-logie dans la pensée cartésienne* (1986; repr., Paris: Presses Universitaires de France, 2004), § 15, pp. 203ff.; English translation: Jean-Luc Marion, *On Descartes' Metaphysical Prism*, trans. Jeffrey L. Kosky (Chicago: University of Chicago Press, 1999), 193ff. See also Jean-Luc Marion, *Réduction et donation: Recherches sur Husserl, Heidegger et la phénoménologie* (Paris: Presses Universitaires de France, 1989), chap. 3, esp. §§ 6–7, pp. 147ff.; English translation: Jean-Luc Marion, *Reduction and Givenness: Investigations of Husserl, Heidegger, and Phenomenology*, trans. Thomas A. Carlson (Evanston, IL: Northwestern University Press, 1998), 97–107.

53. These normative standards (such an amount of a particular substance in such and such bodily liquid, or such a percentage, but also such and such familial antecedents, sociological statistics, chances for treatment success, economic costs, and so on) define a normality, and, by inevitable contrast, also define abnormality. What the concepts of sickness *and of health* mean vary according to the establishment of the standards: tobacco addiction has recently become a disease, like alcoholism in the previous century, while homosexuality has ceased to be one, like hysteria and other, so to speak, administrative diseases. But each time a campaign for prevention is undertaken by the health department, that is to say by a complex technopolitical decision-making entity, a new standard, and thus new abnormalities, and thus new *diseases*, receive their certification. Every man must meet this standard, or see himself declared sick according to this new requirement: thus, all

prevention, however well intentioned it may be (and it is—why doubt it?), constitutes at once both a security for man *in general,* and a *threat* of illness and abnormality for any *particular* man. The continued imprisonment of convicts who have served their sentence, for the reason that they must undergo permanent treatment, registers this implacable evolution. Thus, what Foucault had shown about exclusion induced by the establishing and the definition of psychological and social diseases is subsequently true for the establishment and definition of physiological preventive diseases. At issue there is the *neutral* observation of a situation ambivalent in itself.

54. *Mobilization* is understood here in the sense used by Ernst Jünger in "Die totale Mobilmachung" [Total mobilization], in his *Krieg und Krieger* (Berlin: Junker und Dünnhaupt, 1930), 9–30.

55. This seems to be the gap between consciousness according to Hegel and the worker according to Jünger: "The 'worker' as the unconditioned *servant* torn apart to the point of becoming the unconditioned *master.*" Martin Heidegger, *Zu Ernst Junger "Der Arbeiter,"* in *GA,* 90 (Frankfurt: Vittorio Klostermann, 2004), 6. See the study by Jean Vioulac, *L'époque de la technique: Marx, Heidegger et l'accomplissement de la métaphysique* (Paris: Presses Universitaires de France, 2009).

56. This is without prejudging the legitimacy of ever speaking of a truly proper name: the family name (the name of the *gens*) and the given name (or the Christian name, the name of a patron saint) are indeed always borrowed, and so visibly borrowed that these first names must right away be completed, albeit provisionally and insufficiently, by a surname or surnames; these *sur*names in turn, like an *over*coat, hide and mask the fundamental homonymy (the impropriety, the inappropriation) of the always *im*proper name. See Jean-Luc Marion, *Étant donné: Essai d'une phénoménologie de la donation* (Paris: Presses Universitaires de France, 1998), § 28, pp. 401–4; and Jean-Luc Marion, *Being Given: Toward a Phenomenology of Givenness,* trans. Jeffrey L. Kosky (Stanford, CA: Stanford University Press, 2002), 291–93.

57. Primo Levi lived and described thoroughly the moment when the number, having become the most efficacious tool for the definition (in this case ideological and racist) of man, and thus for the stigmatization of the nonman (the Jew), silences the name of a man by substituting itself for that name: "He is Null Achtzehn. He is not called anything except that, Zero Eighteen, the last three figures of his entry number; as if everyone was aware that only a man is worthy of a name, and that Null Achtzehn is no longer a man." Primo Levi, *If This Is a Man: The Truce,* trans. Stuart Woolf (London: Abacus, 1987), 48. And once the name of a man is abolished, and his humanity thus denied, it becomes possible and even much easier to put an end to him physically, since his status no longer differs from that of a "dog" or a "pig"—in other words, of an animal. The same observation is made by Simone Veil: "Even more than the blows, the dogs that harassed us, the exhaustion, the

hunger, the cold, and the sleeplessness, it was the humiliations aimed at depriving us of all human dignity that, even today, remain the worst in our memories. We *no longer had a name,* but only a *number* tattooed on the arm, serving to identify us." Simone Veil, *Une vie* (Paris: Stock, 2007), 390 (emphasis added). Conversely, getting back a name in place of the entry number marks the recovery of humanity: "We were grouped by nationalities, and a French liaison officer had gathered and verified our identities. It was the first time in months that we were using *our proper names.* We were no longer *numbers.* Slowly we recovered our identity" (ibid., 91 [emphasis added]). See the shameful anecdote: "I must say that once, in an embassy, a high-level French civil servant, pointing at my forearm and my deportation number, asked me with a smile if it was my locker number! After that, for many years, I favored long-sleeves" (ibid., 98).

58. Albert Camus diagnoses this perfectly: "The reality of the present [. . .] is logical crime." He specifies: "In the age of ideologies, we must examine our position in relation to murder. If murder has rational foundations, then our period and we ourselves are rationally consequent." For, "as soon as crime reasons about itself, it multiplies like reason itself and assumes all the aspects of the syllogism." Albert Camus, *L'homme révolté,* in *Essais,* ed. R. Quilliot and L. Faucon (Paris: Gallimard, Pléiade, 1985), 413, 414; and Albert Camus, *The Rebel: An Essay on Man in Revolt,* trans. Anthony Bower (New York: Random House Vintage International, 1991), 3, 4. But one correction is necessary: reason here in fact no longer proceeds by scientific syllogism (which, for Aristotle, assumes that the mean constitutes the definition of the essence at the level of genre, and thus tells us the in-itself of the thing, without substituting its object for it), but by modeling and parameters, in view of producing objects, according to *mathesis universalis* (see above, § 3).

59. Descartes, *Philosophical Writings,* 2:21; and Descartes, *Meditatio II,* in AT, VII:32, line 10. This is confirmed by another of Descartes's remarks: "I take a walk each day amid the bustle of the crowd with as much freedom and repose as you could obtain in your leafy groves, and I pay no more attention to the people I meet than I would to the trees in your woods or the animals that browse there." René Descartes, *To Balzac,* 5 May 1631, in AT, I:203, lines 19–24; and Descartes, *Philosophical Writings,* 3:31. See my study in Jean-Luc Marion, *Questions cartésiennes: Méthode et métaphysique,* chap. 6, § 2 (Paris: Presses Universitaires de France, 1991), 194–99.

60. On the construction and usage of the concept of the "barbarian," see the indications of Rémi Brague, *Au moyen du Moyen Age: Philosophies médiévales en chrétienté, judaïsme et islam* (Chatou, France: Les Éditions de La Transparence, 2006), 141–53; Rémi Brague, *The Legend of the Middle Ages: Philosophical Explorations of Medieval Christianity, Judaism, and Islam,* trans. Lydia G. Cochrane (Chicago: University of Chicago Press, 2009), 107–18, quoting Maimonides (p. 114) among others: "Those who are outside the city are all human individuals who have no doctrinal belief, neither one based on speculation nor one that accepts the au-

thority of tradition: such individuals as the furthermost Turks found in the remote North, the Negroes (*sūdān*) found in the remote South, and those who resemble them from among them that are with us in these climes. The status of those is like that of irrational animals. To my mind they do not have the rank of men, but have among the beings a rank lower than the rank of man but higher than the rank of the apes. For they have the external shape and lineaments of a man and a faculty of discernment that is superior to that of the apes." Maimonides, *The Guide for the Perplexed*, trans. Shlomo Pines (Chicago: University of Chicago Press, 1963), 618–19. See too the indications of Jacques Derrida, *De l'esprit* (Paris: Galilée, 1987), 58–72, on the distinction made by Husserl, who wrote: "We pose the question: How is the spiritual shape of Europe to be characterized? Thus we refer to Europe not as it is understood geographically, as on a map, as if thereby the group of people who live together in this territory would define European humanity. In the spiritual sense the English Dominions, the United States, etc., clearly belong to Europe, whereas the Eskimos or Indians presented as curiosities at fairs, or the Gypsies, who constantly wander about Europe, do not. Here the title 'Europe' clearly refers to the unity of a spiritual life, activity, creation." Edmund Husserl, "Die Krisis des europäischen Menschenstums und die Philosophie," lecture given at Vienna, in 1935, in *Die Krisis der europäischen Wissenschaften und die transzendentale Phänomenologie*, in *Hua.*, VI, 318ff.; English translation: Edmund Husserl, *The Crisis of European Sciences and Transcendental Phenomenology*, trans. David Carr (Evanston, IL: Northwestern University Press, 1970), 273.

61. Baruch Spinoza, "Epistola 50," to Jarig Jelles, in Spinoza, *Opera*, ed. Carl Gebhart (Heidelberg: Carl Winter-Verlag, 1925), 4:240; English translation in Baruch Spinoza, *The Correspondence of Spinoza*, trans. and ed. Abraham Wolf (London: Frank Cass, 1966), 270 (translation modified).

62. "He [the executioner] can kill a man, but he can't change him into something else." This observation, made—and at what a price—by Robert Antelme (*L'espèce humaine* [first published 1957; repr., Paris: Gallimard, Collection Tel, 1978], 230; English translation: Robert Antelme, *The Human Race*, trans. Jeffrey Haight and Annie Mahler [Evanston, IL: Marlboro Press, 1998], 220), rests on the impossibility of denying the uniqueness of the human race: "There is no ambiguity: we're still men, and we shall not end otherwise than as men" (Antelme, *L'espèce humaine*, 229; Antelme, *Human Race*, 219). "[T]he solidity and stability of the species is being put to the test. [. . .] [T]here are not several human races, there is only one human race. It's because we're men like them that the SS will finally prove powerless before us" (Antelme, *L'espèce humaine*, 229; Antelme, *Human Race*, 219). "[T]he thing which, here, is certainly that which requires the most considerable effort to believe, that 'The SS are only men like ourselves'" (Antelme, *L'espèce humaine*, 229; Antelme, *Human Race*, 219–20 [translation modified]). This uniqueness of the human race lies in the fact that its definition, which by defini-

tion is always restrictive qua definition, is not possible, and is opposed to a refusal without any other motive than itself: "The calling into question of our quality as men provokes *an almost biological claim* of belonging to the human race" (Antelme, *L'espèce humaine*, 11; Antelme, *Human Race*, 5–6 [emphasis added]). Thus, one should reflect with much prudence and think a bit about what one says before celebrating, with great joy and trumpet blasts, "the end of the human exception."

63. Robert Antelme showed with the greatest clarity the final stakes of the extermination camps. On the one hand, man finds his "condition as man [. . .] contested by the SS" (Antelme, *L'espèce humaine*, 101; Antelme, *Human Race*, 96; or *L'espèce humaine*, 11; *Human Race*, 5), and hears it said, "*Thou shalt not be*" (*L'espèce humaine*, 79; *Human Race*, 74; see also *L'espèce humaine*, 56; *Human Race*, 51); on the other, he encounters "the clandestine German, the one who thinks that we are men" (*L'espèce humaine*, 66; *Human Race*, 61 [translation modified]), or the Rhinelander who holds his hand out to him in silence or murmurs, "Slowly," to the enslaved workers (*L'espèce humaine*, 80; *Human Race*, 74; and *L'espèce humaine*, 58; *Human Race*, 53), or "the event" of this woman who gives "human bread" (*L'espèce humaine*, 65–66; *Human Race*, 59–60).

64. Gregory of Nyssa, *De hominis opificio*, chap. 11, *PG*, 44, 156b and following; English translation: Gregory of Nyssa, "On the Making of Man," in *Gregory of Nyssa: Dogmatic Treatises*, trans. William Moore and Henry Austin Wilson, vol. 5 of *Nicene and Post-Nicene Fathers of the Christian Church*, ser. 2, ed. Philip Schaff and Henry Wace (Grand Rapids, MI: Eerdmans, 1965), 396–97 (translation modified). And see the beginning of the same chapter 11: "'Who hath known the mind of the Lord?' [Rom. 11:34] the apostle asks; and I ask further, who has understood his own mind? Let those tell us who consider the nature of God to be within their comprehension, whether they understand themselves (εἰ ἑαυτοῦς κατανοήσαν)—if they know the nature of their own mind" (Gregory of Nyssa, *De hominis opificio*, 153d–156a; Gregory of Nyssa, "On the Making of Man," 396). The same result occurs with another argument, in the sermon "Concerning those who have died" (*De Mortuis oratio*) (*PG*, 46, 509b–d): "[J]ust as the eyes see everything of the world, but they cannot see themselves, similarly, the soul explores, searches in a thousand ways, and tracks down everything that is outside of it, yet it is impossible for it to see itself (ἡ ψυχὴ [. . .] ἑαυτήν ἰδεῖν ἀδυνάτως ἔχει). With this in mind, the soul should imitate the eyes. The eyes lack the capacity to turn their own vision on themselves; yet by looking in a mirror at the form and the configuration of their roundness, they see themselves through the intermediary of the icon. In the same way, the soul must look at its own icon and consider as its own that which it sees in the stamp from which it has received resemblance. We should, however, modify the example a bit so that the idea is appropriate to reason; for the icon of the form appearing in the mirror is an imitation of the archetype, while for the stamp of the soul, our idea is the inverse: as the form of the soul is made in

the icon of divine beauty, so it is that when the soul looks at its archetype, then it is itself that it sees with clarity (κατὰ γὰρ τὸ θεῖον κάλλος, τὸ τῆς ψυχῆς εἶ δος ἀπεικονίζεται).” And see as well Gregory of Nyssa, *Against Eunomius* XII, *PG*, 45, 946d and following. Valuable analyses are to be found in Jean Daniélou, *Platonisme et théologie mystique: Essai sur la doctrine spirituelle de Grégoire de Nysse* (Paris: Aubier, 1944), 45ff., 223; and in Walther Völker, *Gregor von Nyssa als Mystiker* (Wiesbaden: F. Steiner, 1955), 132, 182. — Taking up this argument, Basil of Caesarea puts into relation our unknowing of the things of the present world and our unknowing of the Spirit. Gregory of Nyssa, *Against Eunomius* III, 6, *PG*, 29, 668b and following; see B. Sesboüé, ed., Sources chrétiennes, no. 305 (Paris: Éditions du Cerf, 1983), 166ff. We find the theme in John Chrysostom, too: “[W]e do not even know well the essence of our own souls; rather, we do not have any knowledge whatsoever of that essence.” Saint John Chrysostom, *On the Incomprehensible Nature of God*, Homily V, paras. 27ff., *PG*, 48, 740d; English translation: Saint John Chrysostom, *On the Incomprehensible Nature of God*, trans. Paul W. Harkins, Fathers of the Church, vol. 72 (Washington, DC: Catholic University of America Press, 1984), 149. Saint Augustine will powerfully echo this: “[T]here is something of man which is unknown even to the spirit of man which is in him (*aliquid hominis, quod nec ipse scit spiritus hominis, qui in ipso est*), but you, Lord, you know everything about him, you who made him.” Saint Augustine, *Confessions*, X.5.7, p. 182 (translation modified). See my commentary in Jean-Luc Marion, *Au lieu de soi: L’approche de saint Augustin* (Paris: Presses Universitaires de France, 2009), II, § 10, pp. 106–8; and Marion, *In the Self’s Place*, 67–68.

65. Basil of Caesarea, *On the Origin of Man*, I, 7, *PG*, 44, 264b; and Basil of Caesarea, *Sur l’origine de l’homme: Homélie X et XI de l’Hexaéméron*, ed. Alexis Smets and Michel Van Esbroeck, Sources chrétiennes, no. 160 (Paris: Éditions du Cerf, 1970), 182. At issue is the “inner” man, as opposed to “phenomenal (φαινομένον) man,” for we are “double (διπλοῖ)”: could this also be understood in the sense of the split between *I* and *me*?

66. For example, in John Scotus Eriugena, *De divisione naturae* II, 27, *PL*, 122, 584d–585d; English translation: Johannes Scotus Eriugena, *Periphyseon (The Division of Nature)*, trans. I. P. Sheldon-Williams, rev. John J. O’Meara (Montreal: Editions Bellarmin / Washington, DC: Dumbarton Oaks, 1987), 191 (translation modified). But reference is also made here to Gregory of Nazianzus (particularly his *Discourse* 29, *PG*, 36, 93b) and to Maximus Confessor (particularly his *Ambigua* XVII, *PG*, 91, 1229b–d). See the notes of Francis Bertin, trans., in Jean Scot Erigène, *De divisione naturae*, vol. 2 (Paris: Presses Universitaires de France, 1995), 453ff.

67. See, among other passages, the following from Eriugena, *De divisione naturae* I, 3: “For just as God as He is in Himself beyond every creature is comprehended by no intellect, so too is the οὐσία, considered in the innermost depths of

the creature which was made by Him, equally incomprehensible" (col. 443b); English translation: Eriugena, *Periphyseon*, 27 (translation modified). And Eriugena, *De divisione naturae* II, 27: "For the Creator, invisible and incomprehensible and passing all understanding, created His image similar to Himself in all these things. For even our intellect is not known as to what it is (*quid sit*) in its essence either by itself or by any other save God Who alone knows what He has made; but as concerning his Creator [man] knows only that He is (*quia est*) but does not perceive what He is (*quid sit*), so concerning himself he only determines that he is (*quia sit*), but how or in what substance he is constituted he cannot understand" (col. 585b); English translation: Eriugena, *Periphyseon*, 190–91 (translation modified).

68. Eriugena, *De divisione naturae* IV, 7, in *PL*, 122, 771bc; and Eriugena, *Periphyseon*, 417–18. The final formula comes from Saint Augustine, *De ordine*, II, 16, 44, in *PL*, 32, 1015 (and is found again in Dionysos the Areopagite, *Letter* 1, *PG*, 3, 1065ab). But, and such here appears to be the decisive point, the privilege of unknowing (see Jean-Luc Marion, *De surcroît: Études sur les phénomènes saturés* [Paris: Presses Universitaires de France, 2001], chap. 6, § 5, pp. 179–90; English translation: Jean-Luc Marion, *In Excess: Studies of Saturated Phenomena*, trans. Robyn Horner and Vincent Berraud [New York: Fordham University Press, 2002], 148–58) extends here not only to God, but to man, who thus also requires the three ways of mystical theology (which include the negative).

69. Eriugena, *De divisione naturae* IV, 7; and Eriugena, *Periphyseon*, 418 (translation modified). This has to do exactly with what David Tracy calls "the Incomprehensible-Comprehensible God." David Tracy, *On Naming the Present: God, Humanity and the Church* (New York: Orbis Books, 1994), 54.

70. Eriugena, *De divisione naturae* IV, 7, 772a; and Eriugena, *Periphyseon*, 418. On this doctrine, see Bernard McGinn, "The Negative Element in the Anthropology of John the Scot," in *Jean Scot Erigène et l'histoire de la philosophie (Laon, 7–12 juillet 1975)*, ed. René Roques (Paris: Éditions du CNRS, 1977), 315–25; and Werner Beierwaltes, "Das Problem des absoluten Selbstbewußtseins bei Johannes Scotus Eriugena (*Divina ignorantia summa ac vera sapientia*)," *Philosophisches Jahrbuch* 73 (1966): 264–84. Karl Rahner was even able to show, in a convincing manner, that the incomprehensibility of God had the same consequence for the definition of man in Thomas Aquinas. Karl Rahner, "Thomas Aquinas on the Incomprehensibility of God," supplement, *Journal of Religion* 58 (1978): S107–S125.

71. Saint Augustine, *Confessiones* X.5.7; English translation: Saint Augustine, *Confessions*, 182–83 (translation modified), which quotes at the end Psalm 89 (90):8. See Marion, *In the Self's Place*, 67–68.

72. Saint Augustine, *Confessiones* X.17.26; English translation: Saint Augustine, *Confessions*, 194 (translation modified).

73. Saint Augustine, *Confessiones* X.37.62; English translation: Saint Augustine, *Confessions*, 216 (translation modified).

74. Saint Augustine, *De Trinitate* 10.5.7, in *Corpus Christianorum, Series Latina*, vol. 50, *Sancti Aurelii Augustini, De Trinitate Libri XV (Libri I–XII)*, ed. W. J. Mountain and F. Glorie (Turnhout, Belgium: Brepols, 1968), 320. English translation: Saint Augustine, *The Trinity*, trans. Edmund Hill, OP (Brooklyn, NY: New City Press, 1991), 292 (translation modified).

75. Heidegger formulates it this way: Anyone "for whom the Bible is divine revelation" cannot even ask, "Why are there beings at all instead of nothing?" (or any other question), because he "already has the answer" (which, here, is that "beings, with the exception of God Himself, are created by Him"); indeed, "one who holds on to such faith as a basis can, perhaps, emulate and participate in the asking of our question in a certain way (*in gewisser Weise*), but he cannot authentically question (*nicht eigentlich fragen*) [. . .]. He can only act 'as if' (*nur so tun as ob*)." Martin Heidegger, *Einführung in die Metaphysick*, § 1, in *GA*, 40:8; English translation: Martin Heidegger, *An Introduction to Metaphysics*, trans. Gregory Fried and Richard Polt (New Haven, CT: Yale University Press, 2000), 7. As it happens, this always-already known response belongs to "humanism," and thus to metaphysics: "The Christian sees the humanity of man, the *humanitas* of *homo*, in contradistinction to *Deitas*. He is the man of the history of redemption [. . .] as a 'child of God.'" Martin Heidegger, *Brief über den Humanismus*, in *GA*, 9:319; English translation: "Letter on Humanism," in Martin Heidegger, *Basic Writings*, rev. ed., ed. David Farrell Krell (San Francisco: HarperCollins, 1993), 224.

76. Saint Augustine, *Confessiones*, XIII.22.32; English translation: Saint Augustine, *Confessions*, 292 (translation modified)—quoting successively from Romans 12:2 and Genesis 1:24 and 1:26. See Marion, *In the Self's Place*, chap. 6, § 40 (in answer to chap. 2, § 10), 252–60, 62–68.

77. Heidegger, *Sein und Zeit*, § 10, p. 48; English translation: Heidegger, *Being and Time*, 74.

78. Heidegger, *Sein und Zeit*, § 10, p. 48; English translation: Heidegger, *Being and Time*, 74.

79. Friedrich Nietzsche, *Kritische Studienausgabe*, ed. Giorgio Colli and Mazzino Montinari (Berlin: Walter de Gruyter, 1988), vol. 11, *Nachgelassene Fragmente*, Frühjahr 1884, notebook 25 [428], 125. See "For man is more sick, more uncertain, more mutable, less stabilized [*unfestgestellter*] than any other animal, there is no doubt about that." Friedrich Nietzsche, *On the Genealogy of Morals*, III, § 13, trans. Douglas Smith (Oxford: Oxford World's Classics, 1996), 100.

80. Søren Kierkegaard, *Concluding Unscientific Postscript to "Philosophical Fragments,"* vol. 1 (pt. 2, sect. 2, chap. 1), ed. and trans. Howard V. Hong and Edna H. Hong (Princeton, NJ: Princeton University Press, 1992), 130; and Søren Kierkegaard, *Samlede Vaerker*, 3rd ed. (Copenhagen: Gyldendal, 1963), 7:106. The "most" because this most difficult task first appears to be "insignificant" (ibid.).

81. Pascal, *Pensées* (ed. Lafuma), § 131; and Pascal, *Pensées* (trans. Krailsheimer), 35.

82. Friedrich Nietzsche, *Thus Spoke Zarathustra*, "Prologue," § 3, trans. Adrian Del Caro, ed. Robert Pippin (Cambridge: Cambridge University Press, 2006), 5. See also I, § 5, "On the Despisers of the Body"; I, § 13, "On the Friend"; III, § 13, "On Old and New Tablets," 4; IV, § 8, "The Ugliest Human Being"; and so on.

83. Pascal, *Pensées* (ed. Lafuma), § 130; Pascal, *Pensées* (trans. Krailsheimer), 32 (translation modified); and Friedrich Nietzsche, *Ecce Homo*, "Thus Spoke Zarathustra," § 8, in *The Anti-Christ, Ecce Homo, Twilight of the Idols, and Other Writings*, ed. Aaron Ridley and Judith Norman (Cambridge: Cambridge University Press, 2005), 133.

84. Pico della Mirandola, *De dignitate hominis*, ed. G. Tonion, French trans. Olivier Boulnois (1993; repr., 2nd ed., Paris: Presses Universitaires de France, 2004), 12; English translation in Pico della Mirandola, *The Renaissance Philosophy of Man*, ed. Ernst Cassirer, Paul Oskar Kristeller, and John Herman Randall Jr., trans. Elizabeth Livermore Forbes (Chicago: University of Chicago Press, 1948), 227 (translation modified).

85. Pico della Mirandola, *De dignitate hominis*, 6 (corrected); and Pico della Mirandola, *Renaissance Philosophy of Man*, 224–25 (translation modified).

86. Pico della Mirandola, *De dignitate hominis*, 4 (corrected); and Pico della Mirandola, *Renaissance Philosophy of Man*, 223 (translation modified).

87. Saint Augustine, *Confessiones*, IV.14.22; English translation: Saint Augustine, *Confessions*, 66 (translation modified).

88. Voltaire, *Lettres philosophiques*, letter 25, "Sur les *Pensées* de Pascal," III, in *Mélanges*, ed. J. Van den Heuvel (Paris: Gallimard, Pléiade, 1961), 106; and Voltaire, *Philosophical Letters; or, Letters Regarding the English Nation*, ed. John Leigh, trans. Prudence L. Steiner (Indianapolis: Hackett, 2007), 102, 103.

89. Sartre: "As our point of departure there can be no other truth than this: *I think therefore I am.* This is the absolute truth of consciousness attaining itself." Jean-Paul Sartre, *L'existentialisme est un humanisme*, ed. A. Elkaïm-Sartre (Paris: Gallimard, 1996), 57 (first published in Paris by Nagel, 1946); and Jean-Paul Sartre, *Existentialism Is a Humanism, Including a Commentary on the Stranger*, trans. Carol Macomber (New Haven, CT: Yale University Press, 2007), 40 (translation modified). It is precisely this point of departure (which, by the way, is not Cartesian, for Sartre adds, "consciousness attaining itself") that Merleau-Ponty will quickly challenge: "Must we say then that philosophy is humanist? No, if one understands by 'man' an explanatory principle which ought to be substituted for others. One explains nothing by man, since he is not a force but a weakness at the heart of being." Maurice Merleau-Ponty, *Éloge de la philosophie* (first published 1953; 3rd ed., Paris: Gallimard, 1979), 52; and Maurice Merleau-Ponty, *In Praise of Philosophy and Other Essays*, trans. John Wild, James Edie, and John O'Neill (Evanston, IL: Northwestern University Press, 1988), 44 (translation modified).

90. "Every human reality is a passion in that it projects losing itself so as to found being and by the same stroke to constitute the In-itself which escapes con-

tingency by being its own foundation, the *Ens causa sui*, which religions call God." Jean-Paul Sartre, *L'Etre et le Néant* (Paris: Gallimard, 1943), 708; and Jean-Paul Sartre, *Being and Nothingness: An Essay on Phenomenological Ontology*, trans. Hazel E. Barnes (New York: Washington Square Press, 1966), 784. The extraordinary imprecision of the vocabulary and of the formulas is not enough to blur the essential: the *causa sui* constitutes the horizon (in fact impracticable, but at least also *fixed*) of the *cogitatio sui*, untenable and, what is more, not held by Sartre himself. Needless to say, for Descartes, to attribute the *causa sui* to man would have had no sense whatsoever, especially since it was already very difficult for him to assign it to God (which, of course, the "religions" have never done, or dreamed of doing). It would be useless to recall this, if certain imprecise historians of philosophy were not trying to muddle this obvious fact.

91. Heidegger, *Brief über den Humanismus*, in *GA*, 9:321; and Heidegger, "Letter on Humanism," 225, 226.

92. Heidegger, *Brief über den Humanismus*, in *GA*, 9:323, 9:330; and Heidegger, *Basic Writings*, 233–34, 230.

Chapter II

1. René Char, *Recherche de la base et du sommet*, in *Oeuvres complètes* (Paris: Gallimard, Pléiade, 1983), 631.

2. "*Ipsa incomprehensibilitas in ratione formali infiniti continetur.*" René Descartes, *Quintae responsiones*, in AT, VII:368, lines 3–4; and René Descartes, *The Philosophical Writings of Descartes*, trans. John Cottingham, Robert Stoothoff, and Dugald Murdoch, vol. 2 (Cambridge: Cambridge University Press, 1984), 253 (translation modified). Voltaire repeats this nicely: "By the very fact that an infinite being is demonstrated, it is demonstrated to us as well that it must be impossible for a finite being to understand it." Voltaire, *Traité de métaphysique*, chap. 2 in *Mélanges*, ed. J. Van den Heuvel (Paris: Gallimard, Pléiade, 1961), 167.

3. Thomas Hobbes: "Whatsoever we imagine is *Finite*. Therefore there is no idea or conception of any thing we call *Infinite*. No man can have in his mind an image of infinite magnitude; nor conceive infinite swiftness, infinite time, or infinite force, or infinite power. When we say any thing is infinite, we signify only, that we are not able to conceive the ends, and bounds of the thing named; having no conception of the thing, but of our inability. And therefore the Name of *God* is used, not to make us conceive him; (for he is *Incomprehensible*; and his greatness, and power are unconceivable); but that we may honour him." Thomas Hobbes, *Leviathan*, chap. 3 (London: Penguin Books, 1985), 99. In a sense, there is nothing more biblical than this position.

4. See Jean-Luc Marion, *The Idol and Distance: Five Studies*, trans. Thomas A. Carlson (New York: Fordham University Press, 2001); and Jean-Luc Marion, *God without Being*, trans. Thomas A. Carlson (Chicago: University of Chicago Press, 1991), §§ 1–8, pp. 7–24.

5. Blaise Pascal, *Pensées*, in *Oeuvres complètes*, ed. Louis Lafuma (Paris: Seuil, 1963), § 449; and Blaise Pascal, *Pensées*, trans. A. J. Krailsheimer (London: Penguin, 1995), 140.

6. Heidegger establishes not only the finitude of Dasein ("*Ursprünglicher als der Mensch ist die Endlichkeit des Daseins in ihm*") ("[M]ore original in man than himself is the finitude of the Dasein in him") (Martin Heidegger, *Kant und das Problem der Metaphysik*, § 41, in *GA*, 3 [Frankfurt: Vittorio Klostermann, 1991], 141; and Martin Heidegger, *Kant and the Problem of Metaphysics*, 5th ed. enlarged, trans. Richard Taft [Bloomington: Indiana University Press, 1997], 160), but also the finitude of being itself: "*Das Wesen des Seyns ist in sich endlich*" ("Being is in itself finite") (Martin Heidegger, *Schelling: Vom Wesen der menschlichen Freiheit [1809]*, in *GA*, 42 [Frankfurt: Vittorio Klostermann, 1988], 140; and Martin Heidegger, *Schelling's Treatise on the Essence of Human Freedom*, trans. Joan Stambaugh [Athens: Ohio University Press, 1985], 82). See also Martin Heidegger, *Besinnung*, IV, 20, in *GA*, 66 (Frankfurt: Vittorio Klostermann, 1997), 87ff. — One is accustomed to challenging the dialectic between the finite and the infinite as purely metaphysical, by privileging (at least since Feuerbach) a finitude unscathed by any relation to the infinite, or even more by any relation to an infinite anterior to it, the positivity of which would make it possible (according to the thesis of Descartes). The metaphysical origin (Duns Scotus and Suárez) of the distinction of the concept of *ens* into finite and infinite is hardly doubtful, but the real intelligibility of a finitude without the background or the foreground of the infinite remains problematic. Must not this infinite, even and above all if it is nonontic, fulfill a transcendental function toward the finite, and thus finitude? Or if not, then it would be necessary to conceive a finitude not only without the infinite, but also without the finite. Think it if you can.

7. See Jocelyn Benoist in his critique of certain of my previous works: "Is it enough not to be a concept to be God?"; or "It is hardly sufficient, either, not to be an object to be God." Jocelyn Benoist, *L'idée de phénoménologie* (Paris: Beauchesne, 2001), 86, 96. — In taking this objection into consideration here, I am obviously running counter to (albeit provisionally, see §§ 11–13) my own thesis concerning the unavoidable necessity of the counter-experience as the only mode of experience appropriate to the phenomenality of saturated phenomena. See Jean-Luc Marion, *Étant donné: Essai d'une phénoménologie de la donation* (Paris: Presses Universitaires de France, 1998), § 22, pp. 300–309; and Jean-Luc Marion, *Being Given: Toward a Phenomenology of Givenness*, trans. Jeffrey L. Kosky (Stanford, CA: Stanford University Press, 2002), 212–21. For a detailed response to Benoist's objection as such, see Jean-Luc Marion, *Le visible et le révélé* (Paris: Cerf, 2005), chap. 6, "La banalité de la saturation," in particular 150–54, 170–75; and Jean-Luc Marion, *The Visible and the Revealed*, trans. Christina M. Gschwandtner et al. (New York: Fordham University Press, 2008), 123–25, 174–76.

8. Martin Heidegger, *Geschichte der Philosophie von Thomas von Aquinas bis Kant*, in *GA*, 23 (Frankfurt: Vittorio Klostermann, 2006), 77.

9. Immanuel Kant, *Critique of Pure Reason*, A297/B354–A298, trans. and ed. Paul Guyer and Allen W. Wood (Cambridge: Cambridge University Press, 1998), 386.

10. "*Qui autem negant se habere ideam Dei, sed vice illius efformant aliquod idolum etc., nomen negant, et rem concedunt.*" René Descartes, *Secundae responsiones*, in AT, VII:139, lines 5–7; and Descartes, *Philosophical Writings*, 2:99 (translation modified). And also: "Is it possible that [your correspondent (Gassendi)] could not, as he says, understand what I mean by the idea of God, the idea of the soul, and the ideas of imperceptible things? I mean only what he must necessarily have understood himself when he wrote to you that he did not understand my meaning. For he does not say that he had no conception corresponding to the expressions 'God,' 'soul,' 'imperceptible things'; he just says that he did not know what was to be understood by the idea of these things. But if he had any conception corresponding to these expressions, as he doubtless had, he knew at the same time what was to be understood by the ideas—namely nothing other than the conception which he himself had." René Descartes, *To Mersenne*, July 1641, in AT, III:392, lines 11–24; and Descartes, *The Philosophical Writings of Descartes*, trans. John Cottingham, Robert Stoothoff, Dugald Murdoch, and Anthony Kenny (Cambridge: Cambridge University Press, 1991), 3:184–85.

11. Homer, *The Odyssey*, bk. X, line 306: θεοὶ δέ πάντα τε δύνανται (see also XIV, line 445: δύναται γὰρ ἅπαντα). *The Odyssey*, with an English translation by A. T. Murray, in 2 vols. (1919; repr., Cambridge, MA: Harvard University Press, 1966), 1:366, 2:66.

12. "*Nihil est, inquiunt, quod deus efficere non possit.*" Cicero, *De divinatione*, bk. 2, § 41, 86, in *De senectute; De amicitia; De divinatione*, ed. and trans. W. A. Falconer (Cambridge, MA: Harvard University Press, 1923), 468. See: "*[V]os* [the Stoics?] *enim ipsi dicere soletis nihil esse quod deus efficere non possit et quidem sine labore ullo.*" ("[F]or you yourselves often claim that there is nothing which God cannot perform, and effortlessly at that.") Cicero, *De natura deorum*, bk. 3, 39, 92, in *Cicero in Twenty-Eight Volumes*, vol. 19, *De natura deorum: Academica*, with an English translation by H. Rackham (Cambridge, MA: Harvard University Press, 1933), 378; English translation: Cicero, *The Nature of the Gods*, trans. with introduction and explanatory notes, P. G. Walsh (Oxford: Clarendon Press, 1997), 144.

13. Respectively: "*Sed Deo nihil est impossibile, nisi quod non vult*" (Tertullian, *De Carne Christi*, III, in *PL*, 2, 756b; English translation: Tertullian, *Tertullian's Treatise on the Incarnation*, ed., introduction, trans., and commentary, Ernest Evans [London: S.P.C.K, 1956], 9); and Gregory of Nyssa, *De hominis opificio*, XXVI, in *PG*, 44, 224bc; English translation: Gregory of Nyssa, "On the Making of Man," in *Gregory of Nyssa: Dogmatic Treatises*, trans. William Moore and Henry Austin

Wilson, vol. 5 of *Nicene and Post-Nicene Fathers of the Christian Church*, ser. 2, ed. Philip Schaff and Henry Wace (Grand Rapids, MI: Eerdmans, 1965), 417.

14. "*Omnis quippe necessitas et impossibilitas eius subiacet voluntati. Illius autem voluntas nulli subditur necessitati aut impossibilitati.*" Anselm, *Cur Deus homo?*, II, 17, in S. Anselmi Cantuariens, *Libri Duo: Cur Deus Homo*, ed. Hugo Laemmer (Berlin: Gust. Schlawitz, 1857), 79; English translation in Anselm, *Complete Philosophical and Theological Treatises of Anselm of Canterbury*, trans. Jasper Hopkins and Herbert Richardson (Minneapolis: Arthur J. Banning Press, 2000), 376.

15. "*Quamobrem indubitabili fide credendum est, Deum omnia posse, sive faciat, sive non faciat.*" Peter Damian, *Letter on the Omnipotence of God*, X, 1, in *PL*, 145, 610d; English translation in Peter Damian, *Letters, 91–120*, The Fathers of the Church, Mediaeval Continuation, vol. 5, trans. Owen J. Blum, OFM (Washington, DC: Catholic University of America Press, 1998), letter 119, para. 80, p. 383.

16. "*Deus dicatur omnipotens, quia potest omnia possibilia absolute, quod est alter modus dicendi possibile.*" Thomas Aquinas, *Summa theologiae*, Ia, q. 25, a. 3, *resp.*, in Sancti Thomae de Aquino, *Summa theologiae* (Cinisello Balsamo, Italy: Edizioni San Paolo, 1988), 136; English translation in Thomas Aquinas, *Basic Writings of Saint Thomas Aquinas*, ed. Anton C. Pegis (Indianapolis: Hackett, 1997), I:263.

17. Michel de Montaigne, *Essais*, I, 27, ed. Pierre Villey (Paris: Presses Universitaires de France, 1965), 1:179; English translation in Michel de Montaigne, *The Complete Essays of Montaigne*, trans. Donald M. Frame (Stanford, CA: Stanford University Press, 1958), 132. He continues: "[T]o condemn them as impossible is to pretend, with rash presumption, to know the limits of possibility." Montaigne, *Essais*, 1:180; and Montaigne, *Complete Essays*, 133. Montaigne could also be recalling Rabelais: "But tell me, if it had been the will of God, would you say that he could not do it? Ha, for favour sake, I beseech you, emberlucock or impulregafize your spirits with these vain thoughts and idle conceits; for I tell you, it is not impossible with God; and, if he pleased, all women henceforth should bring forth their children at the ear." François Rabelais, *Gargantua*, chap. 6, in *Oeuvres complètes*, ed. Guy Demerson (Paris: Seuil, 1973), 57; English translation: François Rabelais, *Gargantua and Pantegruel*, trans. Thomas Urquhart and Peter Motteux (London: Wordsworth Editions, 1999), 22.

18. "*Infixa quaedam est meae menti vetus opinio, Deum esse qui potest omnia.*" René Descartes, *Meditationes*, 1, in AT, VII:21, lines 1–2; and Descartes, *Philosophical Writings*, 2:14 (translation modified). One could also rely on the determination of God as an "incomprehensible power" who creates even the supposedly eternal mathematical truths. René Descartes, *To Mersenne*, 6 May 1630, in AT, I:150; and Descartes, *Philosophical Writings*, 3:25. Here in particular Descartes follows Montaigne, *Essais* II, 12, pp. 2:523, 2:527–28, 2:540.

19. "*Mihi autem non videtur de ulla umquam re esse dicendum, ipsam a Deo fieri*

non posse." René Descartes, "Letter to Arnauld," 29 July 1648, in AT, V: p. 223, line 31–p. 224, line 1; and Descartes, *Philosophical Writings*, 3:358.

20. John Locke, *An Essay Concerning Human Understanding*, bk. IV, chap. 10, § 4, ed. Roger Woolhouse (London: Penguin, 2004), 548. — The emergence of modern "atheism" naturally has had to assume a residual definition of the nonexisting or presumed not to exist "God" ("O you whose existence is still a problem," bemoaned Sylvain Maréchal, in 1781: Sylvain Maréchal, *Anthologie de la poésie française*, vol. 2 [Paris: Gallimard, Pléiade, 2000], 298); this was precisely the notion of "universal cause," the notion of omnipotence closest to the impossible (as Winfried Schröder has shown, in Winfried Schröder, *Ursprünge des Atheismus: Untersuchungen zur Metaphysik und Religionskritik des 17. und 18. Jahrhunderts* [esp. IV, 2, a] [Stuttgart: Frommann-Holzboog, 1998], 209ff.).

21. Søren Kierkegaard, *Kjerlighedens Gjerninger*, I, chap. 2, C, in *Samlede Vaerker*, 2nd ed., ed. A. B. Drachmann, J. L. Heigergand, and H. O. Lange (Copenhagen: Gyldendal, 1920–36), 9:81; English translation: Søren Kierkegaard, *Works of Love*, trans. Howard Hong and Edna Hong (New York: Harper & Row, 1962), 77. See P. Grosos, "L'existence impossible (Kierkegaard)," *Quaestio*, no. 3: L'existence (Turnhout-Bari: Brepols-Pagina, 2003), 265–79.

22. Emmanuel Levinas, *Autrement qu'être ou au-delà de l'essence* (The Hague: Nijhoff, 1974), 165; and Emmanuel Levinas, *Otherwise Than Being or Beyond Essence*, trans. Alphonso Lingis (1981; repr., Pittsburgh: Duquesne University Press, 1997), 128. — Blanchot noted very clearly the repercussions of Levinas's returns to and inversions of the formula of Heidegger on "the death without expression, the death without any name, the death outside the concept—*impossibility itself*." Maurice Blanchot, *L'écriture du désastre* (Paris: Gallimard, 1980), 112, see also 81, 106, 114; and Maurice Blanchot, *The Writing of the Disaster*, new ed., trans. Ann Smock (Lincoln: University of Nebraska Press, 1995), 68.

23. See my book *Le phénomène érotique: Six méditations*, § 37 (Paris: Grasset, 2003), 297–302; and Jean-Luc Marion, *The Erotic Phenomenon*, trans. Stephen E. Lewis (Chicago: University of Chicago Press, 2007), 191–95. In other words: "*Pero esto tiene la fuerza y vehemencia de amor, que todo le parece posible.*" Saint John of the Cross, *Noche oscura* II, 13, 7, in *Obras completas* (Madrid: BAC, 1974), 667; "The strength and the vehemence of love has this trait: Everything seems possible to it." Saint John of the Cross, *The Collected Works of St. John of the Cross*, trans. Kieran Kavanaugh, OCD, and Otilio Rodriguez, OCD (Washington, DC: ICS Publications, 1979), 359.

24. Jacques Derrida, *Sauf le nom* (Paris: Galilée, 1993), 31; and Jacques Derrida, *On the Name*, ed. Thomas Dutoit, trans. David Wood, John P. Leavey Jr., and Ian McLeod (Stanford, CA: Stanford University Press, 1995), 43. See also Jacques Derrida, *Psyché: L'invention de l'autre* (Paris: Galilée, 1987), 59 and passim. A dossier can be found in H. Rayment-Pickart, *Impossible God: Derrida's Theology* (Burlington, VT: Ashgate Publishing, 2003), but first in John D. Caputo, "Apostles of

the Impossible: On God and the Gift in Derrida and Marion," in *God, the Gift, and Postmodernism*, ed. John D. Caputo and Michael J. Scanlon (Bloomington: Indiana University Press, 1999). His conclusion is accurate: "It can be said in defense of the Kingdom of God that it is not simply impossible, but rather, let us say, *the* impossible." John D. Caputo, "The Poetics of the Impossible and the Kingdom of God," in *The Blackwell Companion to Postmodern Theology*, ed. Graham Ward (Oxford: Blackwell Publishing, 2001); reprinted in *Rethinking Philosophy of Religion: Approaches from Continental Philosophy*, ed. Philip Goodchild (New York: Fordham University Press, 2002).

25. And "God in the church is the completed mask of the impossible." Georges Bataille, *Le petit*, in *Oeuvres complètes*, vol. 3 (Paris: Gallimard, 1971), 47. On this theme, see Kevin Hart, *The Impossible* (Newtown, NSW: Vagabond Press, 2003); and his *The Dark Gaze: Maurice Blanchot and the Sacred* (Chicago: University of Chicago Press, 2004), chap. 4. See also Nicole Gueunier, "L'impossible de Georges Bataille: Essai de description structurale," in *Essais de sémiotique poétique* (Paris: Larousse, 1972); and Jean-Michel Besnier, *La politique de l'impossible* (Paris: La Découverte, 1988).

26. Jules Renard, *Journal, 1887–1910*, ed. Léon Guichard and Gilbert Signaux (Paris: Gallimard, Pléiade, 1960), 217.

27. "*Unde cum Deo nihil sit impossibile, oportet per ea quae in hoc mundo sunt impossibilia nos ad ipsum respicere, apud quem impossibilitas est necessitas.*" Nicholas of Cusa, *Trialogus de possest*, in *Werke*, ed. Paul Wilpert (Berlin: Walter de Gruyter, 1967), 2:66; English translation in Nicholas of Cusa, *Complete Philosophical and Theological Treatises of Nicholas of Cusa*, trans. Jasper Hopkins (Minneapolis: Arthur J. Banning Press, 2001), 2:946.

28. Tertullian, respectively: "*Deum nosse, qui non alia lege credendus est, quam ut omnia posse credatur*" (Tertullian, *De Resurrectione Carnis*, XI, in *PL*, 2, 809b; Tertullian, *Tertullian's Treatise on the Resurrection*, trans. Ernest Evans [London: S.P.C.K., 1960], 31); and "*Et sepultus, resurrexit: certum est, quia impossibile*" (Tertullian, *De Carne Christi*, V, 4, in *PL*, 2, 761a; Tertullian, *Treatise on the Incarnation*, 19). On Tertullian's skillful use of paradoxes, see Willemien Otten, "Christ's Birth of a Virgin Who Became a Wife: Flesh and Speech in Tertullian's *De Carne Christi*," *Virgilliae Christianae* 51 (Leiden: Brill, 1997).

29. On counter-experience, see Marion, *Étant donné*, § 22, pp. 300–302; Marion, *Being Given*, 215–16; and Marion, *Le visible et le révélé*, chap. 6, pp. 170–75.

30. It is not at all evident that such a dependence of the undergoing of self on its counterordeal by the infinite contradicts the primacy of autoaffection, such as Michel Henry defined it. Indeed, it couldn't be the case, unless the infinite were to remain exterior to finitude, as an other to it. On the contrary, the counter-experience of the infinite implies that the infinite affects, right away and first of all, the finite in me. For I am not first of all finite, so as next to find myself affected by the infinite, but rather the infinite affects me more originally than myself (and whatever else

there may *be*), therefore like me *before* me. The original delay of the finite over the infinite exposes temporally what is presented spatially by the inclusion in the (finite) limit of its external bound (access to the infinite).

31. Jules Supervielle, *La fable du monde* (Paris: Gallimard, 1950), 55.

32. "*Sed, qui absque dubio omnipotens est, per impossibilitatem excusari non potest.*" Richard of St. Victor, *De Trinitate*, III, chap. 4, in *PL*, 196, 918; English translation in Richard of St. Victor, *The Twelve Patriarchs; The Mystical Ark; Book Three of the Trinity*, trans. Grover A. Zinn (Mahwah, NJ: Paulist Press, 1979), 377 (translation modified). In his own way, Voltaire sometimes approaches this argument: "The arguments against creation boil down to showing that it *is impossible for us* to conceive of it, that is to say, to conceive its means, but not that it is impossible *as such*; for in order for creation to be impossible, it would first be necessary to prove that a God is impossible; but far from proving this impossibility, one is forced to recognize that it is impossible for him not to exist." Voltaire, *Traité de métaphysique*, 167.

33. The impossibility of the impossible also defines love. See Marion, *Erotic Phenomenon*, § 37, p. 193; and Marion, *Le phénomène érotique*, 299. There cannot be any difficulty here unless one is surprised by the identity of God and love. That it goes without saying nevertheless does not mean that it allows itself to be thought cheaply.

34. Angelus Silesius, *Cherubinischer Wandersmann*, VI, 153, in *Sämtliche Poetische Werke*, ed. H. L. Held, 3rd ed. (Munich: Hanser, 1949), 3:206. I maintain the ambiguity raised by Jacques Derrida: effectively, *Überunmöglichste* "can signify just as well 'most' or 'more than': the most impossible or the more than impossible." Derrida, *Sauf le nom*, 33; English translation: Derrida, *On the Name*, 44.

35. Indeed, one could reasonably argue that Descartes (René Descartes, *Meditationes, V*, in AT, VII:66, lines 2–15; Descartes, *Primae responsiones*, in AT, VII:116, lines 8–19; and René Descartes, *Principia philosophiae*, I, § 16, in AT, VIII: p. 10, line 27–p. 11, line 4) and Hegel (G. W. F. Hegel, *Wissenschaft der Logik*, I, 1, chap. 1, Anmerkung 1, ed. G. Lasson [Hamburg: F. Meiner, 1934], 1:75) respond to Kant correctly: in the case of all the other beings, we have reason to distinguish the concept from the existence; but this "habit" is precisely no longer valid in the case of God, who by definition makes an exception to the rule of common beingness. What is more, Saint Anselm bases his entire argument not on the essence of God (for in sound theology, either it remains inaccessible to us, or God does without it), but on its absence. See my study in *Questions cartésiennes: Méthode et métaphysique* (Paris: Presses Universitaires de France, 1991), chap. 7, "L'argument relève-t-il de l'ontologie?," 221–58; English translation: *Cartesian Questions: Method and Metaphysics* (Chicago: University of Chicago Press, 1999), 139–60. In fact, Kant's refutation presupposes what he had to demonstrate: that if God is, then he is according to the same principles as the other entities, or put otherwise, that he submits himself to the (transcendental) conditions of general experience; in short, that he only

has the rank of an object of experience, among all the others. The Kantian refutation of the "ontological" argument *presupposes* that God is not God; it does not demonstrate it. And without this presupposition, it could not demonstrate that the existence of God cannot be demonstrated a priori. That Kant's counterargument has been able to impose itself as evident attests only to the profound lack of theological cultivation among the majority of modern philosophers, rather than reinforcing it in any way.

36. The point is less that of proving the existence of God than that his impossibility exactly contradicts the definition of the essence and thus of the entity as possibility. As impossible, God is from the outset outside essence, and therefore already outside being [*hors d'être*] (at least outside of the situation of Being as a being) in the sense of ontology (*metaphysica generalis*) within the system of metaphysics.

37. That God does not remain impossible to himself nevertheless does not cast the shadow of a *causa sui* onto the impossible: the *causa sui* enters into metaphysics under the authority of the principle of causality universalized to the point of anticipating the principle of sufficient reason; God must cause himself, because every existence requires a cause, or a reason to do without it (as it happens, his own proper essence considered as an infinite power); thus, the *causa sui* depends on possibility (an essence), in view of fulfilling it to the point of an existence, *complementum possibilitatis*. The issue, then, is an inverse argument from that allowed by the impossible. In one case the conditioned possibility (of the essence) accomplishes existence, while in the other impossibility forbids the impossibility of the unconditioned possibility, without however positing the least existence.

38. Note that Siger de Brabant puts at the head of his *impossibilia* the following: "*primum fuit* Deus non esse." And he argues that "this is the first impossible, since its opposite is the first necessary." See Siger de Brabant, "Die *impossibilia* von Siger von Brabant," in *Beiträge zur Geschichte der Philosophie des Mittelalters*, ed. C. Baeumker, vol. 2 (Münster: Aschendorff Verlag, 1908), 1. But he, too, quickly leads the impossibility (of impossibility) back to the necessity of existence, instead of maintaining it as an absolute possibility.

39. "*Ita ut solus Deus id sit quod esse potest, nequaquam autem quaecumque creatura, cum potentia et actus non sint idem, nisi in principio.*" Nicholas of Cusa, *Trialogus de possest*, 646; English translation: Nicholas of Cusa, *Complete Philosophical and Theological Treatises*, 917 (translation modified). And: "*Deus sit absoluta potentia et actus atque utriusque nexus et ideo sit actu omne possibile esse.*" Nicholas of Cusa, *Trialogus de possest*, 646; English translation: "God is Absolute Possibility, is Actuality, and is the Union of the two (and so, He is actually every possible being)." Nicholas of Cusa, *Complete Philosophical and Theological Treatises*, 917.

40. "*Deum id esse quod esse potest.*" Nicholas of Cusa, *Trialogus de possest*, 646; English translation: Nicholas of Cusa, *Complete Philosophical and Theological Treatises*, 917.

41. "*Nulla creatura est possest.*" Nicholas of Cusa, *Trialogus de possest*, 654; English translation: Nicholas of Cusa, *Complete Philosophical and Theological Treatises*, 928.

42. "*Increata possibilitas est ipsum possest.*" Nicholas of Cusa, *Trialogus de possest*, 654; English translation: Nicholas of Cusa, *Complete Philosophical and Theological Treatises*, 929.

43. "*Esto enim quod aliqua dictio significet simplicissimo significatu quantum hoc complexum: posse est, scilicet quod ipsum posse sit. Et quia, quod est, actu est, ideo posse esse est tantum quantum posse esse actu. Puta vocetur possest [. . .] est Dei satis propinquum nomen secundum humanum de eo conceptum. Est enim nomen omnium et singulorum nominum atque nullius pariter. Ideo dum Deus sui vellet notitiam primo revelare, dicebat: 'Ego' sum 'Deus omnipotens,' id est 'Sum actus omnis potentiae.'*" Nicholas of Cusa, *Trialogus de possest*, 649; English translation: Nicholas of Cusa, *Complete Philosophical and Theological Treatises*, 921. See also: "*supra omne nomen quo id, quod potest esse, est nominabile, immo supra ipsum esse et non esse omni modo quo illa intelligi possunt*" ("above every name by which what-is-able-to-be is nameable[, i]ndeed, above being and not-being [in whatsoever manner being and not-being can be conceived]"). Nicholas of Cusa, *Trialogus de possest*, 653; English translation: Nicholas of Cusa, *Complete Philosophical and Theological Treatises*, 927. Possibility (unconditioned) is here exactly equivalent to an indifference toward the difference between being and not-being.

44. Kant, *Critique of Pure Reason*, A290/B346, p. 382.

45. Thomas Aquinas: "*Deus dicatur omnipotens, quia potest omnia possibilia absolute, quod est alter modus dicendi possibile. Dicitur autem aliquid possibile vel impossibile absolute, ex habitudine terminorum [praedicatum repugnat subjecto]. [. . .] Quaecumque igitur contradictionem non implicant, sub illis possibilibus continentur, respectu quorum dicitur Deus omnipotens.*" Aquinas, *Summa theologiae*, Ia, q. 25, a. 3, *resp.*, in Sancti Thomae de Aquino, *Summa theologiae*, 136; English translation in Aquinas, *Basic Writings*, I:263; see also *Summa contra gentiles*, I, chaps. 22 and 25, in Sancti Thomae Aquinatis, *Opera omnia*, vol. 13, *Summa contra gentiles* (Rome: Riccardi Garroni, 1918), 68–69, 76–77. This limitation of divine omnipotence to what is logically possible will remain the position of Duns Scotus: "*Alio modo 'omnipotens' accipitur proprie theologice, prout omnipotens dicitur qui potest in omne effectum et quodcumque possibile (hoc est in quodcumque quod non est ex se necessarium nec includit contradictionem)*" (John Duns Scotus, *Ordinatio*, I, d. 42, n. 9, in *Opera omnia*, ed. C. Balic [Rome: Vatican Polyglot, 1963], 6:343; and even by way of *potentia absoluta*: see *Ordinatio* I, d. 44, n. 7, pp. 365ff.); and likewise for Ockham (see *Quodlibet* III, q. 3, and VI, q. 6; see Philotheus Boehner, *Collected Articles on Ockham*, ed. E. M. Buytaert [New York: Franciscan Institute, 1958], 151ff; as well as the texts translated by Elizabeth Karger in her article "Causalité divine et Toute-Puissance," in *La puissance et son ombre: De Pierre Lombard à Luther*, ed. Olivier Boulnois [Paris: Aubier, 1994], 321–56]). An exception to the logical

limitation of divine omnipotence is perhaps found in Hugh of Saint-Cher. See Eugenio Randi, "*Potentia Dei conditionata*: Una questione di Ugo di Saint-Cher sulla onnipotenza divina (*Sent. I*, d. 42, q. 1)," *Rivista di Storia della Filosofia* 39 (1984): 521–36.

46. Nicolas Malebranche, *Traité de morale*, pt. II, chap. 9, § 12, in *Oeuvres complètes de Malebranche*, ed. André Robinet, vol. 11, ed. Michel Adam (Paris: Vrin, 1966), 226.

47. Ibid., pt. I, chap. 1, § 23, p. 27.

48. C. Wolff: "*Possibile est quod nullam contradictionem involvit seu quod non est impossibile.*" Christian Wolff, *Philosophia prima sive Ontologia* (Frankfurt and Leipzig: Renger, 1730), § 79; modern edition: Christian Wolff, *Philosophia prima sive Ontologia*, ed. J. Ecole (Hildesheim, Germany: Georg Olms, 1962), 65.

49. Descartes, "Letter to Arnauld," 29 July 1648, in AT, V:223, lines 29–30. See my clarification in *Sur la théologie blanche de Descartes: Analogie, création des vérités éternelles et fondement*, 2nd ed. (Paris: Presses Universitaires de France, 1991), § 13, pp. 296–303.

50. Alexander Gottlieb Baumgarten: "*Nihil negativum,* irrespresentabile, *impossibile, repugnans (absurdum), contradictionem involvans, implicans*"; then: "*Nonnihil est aliquid:* repraesentabile, *quidquid non invovit contradictionem, quidquid non est A et non-A, est possibile.*" Alexander Gottlieb Baumgarten, *Metaphysica* (Halle, Germany, 1739); modern edition: Alexander Gottlieb Baumgarten, *Metaphysica* (Hildesheim, Germany, and New York: Georg Olms, 1982), §§ 7 and 8, respectively; English translation: Alexander Baumgarten, *Metaphysics: A Critical Translation with Kant's Elucidations, Selected Notes and Related Materials*, trans. and ed. with an introduction by Courtney D. Fugate and John Hymers (London: Bloomsbury Academic, 2013), 100.

51. Though he didn't make a habit of it, it must be recognized that, at least once, Suárez perfectly distinguished between the two possibles: the possible for God, and the possible for our understanding (thus explicitly critiquing Thomas Aquinas on this point): "Likewise the natural light of our understanding cannot be the rule to measure what is the possible or contradictory object for God's omnipotence (*non potest naturale lumen intellectus nostri esse regula objecti possibilis vel repugnantis omnipotentiae Dei*); otherwise, it would be necessary to judge as contradictory many things that we believe by certain faith. [. . .] For, even if our understanding recoils and does not have the strength to conceive how that can be done (*concipere quomodo id fieri possit*), it is nevertheless not sufficiently grounded to think that it is impossible or opposed to God, but only [to think that it is] above reason or nature (*non habet sufficiens fundamentum ut existimet illud esse impossibile Deo, vel contra, sed supra rationem vel naturam*)." Francisco Suárez, *Disputationes metaphysicae* XXX, s. 17, n. 13, in *Opera omnia*, vol. 26 (Paris: Vivès, 1861), 210, with an impeccable commentary on Luke 1:37 in no. 14 (ibid.).

52. Martin Heidegger, *Sein und Zeit*, 19th ed. (1927; repr., Tübingen, Germany:

Max Niemeyer, 2006), § 7, p. 38; and Martin Heidegger, *Being and Time*, trans. John Macquarrie and Edward Robinson (New York: Harper and Row, 1962), 63.

53. See Marion, *Étant donné*, § 17, pp. 243–44; and Marion, *Being Given*, 172–73.

54. On birth, besides the works of Paul Ricoeur, Michel Henry, Claude Romano (esp. *L'événement et le monde* [Paris: Presses Universitaires de France, 1998], 96–112 / *Event and World*, trans. Shane Mackinlay [New York: Fordham University Press, 2009], 69–82; and *L'événement et le temps* [Paris: Presses Universitaires de France, 1999], 274–80 / *Event and Time*, trans. Stephen E. Lewis [New York: Fordham University Press, 2013], 213–18), and Jean-Louis Chrétien, see Françoise Dastur's analysis, "Pour une phénoménologie de l'événement: L'attente et la surprise," *Etudes phénoménologiques*, no. 25 (1997); English translation: Françoise Dastur, "Phenomenology of the Event: Waiting and Surprise," *Hypatia* 15, no. 4 (Autumn 2000): 178–89. Also, see some indications in my book *In Excess: Studies of Saturated Phenomena*, trans. Robyn Horner and Vincent Berraud (New York: Fordham University Press, 2002), chap. 2, pp. 41–45; as well as below (in this book), chap. III, § 17, pp. 103–106, and chap. V, § 29, pp. 190–194.

55. According to Claude Dagens's accurate formulation: *Le maître de l'impossible* (Paris: Fayard, 1982).

56. I read, following the Greek text of Nestlé and Aland, παρὰ τοῦ θεοῦ in the genetive and not in the dative, τῷ θεῷ: not "for him," but "from his point of view, from his side." *Novum Testamentum graece et latine*, 25th ed. (Stuttgart: Deutsche Bibelgesellschaft, 1965), ad loc. See, on the two extremes, Strack-Billerbeck, which translates this verse "*von vor Gott her*" (Hermann Strack and Paul Billerbeck, eds., *Kommentar zum Neuen Testament aus Talmud und Midrasch* [Munich: Beck, 1924], 2:100), and Claude Tresmontant, who translates this verse "coming on God's behalf" (*Evangile de Luc*, trans. and notes Claude Tresmontant [Paris: OEIL, 1987], 10).

57. As in the Magnificat, in Luke 1:42 (and Acts 10:37). See Heinz Schürmann's remark, in *Das Lukasevangelium* (Freiburg im Breisgau, Germany: Herder, 1969), 57. — On the contrary, Thomas Aquinas curiously refers Luke's verse ("*on erit impossibile apud Deum omne verbum*") to the possible according to mere noncontradiction: "*id enim quod contradictionem implicat, verbum esse non potest: quia nullus intellectus potest illud concipere.*" Aquinas, *Summa theologiae*, Ia, q. 25, a. 3, *resp.*, in Sancti Thomae de Aquino, *Summa theologiae*, 136. Thus, lowering divine transcendence to the level of the metaphysics of omnipotence, he therefore must limit it as well by what is logically possible: "*sub omnipotentia Dei non cadit aliquid quod contradictionem implicat.*" Ibid., Ia, q. 25, a. 4, p. 137.

58. As in Mark 14:36: "Abba, O Father, all things are possible to you" ("πάντα δυνατά"), where precisely the Father does not at this moment put into operation that which appears as a simple arbitrary and empty omnipotence, in the obvious sense of Jesus's prayer (which he moreover withdraws immediately: "not what I will, but what you will").

59. The point is emphasized by J. Reiling and J. L. Swellengrebel: "The future tense, however, is preferable because it shows that the reference is also to what will happen to Mary" (*A Translator's Handbook on the Gospel of Luke* [Leiden, Netherlands: Brill, 1971], 62); and also by François Bovon: "*Die futurische Form steht im Rahmen einer Theologie der Hoffnung: Gott wird bald die mögliche Unmöglichkeit verwirklichen*" (*Das Evangelium nach Lukas (Lk 1,1–9,50)* [Zurich: Benziger/Neukirchener, 1989], 77–78).

60. Origen, *Contra Celsum*, V, 14 and 23 (see *PG*, 11, 1201b and 1215d); English translation: Origen, *Contra Celsum*, trans. Henry Chadwick (Cambridge: Cambridge University Press, 1980), 274–75, 281 (translation modified). A similar answer is given by Gregory of Nazianzus, *Discours théologique* XXX, 30, 10–11, ed. P. Gallay, Sources chrétiennes, no. 250 (Paris: Cerf, 1978), 243ff. (see *PG*, 36, 116b).

61. Despite Saint Augustine's classic argument: "*[C]erta et immutabilis et efficacissima sit voluntas Dei: quam multa possit et non velit, nihil autem velit quod non possit [. . .]. Non ergo fit aliquid nisi omnipotens fieri velit, vel sinendo ut fiat vel ipse faciendo.*" ("[H]ow sure, unchangeable and most efficacious the will of God is, and how many things he could do but does not will to do, while he wills nothing that he cannot do [. . .]. So nothing happens unless the Almighty wills it, either by allowing it to happen or by doing it himself.") Saint Augustine, *Enchiridion*, XXIV, 95, in *Corpus Christianorum, Series Latina*, vol. 46, *Sancti Aurelii Augustini, De Fide rerum invisibilium; Enchiridion ad Laurentium de fide et spe et caritate; De catechizandis rudibus; Sermo ad catechumenos de symbolo; Sermo de disciplina christiana; Sermo de utilitate ieiunii; Sermo de excidio urbis Romae; De haeresibus*, ed. M. P. J. van den Hout et al. (Turnhout, Belgium: Brepols, 1969), 99; English translation: Saint Augustine, *The Augustine Catechism: Enchiridion on Faith, Hope, and Love*, trans. Bruce Harbert (Hyde Park, NY: New City Press, 1999), 118. Or: "*Neque enim ob aliud veraciter vocatur omnipotens nisi quoniam quidquid vult potest, nec voluntate cuiuspiam creaturae voluntatis omnipotentis impeditur effectus.*" ("For the only true reasons why he is called almighty are that he can do whatever he wills, and that the effectiveness of the will of the Almighty is not impeded by the will of any creature whatsoever.") Saint Augustine, *Enchiridion*, XXIV, 96, *Corpus Christianorum, Series Latina*, 46:100; English translation: Saint Augustine, *Augustine Catechism*, 118.

62. "*Deus omnipotens est; et cum sit omnipotens, mori non potest, falli non potest, mentiri non potest, et, quod ait apostolus, 'Negare se ipsum non potest' (2 Tim. 2:13). Quam multa non potest, et omnipotens est. Et ideo omnipotens est, quia ista non potest. Nam si mori posset, non esset omnipotens; si mentiri, si falli, si fallere, si inique agere, non esset omnipotens, quia, si hoc in eo esset, non fuisset dignus qui esset omnipotens. Prorsus omnipotens pater noster peccare non potest. Facit quidquid vult; ipsa est omnipotentia. Facit quidquid bene, vult, quidquid iuste, vult; quidquid autem male fit, non vult.*" Saint Augustine, *Sermo de symbolo ad catechumenos*, I, 2, in *Corpus Christianorum, Series Latina*, 46:185–86; English translation, slightly modified: Saint Augustine, *Treatises on Marriage and Other Subjects*, ed. Roy J.

Deferrari, trans. Charles T. Wilcox, MM, et al., Fathers of the Church, vol. 27 (1955; repr., Washington, DC: Catholic University of America Press, 1999), 290. See "*Sicut nec potestas ejus [God's] minuitur, cum dicitur mori fallique non posse. Sic enim hoc non potest, ut potius, si posset, minoris esset utique potestatis. Recte quippe omnipotens dicitur, qui tamen mori et falli non potest. Dicitur enim omnipotens faciendo quod vult, non patiendo quod non vult; quod ei si accideret, nequaquam esset omnipotens. Unde propterea quaedam non potest, quia omnipotens est.*" Augustine of Hippo, *De civitate Dei*, V, 10, 1, in *Corpus Christianorum, Series Latina*, vol. 47, *Sancti Aurelli Augustini, De civitate Dei, Libri I–X*, ed. B. Dombart and A. Kalb (Turnhout, Belgium: Brepols, 1955), 140; English translation: Augustine of Hippo, *The City of God against the Pagans*, trans. R. W. Dyson (Cambridge: Cambridge University Press, 1998), 204: "By the same token, His [God's] power is not diminished when we say that He 'cannot' die or err. For this is impossible to Him in such a way that, if it were possible, He would have less power. He is indeed rightly called omnipotent even though He cannot die or err. For He is called omnipotent because He does what He wills and does not undergo what He does not will: if this were not so, He certainly would not be omnipotent. But it is precisely because He is omnipotent that there are certain things that He cannot do [. . .]." In the same sense, we may highlight the effort of Hugh of St. Victor to redefine a possible of a nonontic order: "*Ergo summe potens est, qui potest omne quod possibile est, nec ideo minus potest, quia impossibilia non potest: impossibilia posse non esset posse, sed non posse. Itaque omnia potest Deus, quae posse potentia est; et ideo vere omnipotens est, quia impotens esse non potest*" (Hugh of St. Victor, *De Sacramentis christiane fidei*, bk. I, pt. II, chap. 22, in *PL*, 176, 216); "I say, therefore, that God can do all things, and He can not destroy Himself. For this power would not be power, but non-power. And so God can do all things, to be able to do which is power. And so He is truly omnipotent, because He can not be impotent" (Hugh of St. Victor, *On the Sacraments of the Christian Faith (De Sacramentus)*, trans. Roy J. Deferrari [Cambridge, MA: Medieval Academy of America, 1951], 38). Or that of Thomas Aquinas: "*Peccare est deficere a perfecta actione: unde posse peccare est posse deficere in agendo, quod repugnat omnipotentiae. Et propter hoc, Deus peccare non potest, qui est omnipotens*" (*Summa theologiae*, Ia, q. 25, a. 3, *ad 2m*, p. 136); English translation in Aquinas, *Basic Writings*, 1:264: "To sin is to fall short of a perfect action; hence to be able to sin is to be able to fall short in action, which is repugnant to omnipotence. Therefore it is that God cannot sin, because of His omnipotence." Even in these cases, we may nevertheless doubt that a redefinition, even a critical one, of the possible by itself would be enough to pass to the (im)possible on God's side.

63. And Luke 18:28 or Mark 10:27.

64. Here I follow the remarkable commentary of Jean-Marie Lustiger, *La promesse* (Paris: Parole et Silence, 2002), 24ff.

65. Similarly, for men it is more difficult for heaven and earth to pass away,

whereas for God this remains "much easier (εὐκοπώτερον) [. . .] than for a single dot of the law to become void" (Luke 16:17), which is to say, than for any of that to which God has committed his Word, namely, concerning Christ, and through Christ. In the law, God literally (practically to the dot) risks his word, and thus his Word, Christ. He risks his head and his life—which he will in fact lose.

66. And Mark 2:1–12; and Luke 5:17–26.

67. See below, § 22.

Chapter III

1. Thomas Aquinas, *Summa theologiae*, Ia, q. 38, a. 2, in Sancti Thomae de Aquino, *Summa theologiae* (Cinisello Balsamo, Italy: Edizioni San Paolo, 1988), 185; English translation: Thomas Aquinas, *Basic Writings of Saint Thomas Aquinas*, ed. Anton C. Pegis (Indianapolis: Hackett, 1997), 1: 361.

2. A strange expression because, on the occasion when I say that I give "everything," most of the time in fact I give nothing (nothing real, no thing—a first paradox); and this fact even allows me to give all that I can, namely, myself (almost) without reserve, without holding back (second paradox). But what is the significance of this gift in which I give nothing in order to give myself—precisely not as a thing? What is this unreal gift, total and yet repeatable? From the outset, we find ourselves in an aporia.

3. *Translator's note:* Throughout this chapter, the author makes use of a number of common expressions employing the verb "*rendre*" in order to bring out their rootedness in the notion of returning or regiving. In a typical English translation of most of these expressions, this notion of returning or regiving would either be lost or translated without making use of the English verb "to render": in the instance here, "*sans s'en rendre compte*" would normally be translated as "without realizing it," instead of the literal "without rendering an account of it." But because the literal sense of the French verb "*rendre*" is important to the arguments throughout the chapter, it will be translated literally in most instances. Among other such expressions using "*rendre*" in this chapter, the reader will come to recognize the expression "*rendre raison*" ("to give a rational explanation"); it will typically be translated as "to render reason."

4. On the question of the gift, its possible contradiction, and the critique of my approach to it in *Réduction et donation: Recherches sur Husserl, Heidegger et la phénoménologie* (Paris: Presses Universitaires de France, 1989) (*Reduction and Givenness: Investigations of Husserl, Heidegger and Phenomenology*, trans. Thomas A. Carlson [Evanston, IL: Northwestern University Press, 1998]), see the successive remarks of Jacques Derrida in *Donner le temps*, vol. 1, *La fausse monnaie* ([Paris: Galilée, 1991], esp. 24ff., 72ff., etc.; English translation: Jacques Derrida, *Given Time*, vol. 1, *Counterfeit Money*, trans. Peggy Kamuf [Chicago: University of Chicago Press, 1992], 12–15, 50–52, etc.), my return to the issue in *Étant donné: Essai d'une phénoménologie de la donation* (Paris: Presses Universitaires de France,

1998), 108ff. (*Being Given: Toward a Phenomenology of Givenness,* trans. Jeffrey L. Kosky [Stanford, CA: Stanford University Press, 2002], 74–79), and our debate "On the Gift: A Discussion between Jacques Derrida and Jean-Luc Marion, Moderated by Richard Kearney," in *God, the Gift and Postmodernism,* ed. John D. Caputo and Michael J. Scanlon (Bloomington: Indiana University Press, 1999), 54–78.

5. Here I am taking into account the arguments of Camille Tarot, *De Durkheim à Mauss, l'invention du symbolique: Sociologie des sciences de la religion* (Paris: La Découverte, 2000); and Alain Caillé, *Anthropologie du don: Le tiers paradigme* (Paris: Desclée de Brouwer, 2000).

6. Anne-Robert-Jacques Turgot, *Réflexions sur la formation et la distribution des richesses* (written 1766, published 1768–70), § 31, ed. J.-T. Rovis and P. M. Romani (repr., Paris: GF, 1997), 175; English version: Anne-Robert-Jacques Turgot, *Reflections on the Formation and Distribution of Wealth,* no translator named (London: E. Spragg, for J. Good, Bookseller, 1793), 32.

7. Antoine-Augustin Cournot, *Recherches sur les principes mathématiques de la théorie des richesses* [1839], in *Oeuvres complètes,* vol. 8, ed. Gérard Jorland (Paris: J. Vrin, 1980), 9, 13, respectively; English translation: Antoine-Augustin Cournot, *Researches into the Mathematical Principles of the Theory of Wealth,* trans. Nathaniel T. Bacon (New York: Macmillan, 1897), 10, 16–17, respectively (translation modified).

8. Cournot, *Recherches sur les principes mathématiques de la théorie des richesses,* 8; English translation: Cournot, *Researches into the Mathematical Principles of the Theory of Wealth,* 8 (Cournot's emphasis).

9. More than to Descartes (although one might think of the *Discourse on the Method;* AT, VI:61–62), Augustin Cournot is referring here to Leibniz: "I have already sketched elsewhere [in the *Traité de l'enchaînement des idées fondamentales,* II, chap. 7] the principles of this *superior dynamic* of which Leibniz had the idea, and which shows us, in the laws that govern the work of machines, a proper example for conceiving the much more general laws according to which the perpetual conversion of natural forces into one another is brought about; in the same way one can establish a comparison between the phenomenon of economic production and the work of machines, so as to express the analogies that they present." Antoine-Augustin Cournot, *Principes de la théorie des richesses* [1860], in *Oeuvres complètes,* vol. 9, ed. Gerard Jorland (Paris: Vrin, 1981), 39 (Cournot's emphasis). — But it was Diderot who perfectly saw and stated, in his own way, that the "economy" is inscribed in the unfolding of the *mathesis universalis* in its strictly Cartesian meaning, on which it depends from top to bottom for the radicality of its objectification: "We hold forth, we examine, we feel little and reason much; we *measure everything to the scrupulous standard of method,* of logic and even of truth [. . .]. Economic science is a beautiful thing, but it will stupefy our minds." Denis

Diderot, *Salon de 1769*, in *Oeuvres complètes*, ed. Herbert Dieckmann and Jean Varloot, vol. 16 (Paris: Hermann, 1990), 657. Quotation from René Descartes, *Discourse on the Method*, in *The Philosophical Writings of Descartes*, trans. John Cottingham, Robert Stoothoff, and Dugald Murdoch, vol. 1 (Cambridge: Cambridge University Press, 1985), 117; AT, VI:14, line 1: "the standards of reason."

10. Jean-Baptiste Say, *A Treatise on Political Economy; or, The Production, Distribution and Consumption of Wealth*, 5th American ed., trans. C. R. Prinsep, vol. 1 (Philadelphia: Grigg & Elliott, 1832), 365, 58; translation of Jean-Baptiste Say, *Traité d'économie politique; ou, Simple exposition de la manière dont se forment, se distribuent et se consomment les richesses*, 6th ed., ed. Horace Say (1st ed., 1803; repr., Paris: Guillaumin, 1841), 1:455, 1:117.

11. Karl Marx, *Capital: A Critique of Political Economy*, bk. 1, *The Process of Capitalist Production*, trans. from the 3rd German ed. by Samuel Moore and Edward Aveling, ed. Frederick Engels (New York: International Publishers, 1967), chap. 19, p. 506; chap. 18, p. 500; chap. 6, p. 172; chap. 1, § 4, pp. 84ff. (emphasis added). The excess of surplus value, which does not appear in the exchange's formulation, destroys its equality: this fact contradicts not only social justice, and Ricardo's and Smith's theory of value, but above all invalidates the very notion of a political economy (henceforth dubbed "bourgeois"). Excess—even the invisible excess of surplus value—destroys the terms of exchange, and thus the economy. Certainly, Bataille envisages an economy based on excess: "The solar radiance . . . finally finds nature and the meaning of the sun: it is necessary for it to give, *to lose itself without calculation.* A living system grows, or lavishes itself *without reason*," such that "in practical terms, from the perspective of riches, the radiance of the sun is distinguished by its unilateral character: it loses itself *without counting, without consideration. The solar economy* is founded on this principle." Georges Bataille, "The Economy to the Proportion of the Universe," trans. Michael Richardson, in *Georges Bataille: Essential Writings*, ed. Michael Richardson (London: Sage, 1998), 75, 74; translation of Georges Bataille, "L'économie à la mesure de l'univers," first published in *La France Libre*, no. 65 (July 1946), repr. in Georges Bataille, *Oeuvres complètes* (Paris: Gallimard, 1976), 7:10 (Bataille's emphasis). Yet we can question the legitimacy of wanting to continue to think this excess (without reason or measure) of expenditure in terms of an economy, since this amounts to assuming an economy deprived of exchange, price, and calculation of value; that is, exactly the contrary of what economists understand by this term.

12. Marx relies here on Aristotle's arguments. On the one hand, equality defines justice, and therefore exchange: "[T]he unjust man and the unjust act are unfair or unequal; now it is clear that there is also an intermediate between the two unequals involved in either case. And this is the equal." On the other hand, injustice consists in upsetting equality by appropriating "more" (value): "The man who acts unjustly has too much, and the man who is unjustly treated too little, of

what is good." Aristotle, *Nicomachean Ethics*, trans. W. D. Ross, in *The Basic Works of Aristotle*, ed. Richard McKeon (New York: Modern Library, 2001), p. 1006 (V.3.1131a10–11) and p. 1007 (V.3.1131b19–20).

13. Leibniz firmly insists that this universality of the principle of sufficient reason extends to the contingency of the event. See, for instance: "*No fact* can be real or actual, and no proposition true, without there being a sufficient reason for its being so and not otherwise" (G. W. Leibniz, *G. W. Leibniz's Monadology: An Edition for Students*, trans. Nicholas Rescher [Pittsburgh: University of Pittsburgh Press, 1991], § 32, p. 116 [emphasis added]); or "The principle in question is the principle of the want of a sufficient reason *for a thing to exist, for an event to happen*" (G. W. Leibniz, "Fifth Letter to Clarke," in *G. W. Leibniz: Philosophical Essays*, ed. and trans. Roger Ariew and Daniel Garber [Indianapolis: Hackett, 1989], § 125, p. 346 [emphasis added]). Or again: "*Constat ergo omnes veritates* etiam maxime contingentes *probationem a priori seu rationem aliquam cur sint potius quam non sint habere. Atque hoc ipsum est quod vulgo dicunt, nihil fieri sine causa, seu nihil esse sine ratione*." ("It is therefore established that all truths, *even the most contingent*, have an a priori proof or some reason why they are rather than are not. And this is what the vulgar say: Nothing comes to be without cause; or: Nothing is without reason.") Untitled text described on the contents page by the editor (Gerhardt) as "Ohne Uberschrift, in Betreff der Mittel der philosophischen Beweisführung [Reference to the means of philosophical demonstration]," in Gottfried Wilhelm Leibniz, *Die philosophischen Schriften von Gottfried Wilhelm Leibniz*, ed. C. I. Gerhardt, 7 vols. (Berlin: Weidmann, 1875–90), 7:301 (emphasis added).

14. Without repeating the Cartesian *causa sui*, which submits even God to causality ("*de ipso Deo quaeri potest*," *IIae Responsiones*, in AT, VII:164, line 29; "This question may even be asked concerning God," Descartes, *Philosophical Writings*, 2:116)—or, in God's case alone, to reason—Leibniz nevertheless thinks God as being a reason (His own sufficient reason) for Himself: "*Vides quid ex illo theoremate sequatur,* nihil est sine ratione *[. . .] omnia, quae sibi ipsi ratio cur sint, non sunt [. . .] ea tamdiu in rationem, et rationem rationis, reducenda esse, donec reducantur in id quod sibi ipsi ratio est, id est Ens a se, seu Deum*." ("You see what follows from the thesis: *nothing is without a reason* [. . .] everything that is not a reason for its own existence [. . .] is to be reduced to its reason, and its reason's reason, until it is reduced to what is its own reason, namely, the Being of itself, that is, God.") G. W. Leibniz, *Confessio philosophi*, in Leibniz's *Sämtliche Schriften und Briefe*, ser. 6, vol. 3, *Philosophische Schriften: 1672–1676*, ed. Leibniz-Forschungsstelle der Universität Münster (Berlin: Akademie-Verlag, 1980), 120 (Leibniz's emphasis).

15. Even gratuity can end up doing injury or producing submission—after all, *gratuity* also signifies a tip.

16. Perhaps Blanchot sketches it at times: "To give is not to give something, or even oneself, for then—inasmuch as what one gives has its characteristic feature that no one can take it from you (retrieve it from you and withhold it)—to give

would be to keep and to preserve. Summit of egotism, ruse of possession. [. . .] [T]here would be no gift at all if not the gift of what one does not have [. . .]. Gift of the disaster, of that which can neither be asked for nor given. Gift of the gift, with neither giver nor receiver, which does not annul the gift but which causes nothing to happen in this world of presence and under the sky of absence where things happen, or even do not happen." Maurice Blanchot, *L'écriture du désastre* (Paris: Gallimard, 1980), 83, 84; English translation: Maurice Blanchot, *The Writing of the Disaster*, new ed., trans. Ann Smock (Lincoln: University of Nebraska Press, 1995), 49, 50.

17. It is understandable that the testament is also called a *will* in English, since, if one does not make such a final testament explicit, the legacy could indeed be carried out against the will of the testator.

18. Pierre Corneille: "Cinna, let us be friends! An end to strife! / You were my enemy; I spared your life; / Despite your base designs—that plot insane— / I'll spare my would-be killer's life again! / Let's now compete and time its view deliver / On who fares best—recipient or giver. / My bounties you've betrayed; I'll shower more: / You shall be overwhelmed, as ne'er before!" Pierre Corneille, *Cinna; or, The Clemency of Augustus*, in *Le Cid; Cinna; Polyeuct: Three Plays*, trans. Noel Clark (Bath, UK: Absolute Classics, 1993), V, 3, lines 1701–8. Admittedly, Cinna receives the gift as it is given—but we are in Corneille's world here, not our own.

19. See Pierre-Marie Hasse, "La connaissance du don de Dieu," *Nova et Vetera* 54, no. 3 (1979): 172–90.

20. Yet, Saint Augustine envisions another case than that of my enemy: that of a givee who would have absolutely no need of what I could give him: "The works of mercy will cease; will the fire of love be extinguished? You love a happy man more genuinely for whom you do not have any service that you may render; that love will be pure and much more sincere. For if you render service to a wretched person, perhaps you desire to extol yourself before him and wish him who is the source of your beneficence to be subject to you (*tibi vis esse subjectum; qui auctor est tui beneficii*)." Saint Augustine, *In Epistolam Primam Iohannis Tractatus* 8.5, in *PL*, 35, 2038; English translation in Saint Augustine, *Tractates on the Gospel of John, 112–24, and Tractates on the First Epistle of John, 1–10*, trans. John W. Rettig (Washington, DC: Catholic University of America Press, 1995), 234.

21. See my analysis in *De surcroît: Études sur les phénomènes saturés* (Paris: Presses Universitaires de France, 2001); and *In Excess: Studies of Saturated Phenomena*, trans. Robyn Horner and Vincent Berraud (New York: Fordham University Press, 2002), chap. 5.

22. Fatherhood gives *itself* only to the extent that it gives. It inverts and thus confirms the definition of the gifted [*l'adonné*], who receives *himself* from what he receives. See Marion, *Étant donné*, § 26, in particular pp. 366–72; and Marion, *Being Given*, 266–69.

23. See Emmanuel Levinas, *Le temps et l'autre* [1946–47], published in 1948, citing the 4th ed. (repr., Paris: Presses Universitaires de France, 1991), 82, 85, 86.

24. On the phenomenon's determinations as given, see Marion, *Being Given*, bk. 3, pp. 119–78; and Marion, *Étant donné*, 169–250. I mention only some of them here; but fatherhood also validates the others (anamorphosis, facticity, fait accompli, incident, etc.).

25. See Roland Barthes: "Historically, the discourse of absence is carried on by the woman: Woman is sedentary, Man hunts, journeys; Woman is faithful (she waits), man is fickle (he sails away, he cruises) [. . .]. It follows that, in every man who speaks of the absence of the other, *the feminine* declares itself: this man who waits and who suffers from it, is miraculously feminized." Roland Barthes, *A Lover's Discourse: Fragments*, trans. Richard Howard (New York: Hill and Wang, 1978), 13–14; translation of Roland Barthes, *Fragments d'un discours amoureux* (Paris: Seuil, 1977), 20 (Barthes's emphasis).

26. The subversion of identity by fatherhood therefore marks time according to the direction of the future, because time, like fatherhood, never travels backward. In this way the irreversibility of the father opens time to historicity, because it thereby excludes the return of the same, whether supposedly eternal or not.

27. Michel Henry does this with an exemplary rigor, by opposing reciprocity—"The phenomenon that is at the origin of economy is exchange, a concept impossible to formulate without reciprocity"—to that which goes beyond it—"the non-reciprocity of the interior relationship that links us to God signifies the intervention of a different relationship than those established between humans," that relation precisely where "any human being is a son of God and of God alone [. . .] no living being has the power to bring him- or herself into life." Michel Henry, *Words of Christ*, trans. Christina M. Gschwandtner (Grand Rapids, MI: W. B. Eerdmans, 2012), 28, 34, 35; translation of Michel Henry, *Paroles du Christ* (Paris: Seuil, 2002), 37, 46, 47.

28. Leibniz, *Monadology*, § 31, p. 21.

29. Ibid., § 32, p. 21.

30. See Marion, *Being Given*, §§ 17–18 (and bk. 3 passim). The essential weakness of Donald Davidson's enterprise probably lies in the presupposition that all actions rest or *must* rest on a cause or at least a reason. Not only is this misleading evidence often denied by the most common experiences (where we act most often without *knowing* why, and, what is more, do well in proceeding in this manner), but it flows from an unreserved, noncritical assumption of a preeminently metaphysical position.

31. This gift, which imposes itself to be given and received of itself, could be described, with Roland Barthes (or Hölderlin?), as *adorable*, for "*Adorable* means: this is my desire, insofar as it is unique: 'That's it! That's it exactly (which I love)!' Yet the more I experience the specialty of my desire, the less I can give it a name; to the precision of the target corresponds a wavering [*tremblement*] of the name;

what is characteristic of desire, proper to desire, can produce only an impropriety of the utterance. Of this failure of language, there remains only one trace: the word 'adorable' (the right translation of 'adorable' would be the Latin *ipse*: it is the self, himself, herself, in person)." Barthes, *Lover's Discourse*, 20; and Barthes, *Fragments d'un discours amoureux*, 27. In fact, the ipseity and the pure self of this phenomenon—that which it is a question of loving, hence of receiving, and hence of giving—come to it perhaps from precisely what they liberate from my desire and from its language, which, in this adorable, see only a blinding flash, only a manifest object of an obscure desire.

32. On the transition from "showing itself" to "giving itself," see Marion, *Being Given*, § 6, pp. 68–70; and Marion, *Étant donné*, 100–102.

33. Thus, this remark made by Barthes in passing would take on its full weight: "The gift then reveals the test of strength of which it is the instrument." Barthes, *Lover's Discourse*, 76; and Barthes, *Fragments d'un discours amoureux*, 91.

34. "*Proprius justitiae actus est, unicuique quod suum est* reddere" (Saint Thomas Aquinas, *Summa theologiae*, IIa IIae, q. 58, a. 11, *conclusio* [emphasis added]), referring to Aristotle (*Nicomachean Ethics*, V), who does not, however, use this exact formula.

35. "*Axioma magnum / Nihil est sine ratione / Sive, quod idem est, nihil existit quin aliqua ratio* reddi *possit (saltem ab omniscio) cur sit potius quam non sit et cur sic sit potius quam aliter.*" G. W. Leibniz, *Elementa verae pietatis* [1677–78], in *Textes inédits*, 2 vols., ed. Gaston Grua (Paris: Presses Universitaires de France, 1948), 1:13 (emphasis added). See, among other texts: "*Principium omnis ratiocinationis primarium est, nihil esse aut fieri, quin ratio* reddi *possit, saltem ab omniscio, cur sit potius quam non sit, aut cur sic potius quam aliter, paucis omnium rationem* reddi *posse*" (ibid., 1:25); or: "*Principium* reddendae *rationis, quod scilicet omnis propositio vera, quae per se nota non est, probationem recipit a prior, sive quod omnis veritatis ratio* reddi *potest, ut vulgo ajiunt, quod nihil fit sine ratione.*" G. W. Leibniz, "Specimen inventorum de admirandis naturae generalis arcanis," in Leibniz's *Die philosophischen Schriften*, 7:309.

36. See Oscar Bloch and Walther von Wartburg, *Dictionnaire étymologique de la langue française* (1st ed., 1932; 8th ed., Paris: Presses Universitaires de France, 1989), 546; Alfred Ernout, *Morphologie historique du latin*, Nouvelle Collection à l'Usage des Classes, no. 32 (1st ed., 1914; 3rd ed., Paris: Klincksieck, 1953), § 207, p. 136; and Antonio Maria Martin Rodriguez, *Los verbos de "dar" en latín arcaico y clásico* (Grand Canary: Universidad de Las Palmas, 1999), *ad loc.* This is confirmed by Vincent Carraud, who emphasizes this "fundamental meaning" ("*donner la raison*" [to give reason], *ratio redenda/ratio reddita*, etc.) even in the formulas of the history of metaphysics. Vincent Carraud, *Causa sive ratio: La raison de la cause, de Suárez à Leibniz* (Paris: Presses Universitaires de France, 2002), 27ff., 436, 462, 492n1.

37. *Translator's note:* At various points in this chapter, and especially in these

last few pages, the author plays with the common French expressions "*avoir raison*," which literally means "to have reason" but is normally translated by "to be right," and "*donner raison*," which literally means "to give reason" but is normally translated by "to agree" or "to prove that someone is right" (e.g., *donner raison à quelqu'un*). Thus, the final sentence of this paragraph, "*le don se donne raison*," would be rendered into English according to its common French understanding as "the gift proves itself right."

38. On the determinations of the phenomenon as pure given, see Marion, *Being Given*, bk. 3, 117–78.

39. On the analysis of saturated phenomena, see Marion, *Being Given*, bk. 4, §§ 21–23; and Marion, *In Excess*, passim.

Chapter IV

1. The same goes for anyone who puts his life in danger, ultimately for nothing, or almost nothing (the "adventurer" or the so-called extreme athlete). The question arises, at what point are we dealing here with a figure, though debased yet still a true descendant of the figure of the master in the dialectic of recognition (the slave remaining within the domain of the profane, where one does not destroy oneself)?

2. This was moreover the classical argument (forged by the Reformation, then taken up by the Enlightenment) against a peaceful but also radical figure of sacrifice—monastic vows: to renounce power, riches, and reproduction amounts to destroying goods, which allow the world to live and to increase, and this renunciation even makes one enter into the field of the sacred, in this case into a life that, if it is not outside the world, is at least oriented eschatologically toward the alteration of this world.

3. Aristotle underscores the point: "We assume the gods to be above all other beings blessed and happy; but what sort of actions must we assign to them? Acts of justice? Will not the gods seem absurd if they make contracts and return deposits, and so on?" Aristotle, *Nicomachean Ethics*, trans. W. D. Ross, X, 8, 1178 b 8–12, in *The Basic Works of Aristotle*, ed. Richard McKeon (New York: Modern Library, 2001), 1106–7. The gods do not make contracts, and owe us nothing.

4. The attempts to define sacrifice made by Henri Hubert and Marcel Mauss in the famous "Essai sur la nature et la fonction du sacrifice" (published first in the *Année sociologique* 2 [1898], then in Marcel Mauss, *Oeuvres*, ed. Victor Karady, vol. 1, *Les fonctions sociales du sacré* [Paris: Minuit, 1968]; and Marcel Mauss, *Sacrifice: Its Nature and Function*, trans. W. D. Halls [Chicago: University of Chicago Press, 1964]) are characterized by their poverty, indeed their complete silence on the central (in fact the only) problem of the function and the intrinsic logic of sacrifice (its intention, its mechanism of compensation, its mode of constraint, etc.), in striking contrast with the wealth of details on the workings of a process that in fact remained unintelligible. We thus proceed by pure and simple suppositions:

"[s]acrifice [. . .] was originally a gift made by the primitive [*sic*] to supernatural [*sic*] forces to which he must bind himself" (Mauss, *Oeuvres*, 193; and Mauss, *Sacrifice*, 2 [translation modified]); but it remains to be understood whether and how these "forces" tolerate being thus "bound." The same abstraction and the same approximation obtain in the definition that is ultimately adopted: "Thus we finally arrive at the following definition: *Sacrifice is a religious act which, through the consecration of a victim, modifies the condition of the moral person who accomplishes it or that of certain objects with which he is concerned*." (Mauss, *Oeuvres*, 205; and Mauss, *Sacrifice*, 13.) But what does *consecration* here signify, if not precisely what is to be defined under the term "sacrifice"? Supposing that one understands what it consists of, how does the "consecration" come to "modify" the "moral person" in question? Is the "primitive," then, a "person"? If so, of what "morality"? What modification would we be talking about if it bears on this "person" and (also? at the same time?) on "objects"? In what way can all of this be defined precisely as "religious"? We expect no response to these questions, because they are not even raised. These stupefying approximations lead back inevitably to the features, themselves already highly imprecise, of the Maussian concept of the gift. (1) Sacrifice becomes a simple and banal reciprocal gift, an exchange, that won't acknowledge itself as such—and not yet a gift: "If on the other hand, one seeks to bind the divinity by a contract, the sacrifice has rather the form of an attribution: *do ut des* is the principle" (Mauss, *Oeuvres*, 272; and Mauss, *Sacrifice*, 65–66 [translation modified]); but, once again, what does it mean to bind "contractually" a "divinity" that has precisely the characteristic of being able to recuse itself from any contract and any reciprocity? (2) Destruction is considered, without any explanation, to be endowed by itself with what it takes to seal a contract: "*This procedure* [the sacrifice!] *consists in establishing a line of communication between the sacred and the profane worlds through the mediation of a victim, that is, of a thing that in the course of the ceremony is destroyed*" (Mauss, *Oeuvres*, 302; and Mauss, *Sacrifice*, 97); but who cannot see that the difficulty of such a "line of communication" consists precisely in the fact that the "sacred world" (what should we understand by this phrase?) has no reason to accept it, along with the "profane world"? Or, then, an explanation as to why this sometimes becomes possible is necessary. (3) Moreover, one ends by granting that the supposed sacrifice, in the end, isn't one: "The sacrifier gives up something of himself but he does not give himself. Prudently, he sets himself aside. This is because if he gives, it is partly in order to receive." Mauss, *Oeuvres*, 304; and Mauss, *Sacrifice*, 100. Put another way, ignorance is admitted as to what distinguishes a sacrifice from an exchange, because in fact gift and exchange were already confused with each other.

5. Jacques Derrida, *Donner le temps*, vol. 1, *La fausse monnaie* (Paris: Galilée, 1991), 42; and Jacques Derrida, *Given Time*, vol. 1, *Counterfeit Money*, trans. Peggy Kamuf (Chicago: University of Chicago Press, 1992), 27.

6. See Jean-Luc Marion, *Étant donné: Essai d'une phénoménologie de la dona-*

tion, §§ 9–11 (Paris: Presses Universitaires de France, 1997, 1998), 124–61; and Jean-Luc Marion, *Being Given: Toward a Phenomenology of Givenness*, trans. Jeffrey L. Kosky (Stanford, CA: Stanford University Press, 2002), 85–113.

7. "*Quemadmodum, fratres, si sponsus faceret sponsae suae annulum, et illa acceptum annulum plus diligeret quam sponsum qui illi fecit annulum; nonne in ipso dono sponsi adultera anima deprehenderetur, quamvis hoc amaret quod dedit sponsus? Certe hoc amaret quod dedit sponsus; tamen si diceret, Sufficit mihi annulus iste, iam illius faciem nolo videre; qualis esset? Quis non detestaretur hanc amentiam? quis non adulterinum animum convinceret? Amas aurum pro viro, amas annulum pro sponso: si hoc est in te, ut ames annulum pro sponso tuo, et nolis videre sponsum tuum; ad hoc tibi arrham dedit, ut non te oppigneraret, sed averteret.*" Saint Augustine, *In Epistolam Primam Iohannis Tractatus*, II, 11, in *PL*, 35, 1995; English translation available in *The Fathers of the Church: St. Augustine, Tractates on the Gospel of John, 112–24, Tractates on the First Epistle of John*, trans. John W. Rettig (Washington, DC: Catholic University of America Press, 1995), 154.

8. Martin Heidegger, *Zeit und Sein*, in *Zur Sache des Denkens*, in *GA*, 14 (Frankfurt am Main: Vittorio Klostermann, 2007), 12; and Martin Heidegger, *On Time and Being*, trans. Joan Stambaugh (New York: Harper and Row, 1972), 8.

9. Martin Heidegger, *Die onto-theo-logische Verfassung der Metaphysik*, in *Identität und Differenz*, in *GA*, 11 (Frankfurt am Main: Vittorio Klostermann, 2006), 71; and Martin Heidegger, *The Onto-theological Constitution of Metaphysics*, in *Identity and Difference*, trans. Joan Stambaugh (Chicago: University of Chicago Press, 2002), 64–65 (translation modified).

10. Understood *also* in the trivial French sense, which says *que cela donne* (when it functions, it works).

11. Let us recall that we are dealing here with the three marks of the phenomenon as given. See Marion, *Étant donné*, § 13, 170–71; and Marion, *Being Given*, 119–20.

12. See the analysis of Roland de Vaux, *Les sacrifices de l'Ancien Testament* (Paris: J. Gabalda, 1964).

13. I translate Genesis 18:14 following the version of the Septuagint: "μὴ ἀδυνατῆσεῖ παρὰ τῷ θεῷ ῥῆμα," in conformity with Luke 1:37, which quotes it: "οὐκ ἀδυνατῆσεῖ παρὰ τῷ θεῷ πᾶν ῥῆμα." See in this book § 9, p. 63; § 13, p. 77; and, for other texts, § 23, pp. 146ff.

14. The death of the Christ accomplishes a sacrifice understood in *this* sense: by returning his spirit to the Father who had given it to him, Jesus gives himself up, disappears by making the Father appear, directly (the veil of the Temple that separated God from men is torn at his death: Matt. 27:51). And at the same moment, in Jesus dead, there appears the Christ, Son *of the Father*, gift given up and thus visible as gift: "Truly this was the *son of God*" (Matt. 27:54). See my sketch in Jean-Luc Marion, "La reconnaissance du don," *Revue Catholique International Communio*

33/1, no. 195 (January–February 2008); republished in Jean-Luc Marion, *Le croire pour le voir* (Paris: Parole et Silence, 2010), 179–93.

15. Emmanuel Levinas, "Enigme et phénomène," in *En découvrant l'existence avec Husserl et Heidegger* (1949; repr., Paris: Vrin, 1974), 215; and Emmanuel Levinas, "Enigma and Phenomenon," trans. Alphonso Lingis, in *Emmanuel Levinas: Basic Philosophical Writings*, ed. Adriaan T. Peperzak, Simon Critchley, and Robert Bernasconi (Bloomington: Indiana University Press, 1996), 77.

16. Georges Bataille, *Théorie de la religion*, in *Oeuvres complètes*, vol. 7 (Paris: Gallimard, 1976), 310; and Georges Bataille, *Theory of Religion*, trans. Robert Hurley (New York: Zone Books, 1989), 48–49 (translation modified). Or, in what amounts to the same, Josef Ratzinger writes: "Christian sacrifice does not consist in a giving of what God would not have without us but in our becoming totally receptive and letting ourselves be completely taken over by him. Letting God act on us—that is Christian sacrifice." Joseph Ratzinger, *Introduction to Christianity*, trans. J. R. Foster (1990; repr., San Francisco: Ignatius Press, 2004), 283.

17. Jan Patočka, "The Dangers of Technicization in Science According to E. Husserl and the Essence of Technology as Danger According to M. Heidegger" (1973), in Erazim V. Kohák, *Jan Patočka: Philosophy and Selected Writings* (Chicago: University of Chicago Press, 1989), 332 (translation modified in light of the French translation: Jan Patočka, *Liberté et sacrifice: Écrits politiques*, trans. Erika Abrams [Grenoble, France: Jérôme Millon, 1990], 266).

18. Saint Thomas Aquinas: "*Omne opus virtutis dicitur esse sacrificium* inquantum ordinatur ad *Dei reverentiam*." Thomas Aquinas, *Summa theologiae*, IIa IIae, q. 81, a. 4, *ad 1*; in Sancti Thomae de Aquino, *Summa theologiae* (Cinisello Balsamo, Italy: Edizioni San Paolo, 1988), 1420 (emphasis added). See also Saint Augustine defining sacrifices as "*Opera [. . .] misericordiae sive in nos ipsos sive in proximos, quae* referuntur ad Deum [works of mercy shown to ourselves or to our neighbours, and done with reference to God]." Saint Augustine, *De civitate dei*, X.6, in *Corpus Christianorum, Series Latina*, vol. 47, *Sancti Aurelli Augustini, De civitate Dei, Libri I–X*, ed. B. Dombart and A. Kalb (Turnhout, Belgium: Brepols, 1955), 279; and Saint Augustine, *The City of God against the Pagans*, trans. R. W. Dyson (Cambridge: Cambridge University Press, 1998), 400.

19. One recognizes here the argument of G. W. F. Hegel, *Phänomenologie des Geistes*, I, IV, A, ed. W. Bonsiepen and R. Heede, in *Gesammelte Werke*, vol. 9 (Hamburg: Felix Meiner, 1980), 109ff.; English translation: G. W. F. Hegel, *Phenomenology of Spirit*, trans. A. V. Miller (Oxford: Oxford University Press, 1977), 111–19.

20. See Jean-Luc Marion, *The Erotic Phenomenon*, trans. Stephen E. Lewis (Chicago: University of Chicago Press, 2007), §§ 12–14, pp. 53–66; and Jean-Luc Marion, *Le phénomène érotique: Six méditations* (Paris: Grasset, 2003), 89–109.

21. Vladimir Jankélévitch, *L'imprescriptible*, 2nd ed. (Paris: Seuil, 1986), 50, 55.

22. Ibid., 43 (my emphasis), inverting Luke 23:34.

23. Jacques Derrida, *Pardonner: L'impardonnable et l'imprescriptible* (Paris: L'Herne, 2005), 31. Derrida continues: "I ask whether forgiveness does not begin where it seems to end, where it appears im-possible, precisely at the end of the history of forgiveness" (p. 32). Thus, the same would go for forgiveness as had already been the case for the gift (see above, § 14). On this debate, see Jan-Heiner Tück, "Pardonner l'impardonnable? Jankélévitch et Derrida—à propos d'un débat qui doit rester ouvert," *Revue catholique internationale Communio*, Paris, vol. 30, nos. 5–6 (2006): 101–14. —The seriousness of this debate contrasts with the exemplary superficiality of the analyses of J. L. Austin on the request for excuse ("A Plea for Excuses," in *Philosophical Papers*, ed. J. O. Urmson and G. J. Warnock [Oxford: Oxford University Press, 1979], 175–204); his two significant discoveries—(1) the excuse belongs to those elocutionary acts which seek to produce in the interlocutor an effect that can differ from the obvious meaning of the statement, and (2) the excuse can always be challenged, and thus there is the possibility of impossibility—are irremediably compromised by two distressing insufficiencies: (1) Austin never considers that there may be at least one case of absolute and unconditional agreement about the request for forgiveness: precisely, the case of God (who alone can forgive everything); (2) this inadvertence goes with and is explained by the option of privileging the most trivial or arbitrary grounds for requesting excuse (for example: having crushed a snail, having trod on a baby). It may be that one must first ask to be excused for serious mistakes, and even that the request to be *excused* is at base a superficial euphemism masking the only genuine request: the request for *forgiveness* from a fault.

24. Unless, on the contrary, as Stanley Cavell argues, Lear wishes only to make an exit from love (which he knows he does not know how to practice) precisely so as to enter into exchange (which he knows he knows how to practice), even at the risk, clearly evident to him, of provoking an unjust exchange. For him, the injustice of exchange would be worth more than the unconditionality without return of love. See "The Appearance of Love," in Stanley Cavell, *Must We Mean What We Say?* (1969; repr., Cambridge, MA: Harvard University Press, 2002), 287ff.

25. On the contrary, shouldn't forgiveness (*for*-giveness) be understood as an anticipation of the gift, rather than its repetition after the fact? Probably not, not only because philology does not directly authorize such conceptual inferences, but above all because the prefix instead indicates the radicalization of the first gift to the point of its absolutely radical loss, its dispersion without return of the gift (as in the French *par-don* and the German *Ver-gebung*). Forgiveness conquers every refusal to accept, because it does away even with acceptance, the possible denial of which it overwhelms.

26. On this text and this term "οὐσία," see the reading I proposed in *God without Being*, trans. Thomas A. Carlson (Chicago: University of Chicago Press, 1991),

III, § 4, pp. 95–101; and *Dieu sans l'être*, 2nd ed. (1982; repr., Paris: Quadrige, 2002), 140–48.

27. The distribution is made of a double share for the elder son, and a single share for the younger (according to Deut. 21:15–17), but this early division is neither obligatory nor even recommended (at least according to the prudent opinions contained in the book of Sir. 33:19–23).

28. At issue is precisely the χώρα, which Jacques Derrida in the end puts forward against givenness. The expression χώραν μακρὰν does not mean a large region or land, but a region that is far away (it functions as an adverb, as in v. 20, where the father sees his son "from afar," μακρὰν, as well as in 7:6).

29. Not only does the son find himself reduced to the level of swine, seemingly the lowest (see Lev. 11:7 and Matt. 7:6), but in fact he is beneath them: since they still retain a market value, food is provided for them; but not for their keeper, who thus must live on leftovers stolen from the swine. The son becomes not only subhuman, but subanimal.

30. Certain interpreters refuse to take ἀναστὰς (v. 18) in the strong sense of to raise (oneself) up, like later in the Resurrection account. This is to ignore two pieces of evidence: the son "walks toward himself" ("εἰς ἑαυτὸν") (v. 17), a radical formula that we find also in Epictetus ("Arrian's Discourses of Epictetus," III, 1, 5, in Epictetus, *The Discourses as Reported by Arrian, The Manual, and Fragments*, with an English translation by W. A. Oldfather, in two vols. [Cambridge, MA: Harvard University Press, 1966], 2:6), as well as when Peter "came to himself" (after his miraculous escape from prison at the hands of angels, Acts 12:11); and above all the return of the son is twice described in terms of death and resurrection (vv. 24 and 32, perhaps to be compared with John 5:24 and 1 John 3:14).

31. The correction of certain manuscripts, which complete verse 21 with verse 19 is therefore useless, even misleading; for, as Loisy rightly notes, "the father, moreover, does not leave him time to say more." Alfred Loisy, *L'évangile de Luc* (Paris: Nourry, 1924), 399.

32. Luke 3:22 says more: "This is my son, my beloved, with whom I am pleased," which reinforces further the trinitarian dimension of this proclamation. — The three gifts made to the returned son show as well this status of complete filiation: the robe of honor designates the principal host of the reception (this ought to be meant for the eldest son), the ring indicates the heir who will possess the entire property, and the sandals put on his feet underline not only the son's difference from a servant (who walks barefoot) but also his difference from a visitor (whose feet are washed but who walks without sandals in the house).

33. Or, in the parable of the talents, just as the third servant sees his master as "a hard man" (Matt. 25:24).

34. François Bovon emphasizes this point. See *L'oeuvre de Luc: Études d'exégèse et de théologie* (Paris: Cerf, 1987), 46. This title, emphatic and more intimate than

the one accorded to the younger, also constitutes (like "your brother," v. 32) a response to the way in which the elder refuses to name his brother as such: "this son of yours" (v. 30).

35. *Translator's note:* Here and at several places in chapter 5 (see §§ 25, 28, and 29), different instances of the French verb "*passer*" are used in order to emphasize the sense in which the happening of events is their passing. The French reflexive verb "*se passer*" is normally translated into English by "to happen"; here and elsewhere, the author will use this fact to emphasize the way in which every event that happens "passes [of] itself" in happening.

Chapter V

1. Charles Baudelaire, "A une passante," *Les fleurs du mal*, 93, in Baudelaire, *Oeuvres complètes*, ed. Marcel A. Ruff (Paris: Seuil, 1968), 101; English translation: Charles Baudelaire, *The Flowers of Evil*, trans. James McGowan (Oxford: Oxford University Press, 1993), 189.

2. Of course, Kant maintains the noumena (at least in the positive sense; see below, § 26), which keep the status of object; but in question are rather particular objects, since we cannot know them according to the sole intuition that we have at our disposal, sensible intuition. Descartes avoids this ambiguity (or this inconsistency) by keeping himself from naming as "objects" God or the human mind (the properly metaphysical verities); he thus maintains them as knowable, without submitting them to the method, or more exactly without imposing on them the measure (*mensura*) of the *mathesis universalis*, in a still theoretical rationality (while Kant, in order to conceive them, will have to transpose them into practical reason). See Jean-Luc Marion, *Questions cartésiennes: Méthode et métaphysique* (Paris: Presses Universitaires de France, 1991), chap. 3, pp. 75–109; English translation: Jean-Luc Marion, *Cartesian Questions: Method and Metaphysics* (Chicago: University of Chicago Press, 1999), 43–66; and Jean-Luc Marion, *Questions cartésiennes II* (1996; repr., Paris: Presses Universitaires de France, 2002), chap. 8, pp. 283–316.

3. Rudolf Carnap, "Überwindung der Metaphysik durch Logische Analyse der Sprache," first appearing in *Erkenntnis*, vol. 2 [1932]; English translation: Rudolf Carnap, "The Elimination of Metaphysics through Logical Analysis of Language," trans. Arthur Pap, in *Logical Positivism*, ed. A. J. Ayer (New York: Free Press, 1959), 60–81, at 80. True musicians, says Carnap, have the wisdom to give up *entirely* on dealing with objects by devoting themselves to pure music that is "entirely free from any reference to objects." Carnap, "Elimination of Metaphysics," 80.

4. According to Claude Romano's exact formulation, in *L'événement et le monde* (Paris: Presses Universitaires de France, 1998), 209; and Claude Romano, *Event and World*, trans. Shane Mackinlay (New York: Fordham University Press, 2009), 155.

5. Friedrich Nietzsche, *Beyond Good and Evil*, trans. Judith Norman (Cam-

bridge: Cambridge University Press, 2002), § 285, p. 171; Friedrich Nietzsche, *Kritische Studienausgabe*, ed. Giorgio Colli and Mazzino Montinari (Berlin: Walter de Gruyter, 1988), 5:232; quoted in Romano, *L'événement et le monde*, 68 (English translation: Romano, *Event and World*, 49).

6. *Translator's note:* On the translation of "*se passer*" in this chapter, see the translator's note from the end of chap. 4, n. 35.

7. René Descartes, *Discourse on the Method*, in AT, VI:14, line 1; English translation: René Descartes, *The Philosophical Writings of Descartes*, trans. John Cottingham, Robert Stoothoff, and Dugald Murdoch, vol. 1 (Cambridge: Cambridge University Press, 1985), 117.

8. René Descartes, *Regula II*, in AT, X:362, lines 2–5; English translation: Descartes, *Philosophical Writings*, 1:10.

9. René Descartes, *Meditatio II*, in AT, VII:25, lines 22–24; English translation: Descartes, *Philosophical Writings*, 2:17.

10. Descartes, *Meditatio II*, in AT, VII:31, lines 2–3; English translation: Descartes, *Philosophical Writings*, 2:20 (translation modified). Gassendi sees, rightly, in this reduction a "*detractio formarum quasi vestium*," a stripping away of forms, as when one strips off clothing (AT, VII:271, lines 30ff.). Descartes will defend himself against having "abstract[ed] the concept of the wax from the concept of its accidents," and claims to have only shown how the substance showed itself by means of its accidents ("*per accidentia manifestetur*," in AT, VII:359, lines 3–17). But it is precisely by manifesting itself in this way by means of an instance other than itself that the substance does not manifest itself, or at least it does not manifest *itself*; in other words, in the language of Descartes, it "does not of itself have any effect on us." See René Descartes, *Principia philosophiae*, I, § 52, in AT, VIII; English translation: Descartes, *Philosophical Writings*, 1:210. The thing alone would affect us, but not the object that it has become; we constitute the object, or here we *conclude* it, from its principal attribute. The object has indeed been stripped of its *self*.

11. *Nihil aliud quam* (AT, VII:31, lines 2–3; several other meaningful occurrences are found at VII:45, line 5; VII:49, line 15; and VII:81, line 6) even ought to be understood as a quasi concept, the indicator of the reduction that results in the object. Jean Beaufret said it well: "How does one pass from fantasy to knowledge? Not by turning towards the thing and gazing at it better, but by turning back towards oneself in order, from there, to be able to say to the thing in return: you are nothing other than—*nihil aliud quam*. Thus the famous piece of wax is: *nihil aliud quam extensum quid, flexibile, mutabile*." Jean Beaufret, *Dialogue avec Heidegger*, vol. 3 (Paris: Éditions de Minuit, 1974), 33.

12. Descartes, *Regula II*, in AT, X:365, lines 16–18; English translation: Descartes, *Philosophical Writings*, 1:12. See the other occurrence of the word "*experientia*," a few lines earlier (AT, X:365, lines 1–4).

13. See Aristotle, *Metaphysics E*, 2, 1027a13ff., in *Aristotle in Twenty-Three Volumes*, vol. 17, *The Metaphysics, Books I–IX*, with an English translation by Hugh

Tredennick (Cambridge, MA: Harvard University Press, 1933), 302; and Aristotle, *The Basic Works of Aristotle*, ed. Richard McKeon (New York: Modern Library, 2001), 781.

14. René Descartes, *Regula IV*, in AT, X: p. 377, line 23–p. 378, line 1; English translation: Descartes, *Philosophical Writings*, 1:19 (translation modified). On the translation of *mathesis* [*universalis*], see René Descartes, *Règles utiles et claires pour la direction de l'esprit dans la recherche de la vérité*, trans. and annotated by Jean-Luc Marion, with mathematical notes by Pierre Costabel (The Hague: Martinus Nijhoff, 1977), 156n31, 156ff., and app. 2, pp. 302–9.

15. See the quasi-conceptual occurrences of *tantum* in René Descartes, *Meditationes*, in AT, VII:25, line 23; VII:27, line 13; VII:43, lines 14–15: "perpauca tantum *esse quae in illis* [the ideas of corporal things] *clare et distincte percipio*" follows the reduction to simple material natures; VII:56, line 15; VII:78, line 16; and VII:86, line 2. We already find the same usage in René Descartes, *Regulae*, in AT, X:361, line 18; X:365, line 11; X:368, line 11; X:370, line 14; X:394, lines 12ff.: "*de rebus* tantum *purae simplicibus et absolutis experientiam certam haberi posse*"; X:399, lines 5ff.: "*res ipsas, quae* tantum *spectandae sunt prout ab intellectu attinguntur*"; X:411, line 3; X:413, line 14: "*sed* tantum *abstrahamus ab omni alio, quam quod habeat* [sc. *color*] *figurae naturam*"; X:418, line 14; X:423, lines 1–3: "*intellectum a nullo unquam experimento decipi posse, si praecise* tantum *intueatur rem sibi objectam*"; X:426, line 25; X:429, line 28; X:423, line 15; X:440, line 26; X:444, line 5; X:446, line 6; X:447, line 21; X:448, line 19; X:450, line 13; X:453, line 11; X:461, line 22; and X:467, line 4.

16. This formula appears four times in Descartes, *Meditationes* (AT, VII:71, lines 9 and 15; VII:74, line 2; and VII:80, line 10), amounting to half of all the occurrences of *objectum* in the entire text.

17. Immanuel Kant, *Critique of Pure Reason*, A494/B522, trans. and ed. Paul Guyer and Allen W. Wood (Cambridge: Cambridge University Press, 1998), 512–13.

18. Ibid., A93/B125, p. 224 (translation modified).

19. See Marion, *Questions cartésiennes*, chap. 3; and Marion, *Questions cartésiennes II*, chap. 8.

20. René Descartes, *Regula XII*, in, respectively, AT, X:418, line 2, and X:419, line 6; English translation: Descartes, *Philosophical Writings*, 1:44.

21. Kant, *Critique of Pure Reason*, B138, p. 249.

22. The seal, the stamp, or the mold are no longer (or not yet) the "form," but instead a figure that is *already* material, or rather materialized (a figure given to matter, precisely in order to be able to act upon and weaken it); thus, like all ὕλη, they can only be used and *de-formed*, and thus they have a specific life span, a certain history, and therefore an eventness.

23. G. W. Leibniz, *Principes de la Nature et de la Grâce fondés en raison*, § 7, in *Die philosophischen Schriften von Gottfried Wilhelm Leibniz*, ed. C. I. Gerhardt,

7 vols. (Berlin: Weidmann, 1875–90), 6:602; English translation: G. W. Leibniz, *The Philosophical Works of Leibnitz*, 2nd ed., trans. George Martin Duncan (New Haven, CT: Tuttle, Morehouse & Taylor, 1908), 303. "The principle of causality [. . .] is the father of metaphysics," says Maine de Biran, attributing this formula to J. P. F. Ancillon. "Essai sur le premier problème de la philosophie," in *Mélanges de littérature et de philosophie* (Paris, 1809), in the *Essai sur les fondements de la psychologie* (1812), in *Oeuvres*, ed. F. C. T. Moore, vol. VII/1 (Paris: J. Vrin, 2001), 159. On the relation between sufficient reason and causality, which I do not merge together, see Vincent Carraud, *Causa sive ratio: La raison de la cause, de Suárez à Leibniz* (Paris: Presses Universitaires de France, 2002).

24. Aristotle, *Physics*, III, 4, 203b6, in Aristotle, *The Physics*, with an English translation by Philip H. Wicksteed and Francis M. Cornford, in 2 vols. (Cambridge, MA: Harvard University Press, 1963), 1:222. English translation: Aristotle, *Basic Works*, 259. Clearly, Aristotle remains at a distance from his successors, because he does not reduce plurivocal causality to efficiency, and distinguishes ἀρχὴ (principle) from αἰτία (cause).

25. Francisco Suárez, *Disputationes metaphysicae* XII, Proemium, in *Opera omnia*, vol. 25 (Paris: Vivès, 1867), 372. Causality enters here as the first determination that adds itself to the concept of *ens* and to essence. Suárez justifies this exorbitant privilege with two arguments: causality suffers no exception ("*Est veluti proprietas quaedam entis, ut sic; nullum est enim ens, quod aliquam rationem causae non participet*"), and it is exerted on beings themselves ("*ipsa entis ratio per se ac proprie causatur*") (emphases added). But these two arguments depend on a prior one, which decides everything: causality takes its universality from its abstraction ("*ratio autem causae universalior est et abstractior*") (emphasis added). Such an abstraction provokes precisely the transmutation of the being into an object of poor phenomenality.

26. René Descartes, *Secundae responsiones*, in AT, VII:164, lines 28–29; English translation: René Descartes, *The Philosophical Writings of Descartes*, trans. John Cottingham, Robert Stoothoff, and Dugald Murdoch, vol. 2 (Cambridge: Cambridge University Press, 1984), 116 (translation modified). This is the first of the axioms.

27. Pascal, who specifies: "Thus, since all things are both caused or causing, assisted and assisting, mediate and immediate, providing mutual support in a chain linking together naturally and imperceptibly the most distant and different things, I consider it as impossible to know the parts without knowing the whole as to know the whole without knowing the individual parts." Blaise Pascal, *Pensées*, § 199, in *Oeuvres complètes*, ed. Louis Lafuma (Paris: Seuil, 1963); English translation in Blaise Pascal, *Pensées*, trans. A. J. Krailsheimer (New York: Penguin, 1995), 64. The causal tie thus has as its effect to bring about knowing, which is to say, to transmute things into objects.

28. Kant, *Critique of Pure Reason*, A9/B13, p. 131. See Donald Davidson's rather

serene repetition of this metaphysical principle, undisturbed by any questioning, in his *Essays on Action and Events* (Oxford: Clarendon Press, 1980), 16, 26.

29. Leibniz, *Principes de la Nature et de la Grâce fondés en raison*, 6:602 (emphasis added).

30. Descartes, *Regula XII*, in AT, X:418, lines 1–3; English translation: Descartes, *Philosophical Writings*, 1:44.

31. Descartes, Hume, and Nietzsche having sufficiently demonstrated this paradox, there is no need to dwell on it here. See my analysis in *Étant donné: Essai d'une phénoménologie de la donation* (Paris: Presses Universitaires de France, 1998), IV, § 17, pp. 232–35; and *Being Given: Toward a Phenomenology of Givenness*, trans. Jeffrey L. Kosky (Stanford, CA: Stanford University Press, 2002), 165–67.

32. Kant, *Critique of Pure Reason*, A218/B265, p. 321 (translation modified). Of course it is not by chance that, in the few brief pages that Kant devotes to "elucidating" the "Postulates of empirical thinking in general," he says (to my knowledge) literally nothing about contingency (not even the word), so much does he concentrate on possibility, in order to lead the possibility of phenomena back to the possibility of the objects of our cognition.

33. Ibid., A111, p. 234.

34. "*Complementum possibilitatis*." Christian Wolff, *Philosophia prima sive Ontologia*, § 174 (Frankfurt and Leipzig: Renger, 1730).

35. Martin Heidegger, *Die Grundprobleme der Phänomenologie*, § 15, in *GA*, 24 (Frankfurt: Vittorio Klostermann, 1975), 222; English translation: Martin Heidegger, *The Basic Problems of Phenomenology*, rev. ed., trans. Albert Hofstadter (Bloomington: Indiana University Press, 1988), 156. Levinas says nothing different: "The phenomenological reduction was a radical way of suspending the natural approach, which posits the world as an object, a radical struggle against the abstraction that the object epitomizes." Emmanuel Levinas, *En découvrant l'existence avec Husserl et Heidegger* (1949; repr., Paris: Vrin, 1974), 122; English translation: Emmanuel Levinas, *Discovering Existence with Husserl*, trans. Richard A. Cohen and Michael B. Smith (Evanston: Northwestern University Press, 1998), 102.

36. "*Wenn nicht mehr Zahlen und Figuren / Sind Schlüssel aller Kreaturen, / Wenn die so singen oder küssen / Mehr als die Tiefgelehrten wissen, / Wenn sich die Welt ins freie Leben / Und in die Welt wird zurückbegeben, / [. . .] Dann fliegt vor Einem geheimen Wort / Das ganze verkehrte Wesen fort.*" *Novalis Schriften*, ed. Paul Kluckhohn and Richard H. Samuel, vol. 1 (Stuttgart: Kohlhammer, 1960), 341; English translation in *Great German Poems of the Romantic Era: A Dual-Language Book*, ed. and trans. Stanley Appelbaum (Mineola, NY: Dover Publications, 1995), 69 (translation modified).

37. Friedrich Nietzsche, "Away with this 'World Turned Upside-Down'!" ("*Fort mit dieser 'verkehrten Welt'!*"), *Kritische Studienausgabe*, ed. Giorgio Colli and Mazzino Montinari (Berlin: Walter de Gruyter, 1988), 5:371; English translation:

Friedrich Nietzsche, *On the Genealogy of Morals,* trans. Douglas Smith (Oxford: Oxford World's Classics, 1996), essay 3, § 14, p. 103.

38. Nietzsche, *Kritische Studienausgabe, Nachgelassene Fragmente,* 1888–89, notebook 14, Spring 1888, fragment 105, 13:276; English translation in Friedrich Nietzsche, *Writings from the Late Notebooks,* ed. Rüdiger Bittner, trans. Kate Sturge (Cambridge: Cambridge University Press, 2003), 253. Husserl laid open in greater detail, and with arguments, this "inverted mathematizing interpretation of nature" ("*mathematisierender Umdeutung der Natur*"). Edmund Husserl, *Die Krisis der europäischen Wissenschaften und die transzendentale Phänomenologie,* § 9, in *Hua.*, VI, ed. Walter Biemel (The Hague: Martinus Nijhoff, 1976), 54; English translation: Edmund Husserl, *The Crisis of European Sciences and Transcendental Phenomenology,* trans. David Carr (Evanston, IL: Northwestern University Press, 1970), 53 (translation modified).

39. Wassily Kandinsky, *Complete Writings on Art,* ed. Kenneth C. Lindsay and Peter Vergo (New York: Da Capo Press, 1994), 369–70 (translation modified; emphases added). See Alain Bonfand's commentary, *Histoire de l'art et phénoménologie: Recueil de textes, 1984–2008* (Paris: Vrin, 2009), 119ff. This episode confirms the analysis of the effect of the painting that I had attempted in *Étant donné,* I, § 4, pp. 60–78; and *Being Given,* 39–53. See also the description of the passage of the same colors from the status of object (flag or traffic sign) to that of the painting (of Rothko) sketched in Jean-Luc Marion, *Le visible et le révélé* (Paris: Cerf, 2005), chap. 6, § 4, pp. 157–59; and Jean-Luc Marion, *The Visible and the Revealed,* trans. Christina M. Gschwandtner et al. (New York: Fordham University Press, 2008), 127–28.

40. Nietzsche, posthumous fragment, Autumn 1885, notebook 2, fragment 84, in *Nachgelassene Fragmente,* vol. VIII, 1, pp. 101–2; English translation: Nietzsche, *Writings from the Late Notebooks,* 75–76 (translation modified). Must it be stated once again that, despite contemporary rhetoric (Badiou, Davidson, etc.), the event absolutely cannot be understood as an object, nor as an entity?

41. Kant, *Critique of Pure Reason,* A182/B224 and B233, respectively, 299 (translation modified), 304.

42. Ibid., A290/B346, p. 382.

43. Ibid., A19/B33, p. 155 (translation modified).

44. On this definition of each of the meanings of nothingness, I emphasize that even the last one (the *nihil negativum* as the "empty object without concept") is defined by a default of intuition. See Marion, *Étant donné,* § 20, pp. 274–75; and Marion, *Being Given,* 195–96.

45. Kant, *Critique of Pure Reason,* A249, p. 347. See "The concepts [of reflection] can be compared logically without worrying about where their objects belong, whether as noumena to the understanding or phenomena to sensibility." Ibid., A269/B325, p. 371.

46. Ibid., respectively: A238/B298, p. 356; A258/B314, p. 364; and A245, p. 344.

47. Ibid., respectively: B307, pp. 360–61; B307, p. 360; A246/B303, p. 358; and A255/B311, p. 363.

48. Ibid., A254/B310, p. 362.

49. Ibid., B308, p. 361. At issue is not only the lack of empirical use (A257/B313, p. 364), but of "all use" in general (A247/B304, p. 359).

50. Ibid., BXXVI–BXXVII, 115 (translation modified).

51. Ibid., respectively: A277/B333, p. 375; A288/B344, p. 381; and A278/B334, p. 376.

52. Ibid., A288/B344, p. 381.

53. Ibid., A250, A251, A253, pp. 348, 349.

54. René Descartes, *Les passions de l'âme*, § 1, in AT, XI:328, lines 5–9; English translation: Descartes, *Philosophical Writings*, 1:328 (emphasis added; translation modified).

55. Charles Péguy, respectively: *Un poète l'a dit*, in *Oeuvres en prose complètes*, ed. Robert Burac, vol. 2 (Paris: Gallimard, Pléiade, 1988), 871; and *Clio: Dialogue de l'histoire et de l'âme païenne*, ed. Robert Burac, vol. 3 (Paris: Gallimard, Pléiade, 1992), 1204.

56. Péguy, *Clio*, 3:1208.

57. Nietzsche, *Kritische Studienausgabe, Nachgelassene Fragmente*, 1888–89, notebook 14, fragment 98, 13:275; English translation: Nietzsche, *Writings from the Late Notebooks*, 252 (translation modified).

58. I will not repeat here what I have said about the event in general in *Étant donné / Being Given*, IV, §§ 17 and 21; and then in *De surcroît: Études sur les phénomènes saturés* (Paris: Presses Universitaires de France, 2001) / *In Excess: Studies of Saturated Phenomena*, trans. Robyn Horner and Vincent Berraud (New York: Fordham University Press, 2002), chap. 2.

59. Hume noted quite well how the cause of even the most simple and individual phenomena remains unidentifiable: "[P]hilosophers, who carry their scrutiny a little farther, immediately perceive, that, even in the most familiar events, the energy of the cause is as unintelligible as in the most unusual, and that we only learn by experience the frequent CONJUNCTION of objects, without being ever able to comprehend any thing like CONNEXION between them." David Hume, *An Enquiry Concerning Human Understanding*, ed. Eric Steinberg (Indianapolis: Hackett, 1977), § 7, p. 46.

60. Baudelaire, "A une passante," 101; English translation: Baudelaire, *Flowers of Evil*, 189 (translation modified).

61. This is why, in every good detective novel, especially if a private investigator is involved, the investigation, which ideally must *resolve* the mystery by dissolving its event (without cause, unrepeatable, unpredictable, impossible) into the objectivity of an explanation (in terms of place, time and date, motive or cause, means or weapon, and finally, the one who is guilty), unfolds and advances only according

to the rhythm of what *happens* to the hero: a lucky break, a shot fired, a sudden insight, blow by blow, blow for blow—in short, only by "blows," which is to say, once again, by events. Nestor Burma does not spend his time resolving mysteries (making them disappear); instead, like a good phenomenologist, he spends his time looking at them as phenomena that have happened, reconstructing, in the place of presumed objects, just so many events. He does it only by provoking their bursting forth through and upon himself, in a sense for the first and only time; yet this particular time alone explains the other times of the other events. One could of course say something similar about Proust's narrator.

62. Baudelaire, *Flowers of Evil*, 189 (translation modified).

63. See, among others, the quite convincing analysis of Dominique Fernandez (*Ramon* [Paris: Grasset, 2009]) recounting the contradictions of Ramon Fernandez, who in the space of several years passed from socialist (and almost communist) convictions to an engagement with fascism. By contrast, François Mauriac offers the most lucid review of the responses to the event of this same period. Mauriac, *Journal: Mémoires politiques*, ed. Jean-Luc Barré (Paris: Robert Laffont, 2008).

64. René Descartes, respectively: *Meditatio III*, in AT, VII:52, line 15; *Primae responsiones*, in AT, VII:114, line 7; English translation: *Philosophical Writings*, 2:36 (translation modified), 2:82 (translation modified).

65. Pierre Corneille, *Othon*, 2.2.497, in *Othon, Tragédie par P. Corneille* (Paris: Guillaume de Luyne, 1665), 20 (emphasis added).

66. Emmanuel Housset, *Personne et sujet selon Husserl* (Paris: Presses Universitaires de France, 1997), 29.

67. Claude Romano, *L'événement et le monde*, 100 / Claude Romano, *Event and World*, 73; and Claude Romano, *L'événement et le temps* (Paris: Presses Universitaires de France, 1999), 276 / Claude Romano, *Event and Time*, trans. Stephen E. Lewis (New York: Fordham University Press, 2013), 214.

68. Romano, *L'événement et le monde*, 96 / Romano, *Event and World*, 70. Rather than "*advenant*," it would be better to say "*advenu*" (the one who happened)—that is, *adonné* (the gifted).

69. Saint Augustine, *In Epistolam Primam Iohannis Tractatus*, tractate III, para. 1, *PL*, 35, 1997; in Saint Augustine, *The Fathers of the Church: St. Augustine, Tractates on the Gospel of John, 112–24, Tractates on the Epistle of John*, trans. John W. Rettig (Washington, DC: Catholic University of America Press, 1995), 159. We find Levinas invoking "birth, non-chosen and impossible to choose [. . .], which situates the will in an anarchic world, that is, a world without origin." Emmanuel Levinas, *Totality and Infinity*, trans. Alphonso Lingis (Pittsburgh: Duquesne University Press, 1969), 223.

70. Michel Henry, *De la phénoménologie*, vol. 1, *Phénoménologie de la vie* (Paris: Presses Universitaires de France, 2003), 68. See: "To be born is not to come into the world. To be born is to come into life." Michel Henry, *I Am the Truth: Toward*

a Philosophy of Christianity, trans. Susan Emanuel (Stanford, CA: Stanford University Press, 2003), 59.

71. See Marion, *Étant donné*, III, § 17, pp. 225–44; and Marion, *Being Given*, 159–73.

72. See Marion, *Étant donné*, III, §§ 9–11, pp. 124–60; and Marion, *Being Given*, 85–113; as well as above, § 16.

73. Descartes, *Regula XII*, in AT, X:423, line 3 (following the French translation in Descartes, *Règles*, 49, 245n).

74. Kant, *Critique of Pure Reason*, A252, p. 348.

75. Ibid., A249, p. 347.

76. In this way, we would lay out a new table of phenomena. On the one side, the phenomena of the object type, comprising the poor phenomena (logical forms, mathematical idealities, etc.) and the common-law phenomena (objects of the "natural" sciences, industrial objects, etc.). On the other side, the phenomena of the event type, comprising the simple saturated phenomena (the event in its restricted sense, according to quantity; the idol or the painting, according to quality; the flesh, according to relation; and the icon or the face of the other, according to modality), but also the phenomena of revelation (which combine several saturated phenomena, such as the erotic phenomenon, the phenomena of revelation, Revelation, etc.). This table would complete and complicate the one found in *Étant donné* (IV, § 23, pp. 309–25) / *Being Given* (221–33), by binding saturation and eventness: a phenomenon shows *itself* to be all the more saturated when it gives itself with a greater eventness.

77. Kant, *Critique of Pure Reason*, respectively, B307, p. 361 (translation modified), and A255/B310, p. 362. And also: "They [synthetic a priori propositions] can belong only to the object *as* [*als*] phenomena, and not *as* [*als*] things in themselves." In Immanuel Kant, *Opus postumum*, AA, 22:22. Indeed, the distinction depends in the final instance on a variation in the point of view: "The difference between the concept of a thing in itself and of a thing in the phenomenon is not objective, but solely subjective. The thing in itself (*ens per se*) is not another object [*Objekt*], but another relation (*respectus*) of the representation to the same object [*Objekt*]." Thus "the thing in itself = x does not signify another object [*Objekt*], but only another point of view, negative, starting from which precisely the same object is considered." Ibid., respectively, pp. 26 and 42.

78. Immanuel Kant, *Critique of Practical Reason*, AA, 5:97; English translation: Immanuel Kant, *Critique of Practical Reason*, trans. Mary J. Gregor, in Immanuel Kant, *Practical Philosophy*, ed. Mary J. Gregor (Cambridge: Cambridge University Press, 1996), 218 (translation modified; emphasis added). See "the same action" ("*dieselbe Handlung*") taking on "at the same time" ("*zugleich*") the two statuses. AA, 5:104–5; and Kant, *Practical Philosophy*, 223.

79. AA, 5:102; English translation: Kant, *Practical Philosophy*, 222 (translation modified).

80. Martin Heidegger, *Sein und Zeit*, 19th ed. (1927; repr., Tübingen, Germany: Max Niemeyer, 2006), § 63, p. 361; and Martin Heidegger, *Being and Time*, trans. John Macquarrie and Edward Robinson (New York: Harper & Row, 1962), 412.

81. Heidegger, *Sein und Zeit*, § 33, p. 158; and Heidegger, *Being and Time*, 200.

82. Heidegger, *Sein und Zeit*, § 33, p. 158; and Heidegger, *Being and Time*, 200, 201. Similarly: "This levelling of the primordial 'as' of circumspective interpretation to the 'as' with which presence-at-hand (*Vorhandene*) is given a definite character is the specialty of assertion." Heidegger, *Sein und Zeit*, § 33, p. 158; and Heidegger, *Being and Time*, 201.

83. I have attempted to show this elsewhere in more detail—with the example of the Salle des Actes, which, during an *actio*, can pass from the rank of object to that of an event. See Marion, *De surcroît*, II, § 2, pp. 37–40; and Marion, *In Excess*, 31–34.

84. See the description of these variations by degree in Jean-Luc Marion, "The Banality of Saturation," in *The Visible and the Revealed*, trans. Christina M. Gschwandtner (New York: Fordham University Press, 2008), VII, § 4, pp. 127–33; and Marion, *Le visible et le révélé*, 157–65.

85. See Marion, *Étant donné*, § 17, on "The Event" (*Étant donné*, 225–44 / Marion, *Being Given*, 159–73), as the determination of the phenomenon that gives itself; and Marion, *De surcroît*, 53 ("and thus all other phenomena [. . .]"), 62, 87; English translation: Marion, *In Excess*, 44, 52, 72.

Conclusion

1. Martin Heidegger, *Sein und Zeit*, 19th ed. (1927; repr., Tübingen, Germany: Max Niemeyer, 2006), § 7, p. 28; and Martin Heidegger, *Being and Time*, trans. John Macquarrie and Edward Robinson (New York: Harper and Row, 1962), 51.

2. Edmund Husserl, *Ideas Pertaining to a Pure Phenomenology and to a Phenomenological Philosophy*, I, § 24, trans. F. Kersten (Dordrecht, Netherlands: Kluwer Academic Publishers, 1982), 44 (translation modified).

3. Immanuel Kant, *Critique of Pure Reason*, A51/B75, trans. and ed. Paul Guyer and Allen W. Wood (Cambridge: Cambridge University Press, 1998), 193.

4. Ibid., A50/B74, p. 193.

5. See the discussion of the analyses of Bertrand Russell ("On Denoting") and W. V. Quine (*The Ways of Paradox and Other Essays*, first published New York: Random House, 1966, then Cambridge, MA, 1976) carried out by Phillipe de Rouilhan, *Russell et le cercle des paradoxes* (Paris: Presses Universitaires de France, 1996).

6. Søren Kierkegaard, *Philosophical Fragments*, in *Samlede Vaerker*, 3rd ed., ed. A. B. Drachmann, J. L. Heigergand, and H. O. Lange (Copenhagen: Gyldendal, 1962), 4:204; and Søren Kierkegaard, *Philosophical Fragments*, ed. and trans. Howard V. Hong and Edna H. Hong (Princeton, NJ: Princeton University Press, 1985), 37. See: "[F]or now the understanding's paradoxical passion that wills the

collision awakens and, without really understanding itself, wills its own downfall." Kierkegaard, *Philosophical Fragments*, in *Samlede Vaerker*, 4:206; and Kierkegaard, *Philosophical Fragments* (trans. Hong and Hong), 38–39. Or: "What people have always said is this: To say that we cannot understand this or that does not satisfy science, which insists on comprehending. Here lies the error. We must say the very opposite, that if *human* science refuses to acknowledge that there is something it cannot understand, or, more accurately still, something such that it clearly understands that it cannot understand it, then everything is confused. For it is a task for human cognition to understand that there is something, and what it is, that it cannot understand. [. . .] The paradox is not a concession but a category, an ontological qualification which expresses the relation between existing cognitive spirit and the eternal truth." *Søren Kierkegaards Papirer*, ed. P. A. Heiberg, V. Kuhr, and E. Torstung, vol. 8, part 1 (Copenhagen: Guldendalske boghandel, Nordisk forlag, 1917), A 11 (1847) (the reference is to entry number and year); English translation in Søren Kierkegaard, *Papers and Journals: A Selection*, trans. Alastair Hannay (London: Penguin Books, 1996), 255.

GENERAL INDEX

accident, 148, 157, 168, 177, 189
advertising, 30–31
alienation, 18, 19, 23, 26, 32, 34–35; of thing from itself, 24–25, 39
alterity, 48, 87
Ambrose, Saint, 18
anamorphosis, 114, 186
anarchy, 191, 193
Ancillon, J. P. F., 257n23
Angelus Silesius, 68
animality, 219n50
animal-machine, the, 28–29, 35
Anselm, Saint, 60, 234n35
Antelme, Robert, 222n62, 223n63
apophasis, 52
apperception, 3
Aristotle, 8, 47, 157, 164, 169, 188, 192, 214n13, 243n12, 247n34, 248n3
atheism, 52, 53, 54–55, 56
attention, 97, 102
Augustine, Saint, ix, 16–19, 20, 41, 42–43, 47, 80, 123–24, 125, 188, 191, 212n7, 224n64, 225n68, 251n18
Austin, J. L., 252n23
autarchy, 87, 117, 118

Badiou, Alain, 259n40
Barthes, Roland, 246n25, 246n31, 247n33
Basil of Caesarea, Saint, 38, 224n64
Bataille, Georges, 62, 132, 243n11
Baudelaire, Charles, 155, 182–86
Baumgarten, Alexander Gottlieb, 72
Beaufret, Jean, 255n11
beauty, 175, 176
Beierwaltes, Werner, 225n70
being, 23, 49, 55, 56, 57, 74, 79, 97, 124–25, 132, 150, 159, 165, 174, 189, 191, 198, 201, 202, 204; according to metaphysics, 33, 35; being-in-the-world, 201; being-toward-death, 61, 191; and equivalence with the thinkable, 23, 74; present-at-hand (*vorhanden*), 43, 44, 198, 199, 202; ready-to-hand (*zuhanden*), 116, 189, 198, 199, 202

beings, 2, 17, 31, 51, 52, 61, 69, 70, 77, 102, 108, 109, 122, 123, 124–25, 132, 144, 161, 189, 192, 193, 199, 201, 202, 204
Benoist, Jocelyn, 229n7
Berkeley, George, 218n42
Besnier, Jean-Michel, 233n25
biology, 31
birth, 3, 28, 30, 74–76, 194; as arch-phenomenon, 193; as pure event, 190–93; virginal, 79
Blanchot, Maurice, 232n22, 244n16
body, 20, 28, 29, 110, 204; resurrection of the, 79
Bonfand, Alain, 259n39
Bovon, François, 239n59, 253n34
Brague, Rémi, 221n60

Caillé, Alain, 242n5
call, the, 24–25, 150, 187, 193
Camus, Albert, 221n58
Caputo, John D., 232n24
care, 96, 102
Carnap, Rudolf, 158
Carraud, Vincent, 247n36, 257n23
categorical imperative, 57
causality, 3, 75, 76, 89, 90, 91, 93, 99, 100, 107, 108, 109, 110, 111, 112, 114, 125, 156, 158, 159, 168–71, 177, 180, 181, 182, 183, 184, 191, 192, 197, 199, 257n25; *causa sui*, 49, 117, 124, 228n90, 235n37
Cavell, Stanley, 252n24
Celsus, 79
certainty, 1–2, 3, 4, 5–7, 8–9, 14, 15, 22–23, 84, 101, 147, 156, 157, 163, 164, 165, 166, 185, 194, 205, 206; knowledge without, 3, 205, 206; negative, 1, 5–7, 20, 147, 205–6, 207; positive, 4, 5, 6, 205
Cézanne, Paul, 41
Char, René, 51
child, the, 100–102, 103
Chrétien, Jean-Louis, 238n54
Christian, the, 18, 226n75
Cicero, 60
Clauberg, Johannes, 23
cogito, 6, 13, 14, 20, 35, 201
consciousness, 19, 97–98, 134, 135, 136, 166, 193, 214n13
consumption, 30–31
contradiction/noncontradiction, 83, 98, 144, 180; of conditions of experience, 196, 207; principle of, 3, 7, 59, 72, 73, 74, 75, 77, 78, 104, 105, 106, 107, 156, 173
conversion, 17, 18, 64, 81–82, 147, 148, 151, 154; of the impossible into the possible, 67, 71, 72, 74
Cordelia (Shakespeare character), 141–43
Corneille, Pierre, 190, 245n18
counter-experience, 56, 65–67, 76, 204–5, 207
Courcelle, Pierre, 214n8
Cournot, Antoine-Augustin, 88
creation, 39, 44, 64, 69, 70, 76, 146, 234n32
crime, 33, 36

Dagens, Claude, 238n55
Daniélou, Jean, 224n64
Dasein, 61, 198, 199, 201, 229n6
Dastur, Françoise, 238n54
Davidson, Donald, 246n30, 257n28, 259n40
death, 17, 28, 29, 30, 61, 95, 100, 102, 129, 131, 135, 143, 150, 191, 192, 204
deconstruction, 61
deism, 55
Derrida, Jacques, 61–62, 120, 139, 146, 222n60, 234n34, 241n4, 253n28
Descartes, René, 1, 2, 3, 5–6, 8, 12, 13, 14, 15, 22, 23, 35, 54, 58, 61, 72, 85, 89,

157, 163–64, 165, 166, 169, 170, 172, 173, 174, 181, 188, 195, 214n7, 214n13, 219n52, 230n10, 258n31
desire, 30–31, 46, 87
Diderot, Denis, 242n9
différance, 102, 193
Dilthey, Wilhelm, 157
Dionysos the Areopagite, 225n68
doubt, 1, 9
Duns Scotus, John, 6, 229n6, 236n45

economics, 30–31, 108, 134
economy, 86, 88, 89, 90, 91–93, 94, 97, 98, 99, 103, 105, 109, 110, 112, 120, 121, 149
ego, 13, 14, 15, 18–19, 23, 26, 35, 74, 87, 117, 166, 201, 214n12. *See also* I; self
Enlightenment, the, 5, 248n2
Epictetus, 253n30
epistemology, 3, 30, 48, 54, 56, 164, 171, 189; limits of, 3, 15
equipment (*das Zuhandene*), 197, 198, 199, 202
Eriugena, John Scot, 39, 224n67
essence, 104, 105, 107, 156, 157, 158, 159, 173; of God, 42, 51, 52, 55, 70, 72 (*see also* God); of man, 14, 15, 20, 34, 37, 43, 48 (*see also* man); of myself, 18, 20, 37
ethics, 104, 154, 204
event, 3, 28, 30, 62, 74, 75, 76, 90, 99, 100, 145, 153, 154, 155, 159, 160, 162, 163, 165, 166, 167, 169, 170, 171, 172, 173, 176, 177, 178, 181–88, 189, 190, 193, 194, 195, 196, 199, 202, 203, 204, 214n12; that passes of itself, 181, 182, 183, 184, 185, 186, 187, 193; redounding of the given, 145; response to, 187
eventness, 114, 165, 168, 177, 182, 189, 193, 199, 204, 207
evil, 140, 141
exchange, 29–31, 84–85, 86, 87–90, 91–92, 94, 95, 96, 97, 98, 99, 103, 104, 105, 106, 108, 109, 110, 112, 113, 114, 115, 119–21, 123, 124, 127, 128, 130, 131, 133, 134, 135–36, 137, 138, 139, 140, 141, 142, 144, 145, 147, 148, 149, 150, 152
exclusion, 32, 220n53
existence, 14, 107, 159, 173; of God, 51–52, 235n35
experience, 2, 3, 8, 9, 30, 52, 56, 57, 58, 62, 64, 65, 66, 67, 68, 69, 86, 88, 89–90, 164, 166, 177, 178, 196, 203, 204, 207; lived, of consciousness, 52; transcendental conditions of, 66, 158, 159, 166, 172, 174, 176, 178

facticity, 44, 75, 185, 187, 191, 246n24
fait accompli, the, 114
faith, 45, 78, 96
family, 30
father, the, 100, 101, 102, 103, 105, 148, 149, 150, 151, 152; transcendence of, 100–102, 104
fatherhood, 98, 102, 103, 104, 105, 106, 107, 148, 149, 189, 246n26; as given phenomenon that gives, 99–100, 103, 245n22; as regiving, 101 (*see also* regiving). *See also* paternity
Fernandez, Dominique, 261n63
Feuerbach, Ludwig, 215n22, 229n6
filiation, 104, 149–50
finitude/the finite, 3, 4, 5, 6, 7, 41, 49, 53, 56, 59, 64, 65, 66, 67, 69, 70, 72, 73, 75, 76, 105–6, 156, 159, 167, 171, 204, 205, 206, 228n3, 229n6; infinite, 207; ontic, 3, 191
flesh, 28, 29, 30, 31, 62, 114, 202, 203, 204; autoaffection of, 28, 203–4
forgetting, 19
forgiveness, 62, 82, 132, 133–34, 137–40, 141–43, 144, 145, 146, 147–48, 150,

forgiveness (*cont.*)
151, 152; conditions of possibility of, 139–40, 143; Derrida on, 139, 140, 146; and incommensurability with justice, 140; and injustice, 133–34, 137–39, 142; Jankélévitch on, 138–39, 140, 146; as parallel to sacrifice, 153; phenomenality of, 134, 143; trinitarian status of, 151, 153
Foucault, Michel, 220n53
Francis of Assisi, Saint, 108
freedom, 18, 35, 93, 97, 112, 114, 174, 175, 176, 192, 196, 197, 206
Freud, Sigmund, 214n12

Gassendi, Pierre, 257n10
gift, the, 3, 30, 31, 41, 62, 76, 78, 81, 83–90, 92, 94, 95, 96, 100, 101, 103, 107, 110, 112, 113, 115, 117, 120, 121, 122, 123, 124, 125, 127, 128, 129, 130, 131, 132, 133, 134, 136, 137, 140, 141, 142, 143, 145, 146, 147, 149, 151, 154, 189; abandoning or giving up of [*l'abandon*], 118–21, 122, 127, 128, 130, 131–32, 133, 134, 135–36, 137, 138, 144, 185; acceptability of, 110, 111; acceptance of, 119, 120; and economy of reciprocity/exchange, 84–85, 86, 87–93, 96, 97–99, 102, 103, 104, 105, 108, 119–20, 123, 127, 130, 133, 148, 150, 151; as forgiveness, 148, 150; givability of, 109, 111; that gives itself, 107–11, 114, 121, 124; horizon of, 94, 114; nonobjective and nonobjectifiable, 96–97, 98, 102; as paradigm of phenomenality, 112; redounding of, 127, 131, 132, 145, 146, 147, 150, 151, 152, 153; reduced to givenness, 100, 101, 102, 103, 104, 105, 106, 108, 109, 110, 111, 114, 121, 126, 128, 130, 134, 143, 144, 147, 148, 193; of self, 97; self of, 111, 114; unconditioned freedom of, 121
gifted, the [*l'adonné*], 76, 104, 106, 186; son as, 104
Giraud, Vincent, 220n45
givee, the (or recipient), 84–85, 87, 91, 94, 95, 97, 101–2, 105, 107–8, 109, 110, 111, 120, 121, 122, 123, 124, 127, 132, 133, 134, 135–36, 137, 143, 144, 145, 146, 151, 153, 193; anonymous, 95–96, 98; as enemy, 96, 98, 138, 143
given, the, 41, 85, 86, 91, 95, 97, 100, 102, 103, 104, 110, 112, 120, 121, 122, 123, 124, 125, 126, 127, 130, 132, 143, 144, 145, 146, 149, 150, 152, 155, 156, 202
given-ness, 100, 126, 127
givenness, ix, 7, 61, 86, 93, 94, 96, 97, 98, 99, 100, 101, 102, 103, 106, 108, 109, 110, 111, 112, 113, 114, 121, 122, 125, 126, 127, 128, 132, 133, 134, 143, 144, 145, 146, 147, 148, 153–54, 189, 193, 201, 202, 207; coming-over [*Überkommnis*] of, 124–25, 126, 127; process that passes of itself, 153–54. *See also* reduction
giver, the, 84–87, 90, 91, 94, 95, 97, 101, 102, 105, 107–8, 109, 111, 117, 121–22, 123, 124, 125, 126, 127, 128, 130, 131–32, 133, 134, 135, 137, 138, 140, 143, 144, 151, 152, 153, 193; gift without, 95, 98, 100, 102, 126, 143, 144, 145
God, 14, 15, 18, 19, 25, 38, 64–66, 90, 103–4, 123, 127, 128–31, 132, 146–47, 188, 199, 205; as *causa sui*, 49, 54; concept of, 52, 53, 54, 55, 56, 57, 58, 69; counter-experience of, 56 (*see also* counter-experience); death of, 51, 54, 55, 115; death of the death of, 55; definition of, 55, 60; essence of, 51, 52, 55, 59, 69, 70, 72; as eternal, 53, 70; existence of, 51, 52, 57, 59, 64, 69; experience of, 56, 57–58; as Father, 103–4; fidelity of, 78, 79, 80; human knowledge of,

39–40, 59, 71, 206; illusion of, 58; impossible as domain of, 62, 63, 64, 66, 67, 68, 69, 73, 74, 75, 78, 79, 129, 147; impossibility of (the phenomenon of), 52, 53, 55, 56, 57, 58, 59, 60; impossibility of impossibility for, 68; inaccessibility of, 51, 74; Incarnation of, 79; incomprehensibility of, 38, 39, 40, 41, 45, 48, 56, 69, 206; irreducibility of question of, 57, 58, 59, 60, 67, 68, 74; Kingdom of, 80–81; love of, 80; man as image and likeness of, 39, 40–44, 45, 48; omnipotence of, 60–61, 68, 70, 71, 72–73, 77, 78, 79, 80, 82, 129, 147; ontological proof of the existence of, 69; possibility of, 52, 53, 59, 71, 74; power of over the possible, 63, 65, 70–71, 73, 78; will of, 43, 47, 60, 61, 71, 80, 231n17, 238n58, 239n61, 240n62; word of, 78, 79, 80
gratuity, 87–88, 90, 91, 92, 93, 94, 113, 244n15
Gregory Nazianzus, 224n66, 239n60
Gregory of Nyssa, Saint, 38, 39, 60, 223n64
Gueunier, Nicole, 233n25

Hart, Kevin, 233n25
Hasse, Pierre-Marie, 245n19
health, 28, 29, 219n53
Hegel, G. W. F., 24, 32, 42, 157, 234n35; dialectic of master and bondsman, 32, 134–36, 248n1
Heidegger, Martin, 3, 43, 44, 49, 57, 61, 73, 111, 113, 116, 124–25, 132, 173, 188, 194, 197, 198, 201, 202, 215n21, 219n52, 226n75, 229n6
Henry, Michel, 191–92, 233n30, 238n54, 246n27
hermeneutics, 147–48, 151, 157, 158, 192, 194, 196, 197, 198, 202, 203, 204, 205
history, 184
Hobbes, Thomas, 228n3
Hölderlin, 246n31
Homer, 60
Housset, Emmanuel, 190
Hubert, Henri, 248n4
Hugh of Saint-Cher, 237n45
Hugh of St. Victor, 240n62
human, the, 29
human exception, the, 15, 21
humanism, 27, 48–50, 226n75
humanity, 22, 26, 27, 36, 37, 38, 42, 43, 48, 91, 206
Hume, David, 6, 258n31, 260n59
Husserl, Edmund, 52, 61, 98, 157, 202, 203, 214n16, 222n60, 259n38; "principle of principles" of, 202

I, 15, 16, 17, 19, 22, 23, 24, 30, 34, 35, 41, 190; definition of, 18, 20, 27, 29; of the other, 25, 35; paradox of, 13, 20, 41, 190 (*see also* paradox); as question to myself, 17, 18, 19; self-identity of, 109; thinking, 8–9, 11–12, 23, 48; as thinking thing, 10, 14, 16; transcendental, 3, 9, 12, 15, 36, 166, 186, 202, 214n13. *See also* me
icon, 38, 43–44, 45, 114, 204
identity, 34, 41, 101, 189, 191; principle of, 33–35, 80, 103, 104, 105, 106, 107, 109, 113
ideology, 33, 36, 49, 55, 58, 158
idol/idolatry, 42, 45, 49, 54, 55, 57, 58, 61, 62, 69, 114, 199, 202, 203, 204, 206
immemorial, the, 19, 75, 190
impossible, the / impossibility, 5, 6, 20, 45, 51, 52, 72, 82, 100, 101, 106, 146, 178, 187, 199, 203, 206; counter-experience of, 65–66; as definition of limit between man and God, 62, 64, 71; event as, 182; of forgiveness,

impossible, the / impossibility (*cont.*) 139–40; of God, 52, 53, 55, 56, 57, 59, 60 (*see also* God); as God's domain, 62, 63, 64, 66, 67, 68, 69, 71, 73, 74, 75, 77, 78, 79, 81, 129; impossibility of impossibility for God, 68, 69, 71, 79, 81; on man's side / for man / from man's point of view, 63, 64, 65–68, 70, 71, 73, 74, 75, 77, 79, 80, 81, 82, 147; metaphysical, 15, 56; possible, 59, 111; of possibility, 61; of self-knowledge, 21, 22; trace of, 65, 66; undergoing of, 60

(im)possible, the, 71, 72, 73, 74, 75, 76, 77, 78, 79, 80, 81, 82, 140, 147, 193

incident, 114

indefinition, 37; of man, 39, 41, 44

indeterminism, 113

infinite, the, 3, 6, 14, 25, 41, 46, 49, 54, 64, 66, 75, 207; counter-experience of, 66, 67; counterordeal of, 66, 67; God as, 14, 40, 41, 56, 73, 188, 228n3; possibility, 70

injustice, 133–34, 136–40, 142, 143, 145, 146, 147; and violence, 136–37, 138, 139–40. *See also* forgiveness

intentionality, 17, 34, 52, 181, 186, 187, 205; reversed, 186, 204

intuition, 2, 5, 10, 11, 12, 23, 48, 52, 56, 57, 68, 69, 102, 112, 155, 166, 178, 179, 185, 194, 195, 196, 199, 202, 203, 204, 205; intellectual, 195, 196; sensible, 195, 196

intuitus, 23, 160, 163

invisible, the, 7, 38, 43–44

ipseity, 18, 19, 37, 87, 97

Isenheim altarpiece (Matthias Grünewald), 44

Jankélévitch, Vladimir, 138–39, 146

Jesus Christ, 18, 43, 62, 80, 81, 82, 139, 152; resurrection of, 63, 82

Jews, Nazi extermination of the, 138–39

John Chrysostom, Saint, 224n64

John of the Cross, Saint, 232n23

Jünger, Ernst, 220nn54–55

justice, 85, 90, 91, 94, 104, 108, 112, 114, 133, 137, 140, 143, 148, 149

Kandinsky, Wassily, 175, 176, 177

Kant, Immanuel, 3, 5, 6–7, 10–12, 15, 23, 52, 69, 157, 164, 166, 167, 169, 170, 172, 177, 178–80, 194–97, 203; anthropology of, 12–13, 15, 25; concept of negative magnitudes of, 6–7

Kierkegaard, Søren, 46, 61, 207, 263n6

killing, 36

King Lear (Shakespeare character), 108, 141–43

knowledge, 1–3, 4, 8–9, 18, 62, 157, 159, 165, 205; according to categories of beings, 156, 157, 161, 166, 189, 195, 196; boundaries/limits of, 6, 21, 67, 157, 206; certain, 3, 5, 156, 205 (*see also* certainty); without certainty, 3, 206; by clear and distinct ideas, 22, 37, 158, 187; by concepts, 22, 24, 25, 36, 42, 48, 52, 74, 75, 76, 77, 89, 156, 158, 166, 203; of God, 39–40, 59, 71, 77, 206; God's, 77; of man, 12–13, 16, 20, 21, 36, 39, 48, 206; without an object, 2–3, 20, 158, 171; of objects, 2, 3, 4, 6, 23, 24, 36, 38, 156, 157, 164, 170, 174, 205; of oneself, 10, 11, 20, 21, 22, 48, 67, 206; practical, 188; process of, 9; theoretical, 188; of unknowability/incomprehensibility, 5, 20, 38, 39, 40, 53–54, 56 (*see also* unknowable, the: unknowability)

language, 4, 9; categorical use of, 4

law, moral, 57

Leibniz, G. W., 8, 16, 26, 104, 107, 112–13, 169, 242n9, 244nn13–14, 247n35

Levi, Primo, 222n57
Levinas, Emmanuel, 10, 132, 232n22, 246n23, 258n35, 261n69
life, 28, 96, 102, 103, 143, 149, 192, 204; invisibility of, 192
living one, the [*le vivant*], 31, 35, 49, 76, 190, 191–92
Locke, John, 20, 61
logic, 1, 33, 58, 59, 61, 67, 71, 72, 73, 79, 104, 106, 110, 116, 121, 135, 136, 137, 140, 141, 142, 143, 147, 152, 186, 207
Loisy, Alfred, 253n31
love, 36, 79, 80, 84, 97, 136, 141, 142, 143, 188
Lustiger, Jean-Marie, 240n64

magnitudes, negative, 6
Maimonides, 221n60
Maine de Biran, 257n23
Malebranche, Nicolas, 20, 72
man, 8, 12, 15, 22, 31, 33, 197; as *animal rationale*, 14, 43; as aporia for metaphysics, 13; autonomy of, 48–49; as *causa sui*, 49; defined by *logos*, 43; defined in general, 29, 31; definition of, 13, 15, 16, 21, 25, 27, 31, 33, 35, 36, 37, 38, 41, 42, 43, 45, 46, 47, 49, 50, 206; dignity of, 91; disappearance of, 15; as "economic agent," 29–31; as embryo, 32; essence of, 14, 15, 21, 25, 44, 46, 47, 48, 49; freedom of, 13, 18, 47; as gifted with reason, 12; as giver of names, 24, 25; heteronomy of, 48; identity of, 25, 32, 33, 35, 41; as image and likeness of God, 39, 40–43, 44, 45, 48, 50; as incomprehensible/unknowable, 22, 37, 38, 46, 48; as mentally ill, 32; as object, 26, 27; as political object, 32, 36; possible as domain of, 62, 63, 64, 65–68, 73, 77, 81, 82; as saturated phenomenon, 48, 49; standing out ecstatically, 49; as thinking thing, 16 (*see also* thinking); as undefinable, 41, 42, 46, 47, 206; as "undocumented," 32, 33–35; "What is man?" 26–27, 36; "Who is man?" 27
Maréchal, Sylvain, 232n20
Marx, Karl, 89–90, 243n11
Mary (mother of Jesus), 78, 79
maternity, 193
mathematics, 1, 88, 164, 165, 166, 214n7
mathesis universalis, 9, 23, 89, 165, 166, 174
Mauriac, François, 261n63
Mauss, Marcel, 248n4
Maximus Confessor, 224n66
McGinn, Bernard, 225n70
me, 17, 19, 190, 192, 224n65; as object, 11, 12, 16, 20, 26, 27, 34, 48, 214n16
memoria, 19
memory, 19, 40, 75, 187, 190
Merleau-Ponty, Maurice, 227n89
metaphysics, 5, 7, 13, 33, 34, 36, 44, 45, 49, 51, 52, 56, 58, 60, 61, 62, 63, 69, 71, 72, 73, 75, 77, 80, 82, 89, 99, 104, 107, 111, 112, 113, 156, 157, 158, 160, 161, 169, 170, 174, 176, 177, 178, 182, 191, 192, 193, 201, 203, 205, 207
mind, 14, 20, 22, 39, 58, 73, 163, 203; omniscient, 113; transcendental, 157
mineness (*Jemeinigkeit*), 26–27
Montaigne, Michel de, 20–21, 61, 216n24, 217n38
morality, 110
mother, the, 100–101
mysticism, natural, 53

names, naming, 24, 25, 32, 42, 101, 102; as definition, 25; divine, 25, 42, 52, 62, 63, 70; improper, 32; through numbers, 32; proper, 32, 220n56
nature, 12, 20, 40, 46
neo-Kantianism, 173

Nicholas of Cusa, 63, 69–71
Nietzsche, Friedrich, 45–46, 157, 159, 174, 176–77, 182, 214n12, 258n31
nihilism, 1, 33, 39, 51, 112, 115, 207
nonknowing, 6
nonobject, 158–62, 179
nothingness, 178–79, 202
noumena, 57, 86, 178, 179, 181, 194, 195, 196, 197
Novalis, v, 174
numbers, 174; registration by, 24–25, 32, 33, 35

object, 2–3, 4, 7, 8, 9, 10, 12, 15, 17, 22, 24, 44, 52, 57, 59, 66, 86, 88, 89, 90, 102, 105, 108, 109, 122–23, 126, 127, 144, 155–58, 160, 161, 162, 164, 166, 167, 170, 173, 175, 179, 180, 184, 185, 186, 188, 189, 190, 192, 193, 194, 195, 196, 197, 199, 201, 202; according to modality, 167, 171–72; according to quality, 167–68, 173; according to quantity, 167, 173; according to relation, 167, 168–69, 173; as alienated being, 24, 35; conditions for thinking, 172, 174, 179, 180; constitution of, 4, 5, 15, 34, 48, 156, 158, 165, 185, 186, 201, 205; economic, 29, 31, 88, 89, 90; in general, 178, 179, 181; gift without an, 96–97; in itself (or object = x), 180; knowledge of, 2, 3, 4, 23, 156–57, 164, 180, 189; knowledge without an, 2–3, 7; man as, 13, 16, 22, 26, 27, 29, 37, 48; me as, 11, 12, 15, 16, 20, 22, 26, 37; medical, 27–29; mode of being of, 23; as paradigm of the phenomenon, 207; political, 32; present-at-hand (*Vorhandene*), 198, 199, 202; of pure knowledge, 9; technological, 200
objectification, 3, 27, 28, 31, 194, 201, 202
objectness, 111, 156, 157, 173, 179, 180, 189, 190, 202
ontology, 23, 69, 124, 125, 170, 201, 235n36, 264n6
onto-theo-logy, 52
Origen, 79
other, the, 25, 37, 48, 62, 116, 117–19, 120–21, 135, 138, 205; death of, 61; face of the, 8, 36, 41, 114, 202, 204; hatred of, 136; love of, 136
Otten, Willemien, 235n28
οὐσία (ousia), 148, 149, 150, 157, 159, 160, 252n26

paradox, 19, 42, 56, 59, 60, 62, 63, 66, 68, 71, 106, 135, 142, 168, 183, 196, 201, 205, 207; of birth, 76, 190, 193; of a givenness without monstration, 193; of the I, 13; of self-unknowing, 20–21
Pascal, Blaise, 20, 46, 55, 169, 188
paternity, 3, 101, 189, 191, 193
Patočka, Jan, 132
Péguy, Charles, 181, 182
Peter Damian, Saint, 60
phenomenality, ix, 56, 90, 113, 128, 158, 162, 179, 181, 197, 201; broadening of, 202–3, 204, 205, 207; of the event, 171, 172, 176, 178, 194, 199; of forgiveness, 143; of gift, 98, 102, 106, 109, 110, 111, 125, 143; gift as paradigm of, 112; of givenness, 103, 127, 145, 153; of the giving up [*l'abandon*], 128; of nonobjects, 158, 161, 162, 171; nonstandard, 66; of objects, 158, 161, 162, 163, 166, 167, 168, 174, 176, 178, 179, 194, 199; variation by hermeneutical variation, 197–99
phenomenology, 61, 104, 128, 130, 131, 191, 192, 199
phenomenon/phenomena, 56, 178, 179, 181, 182, 190, 194, 195, 196, 197, 202;

of birth, 75–76; common-law, 195, 203, 262n76; erotic, 31, 61, 62, 136, 187; of the event type, 188, 262n76; gift as, 98, 103, 106, 109, 110, 111, 112, 121, 122, 123, 124, 151, 185; as given, 100, 112, 114, 155; of God, 59, 62, 68; impossible, 51, 52, 56; naturally reduced, 98–101, 103, 189, 194; objective, 156, 157, 159, 160, 161–62, 181, 188; poor, 161–62, 163, 171, 172, 173, 181, 195, 196, 199, 203, 262n76; possible, 52; reversed, 21; saturated, ix, 48, 49, 66, 112, 114, 145, 181, 185, 195, 196, 199, 202, 203–4, 205, 207, 262n76; self of the, 201–2; showing itself as it gives itself, 110–11, 112, 114, 176, 182, 184, 193, 200; showing itself from itself, 39, 107, 110, 111, 112, 114, 155, 159, 171, 173, 175, 176, 178, 182, 184, 193, 200, 201; subjective or non-objective, 156–60, 161, 162, 181; as synthesis of intuition and concept, 52–53, 166, 172, 178–79, 180, 195, 203

philosophy, 10, 13, 38, 42, 45, 56, 57, 58, 82, 104, 149, 206, 207; modern, 52; transgressive of metaphysics, 63

Pico della Mirandola, Giovanni, 46–47

Plato, 216n24

politics, 32, 34–35, 36, 187, 199

possibility / the possible, 22, 102, 104, 105, 109, 111, 112–13, 173, 178, 182, 186, 187, 191, 199, 206; as actualization of the impossible, 72–74, 76, 77, 81, 82; conditions of, 15, 88–90, 156, 158, 172, 176, 177, 184; of forgiveness, 139–40; of God, 52, 53, 59 (*see also* God); on God's side / for God / from God's point of view, 63, 64, 65–68, 71, 72, 74, 75, 76, 78, 79, 80, 81, 82, 147; of impossibility, 61, 62, 63, 64, 72, 100, 106, 111; infinite, 70; as man's domain, 62, 63, 64, 68, 71, 75, 76, 78, 79, 80, 81, 82; pure, 99; as trace of the impossible, 65, 74, 76

poverty, 91, 92

prayer, 18

presence: as happening that passes of itself, 165, 184, 189; persistence in, 11, 163, 165, 177, 184, 185, 189

princess of Clèves (Madame de La Fayette character), 108

procreation, 99, 100, 103

profane, 115, 116, 117

progress, 4, 49–50

proscription, 26, 29, 31, 32, 33, 35, 36, 48

Proust, Marcel, 199, 261n61

psychiatry, 31

Quignard, Pascal, 24

Quine, W. V., 263n5

Rabelais, François, 231n17

racism, 33, 36

Rahner, Karl, 225n70

Ratzinger, Josef, 251n16

reason, 19, 26, 31, 33, 36, 55, 58, 59, 86, 90, 91, 93, 94, 99, 107, 108, 109, 160, 162; boundaries/limits of, 6, 60; broadening of, 201, 207; foreseeable, 3, 99; as gift, 12, 111, 113–14, 156; of gift, 98, 105; metaphysical, 7, 33, 111, 113; practical, 187–88, 196; principle of sufficient, 3, 7, 35, 80, 94, 95, 98, 107, 108, 110, 111, 112, 113, 169; *ratio cognoscendi*, 159, 161; *ratio essendi*, 159, 161; rendering of, 112–14, 169, 170, 171, 182, 183, 184; theoretical, 187–88

recognition, 31, 85, 87, 95, 96, 134–35, 192, 248n1

Redemption, 79

reduction, 2, 3; of event to object, 169–70, 171, 172, 194; of gift to givenness, 98, 102–3, 106, 108, 109, 110, 111, 112,

reduction (*cont.*)
113, 126, 128, 130, 144, 147, 148, 193; to givenness, 93, 94, 97, 101–2, 104, 110; naturally to eventness, 189, 194; naturally to givenness, 98–99, 106, 148, 189; to objects, 2, 3, 29, 164, 166, 172, 180, 181
Reformation, the, 250n2
regiving, 101, 112, 113, 120, 127, 130, 131, 132, 140, 142, 143, 145, 146, 153; fatherhood as, 101; as forgiveness, 132, 133, 143, 147, 151 (*see also* forgiveness)
Reiling, J., 239n59
religion, 13, 59
Renard, Jules, 233n26
response, 193
revelation, 57, 205
Revelation, 62, 63
Richard of St. Victor, 68
Rickert, Heinrich, 173
Ricoeur, Paul, 240n54
Romano, Claude, 159, 190–91, 238n54
Rouilhan, Phillipe de, 263n5
Russell, Bertrand, 263n5

sacred, 115, 117
sacrifice, 115–20, 125, 128, 129, 131, 132, 133, 144, 153; as abandonment or return or giving up of gift to givenness from which it proceeds, 126, 127, 128, 130, 131–32, 144; according to the sociology of religion, 119; as dispossession of a good, 118–19, 126; as effecting the redounding / regiving [*redondance*] of the gift, 127, 131–32; human, 129; as parallel to forgiveness, 153; reduction of, to givenness, 121; understood as destruction, 116–19, 120, 126, 128, 130, 131
sacrificer, the, 119
sacrifiement, 115, 117
Sartre, Jean-Paul, 49
saturation, ix. *See also* phenomenon/phenomena: saturated
Say, Jean-Baptiste, 89
Schröder, Winfried, 232n20
Schwärmerei, 5
science(s), 1–2, 4, 6, 8, 9, 12, 21, 22, 36, 156, 157, 158, 159, 174; certain, 1–2, 5, 8, 9, 36, 165; "hard" or exact or natural, 1, 4, 157, 158; human, 1, 12, 157, 158; limits of, 5, 21; of *ontologia*, 23; social, 1, 89, 157
Scripture, 45; synoptic gospels, 63, 64
self, 10, 11, 12–13, 15, 16, 17, 18, 19–21, 22–26; of a phenomenon, 201–2 (*see also* phenomenon/phenomenon: self of the); self-equality, 110, 191; self-identity, 89, 106, 109; self-sufficiency, 109; undergoing of [*l'épreuve de soi*], 28, 64, 66, 104, 204, 233n30. See also *ego*
Shakespeare, William, 141–43, 148
sickness, 28
Siger de Brabant, 235n38
signification, 52, 53, 68, 203, 205
sin, 41, 80, 82, 123, 150
Smith, Adam, 89
solidarity, 91, 96, 105
soul, 20, 41
space, 2, 10, 11, 53, 166, 167, 168, 177, 202
speech, 192, 204
Spinoza, Baruch, 8, 20, 213n2
spirituality, 31
sports, 31
Suárez, Francisco, 169, 229n6, 237n51, 257n25
substance, 11, 12, 14, 77, 148, 157, 168, 177, 189
Supervielle, Jules, 67
Swellengrebel, J. L., 239n59

Tarot, Camille, 242n5
technology, 9, 32, 168, 200
Terence, 37
terrorism, 116, 117
Tertullian, 60, 63
theology, 38, 42, 44, 45, 48, 52, 53, 76, 104, 123, 125, 128; mystical, 52; rational, 56; speculative, 53, 56
They, the, 30, 216n12
things, 3, 5, 25, 164, 165, 192; denying the self of, 25; objectified, 5, 24, 25, 163, 170; present-at-hand (*vorhanden*), 3; ready-to-hand (*zuhanden*), 3, 144; in themselves, 179–80, 196, 197; as thought, 11, 16, 25, 166
thinking, 8, 66, 77, 166; conditions of, 172, 173; me, 9–10; thought, 13, 15, 214n12
Thomas Aquinas, Saint, 61, 69, 70, 72, 83, 112, 132, 238n57, 240n62
time, 2, 10, 11, 53, 96, 97, 102, 124, 155, 161, 163, 165, 166, 167, 168, 177, 185, 186, 189, 193, 197, 202
Tracy, David, 225n69
transcendental appearance, 58
Tresmontant, Claude, 238n56
Trinity, the, 153
truth, defined as *adequatio*, 203
Tück, Jan-Heiner, 252n23
Turgot, Anne-Robert-Jacques, 88
Turner, J. M. W., 204

Umwelt, 17, 216n28
unconsciousness, 19, 40
unexpected arrival (*arrivage*), 114, 184–85
unknowable, the, 2, 40; unknowability, 5, 37

Vaux, Roland de, 250n12
Veil, Simone, 220n57
vengeance, 96, 141, 142
Villon, François, 8
Vioulac, Jean, 220n55
Völker, Walther, 224n64
Voltaire, 47, 234n32

wealth, 88, 89, 96
will, the, 18; power of, 18
witness, 186
Wolff, Christian, 72
world, 10, 12, 17, 22, 63, 79, 81, 82, 107, 109, 116, 117, 174, 175, 176, 192; logic of the, 18

χώρα (chora), 149, 150, 253n28

INDEX TO BIBLICAL PASSAGES DISCUSSED

Gen. 1:24, 42
Gen. 1:26, 42
Gen. 2:19, 24, 25
Gen. 2:23, 219n51
Gen. 4:5, 131
Gen. 18:11, 129
Gen. 18:14, 62, 250n13
Gen. 21:1–3, 129
Gen. 21:7, 8, 9–14, 129
Gen. 22:1–19, 128, 130–31

Exod. 12:11–15, 129
Exod. 12:29–30, 129
Exod. 13:2, 129
Exod. 15:4, 79
Exod. 20:4, 42
Exod. 22:29–30, 129
Exod. 34:19, 129

Lev. 11:7, 253n29
Lev. 11:44, 81
Lev. 19:2, 81

Num. 18:14, 129

Deut. 21:15–17, 253n27

1 Chron. 29:14, 127

Job 38:4, 44–45

Sir. 33:19–23, 253n27

Matt. 5:48, 81
Matt. 7:6, 253n29
Matt. 9:1–9, 82
Matt. 19:17, 147
Matt. 19:20–26, 63, 80–81
Matt. 19:26, 146
Matt. 25:24, 253n33
Matt. 26:40, 146
Matt. 27:51, 250n14
Matt. 27:54, 250n14
Matt. 28:19, 82

Mark 2:1–12, 241n66
Mark 2:7, 82, 146
Mark 10:19, 147
Mark 10:27, 63, 240n63
Mark 14:36, 62, 238n58

Luke 1:24, 77
Luke 1:37–38, 77–78, 79, 237n51
Luke 1:42, 238n57
Luke 3:22, 253n32
Luke 5:17–26, 241n66
Luke 15:11–32, 148–53
Luke 16:17, 241n65
Luke 18:19, 147
Luke 18:28, 240n63

John 1:18, 43, 53
John 5:24, 253n30
John 15:14–15, 152
John 17:10, 152
John 17:21, 152

Acts 10:37, 238n57

2 Cor. 5:21, 146

Col. 1:15, 43

1 Tim. 6:15–16, 63

1 John 3:14, 253n30